I have created a fundraising page with the Against Malaria Foundation which supports their good work in combatting the disease. You too can donate money or nets, by creating your own fundraising page webpage is http://www.AgainstMalaria.com/Lawri

Why malaria?

From a personal point of view, having suffered from malaria in Ghana, it is a horrible disease. Never before had I felt such weariness and general poorliness as the days I spent, lying down, afflicted by it. I saw friends, colleagues and children in my classes occasionally come down with it. In Ghana, I and they were among 8 774 516 confirmed malaria cases in 2012, according to the WHO.

Globally, malaria kills more than half a million people every year.
- 70% of the deaths are children under 5 (That's the equivalent of <u>seven 747s of children</u> dying from malaria each day)
- Malaria is the world's single largest killer of pregnant women
- 90% of the deaths are in sub-Saharan Africa

Yet malaria is totally preventable and treatable. **Nobody need die.** Prevention is better than treatment.
- The most effective means of prevention is sleeping under a mosquito net
- Specifically a Long-Lasting Insecticide treated Net (LLIN)
- Each net costs $3/€2.50/£2
- Every 50-500 nets distributed and installed equals 1 life saved

Why the Against Malaria Foundation (AMF)?

1. AMF is highly cost-effective at using donor funds to prevent illness and avoid deaths from malaria.

They do this in three ways: First, AMF has a clear focus on a specific intervention, anti-malaria bednets, and particularly long-lasting insecticidal nets (LLINs). Anti-malaria bednets reduce illness and prevent deaths. This means the potential impact on lives saved and health improved per dollar donated is high.

Second, AMF has an operating model that has proved highly effective: a lean organisational structure, significant leveraging of technology and many pro bono partnerships with leading organisations. This means AMF's costs are exceptionally low.

Third, AMF places great emphasis on the accountability of distributions to ensure the potential impact of distributing nets is realised and people are demonstrably protected. They report transparently and in detail.

2. All three of, arguably, the world's leading independent charity evaluators rank AMF highly.

The Life You can Save: http://www.thelifeyoucansave.org/WheretoDonate.aspx

Giving What We Can: http://www.givingwhatwecan.org/where-to-give/recommended-charities

GiveWell: http://www.givewell.org/international/top-charities/AMF

Contents

Author's notes	4
Map of Ghana	6
Local area map	7
Prologue	8
Chapter 1 – A new home	12
Chapter 2 – In at the deep end	31
Chapter 3 – Capital calling	49
Chapter 4 – A new arrival	65
Chapter 5 – Independence Day	80
Chapter 6 – Church comes to us!	100
Chapter 7 – Travelling the country	119
Chapter 8 – The joys of Spring Break	142
Chapter 9 – Goodbye my friend	163
Chapter 10 – Mr Loren	184
Chapter 11 – Auntie Gifty's house	203
Chapter 12 – Nana Kweku Fianko Bekoe	225
Chapter 13 – The Beautiful North	241
Chapter 14 – A faltering start to term	255
Chapter 15 – Back in the thick of teaching	275
Chapter 16 – Jaunts away, and meeting the police	295
Chapter 17 – The exams and the election	317
Epilogue	336

Author's notes

English is the official language of Ghana. It exists alongside local dialects too numerous to record in full. The main ones are Twi (pronounced *'Chwee'*), which is spoken across much of the central and southern areas, Ga – alongside and secondary to Twi – in Greater Accra, Fante in the Central and Western Regions, Ewe in the Volta Region and Dagbani in the north. Pronunciation is generally straightforward, with a few exceptions. The letters 'kyi' and 'kye' are both pronounced 'chee', so Sakyi, the name of a boy at Wonderful Love School, comes out as 'Sachee'. Mole National Park is pronounced 'Mo-lay', rather than as for the rodent. In occasional cases, the first of two adjoining consonants are silent, and make the first half of the following syllable more explosive. 'Dagbani', for instance, is pronounced 'Da-Bani', with emphasis on the 'Ba'; in the Volta Region, towns such as Kpando are pronounced 'Pando', with the 'Pa' sounding as if it has almost been spat from the speaker's mouth.

Names of the Ghanaian people in the book are those by which they were most commonly known. At birth, Ghanaians are given an English name and a Ghanaian name, which reflects the day of the week on which they were born. Either can be used as the first name of choice. A summary is here.

Day	Male name	Female name
Monday	Kojo, Kwadwo	Akosua
Tuesday	Kwabena	Adwoa
Wednesday	Kweku	Abena, Mabena
Thursday	Yaw	Akua
Friday	Kofi	Yaa
Saturday	Kwame	Afua, Efua
Sunday	Kwasi	Ama

Whilst I have endeavoured to check the accuracy of any facts I picked up whilst in Ghana, I cannot guarantee the validity of all of the histories I present. In a few cases, there is no printed or internet reference available; local word of mouth is the best I can manage. Finally, conversations (and their contextual situations) are not recorded verbatim, but as I remember them.

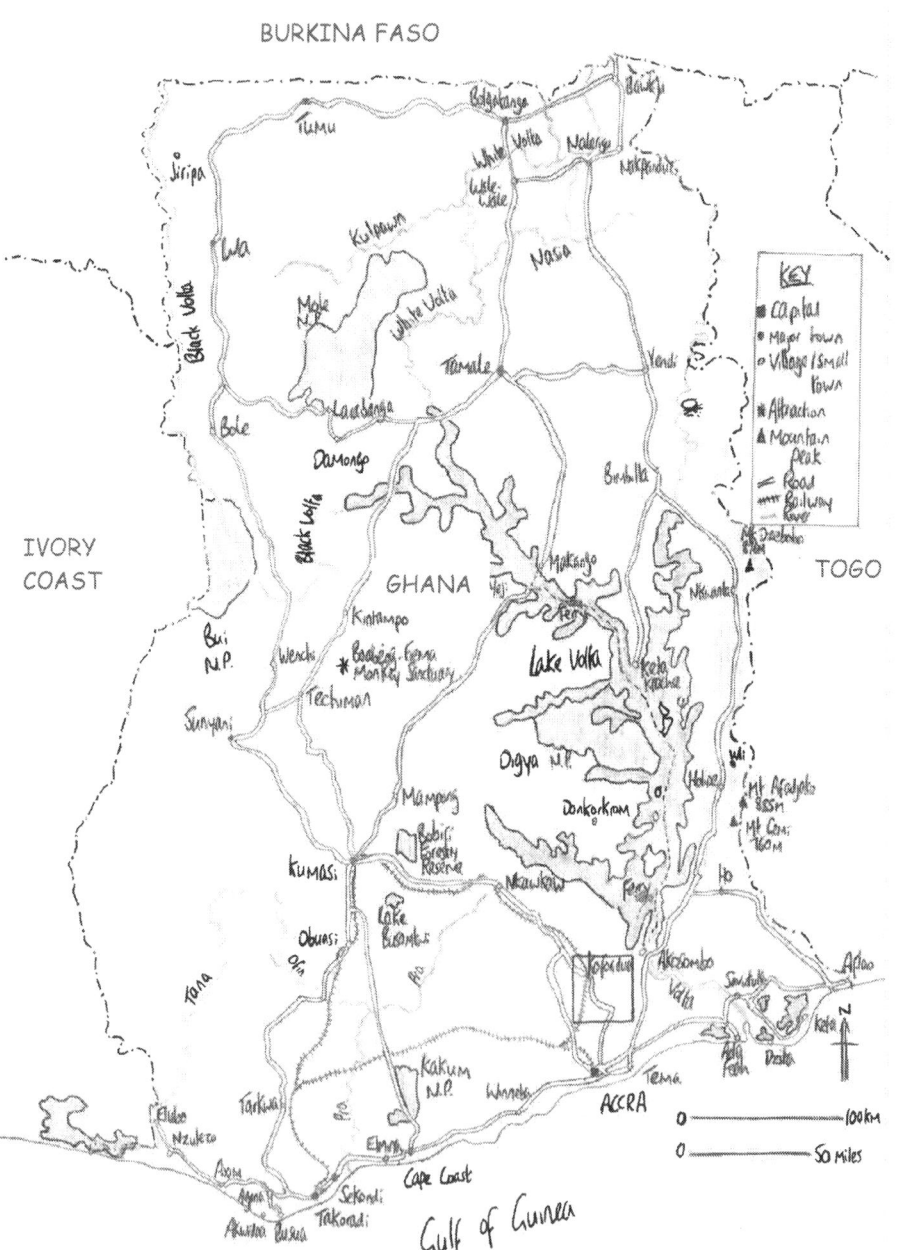

Local area

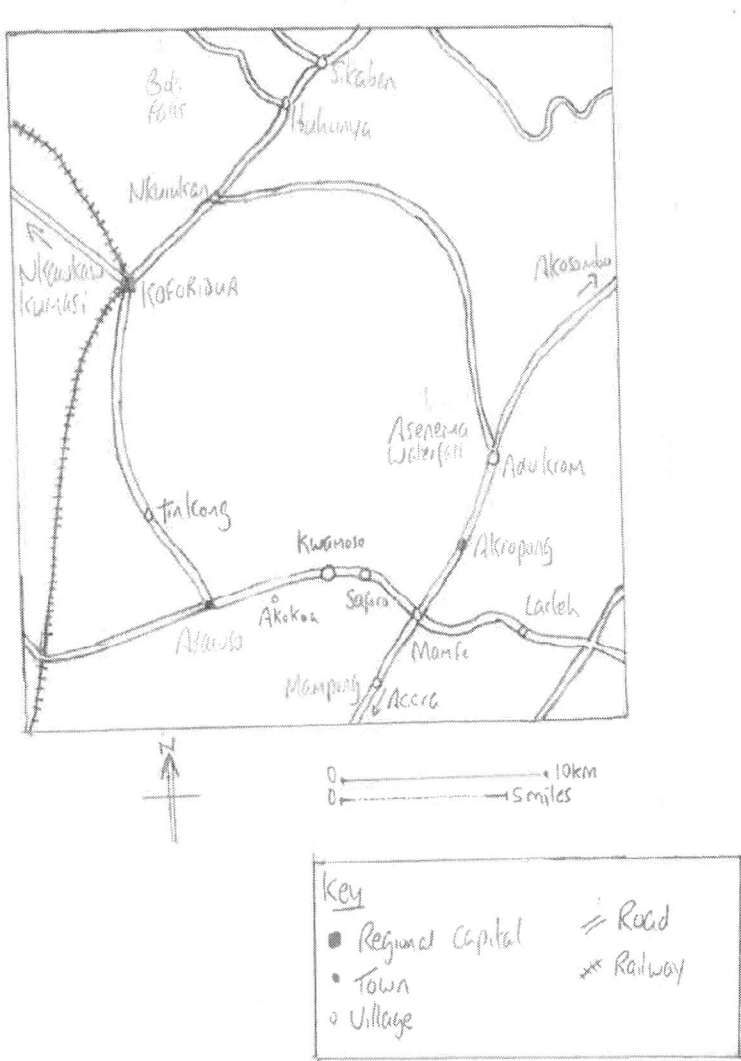

Prologue

"What was it like?"

The question was so vague that, despite its simplicity, it caught me unawares. Where to begin?

I pondered a second and put my pint back on the pub table. Various memories of the previous ten months of my life came flooding back.

In my mind, I was stepping out of the Rev's house in the village of Kwamoso, tucked away in the folds of the Akwapim Hills in Ghana's Eastern region. The air was cool now, but it was only six o'clock in the morning. The sun still had plenty of time to burn through the slight mistiness that hung over the hills in the middle distance. Pretty soon it would be not only hot, but intensely humid too. Hopefully, there would be some water sachets in the storage hut that the family used to keep the pots, pans and food in.

Nana's gospel music, which had been playing over the loudhailer for the previous two hours (Ghana is one of the most Christian countries in the world), was coming to an end. He was playing his favourite song – a little ditty called *Safnat Panea* – with which he always finished. I paused a moment and looked at this fantastic little community of which I was a part.

Immediately to my right, the Rev's thin, wiry body was wrapped in his chief's toga. He slouched on his wooden seat, his bare feet resting on a small table. He waved his hands to reinforce the words that were coming out of his mouth, although, strictly speaking, that was totally unnecessary. I was unsure of what opinion he was expressing to Nana Addo – the King of Kwamoso – and the other chiefs who, together, were the source of authority in Kwamoso, for he was speaking in Twi. However, whatever his point was, he was putting it across perfectly well with the passion of his voice alone. His hairline had long ago receded, and the hair that did remain was largely grey; his sight was failing too: in these respects he was a fragile man. Yet his sense of humour and all round charm gave him great strength of spirit.

To my right, Dora was giving Samson a bath with a bucket of water that she had drawn from the pump the evening before. She had probably had to exert a great degree of energy in the minutes previously in order to make this possible. Samson liked having a bath as much as any other four-and-a-half-year-old boy, which is to say that he regarded it as a particularly unfair form of punishment. How far had he managed to run this morning, I wondered, before his mother caught him and led him to his soapy fate?

In front of me, Dennis, Eunice and Peace were bent over double, using brooms made from reeds to sweep the living area of dust. Oh, there was plenty of that. Dark red in colour, it got everywhere. With one hand behind their back, the three teenagers worked quickly and efficiently. Discarded water sachets, paper and general detritus were put into a yellow container that had once held palm oil, and taken to a corner. Someone would light a fire to burn it later. There were no bin collections, you see. There were no bins to collect, nor binmen to collect them. I hoped that it wouldn't be Samson in charge of the fire that afternoon. He had revelled in the responsibility a while back, pushing the rubbish into the flames with a stick; everything had burned very quickly. He *was* a touch young, though…

Auntie Gifty was wandering across the open space, past the central platform, towards *Obruni* Castle. Further away, Kofi Bosh was sitting in front of his house on a plastic chair. Two buckets of water in front of him, and a pile of clothes to his side, indicated that it was a laundry morning. When Nana had finished his music, Bosh would turn his own sound-system on and play some trendier tunes.

I had a rough plan of the day mapped out in my mind. I would teach my Maths and French lessons at Holy Hills School as usual, in all likelihood. There was the smallest of chances that Pastor Robert would at some point appear, wearing one of his multi-coloured shirts, and call us teachers for a meeting with the Rev. It happened from time to time. On the other hand, Mr Maxwell might send some of the children to the pump to fetch water, or have them cut the grass with their machetes. Whatever else would go on, over First Break I would sit and have a chat with Mr Daniel in his office. It was a well-ventilated place, which teachers and children were welcome to enter at any time. It was furnished with a desk that Daniel would move from Form 3's classroom, and was missing a door. Since it was, actually, just a clearing in the shade of one of the bigger trees around the school grounds, none of this was surprising. Had there been a door, mind, it would have been open all the time. If only all offices could be like that one…

No, perhaps that was not the right place to start. I did not want to paint some perfect picture of the so-called purity of African village life. Nor did I have any intention of letting my answer perpetuate that patronising, stereotypical, and outright wrong view of African children. "Over there," as more than one of my former colleagues at the high school where I had worked had put it, "You'll find it so much more rewarding. You'll be teaching students who are so much more motivated. They'll really value their education and work hard."

Er, no.

Teenagers are teenagers, after all.

If any of them had a chance to avoid doing something that they did not fancy, they would do their best to take it. If there was a way to do something that they knew they probably should not, they would try to find it. Homework? If you're lucky. Revision? No chance. A game of football? Brilliant!

Yet beginning there, or with the laziness and incompetence that some of the teachers at the Rev's Mount Zion Primary school sometimes displayed, would probably have come across as unduly negative, and create totally the wrong impression. Also, someone on another table may have overheard the conversation and got all offended. The last thing I wanted on my return to Britain was an argument with an eavesdropping stranger. That would not have been good. Not good at all.

Instead, the images of Ghana's stunning scenery fell over themselves in my memory. Dzita, that palm tree-lined beach that will forever stay in my mind as heaven on Earth, picked itself up first. Even when heavy drops of rain fell there and splashed into the waves the second time I visited, it was beautiful – the sort of place where time really should have made an exception and stopped itself. I remembered the slave castles at Cape Coast and Elmina. Tastefully renovated, they convey, as best as is possible, an insight into the horrors of the transatlantic slave trade. And, of course, how could I ever forget standing underneath the Volta Region's Wli waterfall, its pure, clear water smacking down onto my head and shoulders? Even without that experience, walking to it through part of the mountain range separating Ghana from its eastern neighbour Togo had been incredible.

Then there was the incredible, spectacular north. The kraals, termite hills and lack of palm trees presented a very different landscape to that of the Eastern Region. Together with the friendliness of the people I spoke to in the northern areas, who outdid even the rest of the country in terms of their hospitality and general decency, these features made the August school holiday forever memorable. I never quite fell in love with Ghana, although for a week up in the north I almost did.

Or should my reply start with the people whom I lived with, and thought of so fondly? Mr Maxwell, Mr Daniel, Mr Sam and Madam Paulina made every day at Holy Hills School an adventure. They were aided and abetted by Yaw, Ishmael, Belinda, Benedicta, Bismark and the rest of the children in my classes. The Three Ds – Daniel, Dorothy and Diana – at Wonderful Love School were inspirational to the children there. At home in Kwamoso, the Rev's family were as warm with me as they were with everyone else in the community. And then there was Lene, with whom I shared experiences good, bad and ugly over three fabulous months.

The question was still hanging in the air. It really deserved better than a cliché, or an abundance of adjectives impossible to quantify and therefore meaningless. After all, I had left a History teaching job which I had thoroughly enjoyed to spend almost a year in the unknown. Five weeks of exploring in South Africa had preceded my time teaching in Ghana.

I took a sip of my pint. "Life was exactly the same as here. But just in a totally different way."

"How do you mean?"

This time, my answer *would* start with a cliché. Never mind.

"Oh, you could write a book about it."

Chapter 1 – A new home

As the aeroplane began its descent through the black evening sky into Accra's Kotoka International airport, I was gazing through the window at the huge mass of lights below. This encompasses not only Ghana's capital city, but a huge expanse of developing world urbanisation. Settlement sprawls, like a slumbering teenage giant, for twenty miles or so along the coastline, and takes in cities substantial in their own right. Tema and Kasoa touch the Gulf of Guinea; inland lie Ashaiman and the wonderful, haphazard, Madina.

I did not realise the complexity of this human geography, though, as the cities' bright lights grew closer. In fact, the main thing running through my mind during those moments was the hope that the plane would touch down before my usual landing nausea reached the sick-bag stage. Fortunately, with help from a decent dose of travelling tablets, the contents of my stomach were still in place when we came to a halt. Strolling through the aircraft doors, I went smack-bang into what felt like a brick wall. This was my welcome to the humidity of equatorial Africa: even at half past eight in the evening, the atmosphere was sapping. It was a feeling that would last: ten months later, walking out of the airport terminal to board my flight back to Britain, Accra's sweltering evenings were still a shock to the system.

I was greeted at the Arrivals hall by a short, squat Ghanaian called Nyemi. He worked for the volunteering company with whom I would work for the next three months. Beside Nyemi stood a tall, wiry westerner. He turned out to be a German volunteer named Chris, whose flight had arrived shortly before mine. Nyemi energetically welcomed me by shaking my hand more times than I could count. Each time, he finished by sliding his middle finger along mine and then making a click with his thumb. Eventually, I cottoned on the idea that a Ghanaian handshake involves a bit more than a British one, and reciprocated with the finger-clicking. The look of joy that came over Nyemi's face when we made a good loud snap was one that I would see from so many people over the rest of the year.

Nyemi beckoned Chris and me to follow him, and ducked and weaved his way through the throng of people crowding Arrivals. All the while he was telling me and my new-found Teutonic buddy all about the heat, Ghanaian women and how we should get married, and football. Following Nyemi as he turned left and right, seemingly at whim, two thoughts occurred to me. The first was how my backpack seemed a lot heavier in this draining humidity than it had whilst holidaying over the previous month in South Africa; the second was Nyemi's friendliness and gregariousness, traits that I would see from the overwhelming majority of Ghanaians throughout my time in the country. Of course, with it being Nyemi's job to welcome people to Ghana on behalf of the volunteering company, he had to come across this way, but very little training would have been required.

As I was pondering this, by now outside the terminal building, I heard Nyemi's voice urgently calling me. What, I wondered, had made him so excited?

"Lawrie," he implored. "I'm having a question for you: on what day were you born?"

Why on earth was asking me this, standing in the car park of an international airport?

"Wednesday," I replied, in a tone that probably reflected this thought.

"Then you are Kweku!" he beamed, before grabbing my hand and pumping it into submission again. "You'll find six wives here in Ghana, Kweku! No, seven!"

With that, he turned and waved his hand in the general direction of the taxis crawling through the car park. What sounded like a mini shouting match then began, between Nyemi and the first driver to have stopped. Ten seconds or so later, he turned to us, and announced, triumphantly: "I've got us a good price to where you are staying tonight!" In the next instant, he was herding Chris and me into the back of a clapped out saloon car, which had orange panels adorning its front and rear wheel arches.

Taxis, he explained to us breathlessly, are identified by these orange panels, "That's what is making them different from private cars." What a brilliant idea, I thought, as the partly Tango-ed vehicle veered its way through the night and Nyemi began talking about something else. We passed all sorts of sights, the first indications of many that Ghana is a 'developing country' in every sense of the phrase. Two abiding images remain with me. First, the *Golden Tulip* hotel (where rooms start at $200 a night), lit up like the *Ritz* and boasting a gateway that the landed gentry of Britain might sit up and take notice of, passed on the right. Then, at the next set of traffic lights, a little boy of no more than eight or nine tapped on the window. Dressed in rags and carrying a little pot, he was asking for small change. The contrast could not have been starker.

Sometime later, after Chris and I had established that we would each be working as teachers in the Akwapim Hills, and mulled over the initial impression that Accra was very different from Europe, the taxi stopped.

"This is where you are staying tonight," grinned Nyemi. He led us into a concrete building which I later found out was called, for reasons I never learned, the 'Pigfarm'.

Nyemi shepherded us into a hot little room with two single beds. "You are waking up at five tomorrow morning. Goodnight!" he exclaimed, before a finger-snapping handshake signalled his departure.

Five o'clock.

That seemed very early.

Once inside our room, Chris and I restarted the chat that had been developing in the taxi. Discussion soon turned to the ceiling-mounted fan that Nyemi had turned on for us. We were thankful for its cooling powers; the only trouble was the noise. The fan's motor sounded very much like the engine of a van that had been driven too far, too fast, for too long. It was clear that we would not have much sleep. An Anglo-German decision, that it would be less bad to lie semi-awake in a room that was too hot than too noisy, was made; the fan was turned off. Liberated from the din, our conversation turned, as is inevitable with twenty-something blokes, to football, women, and varieties of beer, before at some point sleep took hold.

Five o'clock arrived rather sooner than I felt it should have done; in spite of the stuffiness of the room, it disturbed me from a reasonable kip. After a quick breakfast of tea and toast, Chris and I were bundled into another orange-panelled taxi shortly after dawn. Our journey up to the Akwapim Hills and the village of Kwamoso, where I was to live for (at this point) the next three months, had begun. Driving through the backstreets of Accra, I attempted to take in what I saw. On either side of each narrow street, traders were setting up their stalls. Occasional games of football went on between kids who may or may not have been about to get ready to go to school. Wide gutters ran along the edge of the roads, to drain excess rainwater and waste of many varieties.

Exciting as this was, what really struck me was how little visibility there was, streets blurring into a haze not too far in front of us. Wrongly, I guessed that it was smog caused by different forms of pollution. It was actually, our driver explained, the effects of the Harmattan season. From the end of December until late February, winds blow Saharan dust and sand south, blotting out the landscape for all but half a mile in the countryside and much less in the towns. The mornings, he told us, are always worst for visibility because of cloud cover, which hangs low until the sun burns it away.

At some point on the way, the streets and traffic of Accra turned seamlessly into those of Madina. Madina seemed, by some distance, to be the most chaotic place I had been to. The main road through it was roughly seventy metres wide, and made of almost-blinding red dust. Each passing vehicle threw a little more of it into the air, where it mixed with the Harmattan to add to the sense of confusion. The road was divided, into what were effectively several separate sub-roads running in parallel, by lengths of kerbstones. Each sub-road, in turn, was unofficially divided into lanes by the collective imagination of the drivers.

Looking back, however, it was totally ordered chaos. Ordered in the sense that everyone on the road knew in which 'lane' they needed to be, and seemed to adhere to a simple highway principle. This was that if they beeped the horn often enough and for long enough, and were reasonably assertive with where they placed their vehicle, space would open up for them to move into.

Of course, I only realised how Madina's road 'system' worked much later. In that moment, it seemed to be complete, unrestrained madness. Masses of people walked along dodging the traffic. They were either casual pedestrians or roaming traders. Most of these were hawking water, plantain chips, bread, or phone credit. The rest seemed to use the *modus operandi* that if something could be carried, it could be sold. Clothes, electricals, you name it, there was someone carrying a basket of it on his or her head. Next to the bus station was a piece of wasteland, on which lay a few small, partly-built structures. Painted onto the stonework of one of these was a public order notice. It read: "Do not urinate here."

Blimey.

During our jerky journey through Madina, I discovered just how much Ghanaians love football. Many people in Ghana support Chelsea, on account of Ghana's most famous player, Michael Essien, having had a successful stint on the club's books. The sport was even higher in people's thoughts at that time: the African Cup of Nations was in full swing, with Ghana due to play Zambia in the semi-final a day or two later.

The mention of the tournament set our driver off on an emotional roller-coaster. At length, he detailed the strengths and weaknesses of most players in the squad, how so-and-so should be played higher up the field, how someone else is wasting a space in the team and so on. He spoke with an increasingly animated voice, whilst turning around in his seat towards us at ever-widening, surely unlawful angles.

Imagine, for a second, how many British males morph into football experts for the duration of a televised tournament. We sit in our armchair, or prop the bar up, expounding theories of England's formation, the balance of the team and the lack of a left winger. Multiply this tenfold, and you have a rough approximation of Ghanaian passions.

Some time passed, Madina's dust was replaced by another tarmac road, and the traffic that had helped to give the town its flavour turned off in one direction or another. Still deep in conversation about the football, we entered the Eastern Region at a toll booth populated by police and hawkers, and began the climb into the Akwapim hills. The landscape and atmosphere changed here, as the hubbub of the city gave way to a smaller set of communities and a more easy-paced existence. After thirty minutes or so of relative peace, the taxi stopped just outside the little town of Mamfe, and Chris and I said hello to Augustine.

Augustine turned out to be a fantastic bloke of twenty-eight. Tallish, with a circular ringworm[1] scar about the size of a ten pence piece on the right side of his head, he shook us each enthusiastically by the hand, clicked our middle fingers, and

---

[1] Ringworm is a fungal skin infection – related to athlete's foot – which leaves an ugly-looking ring-shaped mark. It is common on the head and face. Ringworm is remedied fairly easily with anti-fungal cream. However, left untreated, as with Augustine, it often leaves permanent scarring.

explained how we were close to Kwamoso. The taxi drove through Mamfe, around the roundabout at its centre, known locally as 'the Circle', and down the hill on the other side. Throughout, Augustine was saying much the same as Nyemi had the previous evening, with similar vivacity. After ten minutes of blind corners and pot-hole dodging excitement, we turned onto a dirt road at a place that Augustine called Quarters Junction, and bounced through the village of Kwamoso.

Holy Hills Complex is nestled in the southern corner of the village of Kwamoso. It is an open space, with a number of blue and white houses dotted around its perimeter and an off-white circular platform at its centre. Holy Hills Primary and Junior High School lies just outside the ring of houses, on the side closest to the Junction. The biggest house belongs to Nana Samuel Fianko Bekoe, the chief of development for the village of Kwamoso. Augustine explained that he was known as 'the Reverend' to the villagers, on account of his leading Kwamoso's branch of the Mount Zion church. He, the King of Kwamoso – a chap called Nana Addo – and the other local chiefs used the platform periodically, for the more official of their regular meetings; the more humdrum meetings took place just outside the Rev's front door.

The Rev was not around when we arrived, and so it was his wife, Florence, who greeted Chris and me as we stepped out of the taxi. Florence was an imposing figure. Around 5'5" tall, she measured about the same around the shoulders and waist. A deep booming voice, and a stance that would not be out of place in a rugby front row, added to her authoritative air. Yet that no-nonsense manner belied a hugely endearing personality. Florence introduced herself and gave Chris and me the seemingly compulsory pumping handshakes. She boomed with empathetic laughter when I told her about my experiences in her country so far. Turning around, she beckoned us to follow her into her home, and towards the bedrooms that we were to have. We dropped our bags off, and returned to the front door, where Augustine was waiting to take us to Koforidua, the capital of the Eastern Region. The town's proper pronunciation is '*Koff-or-id-u-a*'. Since that is a bit of a mouthful, Augustine explained, it is often bastardised to '*Kofordia*', or referred to by its local nickname: the nice and simple 'Koff-Town'.

The journey provided my first experiences of the tro-tro.

Effectively, a tro-tro, or tro for short, is a van with seats. It got its name from the Ga word for three, since prior to Ghana's independence from Britain in 1957 people in the Gold Coast colony paid three pence for a ride on the wagons which passed for local transport. Depending on their size they seat, in theory, either twelve, fifteen or twenty-three people, although in practice adding an extra one or two is not uncommon. This 'overload' is frowned upon by most passengers, although is grudgingly accepted. Only occasionally would there be the odd passenger who registered complaints, which were made loudly until he or she realised that, alone, argument would come to nought.

Tros operate, under a variety of different names, across Africa. They are used in the same way as we in Britain use buses, and can cover any distance: from the short hop from the nearby town of Akropong to Koforidua, to travelling half-way up and down the length of the country. Much more frequent than Ghanaian buses, and covering far more routes, tros are the main mode of transport for most people. Tros leave the tro-tro station when they are full (usually) and plod along the roads until they reach their destination, dropping off and picking up when they need to. Each has a driver, and a 'mate' who sits next to the sliding side door.

Mates are always men (actually, that is not quite true. Just once I had a ride in a tro with a female mate). They almost always have bulging arm muscles, and often wear one of the fake football shirts that are sold on the streets of most towns. The mate's job description is fairly lengthy. His main task is to collect the fares of each passenger. Fares between places are fixed, although never displayed, so the mate has to know how much to charge between each town on the route, and give out change accordingly once everyone has paid.

The mate is also in charge of filling the tro with passengers; to be viable, each vehicle needs to be full most of the time. This is a fairly simple process: at the station, the mate stands next to the tro and rhythmically – or not – shouts the destination at the top of his voice. On the journey, he leans out of the window, sometimes at the most precarious of angles, and does the same. For example, if the tro is bound for Koforidua and has a few empty seats, the mate yells "*Kofordia-fordia-fordia*" whenever he sees someone walking or standing in the road, until his attention is reciprocated or waved away. As the tro stops the mate opens the sliding side door, jumps out, and gestures where he wants the new passenger to sit. Then he jumps back in, gives the driver a shout of '*bien ko*' (pronounced with a short 'o' sound, as in 'cockerel'), meaning 'let's go', and slides, or heaves, the door shut.

The mate also serves as a general assistant to passengers. Many times I sat on a tro ready to leave the station, when a passenger would give the mate money to buy a water sachet, phone credit, or anything else that he or she fancied from one of the many hawkers that ply their trade in the station.

Explanations and questions flowed out of Augustine's mouth once we had boarded the tro to Koforidua. He took great delight in pointing out the little market town of Adawso. Very originally, the name means 'market' in Twi (there are many places across the country called Adawso). It looked thunderously busy today, a mass of stalls and people presenting a quite formidable scene. "Tuesday is market day," Augustine beamed, and explained that, on Tuesdays and Fridays, this otherwise quiet town transforms into a major trade hub. What we could see was only part of it, apparently; away from the scores of people selling fabrics and other products from their stalls, tailors and dressmakers beaver away in their own little wooden huts, making all sorts of garments to order.

A bit further on we passed a signboard for a little school called Mount Zion Primary, at the edge of a village called Tinkong. Augustine dropped into conversation that the Rev was the proprietor of that school, as well as Holy Hills School in the complex. Pretty soon, the tro chugged through Tinkong itself. Augustine excitedly showed us the front of the Mount Zion care home and orphanage. Someone from the volunteering company whom I had not yet met, called Suzy, had a hand in it, he said, although the Rev was ultimately in charge of this place too.

Clearly I was living in the house of an influential man.

What I had come to notice about Augustine is that, by heck, the man could talk. His description of the sights and sounds of the Eastern Region was all a bit much to take in. However, if I thought I had heard him so far, once we got near to Koforidua Augustine seemed to change gear. He launched into a detailed analysis of the layout of the town centre, explaining that it was based around sets of traffic lights on the main street. These are numbered, in the consciousness of Koforidua's inhabitants, from the 'first lights' to the 'sixth lights'. So to find, for example, the post office, one has to turn left at the fifth lights. So wrapped up in this was Augustine, that we had already passed the second lights when he started pointing out where each of them was on the ground, rather than in his mind's eye.

I considered briefly that each set of lights would have its number indicated on it. Getting out of the tro and looking around, this proved to be wishful thinking. It would be best to follow Augustine and keep my eyes and ears open. Over the next hour and a half or so, Chris and I were treated to an eye-opening tour of the regional capital. When we were on the main street it was reasonably easy to navigate, but in the maze of side-streets that Augustine led us down later on, my sense of direction deserted me. All around, people were selling all sorts of products out of wooden stalls or modified haulage containers. As well as enormous quantities of fake replica football tops, there were jeans, soap powder, various different electrical items and all sorts of different foodstuffs. It was something of a surprise when we re-emerged at one of the sets of traffic lights a while later, to make our way back to the tro station and then to Kwamoso. In that time, I had been introduced to the Ghanaian shopping experience, and gained an insight into the techniques of negotiating with the traders for a 'good price'.

I had brought to Ghana only two school-appropriate shirts. Over a rather-more-spicy-than-expected tilapia – local fish – stew in a chop bar near the start of our tour, I had asked Augustine whether he agreed that it would be a good idea to look for a few more. He did. The upshot was that after a brief spell of window-shopping, for want of a better phrase (there was not a window in sight), I had made two new additions to my wardrobe. One was a brown and cream affair, which Chris rolled his eyes at, but I fancied was pretty stylish. The other was a red and white-checked number, which, Augustine assured me, was the height of men's fashion. Some haggling by my chaperone meant that I paid nine cedis – just under £4 – for the pair.

My purchases were carefully placed in a plain black carrier bag and handed to me. Walking around afterwards, I noticed that just about everybody had at least one of these bags their hands. Augustine explained, somewhat surprised that I had asked, that these were standard issue at Ghanaian shops. As if to prove the point, he motioned towards a man buying a skewered sausage from a grill on the pavement across the road. This, too, was put into a – smaller – black bag, before being passed to the customer.

Returning to the Rev's house from Quarters Junction, the effects of Koff-Town's attack on my senses were gradually replaced by the realisation that I had not yet arranged my new room. Slightly wearily, I began to do so. Shortly after starting, I noticed that my new brown and cream shirt was actually not quite as dashing as I had first thought. In fact, the more I looked at it as it hung on its hanger, the more I realised that it was downright ugly.

Oh well. I had bought it, so it was going to get worn.

Enough time had passed for me to have transferred most of the contents of my backpack to the shelf in the corner, but not enough to hang my mosquito net, when there was a tap on the door. I saw before me a short, powerful-looking lad who I estimated to be about sixteen. Two ceremonial scars ran horizontally for about an inch across each cheek. We had a chat, and I asked him what he had been learning about in school. His response was unforgettable: he let out the most delighted, carefree laugh I had ever heard, each audible gasp getting more and more high-pitched. It was fortunate that the windows were wooden frames with mosquito netting stretched over them. Had they been glazed, the sound might well have shattered them.

I had met Kofi Bosh, a twenty-two-year-old odd-jobber and possibly the most laid-back person alive. Over time, Bosh revealed himself to be a powerful football player and a thoroughly entertaining joker and teller of tall tales. He loved to play cards and blag about the amazing strength of his usually crap hand. He also had a hilarious, but for him unfortunate, knack of having the occasional very good hand and still losing out. I lost count of the amount of times I had to say "Thank you" to people in the complex, but a disproportionate number were to Kofi Bosh. During the ten months that I lived in Kwamoso, Bosh's general good sense, along with skills in carpentry and physiotherapy, helped me out of various sticky situations.

Once Chris and I were ready, Bosh introduced us to the neighbours in the complex and then took us around the rest of the village. This took time, mainly because there was a great deal to see and take in. Added to that, everyone had something to tell to Bosh: an important message, a joke, or just general chit-chat. In between the conversations, Bosh did a splendid job of showing us the important places: the football pitch, the clinic and pharmacy, the path down to the water pump, and Club 29. This was the spot bar, or pub.

The last port of call was to pop over the main road to the other half of the village, a section called Habitat, which was partly built by an American NGO. There, we met a brown-haired Dutch girl called Merel, and a Swiss chap, Martin, who bore a striking resemblance to the Hobbit. They too were volunteers living in the Rev's house.

The point of the visit to Habitat was to drop in on some sort of party for the local children, from age four onwards, which was winding down. It was here that I noticed that all children, boys and girls, had shaved heads. I quickly came to regard it as totally normal to see children with incredibly short hair, but was a surprise on the first evening. It happens for a few reasons. Most importantly, it allows parents to identify ringworm. Short hair is also easy and quick to clean, and requires little of the water that is fetched every day from the pump. Finally, Ghanaians think that it gives children a neat and tidy appearance. Being used to youngsters having different hairstyles and still looking neat and tidy, I was less sure about that one, but each to their own.

From a practical point of view, it made distinguishing between one child and the next rather tricky in the first few days, particularly the younger ones. Pretty soon, however, facial features and mannerisms made each child just as recognisable as varying hairstyles would have.

Chris and I were thrust in the party action as soon as we arrived on the scene, by kids eager to discover who we were. As the local pop music blared, I demonstrated to the children that I was a dreadful dancer. They did not seem to mind; in fact, they thought it was great. As the twilight set in, I was being inducted in the moves of Ghana's most popular dance, the *Azonto*. The left foot is kept fully on the ground, whilst the right is raised on tiptoes and pivots from side to side. The left hand is held in front of the groin, and the right forearm is moved diagonally up and down. It looks fairly elegant, when performed by someone other than me.

Shortly before dusk, I moseyed back to the complex in the company, or care, of a group of the kids who lived in the blue and white houses of Holy Hills Complex. They wandered along remarkably slowly; I reckoned that my ninety-year-old aunt would have considered them sluggish. Ghanaians, however, do not rush, except in the most remarkable of circumstances. I found myself talking to three of the older ones who had helped to expose the multiple weaknesses in my dancing prowess. Peace was a bull of girl, who at thirteen could have passed for several years older, and who possessed a voice far louder than her name suggested it should have been. Ishmael was a fifteen-year-old boy with a wiry frame and a fondness for bling. He moved around with his arms and legs waving all over the place, and shared Augustine's trait of speaking at a zillion miles per hour.

The third, Eunice, was a tall, elegant fifteen-year-old. She was also remarkably strong, as she demonstrated by putting Ishmael in a headlock and throwing him on the floor (he had apparently said something, in Twi, that she disagreed with). This was despite a quite marked limp, which required us to drop back from the rest of the group so she could keep up.

Concerned for the girl's welfare (even though she had just floored an older boy), I asked her what was wrong. She had a bad knee, she replied, and rolled up her long skirt to reveal a hideous-looking green scab covering half her kneecap. I was appalled by it, and asked her how long it had been that way. As a first indication of these kids' toughness, she replied that it had been "paining" her for two weeks, but had only been green for a few days. In any case, she was not worried about it because she would be getting medicine soon.

Sure enough, without any fuss, in a few days the infection was going down and she was walking around as normal. Her family had had to save money for whatever the treatment was that she ended up taking, which is why she just had to get on with it for so long. It made me think about how lucky we are in Britain that we can get the things we need to make us feel better without thinking about it too much. We moan a lot about the *NHS*, but we forget that in many places around the world people just do not have access to free healthcare. They have to grin and bear it until they can afford the treatment.

Dong! Dong- dong- dong! Dong- dong- dong! Dong- dong- dong! Dong!

What on earth was this?

Whatever it was, it had brought deep sleep to a premature end.

It was five o'clock. This, I learned soon after, was going to become the new waking up time. Each morning at that hour, one of the children living in the complex would take his or her turn – although it was usually boys – to ring the bell signalling the start of the daily Church service. The bell was actually an old car wheel which hung by a wire from the branch of a tree; it was struck with a black metal rod.

The children quite enjoyed their turn as the bell-ringer. They were wide awake already. Their day started shortly after four o'clock doing jobs for their families, usually sweeping the house and surrounding area, or washing clothes. They saw ringing the bell as a bit of a break. More importantly, it represented a chance to make a loud noise.

Show me a child that willingly passes up the chance of that!

The most enthusiastic bell-ringer was a boy of eleven named Yaw. Yaw came from the poorest family in the complex and lived in a tiny house with one room, along with his parents, younger sister Mabena, and toddler brother Elahji. It was easy to tell when it was Yaw's turn to ring the bell. He struck the wheel with even greater vehemence, and a good few more times, than anyone else ever did.

The service took place in a small chapel near to the school library. It consisted of a lot of rather throaty singing, and almost constant banging of drums. As wake-ups go, I reckoned it was the worst sort possible in the context of a village setting; although given half a year I would find myself proven very wrong.

My second morning in Ghana began at half past five with a bath. In the small washroom beside the Rev's house, I drew a bucket of water from the storage container and threw it over myself. It was a shock to the system that first time; however, with the temperature being high even before dawn, after a few days I came to enjoy the bucket shower as a thoroughly refreshing way to begin the day.

A few hours later, I made my first visit to Wonderful Love School, where I would work for the next three months. I was not quite sure how to hail a tro yet, since I had not paid sufficient attention on the way to Koff-Town the previous day. Luckily, the Suzy whom Augustine had mentioned in passing had phoned before breakfast. She had very kindly arranged not only to meet me at Quarters Junction, but also to take me along to the school itself. Suzy was the *Obruni* (the Twi word for 'foreigner') on the volunteering company's staff. Hers was the unenviable job of trekking around local schools and day care centres offering friendly assistance to any volunteers, or local staff, working in them.

Of average height and build with no discernible regional accent, Suzy came across to begin with as rather bland woman. I reckoned her favourite colour to be grey, and that her idea of a good time would be discussing the relative merits of different methods of teaching young children to count. However, she was new in the job. By her own admission, months later, in a smashing little bar called Palm Hill (which lay just off the road between Mamfe and Akropong), she was smothering herself with the blanket of total professionalism under which the air of levity and humour did not flow. Once this blanket had been cast off after five weeks or so, from time to time we had a good laugh. These occasions became more frequent after I had finished working with the volunteering company towards the middle of the year.

Suzy held her arm out and waved her hand in an up-and-down movement from the wrist at the first tro which appeared around the bend in the road. It acknowledged her with a flash of its headlights and carried on its merry way: it was full. Not to worry, I she assured me rather plainly, another would be along soon.

Sure enough, before I could nod or give a murmur of agreement, another tro (this one with two large cracks in its windscreen) lurched around the bend. Suzy waved her hand again. The driver flicked his indicator and stopped next to us. We scrambled on, said, "*Meda ase*" (thank you) to the mate, and sat down.

Off we went, plodding along the road towards Adawso and Koforidua. Without Augustine jabbering away non-stop, I noticed that the road meandered this way and that, through three or four similar-looking villages. At intervals along the roadside, people sold their wares from either wooden benches or stalls made from bamboo. One young lad, certainly of school-age, was holding out some variety of dead animal that he had killed – 'bushmeat', as it is known, is commonly eaten across West Africa.

Before too long, a tap on the shoulder from Suzy announced that we had arrived at Akokoa Junction; it was time to get off. I took in the scene through the window, and hoped that, in the absence of any distinguishing features, I would remember what Akokoa Junction looked like for the next day's solo journey.

Walking up the dirt road from the junction to the school, Suzy told me all about the class that I would be teaching. She reeled off the many qualities of Daniel, Class 2's teacher, and moved on to expound a few theories of hers about planning lesson activities. It sounded like this was something that she spent all night, every night, reading about as evening entertainment; rather than it being a necessary part of her job.

Daniel turned out to be almost exactly as Suzy had described him, except vastly more interesting. Very slight, his face exuded charm and friendliness. He had eager, bright, eyes which looked as if they might have had sparklers behind them. His arms seemed to be made out of elastic as he waved them at me in greeting. He caught my right hand in his and gave it, as I had become used to, a hearty shaking. He hooted with glee when we made a deep, almost resonating snap from the finger-click, and told me that I was his brother. I felt certain that we were of different parentage, but before I could comment, Daniel expounded that Ghanaians use the terms 'brother' and 'sister' to describe friends, or even acquaintances. After he had quizzed me about my day of birth and reminded me that I was a Kweku, Daniel – born on a Monday and therefore named Kojo – took me down to meet his "sisters". These were Diana and Dorothy, the teachers of Nursery and Class 1. On the way, he told me all about the school and children in it.

Daniel had founded Wonderful Love almost a year earlier, he explained, since there was no other school around the village for the children to go to. Six months previously, at the start of the current academic year, many more children had joined the school, as had Diana and Dorothy.

In appearance, these two were almost total opposites: Dorothy slim and quite dashing, but with a facial expression that might have frozen a mug of tea; Diana much broader, with almost maternal warmth exuding from her round face. Virtually their only similarity was a taste for an extravagant hairstyle. Dorothy's braids were as impressive as any I had seen; whilst Diana appeared to insist upon emptying enough hairspray onto her black and purple bob every morning that she might have kept Ghana's *L'Oreal* rep in business by herself.

The children, Daniel assured me, were willing and enthusiastic, although – since the school had been open for such a short time – spoke little English. "Fear not though, for by God's grace, you'll teach them many things," he enthused, his eyes still gleaming. Daniel turned, and asked a small boy to ring the bell for the end of break. A gigantic grass stain, acquired from the school's football pitch, invaded the youngster's green and white-checked school shirt.

"This is Collins, our bellboy," he beamed, as he did when talking about any of the pupils. Collins picked up the hand bell, gave it a hearty shake, and opened his mouth to reveal a set of yellowish-brown teeth, before yelling at the top of his voice, "Break over *pleeeaaase!*"

This sparked off a mad rush of youngsters to their classroom, around half of whom shrieked '*Obruniii!*' as they raced past me and into their respective classrooms. It would become frequent, walking along streets in many areas of the country, to hear that word called out by adults and children alike.

Usually it was a genuinely friendly greeting from people who rarely see a white face and were expressing their excitement, as was the case here. Often, it was a statement of fact, a simpler way of saying 'Oh look, there is a foreign person'. Sometimes, with '*Ete sen?*' (How are you?) tagged onto the end, it was a little test to see if the foreigner in question knew any of the Twi language and, even better, could respond with an '*E ye*' (I'm fine). Very occasionally there is a hint, or more, of a challenging tone behind it; a tiny minority of people dislike the idea of foreigners living and working in their country. It is, by the way, an infinitely smaller proportion than of British people objecting to foreigners living and working in the UK.

The first thing that I needed to do with Class 2 was to tell them my name. I took a deep breath, and began. "Good morning Class 2."

"Good morning," the children replied, before most fell silent; some tacked 'Sir', or '*Obruni*', onto the end of their utterance.

"My name is Lawrie. My name is *not* '*Obruni*'. What is my name?"

"Lawrie!" Class 2 responded cheerily.

"Good! And what is *not* my name?"

There was a long pause before a bright young boy called Morgan, who sat at the back with the expression of a lovable rogue on his face, piped up. "*Obruni!*" he chirped. "Your name is not *Obruni!*" The rest of the class joined in, almost singing, "Your name is not *Obruni!*"

I was delighted, and told them so, but Daniel knew more about Ghanaian schooling than I did, and added "Clap for yourselves!"

An exultant bunch of nineteen children (three were missing, Daniel explained: two boys called Peter and Thomson, and a delightful little girl called Jennifer) exploded into a brisk routine of 'clap, clap, clap-clap-clap, clap'. It was, and remained, lovely to see the children engage in a concerted act of congratulation for shared or individual achievement. There was none of the too-cool-for-school attitude that often blights British youngsters.

I scanned Daniel's classroom. Of the little wooden chairs around the tables, one was vacant.

"Daniel, didn't you say that there are twenty-two in Class 2?"

"That's right."

I pointed out the numerical disparity. Daniel nodded and looked earnest. It transpired that Jennifer was off with a minor infection, but Peter and Thomson almost never came to school because they had to help their family with farming. I was to see Peter twice and Thomson five times from February to May.

"What happens if, just by chance, they do come in?" I asked.

"Oh, it's no problem. They just sit wherever there's a space. If there are more than twenty, one of them just shares with someone else."

I glanced down at a chair. It was tiny. I thought briefly of how my last Year 10 class would have liked sharing such a seat with a classmate.

They wouldn't have liked it at all.

I had a watching brief that first day, and absorbed tricks too numerous to mention about teaching not just primary school children, which I had only occasionally done, but those who have very limited English. My intended study of the scheme of work for English and Maths passed me by as Daniel went to work. In a mixture of English, brilliantly animated gesticulation, and Twi for a complicated bit, he taught names and spellings of the colours. The lesson ended with a game where children stood up and identified the colours of different parts of the classroom.

Over an hour had passed by in an instant, and I wondered how I could ever do anything approaching what I had seen. Despite my years in classrooms, it was an automatic reaction, on seeing a 'natural' teacher doing it so brilliantly and instinctively, to have a few doubts about how to follow it up. Daniel allayed those little worries straight away. I could teach, he said, in a different way to him; the children would love learning no matter how topics were taught. More pertinently, he told me earnestly over Second Break that he, Dorothy and Diana were so grateful to have me there to teach in 'English only'. It would improve the language skills of the children, who live in a country where not speaking the official language is a huge barrier to getting on in all walks of life.

The only problem with English lessons was that the youngsters did not have books to write in. Lessons had to be conducted using the whiteboard and flashcards, and all of the children's work was done in spoken form. It was a source of some frustration when I came to draw up the end of term English exam at Easter. Half of it had to be modified when I realised that the very need to be *writing* answers in English would be too difficult for many of the class.

School closed at half past one, following a brief downtime session after Second Break. I thought that a bit early, but Diana assured me that the children's parents were happy with the arrangement.

I found it a shame though. The children at Wonderful Love had such sweetness, innocence and love of learning. Lessons could have carried on for perhaps an hour and a half longer, and ended at three. The literacy, numeracy and all round education of these children would have improved rapidly. It would have given them just as much of a chance to succeed in their lives as the setting up of the school had allowed in the first place.

Yet, as Peter and Thomson proved, the reality is that parents often rely on their children, to help earn money to keep the family afloat. Most were glad that the school existed, but also needed to strike a balance. A child knowing the difference between a noun and an adjective does not put tonight's meal on the table.

That evening, Kofi Bosh and his best friend David took Chris, Merel, Martin and me to Club 29, the spot bar. David lived in another part of Kwamoso, and was for some reason known as King David. The semi-final of the African Cup of Nations was about to kick off, between the 'Black Stars' (the Ghanaian team's nickname) and Zambia. The bar looked on as Ghana missed an early penalty and spurned a couple of chances soon after. There was a collective groan when Zambia took the lead early on, and again, louder, when Ghana's star striker Asamoah Gyan ("Just give him the ball and we'll score, man. It's easy!" King David had said as we sat down) was substituted early in the second half.

The bar rallied again as Ghana had a series of shots on goal, but with ten minutes to go Zambia scored. King David, like most others, visibly shrunk in his seat. The final whistle was met with disappointment, rather than anything else. Ghanaian people love their team and their national sport. They felt, in a more honest way than we in Britain do in the build up to a tournament, that their team would win the competition for the first time in nearly thirty years.

Most people left, but I persuaded Bosh and King David to stay on for the second semi-final between Ivory Coast and Mali. There was more disappointment for them when Ivory Coast completed a fairly straightforward win; they were denied a final between Ghana and her western neighbour.

Chapter 2 – In at the deep end

The business of being woken up at five in the morning didn't get any nicer with time, but at least after the first few mornings the church bell did not give the same shock to the system as it had previously.

I slowly but surely got into the routine of getting up around six, the prospect of a busy day ahead meaning that I did not mind too much lying awake for an hour. In that time, the service would begin, build up to a climax, and end in cheering and clapping from the congregation.

After a bath, I would have breakfast with the other volunteers in a square wooden structure which was known to all as '*Obruni* Castle'. Bosh had built it some years before, after the Rev accepted an invitation from the volunteering company to host foreign volunteers. *Obruni* Castle served as the dining room and general living space for the volunteers. Three tables provided plenty of space to eat, read, play cards and, for me and the other teaching volunteers, to prepare lessons. The children also used it to do homework, and most people in the complex came to have a chat there at some point. It was a social place.

The Rev's sister Gifty, or Auntie Gifty to anybody younger than her sixty-odd years, was in charge of cooking for everyone who lived in the Rev's house. Gifty had a similar aura to Florence, although her authority did not come through physical size. Calmness, an easy smile, and a purposeful stride give the fairly diminutive Auntie Gifty her presence.

Gifty's daughter had for some reason moved to Kumasi, a city around a hundred miles away from Kwamoso, some years before. She had left three children behind, who lived with their grandmother and loved her to pieces. Eighteen-year-old Esther had finished Junior High School, or JHS, the spring before I arrived in Kwamoso, Collins – two years younger – was in Form 2, the second of three years of JHS, and Mabena was a tiny girl who looked far younger than her eight years. She was known as Little Mabena, to differentiate her from Yaw's sister, who, slightly confusingly, was the same age, although bigger.

It was Auntie Gifty who gave me my first practical use of Twi phrases: *Wo ho te sen?* and *Ete sen?* (each mean 'How are you?'); and the standard replies *Me ho ye*, or simply *E ye*, meaning 'I'm fine'. Each morning she would greet the volunteers with one of the two questions. Her face would break into a toothy smile of delight when she received the correctly pronounced answer.

Unfailingly, Auntie Gifty would bring bread, jam and tea to *Obruni* Castle for the volunteers' breakfast. We would sit for quite a while after everyone was full, with all sorts of conversations going on between the westerners, Kofi Bosh, the Rev (who sometimes came to say hello), and his delightful young daughter, Debra. A precocious, instantly likeable eight-year-old, Debra had an excellent command of English. She was full of questions for the volunteers, about our home countries, and what we would do during each day. She clearly listened with a keen ear, she frequently asked us follow-up questions days later. The teenagers, Eunice, Ishmael and Peace, would also sometimes drop by for a quiet (less so in Peace's case) word, on their way to school.

The Rev's eldest son Kofi would show up at the breakfast table occasionally as well. Rarely have I met anyone more laid back than Kofi, or BraKofi as he was known by everyone living in the complex (*Bra* means 'come' in Twi, it was tacked to the start of his name because Kofi was always coming and going). BraKofi was a brilliant mathematician. For a number of years, he taught JHS classes at Holy Hills, until he had a huge row, over something trivial, with the Religious and Moral Education (RME) teacher, Paulina. The upshot of this was that he decided to devote more time to a nascent career in construction, and teach far fewer lessons. He and Paulina had had an on-off relationship for some years; the row had heralded another – slightly longer – 'off' period.

One would never guess BraKofi's mathematical ability from looking at him. He had the appearance of a seasoned slob. His customary vest, trousers and flip-flops looked as though they had fallen onto him at some point after he had got up, rather than having been put on in a deliberate act of dressing. He would shuffle along, ask how we were doing, crack a few jokes, and shuffle off again. Underneath it all, though, was a highly intelligent man.

Over the next few weeks, I settled into village and school life. I began to feel less like the foreigner, and more like a member of the strong community that was the Holy Hills Complex. Just in case I ever forgot, though, I continued to be reminded of my foreign-ness by the numerous calls, mainly from children, of '*Obruni!*' every time I ventured further than Quarters Junction.

I took a tro every morning from the Junction to Wonderful Love. Tros do not run to any schedule. It was the luck of the draw as to how long would be spent waiting for one, with space available, to come around the bend in the road. Usually it would be no longer than five minutes, although there was a quiet piece of advice on my first Friday from Bosh. I had waited three or four times longer than normal when he appeared at my side. Full tro after full tro had flashed its headlights at me. Most had trundled past with all sorts of things – mainly huge bunches of plantain or sugar cane – sticking out of their boots, weighing them down almost to the point of scraping the tarmac. Fridays and Tuesdays were market days at Adawso, he reminded me; the stallholders had to get set up. I would need to get to the Junction a bit earlier.

The rides on the tro were often eye-opening. One morning, not long after I had arrived in Kwamoso, I found myself sitting next to a fellow with a physique resembling the proverbial outhouse.

"*Obruni!*" he grinned. "*Wo ho te sen?*"

I grinned back. I knew the answer to this one. Thank you Auntie Gifty! "*Me ho ye.*"

I gambled, perhaps recklessly. "*Wo en swe?*"

His grin widened with excitement; my gamble had paid off. "*Misu me ho ye!* You know Twi!"

I didn't want to get his hopes up too much, since this last statement wasn't even approaching the truth.

"A bit," I offered.

"You know Twi!" he repeated, his enthusiasm undimmed. I'm sure he would also have grasped my hand and shaken it into finger-clicking submission had we not been too tightly squeezed together. "I like you," he beamed. In the ensuing discussion, he offered me not only a trip around Koforidua, but also a meal at his home that evening, before I disappointed him by getting off at Akokoa Junction and making my way to school.

Once I had arrived at school each morning, I had to factor in time to get mobbed. Children who arrived earlier than the teachers broke off their games of football when they saw any of the 'Three Ds' – Daniel, Diana and Dorothy – or me. They ran headlong into us and reached up to take bags, or anything else that we carried, to the classroom. Most days, there would be three or four children clutching part of a bag handle. Not everyone managed to get their little fingers around something that could be carried. These children would instead grasp an arm, wrist, finger or leg, and lead whomever they had hold of to be reunited with his or her bag. As the *Obruni*, and a new one at that for the first few weeks, most of the children found my presence doubly exciting. More than a few times I had to steady myself as children such as Wisdom, Collins, Ansah, Jennifer, Patience and Regina attached themselves to me, almost pulling me down as we happily staggered our way towards Class 2's room.

One morning when I had arrived first, Wisdom jumped at me and thrust his arms towards me in delight. Only just seven years old, Wisdom was the youngest in the class, and was instantly recognisable by his wide eyes and flat nose. Not knowing quite what to do, I took his arms, lifted him off his feet and whirled him around in the air as he whooped in excitement. It was almost a grave error; Ansah was standing closer than I thought. Having narrowly avoided being booted in the face as Wisdom's feet whizzed past, he demanded a turn as well. It took a pretty good feat of escapology to nip into the classroom after I had given six or seven of Class 2 a go, including Wisdom, who had sneaked a second turn. I dizzily rooted through my folder for the flashcards that I intended to use to teach the class verbs. In future, I decided, I would limit 'whirlytime', as it became known, to just a couple of children.

Another day Wisdom wandered into the room whilst I was finalising my decision on which order to teach the different fruits and vegetables in, and announced proudly that he could spell his name.

"Please, give me marker," he enthused, and eagerly took the whiteboard pen from my hand when it was proffered. With a little help from an older boy in Class 2 called Sakyi, Wisdom drafted and re-drafted his name, changing the '6' in the middle of the word to something more resembling a 'd'. All he had to do to finish, I advised him, was to make sure that every letter except the 'W' was in lower case. His little face radiated with pleasure when 'Wisdom' was finished in green pen on the board.

"That is me", he beamed. "I am Wisdom". I grinned at him, resolved that we would finish the fruits with 'pineapple' (partly because it was the longest word and partly because it was my favourite local snack), and nodded.

"That's right. You are Wisdom," I replied, in a tone that I hoped showed my pride in him and his spelling. He was about to reply, I think, but at that moment Collins rang the bell and Wisdom charged outside to line up with the rest of Class 2 for assembly.

Assemblies at Wonderful Love (and the Rev's schools) had a hugely formal, fairly militaristic structure. Children in each class lined up in two roughly equal rows, boys and girls, with the teacher on duty acting as a kind of Regimental Sergeant Major. First up was the singing of the 'Morning Song', the gist of which is that, in the morning, children get up and come to school after having said their prayers. Next was a rendition of the first verse of the national anthem; Daniel and Dorothy in particular insisted on it being sung with great gusto. Right hands over hearts, Class 2 especially belted out 'God bless our homeland Ghana' and the following lines with huge vigour.

This was followed straight away by the national Pledge of Allegiance, about being faithful and loyal to Ghana. When the sun beat down, as it did most mornings, it seemed to me to be an enormous act of loyalty on behalf of the children just to make it that far through the morning's proceedings.

There was a short lull in the singing at this point whilst the RSM checked the cleanliness of pupils' uniform and (strangely I thought at first) fingernails. Hygiene, though, is a huge issue for teachers, because of infections brought on through children biting or sucking dirty fingernails. Dorothy especially appeared to love this part of the morning. She would bustle from child to child and administer a small smack to the hand of anyone who fell outside her requirements. Finally, when Dorothy was satisfied that everyone's uniform and fingers were in good condition, Abigail in Class 2 was asked to "Give us the theme for a marching song."

Abigail decided which song she fancied, from a choice of eight or so. The three classes would be sent marching and singing their way to their respective rooms, to sit down and get ready for their teacher. Daniel encouraged (and entertained) the children by marching alongside them towards Class 2's room, arms and legs swinging away exaggeratedly, as if each limb were an overexcited pendulum inside a grandfather clock.

Marching songs were short verses, repeated over and over again. They covered different themes. Some concerned the importance of going to school and learning; another had the wonderful lines: 'The day is bright / Is bright and fair / Oh happy day / The day of joy.' Others still were about going to war and fighting battles. This glorification of war never sat well with me, although I came to understand the reasons for it.

Daniel explained that when Ghana won its independence from Britain, it was the first sub-Saharan African colony to do so. The first president, Kwame Nkrumah, saw emphasising the military as the way to show both national and pan-African strength. It became custom to instil patriotic pride in all schoolchildren through performing marching songs, as well as by singing the national anthem and taking the Pledge. Marching, Daniel persuaded me, teaches children that they may need to one day fight to protect their nation's stability or independence.

Like so many things in Ghana, this is simply different from Britain, and I – like anyone else visiting the country – was in no position to criticise. We take for granted the peace and security that we have in our country. People in this part of the world do not; they are taught to value and treasure it.

The major problem of it all, I felt, was that the children's English was so limited. They had little or no idea what the words of the national anthem or the Pledge actually meant. They are learned by heart in the first term that children are in school, without proper translation to Twi. Even children in the Rev's Junior High School did not understand the meanings of some of the rarer or more complicated words that they repeated.

A group of children every day would sweep the classrooms before assembly using brooms made from reeds, tied together at one end with twine. It amazed me to begin with how they did this pretty much spontaneously, but it was instilled in them from their first day of school. With no cleaning staff, it was the children's responsibility every morning to clear out the red-brown ground-dust from the floor – the dust seemed to get everywhere over the course of the school day. Each pupil had to take a turn; they quite happily accepted their ten minutes or so of bending over to sweep. Abigail, ten years old and as bright as a button, worked like a Trojan each morning; most vacuum cleaners would not get rid of dust more quickly than her in full swing.

Patience, on the other hand, was a total scatterbrain. Never, I am certain, had a child been so inappropriately named, not even Peace. After a few strokes of the broom, she would forget entirely what she was doing and where she was, before one of us chivvied her to "Hurry up and sweep the room." This command, like virtually every other that Ghanaian teachers gave, was totally unsubtle; it was something else which took me by surprise. I expressed to Diana that I was used to asking, rather than telling, a child to do something. She was incredulous. And I hadn't even told her that use of the word 'please' is recommended. I'm not sure that she would have kept a straight face at that one.

"The children have to be taught not to be stubborn and lazy," Diana explained. "Patience is a lazy girl, she doesn't like to work."

With that, she turned to Patience, who to nobody's surprise was waving her broom around her head again, and scolded her once more.

I dubbed Wednesday 'Pray Day'. After assembly, the school would sit down in Diana's Nursery classroom for Worship. The Three Ds would take it in turns to lead pupils through an intensive, and extensive, repertoire of hymns and prayers. Groups of children, mainly the Class 2 girls, would shake and beat tambourines in time with the melody. The rest of the children stood up, and sang, mouthed or remained silent. For the first ten minutes, Worship was quite a spectacle, before the Nursery children lost interest and began fidgeting, poking each other and scuffling. It had turned into an act of crowd control after three or four songs. By this time, most of Class 1 had become restless as well, and Class 2 were either losing concentration or, as with Abigail and Bless, trying in their own little way to restore a semblance of order.

Fortunately, we would break off from singing before anyone did anything too daft. One of the Ds would write a verse of the Bible on the board for children to practice and memorise. One Wednesday morning Dorothy wrote the words 'Psalm 23, Verse 1' on the board, very carefully and deliberately. I had a feeling, from my own RE lessons in the dim and distant past, that this psalm was one of the more famous ones. I had, however, no idea what was about. Over the following thirty-odd minutes, it was drilled into me not only that 'The Lord is my shepherd', but also that 'I shall not want', as the children learned the lines off by heart.

As an atheist, Worship was the only part of the school week that I had to learn to like. I was fine with clapping in rhythm with the hymns and encouraging those in Nursery or Class 1 who were flagging. I also quite enjoyed getting involved in the singing. The problem was that the Worship sessions lasted too far long to hold the children's interest for its duration, and became, to me, pointless.

I enjoyed the odd theological chat with Daniel: it was interesting to hear him explain his beliefs and the reasons that he held them so strongly. It allowed me to strengthen my own views when I countered him. One Friday morning, for example, I expressed that, for me, it was difficult to believe in something that I cannot see for certain is there. In response, Daniel asked me if I could see my mind. "Of course not," I replied.

"So how do you know it is there?"

Cue a mini debate about science and technology against belief. It was a fairly passionate affair, which only ended when Collins, after asking Daniel two or three times, took it upon himself to ring the bell for "Assembly *pleeeaase!*"

Whilst the classroom, in terms of its general appearance, was always in perfect condition at the beginning of the day, the same could not be said for the tables and chairs at which the children sat. They were covered in pen markings and scratches, created by children working out sums and practicing the formation of letters in rough, before applying them to whatever they were writing on. Tables, at Wonderful Love and the Rev's schools, were used in place of scrap paper by teachers and students alike. It amazed me that this was the case, such was the fastidiousness with which everything else in the classroom was kept clean.

Nevertheless, this was how it was. Once the children had sat down, lessons would begin. "Good morning Class 2. How are you?" either Daniel or I asked, as all teachers, in every Ghanaian school, do. The children replied, "We are fine, thank you, and you?" The teacher would be "Also fine," or "Doing well." It was a lovely routine, even though it was one that had been learned by rote.

The first lesson each day was 'News Time'. This was the equivalent of registration in British schools. Either Daniel or I started a discussion with the children on the issues of the day. With no electricity in Akokoa, only families with battery radios heard the news broadcasts. The issues of the day, therefore, usually extended to what the children had eaten that morning for breakfast. We would walk around the room and address each child in turn.

I noticed two things about this, one far more mundane than the other. Firstly, many of the children ate rice at breakfast time. More gravely, each morning the same little voices would pipe up, "I did not eat" when their turn came. Daniel made light of it, since he often had not had breakfast either. With a friendly rub of their head or squeeze of their cheek, he would tell them to make sure they bought something at break; a stall next to the football pitch sold food.

Each day it was the same children whose concentration would fade once the lesson before First Break had entered its final fifteen minutes or so. Unsurprisingly, it was largely those who had gone without breakfast. Fortunately, genuine hunger was not a problem at Wonderful Love (or across the Akwapim Hills). The fish, rice and banku – a doughy-looking, pretty unpleasant-tasting substance made from cassava and corn – that the school stall sold was slightly cheaper than at the markets in the towns. The children had plenty of time for a good tuck in; at least until the start of the next instalment of the football match that had begun before school got underway.

I usually taught English after First Break. According to the timetable, the lesson lasted an hour and a half. The Three Ds enjoyed breaktimes, however, and did not feel the need to be unnecessarily constrained by a little thing like a schedule. Often, Collins would not be called upon to fulfil his duties as bellboy until way after break was due to finish. My lesson frequently lasted closer to an hour.

One of the first English lessons I taught was on alternative ways of opening a conversation. The repetition of 'I am fine' had been bugging me for a few days, and I had knocked up some flashcards bearing alternatives. Over the final few moments of breaktime, I was moved to add ways of saying 'I am not fine'. Not that it was a phrase that I had heard from the children; in fact it was quite the opposite which gave me the inspiration.

A young girl called Rebecca, in Dorothy's class, had fallen over and given herself a nasty-looking gash on the knee. I was closest to her at the time, having wandered over to the food stall for a water sachet. Since she did not possess sufficient English to explain what happened, there was no point in asking her, particularly in her state of distress. I tried to comfort her by asking, "How are you?" This turned out to be an utterly silly question. Sniffing back the tears and trying to get her breath back, she gasped, "I am fine, thank you, and you?"

I paused, speechless for a second, before giving her the answer that she was used to.

"I am also fine," I murmured, before deciding that I should do something more useful. I helped her to her feet, and then to the first aid box that Dorothy kept in her desk drawer. She howled in agony as a mixture of hydrochloric acid and water cleaned the residual dirt from her wound. Asking 'How are you?' at this point would have been even dafter than, in hindsight, it had been out on the field. I kept silent and pulled faces at her instead to take her mind of the pain. By the time I had given her a plaster, she seemed happier; if still rather less than 'fine'.

That was the backdrop to Class 2 zooming virtually *en masse* into our classroom, sitting down and telling me that they were 'Fine, thank you, and you?' before the lesson began. A look of astonishment appeared on the faces of most children as I broke it to them that there are other ways of expressing how one feels. Collectively, they wondered what on earth I was talking about.

I drew three faces on the board, one with a big smile, one with a straight line for a mouth, and one looking unhappy. Pretty soon, the majority of the class were *au fait* with terms to express very positive conditions such as 'I am very well', 'I am great' and 'I am super', and we had given a number of 'clap, clap, clap-clap-clap, claps'. It was a bit harder to explain the middle category, which was headed with the straight line-mouth, but eventually we got there. They liked the idea that 'I am OK', since 'OK' is also used in Twi (I wondered briefly how many languages in the world do *not* use 'OK'). Patience developed a fondness for 'I am alright'. Over Second Break, I related this to Diana, who joked that it was because Patience considered herself 'right' all the time.

I hit a stumbling block when we got to the last category, with the unhappy face. It was news to Class 2, I think, that expressing negatives to a teacher was acceptable. Little John, who might well have been a fair way along the Autism spectrum, was particularly unhappy with the concept. It took a good while to win him round. After much perseverance and many 'clap, clap, clap-clap-clap, claps', Class 2 had picked up 'I am not so good' and the like, and had practiced using them all until Collins rang the bell for Second Break.

The next day was a Friday. I made sure that I, rather than Daniel, began 'News Time'. Instead of asking the class together, 'How are you?' I asked children one by one. My heart began to sink as child after child replied, 'I am fine, thank you, and you?' Looking back, the context was the wrong one, since at the beginning of the day children are trained to give that standard answer.

To remind the children of the alternatives, during that morning's English lesson we had a series of games. Pupils used different flashcards to pronounce each 'I am…' phrase. One of them would then come to the front and blu-tak it under the correct one of the three faces which I had re-drawn on the board. At breaktime, several 'clap, clap, clap-clap-clap, claps' later, the youngsters stood behind their chairs and filed out row by row; I hoped that at least some of what they had learned might be retained.

My first weekend in Ghana passed – quite eventfully, it turned out, with an eye-opening trip to Accra on the Saturday. I was curious, not to say prepared for the worst, as to whether any pupil would be anything other than 'Fine, thank you, and you?' on Monday morning.

The opening scene, of having numerous children hurl themselves at me and gradually disentangle themselves from my arms, legs, feet and bag, played itself out. A semblance of calmness had descended. I collared Bentil as he wandered past the classroom door. Bentil was a bright ten-year-old boy with an enchantingly mischievous glint is his eye. He and Morgan were the prime 'not-quite-troublemakers' in the class. Most disturbances were caused by children spotting something unusual, like a lizard running along the top of the classroom wall, in the gap between it and the corrugated iron roof. Whenever this happened, it was a decent bet that either Bentil or Morgan had been the one to have spotted it.

"Good morning Bentil," I said, secretly imploring him not to let me down in his answer to my next question. "How are you?"

Maybe he had read my mind: "I am very good," he answered, "And you?"

I was ecstatic, but decided that it was probably wise not to show it.

"I am also very good, Bentil, thank you." I tapped my head. "You remembered our lesson." He nodded, grinned, and continued making his way down to find a reed broom to sweep with. Encouraged, I found a few more of Class 2 and asked them the same question. Of course, some had forgotten about Friday's lesson.

Patience, for one, skipped past waving her broom around her head, and almost sang her response of "I'm fine…." Yet more than I expected told me that they were 'very good', 'very well' or 'super'. For Wisdom, 'I am super' became the new 'I am fine'; most mornings he would catch my eye and seize his chance to show off his new one-liner.

English lessons continued to provide gradual progress, much to Daniel's delight. On an almost daily basis, he told me how well he thought so-and-so was developing his or her command of the language. I was almost as pleased as Daniel with Class 2's improvement: fairly soon they could say more than when I had first met them. By the time I had to leave them, it was possible to have brief conversations about parts of their daily life at home and at school.

I had agreed with Daniel when I arrived that I would also take on Creative Art and Mathematics with Class 2. I was slightly reluctant to teach Creative Art. I had never described myself as 'creative', and my own memories of Art lessons as a child were of applying paint, pastel and clay as much to my school uniform and table as to the piece that I was working on. Yet Daniel's enthusiasm, bordering on insistence, led me to take a deep breath, convince myself that it would be good to get out of my comfort zone, and say 'Yes'.

I was, and remained, grateful that Creative Art occurred only once a week, on a Monday morning at that, which got it out of the way. The timetable told me that it should have happened on a Wednesday after First Break as well. However, I almost always used the late finish to breaktime to wangle my way out of it, once Collins had finally been summoned to ring the bell.

Mathematics followed Creative Art on Wednesday mornings. I would look at Daniel, sigh, and point out with mock regret that the extended breaktime had eaten into much of the lesson. "And Maths is more important for their lives, isn't it?" I would add.

This did the trick, and I would wander over to Class 2's room at the end of break feeling that, once again, I had got away with it.

To be fair, though, Maths was far more important than Creative Art to these children. It was a practical skill which they would need to use in later life. The first job with Class 2 was to challenge them to add together numbers greater than ten, and over time we moved on to sums which involved carrying the one.

Moreover, Maths really enabled me to get the best out of the children. Numbers are universal, and there was less of a language barrier since the English names for numbers are used far more widely than their Twi counterparts.

Maths lessons also allowed me to see, not in the way I had hoped, how open and helpful the children were towards each other. Abigail, Bentil, Sakyi and Morgan were frequently the first to finish their sets of sums, and they invited their classmates to come and copy. All parties were most put out when I asked them, then told them, to go back to their seats.

"But Morgan has the answers," they protested. It was just about the only issue for which I had to use strict tones with Class 2. To them, they were just receiving help from, or giving it to, their mates. Why on earth I should I have a problem with that?

I thought I had had success when, a few lessons in, children usually only left their seats to fetch one of the class pencil sharpeners or rubbers. They probably had a sneaky look at their friends' answers whilst they were at it, but I could turn a blind eye to that.

Then the penny dropped: with about five minutes of an activity left there was a whizzing noise. It sounded suspiciously like an exercise book being propelled across the floor, and turned out to be exactly that. Patience sat herself back upright in her chair, clutching a Maths exercise book. She noticed me lowering myself down to meet her (rather guilty-looking) eyes.

"Is that book for you?" (which means 'Is it yours') I asked her. I used that teacherly tone of voice, which is reserved for occasions when a child should have the sense to realise that he or she has been caught red-handed.

"Yes, Sir Lawrie," she answered, a touch too sheepishly for her own good. She thrust her forearm and hand over the word 'Abigail' on the front cover.

"Are you sure?" I asked, in my teacherly tone again.

"Yes, Sir Lawrie." Patience opened the exercise book to reveal Abigail's neat handwriting, a stark contrast to her own up-and-down scrawl.

"Well, you've down very well, let me see." I manoeuvred Abigail's book so that I could see the sums. "Yes, all correct." Patience smiled, until I picked the book up and tapped her arm with it. As I returned the book to its rightful owner, I complimented Abigail on her work loudly enough that the rest of the class knew exactly what had happened. At roughly the same time that Patience's face fell, I noticed Ansah returning Bentil's book to him under the table.

The stage had been set. I made my mind up that I was not going to tolerate this carrying on, however acceptable it might have been to everyone else in the room. Through a little chat which appealed to their better nature, I persuaded them that it most definitely was not right to copy their friends' work.

That did enough to strike a chord for the rest of the lesson, although not enough to last until the next time Maths took place. A similar trick was pulled, which necessitated a similar, slightly sterner, chat with the class. This was repeated over the next few lessons.

In the end, I grudgingly chose to settle for being eagle-eyed during Maths exercises. A disproving eyebrow was raised at anyone who looked as though they were about to call for a book, and I quietly admonished those who were caught. Kids are kids, copying was the culture, and Class 2 were good-natured enough to know a fair cop when they were the recipient of one. Equally, I was realistic enough to know that I had probably given a fraction of the quiet admonishments that were due.

The Three Ds were keen to get to know me better, just as I was with them. We chatted away at breaktimes, and before school. Mostly it was thoroughly pleasant, although had its tricky moments. Diana was standing outside her classroom directing the sweeping one morning in my first few weeks. She got to the point straight away.

"Are you married?"

"Er, no," I replied.

"Why not? You're twenty-five, aren't you? That's old enough to be getting a wife."

"Twenty-six," I confessed. "But I haven't found the right woman yet." She laughed, and I swallowed pretty hard, remembering Nyemi's prediction that I would have seven 'wives' (after several months I came to the tentative conclusion that the term is used to describe a girlfriend as well as a spouse, in a similar way to how 'brother' and 'sister' are used to mean friends). Was this going to be a proposal? I hoped not: Diana had a lovely personality and a fantastic sense of humour, but was not my type at all. The thought flashed through my mind of how awkward the next few breaktimes would be should I turn her down. Just as importantly, my best mate Dan had constantly told me – with charming phraseology – in the weeks before I left Britain that I was going to "Meet an African bird and stay there." I was determined to prove him wrong.

"I'll find you a woman," she exclaimed, "I am having friends in Akropong who you'll like."

"Thanks Diana, but I'm sure I'll find someone myself one day," I protested.

It fell on deaf ears. Diana gave me a detailed run-down of the various merits of all her friends, her sister, and then her sister's friends.

She was in full flow about how some acquaintance or other of hers cooked excellent fufu (another doughy substance made from mashed up cassava plant that, served with fish or chicken, is quite tasty) and would be a willing and obedient wife. Abruptly, she concluded her mental matchmaking and looked me in the eye. This could have proved a difficult moment. What, I wondered, was coming next? In my mind, I went through five or six excuses that I could possibly use to avoid a date with one of Diana's friends or relations. Each was less plausible than the previous.

Diana doubled over in fits of giggles, and summoned Collins to ring the bell. I had escaped.

That afternoon, back at home, I found myself in at the deep end again. Merel, Martin, Chris and I were standing by the platform chatting about the day's excitement at our respective workplaces, when Peace and Eunice strolled towards us. Each was holding a 25-litre container. These had originally been full of palm oil, used for cooking, but were re-used to carry water. The girls were making a trip to the pump. They stopped, and asked if we wanted to come and help.

"Ooh, this looks fun!" squealed Merel, excited at the idea of carrying something on her head.

"It looks heavy to me," I replied, trying to kerb her enthusiasm.

It was going to be hard work, especially nursing a shoulder that I had hurt a week before I landed in Ghana. A fairly drunk Afrikaner in a Durban bar had decided that I had been in his way. After a brief stream of obscenities, he had knocked me quite unexpectedly to the floor before I could begin to explain that, if I had in any way obstructed him, it had been purely accidental. It was still pretty painful to raise my arm above shoulder height.

Unfortunately, Merel, Martin and Chris were not to be put off. Not wanting to look like a shirker, I took hold of a container and followed the others to the pump. Along the way another of the kids living in the complex, Dennis, caught us up with an open plastic basin. A smashing lad of fifteen, Dennis was an adopted child of the Rev. He spent most of his time after school (a late starter, Dennis was in the final year of the primary section) working in some way: either fetching water, sweeping the area around the houses or performing some other manual task. Consequently, he possessed muscles in places that I had not realised a human body could house them.

After a couple of minutes' walking, we arrived. The pump was a big meeting point for the local children. Their parents sent them to fetch water most afternoons. They had their fun as they waited, pushing in front of each other, pretending to nick each other's full buckets or containers, and generally larking around. A band of three *Obrunis* showing up with a container each was totally unexpected, however, and they gathered around us.

"*Obruni*, can you pump?" one little boy of around ten asked.

"Can you carry?" another voice piped up.

"We'll see," I replied. It would probably be best to keep their expectations of me as low as possible.

The kids watched on, as did Peace, Eunice and Dennis (who were probably just as curious to see how we fared as the other kids). We won their approval when we filled our containers with water, and then screwed the lids back on. Dennis scooped up his full basin as easily as if it was holding fresh air, balanced it expertly on his head, and tended to the volunteers. He helped us to lift the containers onto our heads, and then gave Peace and Eunice a hand with theirs. A pertinent question now presented itself: how was I going to keep the thing balanced?

How indeed?

After much wobbling, I took a few steps forward, holding on to the container handle with my good arm. Dennis was long gone, although waited for us half-way along the path. Merel, with a slightly smaller container, seemed to be doing fine, and had gone quite a way as well; Martin too seemed to be getting by without much trouble. Chris had managed to avoid having to either pump or carry, and was deep in conversation with Eunice. I was lagging behind, swaying to and fro and side to side quite alarmingly. I decided that my head was not built for carrying water. I plonked my container unceremoniously down, and carried it for a while with one hand, then for a shorter time with the other (the one at the end of the arm connected to the bad shoulder). Eventually, I took it in both, almost hugging it. Peace and Eunice were in stitches when they turned around and saw me.

"How do you manage," I asked them between breaths as we sloshed the water into the big blue container next to the Rev's bathroom later on, "To do that?"

"It's easy", one of them replied.

I disagreed with that, but on the other hand, as they explained, they had fetched water virtually since they were old enough to walk to the pump. As young children, they had carried it in small bowls; as they got older they took larger amounts. With practice, it becomes far easier, as I was to discover to my relief later in the year. Dennis, Peace and Eunice skipped back to get another load each, whilst Merel, Martin, Chris and I retreated to the easier existence of having a natter in *Obruni* Castle.

Chapter 3 – Capital calling

"Be careful," I was warned. "It is dangerous there. Lots of people there are robbers."

I had learned over the years that when this type of statement comes out of the mouth of anyone with 'local knowledge', in whatever form it takes, it is sensible to listen. This particular Saturday morning, the mouth in question was Debra's.

"They will rob you." She emphasised 'rob', as if to clarify.

This was her advice for me when I told her that I was planning a day trip to Accra, Ghana's noisy, bustling and colourful (in most places) capital. It was my first weekend; not knowing how long I would be spending in the country beyond the three months with the volunteering company, I had resolved to see as much of it as I could. More practically, I had some travellers' cheques to cash. Infuriatingly, this simple task could only be performed in the capital.

The Rev had expressed surprise that I was going alone, as had Auntie Gifty and Bosh, but I reassured them that I was used to, and liked, travelling to new places by myself. In any case, everyone else was either busy or did not want to go. I pottered off to Quarters Junction, with the guidebook in my bag, and flagged down the first tro that chugged around the corner. The mate was leaning out of the window above the tro's sliding door, at a most improbable angle. More than that, he was making a bizarre pointing motion with his right hand. It was as though there was something of major importance happening over his head, or on the other side of the road. There didn't appear to be, and I scrambled on, said *meda ase* to him, and sat down.

This was going well.

The pointing motion, I discovered a few days later after a chat with Bosh, is an indication of the tro's destination. The mate points in the direction that the tro will take at the next main junction. When the mate points left, over his head, (since vehicles drive on the right hand side of the road) it signifies a left turn. A right turn is signalled by pointing towards the near side of the road.

The tro lurched forward. The mate had a short wrestling match with the door, finally hauling it closed as we rounded the bend and headed away from Quarters

Junction. The logistics of the journey down to the capital were simple. A change at Mamfe would take me straight through to one of the transport hubs in the middle of Accra, known as Tema station. Bosh reckoned that, allowing for traffic, it would take around two hours, so there was plenty of time to have a flick through the guidebook on the way and plan a rough route to take to see the sights.

Mamfe lies just over the summit of a pretty steep hill, and the tro's engine complained noisily as we creaked around the sharp bends leading to the town. Just when the engine sounded ready to give out, the road grew flatter and dipped slightly down. We picked up speed past Mamfe Girls Senior High School, the police station and the post office. With the roundabout known as 'the Circle' approaching rather too rapidly, the driver slammed on the brakes, beeped his horn, and made the sharp left that led to Mamfe's tro stop and on to Akropong. I, like most others, scrambled out; unlike most others, I banged my head on the low door frame. I had done that a few times getting in and out of tros, it was becoming a painful habit which I really needed to get out of.

I crossed the road, to be on the side for Accra, when I was accosted by a large muscular man in a fake Chelsea shirt.

"*Obruni, Wo ko en?!*" he demanded loudly.

What was he saying?

"*Wo ko en?*" his voice boomed again.

I decided that this must mean something to do with going somewhere. I suddenly felt I should have looked up some more Twi before I arrived in Ghana.

"Er, I'm going to Accra," I mumbled hesitatingly.

The large muscular man pointed at a bigger-than-usual tro waiting a few metres away with its engine running. Thick, black smoke belched out of its exhaust. Clearly this guy was the mate.

"Sit down," he commanded.

I ambled over and peered inside. It was nearly full. We would not be waiting long. This door frame also had a lot more headroom than most, which was a bonus.

The large muscular mate shouted something, and soon all of the remaining seats became occupied – the last by the mate himself. A few moments later, another large man opened the driver's door and climbed in. We got moving, rounded the

Circle, and the mate yanked the door shut. Opening the guidebook, I quickly pieced together a route in my mind. It went from Tema station, past Independence Square, and then along a series of roads to Liberation Square, the market at Nkrumah Circle, and on to the central part of Accra. Here, the guidebook promised me, I would find plenty of banks for the traveller's cheques. After I had exchanged these for cedis, I would have a look at Ussher Town and James Town, the two most prominent districts of central Accra, and head back to Tema station.

Simple.

Dust began to be blown in through the open windows, which passengers quickly shut. I realised that we had arrived in Madina. The tro's gears grinded as we speeded up, slowed down, stopped and started, not quite all at the same time but near enough. A maelstrom of humanity bustled around in the dust, whilst cars and taxis beeped their horns expectantly. The driver drew up to the side of the road and came to a halt. This is Madina, I thought to myself, musing that this seemed quite a decisive halt. Everyone got out. Clearly this was the end of the ride.

This is Madina.

It should not be the end of the ride.

The large muscular mate sensed my predicament. He pointed in the direction of the many tros that were parked up at various different angles in the space around us.

"Accra? Go to that car," he advised.

"This one here?" I ventured, pointing uncertainly at the closest one.

"No, no! That car. Orange one."

Aha. There was only one orange vehicle that I could see. It was another large tro, and it bore the legend 'Peace man' on the back windscreen. It was almost full. I thanked the mate and jogged forward as the orange tro began to set off. Its mate looked to be in a world of his own, leaning out of the window yelling something totally incomprehensible.

"Accra?" I asked hopefully.

"Sit down," he grinned.

I was in the process of doing this, when the engine fully kicked in and we accelerated away. Barely twenty seconds had passed since I had been sitting in the previous tro, not knowing what to do next. The driver sent us careering along all sorts of little backstreets, and through improbably small gaps which appeared in the traffic. The mate had not stopped yelling, or grinning. To take my mind off the thought that it would be dreadfully sad to perish in a road accident before I had been in the country a week, I strained my ears to make out what he was shouting.

"*Accra-cra-cra-cra-cra, Tema-Station-Cra-cra!*" he bellowed, his smile extending across the width of his face and his eyes twinkling.

Almost certainly to the driver's disappointment, the tro was forced to slow down as we came to a vast three-lane roundabout. We followed all sorts of vehicles edging around it and onto the Accra road, crawling along behind the traffic in the nearside lane. The mate, still grinning, continued with his lusty "*Cra-cra-cras.*" A lone would-be passenger stood on the pavement a hundred metres ahead, arm outstretched. In front of us, a tro flicked its indicator, signalling its intention to stop and pick this bloke up.

Our driver had other ideas. He flicked his indicator to overtake, spotted a gap in the traffic of a shade more than a tro's width, and gunned the throttle. We zoomed past the slowing tro in front of us and cut back into the nearside lane.

"*Cra-cra-cra!*" hollered the mate, grinning ever more widely. We stopped, the bloke scrambled on, and we spluttered back into the queue of vehicles.

"*Cra-cra-cra!*"

The tro veered around a corner, faster than it probably should have, and along a tiny street with open gutters at each side.

"*Tema Station-Cra!* Last stop!" bellowed the grinning mate. We had arrived.

I stepped off the tro, scanned the station for indications of where I should go to for the journey home, and found that there were none. Tema station looked vast, as well; I realised that getting back might not be as easy as coming. I decided that I would cross that bridge when I came to it, and wandered out of the station. The mate, grin still fixed in place, was now yelling "Madina-Madina-Madina!" at the top of his voice. I could still hear him, although perhaps only as a ring in my ears, as I walked out onto the tiny street. I need not have bothered having a bath that morning. Sweat was pouring down from just about everywhere after the heat, not to mention excitement, of the tro ride.

Independence Arch loomed into view once I had got away from the station. A greyish-creamish, no-frills version of the *Arc de Triomphe*, at its top sits a huge black star, the symbol of African nationalism. The national motto, 'Freedom and Justice', is inscribed underneath it. The Arch stands in the centre of a roundabout, flanked on each side by the national sports stadium and Independence Square. Whilst the stadium has an appearance which is purely functional, the square has an incongruous charm to it which, though difficult to place, is certainly there.

Open at its near end, the three other sides have stadium-style banks of seating along them. The far end is dominated by a curved structure made from three thin half-oval pieces of concrete, which hold up a balcony. Yellow and cream in colour, like the banks of seating which extend from it, it looks somewhat reminiscent of a *McDonald's* logo. I doubt that this was what Ghana's leaders intended in 1957, when they were sifting through plans for a monument to celebrate their new-found sovereignty. Yet sitting down looking at it, and the statue to the Unknown Soldier on the other side of the square, a real sense of national pride was given over by the surroundings. The flags fluttered against the grey sky which typifies the Harmattan season. An air of contentedness came across me in the peace and quiet of it all.

It would be easy to get carried away with this, and put the rose-tinted glasses on. However, I went to Independence Square a number of times subsequently. The feeling came back every time. It wasn't always deserted, or even quiet, either. The place is not everyone's cup of tea – the guidebook used the word 'Ugly' at least once – but I liked it.

Osu Castle is the seat of Ghana's Government, and getting closer than four hundred yards or so to take a peek at it is impossible. The little road that I was standing on, slightly further away still, gave as good a view of it as I was going to get. I had read in the guidebook that photographing the castle is not allowed. Surely, though, no-one would mind, or even notice, a little point-and-shoot?

I was standing about a foot behind a sign which read "NO PHOTOGRAPHY BEYOND THIS POINT". This, I decided, was therefore a perfectly legal vantage point. I had a very quick snap, which showed the castle as a small blob in the background. Photo taken, I made to leave. A shout attracted my attention.

"Give me your camera!"

Oops.

"You! Come here! Give me that camera!" it repeated.

It was a booming voice, the sort that should not be ignored. I looked up and discovered that it belonged to a big, official-looking gentleman in a suit. I made my way over, hoping that some negotiation could take place.

"Give it to me!" He snatched it.

I thought that was a bit unreasonable, since snatching had not been mentioned. Without thinking, I snatched it back.

It reckoned it might have turned unpleasant at this point, so I offered to delete the picture, which, on closer inspection, did not really show anything of the castle. If it mollified him at all, it was not by much.

I forget his exact words, but it will suffice to say that he gave me a thoroughly good rollicking. The prospect of my arrest was mentioned, as was deportation. I stayed silent; it seemed the wisest thing to do. When he had finished telling me off, he snarled at me to get out of his sight.

Taking that as permission to leave, I was only too pleased to do so. I retreated, thoroughly chastened. I was clearly well out of order taking a picture of the place, but it is a shame that there is such hostility to photography of public buildings. A couple of times, innocent pictures to show to friends and family, of interesting things that I had seen, could not be taken. I discovered later that it is borne of a worry that westerners will use the pictures to exploit the country, or to be negative about Ghanaian life. For the overwhelming majority of foreigners who I spoke to, this was completely the opposite of their intentions.

Then again, it is not the westerners' country. The Ghanaians make the rules and visitors should stick to them.

Another discovery was that almost all Ghanaian banks do not open on a Saturday, although I eventually found one that did. There was a long queue, but I did not mind. It was nice to be in an air-conditioned building, and the line was moving steadily enough. Steadily enough, that is, until one customer took an inordinately long time to get whatever he had come for. After twenty or so minutes, I decided to check with a passing clerk whether I could change traveller's cheques in the branch. I was directed to sit down and wait for an advisor, who then told me that, sorry, no, it would be impossible at this branch, or any others that were open that day.

That was that. Off I went.

The traveller's cheques remained unchanged, for one reason or another, all year.

Nkrumah market covers a vast space on all sides of a larger than average roundabout, Nkrumah Circle. Despite its size, that day the roundabout seemed fairly insignificant in the midst of the mass of humanity that threw itself around its outside, to-ing and fro-ing, and generating all types of noise and excitement. I took a deep breath and entered the scrum.

Albeit far larger, Nkrumah market is typical of Ghanaian markets. Sellers of just about every product imaginable sit and chat amongst themselves when they are not busy trading or calling over potential customers. As a foreigner, I was a potential customer in every stallholder's eyes; including, though I was unsure why, a seamstress who made only women's dresses. It took a while to get used to the hubbub, as I trooped around the stalls trying to make it look as if I had not heard the cries of '*Obruni*, come and buy my…!' Once I *had* got used to it, walking around was good fun. I had never imagined that so many crowded stalls could exist in such a small space, and could be looked at by so many people.

I was puzzled to hear a couple of them shout 'Kwasi' in my general direction. I guessed, to begin with, that they were trying to get the attention of someone, perhaps behind me, who was born on a Sunday. After the fourth or fifth different instance, though, that seemed too much of a coincidence. I smiled weakly, for want of any more meaningful gesture, as someone else called out 'Kwasi Bruni' – perhaps they *had* all been talking to me. It was a complete mystery, and all added to the sense of a mini-culture shock, although one that I could get out of simply by walking out of the market.

Simply by walking out of the market.

That proved to be easier said than done when I decided I had seen enough for the day. The trouble with wandering down passages and in between stalls is that all sense of direction is lost. I turned this way and that, back and forth, to no avail. A couple of times I asked the friendly stall-owners the way out, but advice such as, 'Turn left at the shoe shop' can only get you so far, when there are several traders selling footwear.

Lost deep in the bowels of the market, there seemed little chance of getting out any time soon. With roofs over the stalls, it was impossible to use the sun (which was behind the clouds still in any case) as a compass, like the old explorers used to do on their ships.

Forget Henry the Navigator and his mates out at sea. I felt *all* at sea.

Suddenly I heard an engine. Judging by the spluttering that it made, it was a fairly old variety of diesel. Last time I'd experienced that had been... on a tro-tro! With a little whoop of excitement, I made my way in the direction of the noise and found myself at a small tro station. It was not too hard after that to find the road which led back to the centre. I was back on my planned route!

Time had ticked on more quickly than I thought it would do; Ussher Town and James Town would have to wait until another day. After a walk that was a bit longer than expected, I arrived back at Tema station.

I remembered my thoughts regarding getting home when I left Tema station some hours ago: I'll cross that bridge when I come to it. After all the excitement of the rest of the day, this was a bridge that was eminently crossable. Sure enough, before too long I was met by yet another large man.

"*Wo ko en?*"

Brilliant. Not only did I understand the question, I also knew that he was a tro mate.

"Mamfe," I replied.

"Come."

I followed the large man, assuming that, since he was taking time out to lead the way, my tro was fairly close. It was not. Yet, despite the size of the station, he walked me most of the way across it, right to the door of the Akropong-bound tro.

He explained to the Akropong mate that I was going to Mamfe, would he mind letting me out at the Circle? It was typical of the conduct of mates. They would appear in my path '*Wo ko en*'-ing loudly; yet when my destination was different from theirs they would be unblinking in leading me to the correct part of the station.

Seated on the tro, I noticed a familiar face climb in and sit down next to me. It was Daniel. His eyes lit up, and we shook hands, generating a sharp snap as we clicked each other's fingers.

"What are you doing in Accra?" he asked.

"Just a visit for the day, to see what it's like," I answered.

"And how do you see it?"

I hesitated, and tried hard to arrange the day's events into some sort of chronological order. "Well, it was interesting…," I began, and explained the ups and downs of my adventure through the capital.

By the time we had pulled out of the station and had begun the slog back up to the Akwapim Hills, we had moved on to other matters. Daniel's evening plans were similar to mine. The Black Stars were to play Mali in the third place play-off of the African Cup of Nations. It was being shown on TV. Daniel was going to watch it at his friend Edward's house; I hoped to watch it… somewhere. I felt a bit impolite declining Daniel's invitation to join him, but I had promised the Rev that I would be back early.

"Anyhow, you've been in Ghana some time now," Daniel said. "What do you know about it?"

I had read the potted history in the guidebook shortly before I arrived, but it was a bit hazy after all the excitement of this new environment. I was about to regurgitate the limited number of facts that were dragging themselves to the front of my mind, when Daniel seized the moment to tell me a story. Brilliant at this with Class 2, he kept me hooked throughout.

He began by explaining how Ancient Ghana – which actually lay considerably further north than the present-day nation – had been absorbed into the more powerful empire of Ancient Mali. Use of the term 'Ancient' seemed something of a misnomer, since we were only talking eight hundred years previously. However, Daniel was far too animated for it to be worth taking him to task over semantics. Through migration of various West African peoples, and the influence of Islamic traders, there were by 1400 many thriving peoples, notably the Akan, Ga and Dagboma, settled in villages across what is now Ghana.

I shifted a little uneasily in my seat when Daniel started talking about the arrival on the coast in 1471 of the Portuguese; although, since we were crammed in quite tightly, I doubt that he noticed. The first Portuguese arrived at what they called *Da Costa de el Mina de Ouro*, or the Coast of the Gold Mines, which is now the town of Elmina. They were led by a man, born on a Sunday, surnamed Bruni.

That seemed somehow familiar.

"Someone called me 'Kwasi Bruni' earlier!"

"Yes, they were talking to you. Every foreigner is Kwasi Bruni. It's where *Obruni* comes from." Daniel appeared amazed that I did not know this.

Taking my 'well-I-nevers' in his stride, Daniel ploughed on. I was still a bit surprised by Kwasi Bruni, and so I missed quite a bit about Islamic slave traders having taken people from North and East Africa to the Middle East. This had carried on for centuries, long before Europeans had sailed their ships towards equatorial waters.

"So it was nothing different here when you people came," he stated matter-of-factly.

This regained my attention. I put Kwasi Bruni to the back of my mind, and wondered what Daniel's tone would be as he talked about the slave trade. It was inevitable that he would cover this, such a significant part does it play in the history of Ghana, indeed much of West Africa.

To my relief, he was on the whole quite neutral, although I had a feeling that he was holding a few of his thoughts back. I had taught the slave trade to many a class in Britain, whose interest and ability ranged widely. Talking to Daniel, though, was a fantastic lesson in what had happened, why, and with what consequences.

By the way he took a deep breath to organise his thoughts, this was an interest of his, and he was going to go into quite a bit of detail. To begin with, the Portuguese, Dutch and British were interested in mining the gold that lay inland. They sought, and usually achieved, friendly relations with the various kings and chiefs that they encountered on the coast. Materially, the gold industry initially benefitted both the Europeans and the tribal leaders, at least in the sense that there was reasonably fair exchange of commodities. Socially, though, the guns and alcohol (not that alcohol and drunkenness were unheard of in tribal life; there were African liquors prior to the European arrival) that were passed to tribes came to cause multiple problems in the Fante, Ashanti and other kingdoms who thought that they were benefiting from them.

The Europeans had quickly built castles and forts on the coast. They obtained written permission from the local leaders for this – sometimes, Daniel explained, granted after more than a hint of pressure. Some, like the Portuguese St. George's Castle at Elmina, which was later greatly extended by the Dutch, are still standing and are maintained. Others, like the Dutch fort at Moree, and the British at Prampram, are ruined, and only traces are visible, small reminders of what happened at each place once the descent into trading humans began.

It was the British who started this. London was fed up with seeing the Portuguese and Dutch take the lion's share of the gold trade. The newly-formed Royal Africa Company took over the forts that Britain had either built or, more often, aggressively seized from the Dutch. The merchants saw African people captured in tribal wars, far away from the coastal areas, as an even more profitable commodity than gold. When the slave trade started in earnest, spontaneous marauding of other tribes' defenceless villages (using European guns) began, meaning that conflict, formalised or not, was a daily threat for anyone living within the expanding range of aggressor tribes. A violent, tragic downward spiral started. The trade from the raids resulted in people being exchanged for more tools with which to inflict more violence; its profitability led to attacks on communities over a wider area.

Chained and split apart from their parents, children and siblings, life for the captured Africans in the likes of Cape Coast and Elmina castles became horrendous. To say the very least. Only when I had seen the dungeons of these castles did it begin to sink in as to what the existence in these places must have been like. Even after this,

I knew that I still had not really gained any more than a semblance of real understanding of the slave trade's horrors. And I have never seen the inside of a slaving ship either, where they were treated with even greater brutality on the way across the Atlantic. Hundreds of thousands died. Daniel's voice wavered slightly as he explained how well over five thousand captured humans passed through British forts alone every year in the eighteenth century.

Meanwhile, the Dutch had taken note of the huge profit that slave trading generated. They quietly abandoned the gold trade in favour of humans. The Danes set up slave castles as well, accounting for thousands more Africans losing their families, homes and everything else that they once possessed. It is reckoned that twelve million people were forcibly uprooted to the New World, although it could easily be even more than that. The Portuguese had long since packed their bags. This was not out of morality, Daniel hastened to add; they were not getting a look-in on the trade, having sold their forts or lost them to attacks by the Dutch and British. Portuguese slave trading continued further south.

Denmark banned slave trading in 1804. Britain did likewise in 1807 and by 1817, the Dutch, Portuguese and French had followed suit. Thereafter, there was a clampdown on illegal slave trading through European patrols.

I knew that this had merely opened the door for other problems, and Daniel carried on, giving me a much greater insight into these than I had already.

Although slavery had ended, he explained, contact with Europeans had not. Wars followed, between the Fante tribe which held sway on the coast, and the Ashanti which was dominant inland. The British got involved on the Fante's side, looking to maintain a balance of power, and gave the Ashanti a number of beatings. There was peace until 1873, when the leading lights in Westminster decided that it would be nice to control more of the Gold Coast than just its castles (all of which Britain had bought from the other European powers by the early 1870s). Britain declared the coastal area a colony in 1874, although left the interior to the Ashanti.

The 'Scramble for Africa' disrupted the restored peace. The French were eyeing Ashanti lands up, so Britain sent soldiers to the Ashanti capital Kumasi. King Pampreh I and his advisors were exiled to the Seychelles. The Brits also demanded the Golden Stool, upon which all Ashanti kings were (and still are) crowned. The canny Ashanti had seen this coming, Daniel chuckled. They had made a fake, and handed this one over instead, hiding the real one.

The Queen Mother of Ejisu, Yaa Asantewaa, was one of few that would not take Britain's encroachment onto Ashanti territory lying down. In 1900, she attacked Britain's new fort in Kumasi. Heavy fighting followed, the upshot of which was that Yaa Asantewaa joined Pampreh I in exile in the Seychelles, where she died in 1921. The Ashanti kingdom was added to the Gold Coast colony.

After skipping a few more years of Imperial rule, Daniel mentioned a good old British hero. Winston Churchill, among others, proclaimed during the Second World War that the purpose of the struggle was to allow oppressed people to choose the government which ruled them. Although, rather hypocritically, Churchill had no intention of letting the British Empire slip, he did allow parts of the colonial Legislative Council to become elected. Few people were qualified to vote under Churchill's franchise, however, and most locals saw through the move. Kwame Nkrumah, for example, was one such.

Daniel paused. He looked as though he was about to say something shocking. He was. On 28th February 1948, he continued, Nkrumah organised a peaceful demonstration in Accra, near the site of what is now Independence Square. British soldiers shot and killed fifteen people – the road leading to Independence Square at the time of our conversation bore the name 28th February Avenue in commemoration of the atrocity. "Your people blamed Nkrumah and put him in jail," Daniel said, slightly crossly. At the same time, though, the British realised which way the wind was blowing. Downing Street began to accelerate the moves to independence.

Nkrumah was released, and founded the Convention People's Party. He led strikes and boycotts throughout the colony, demanding "Self-government – now!" Although this saw Nkrumah reunited with the clink, the British had the sense to allow a proper election for the Legislative Council. The CPP stormed to victory, and Nkrumah was again released from jail. The force was well and truly with him, and he won convincingly in the colonial elections in 1954 and 1956, on the promise of securing first self-government and then full independence. On 6th March 1957, the Gold Coast colony became the Republic of Ghana.

"And you'll see the celebrations for Independence Day soon", Daniel beamed, changing the subject to something less heavy. "And what celebrations they are as well." I did some calculations; 6th March was just over three weeks away. What would lie in store on that day?

I had several questions for Daniel, but, as all good teachers do, he had clearly decided that my brain had reached its capacity for absorbing information. He returned to conversational mode.

"The Black Stars will score Mali tonight," passion flooding out of his mouth and washing the words into my ears. "Gyan is too good for their defence."

I nodded, despite disagreeing with him. Having seen highlights of some of their games before the semi-final, Ghana looked a shadow of the powerful side that had been so close to making the World Cup semi-final a few years previously. This, though, was not the moment to be critical of the team, much less of its leading player.

I was drenched by Daniel's optimism by the time we arrived at the edge of Mamfe. He broke off our chat and tapped the mate on the shoulder.

This was his stop, he would see me on Monday, God willing, and I should enjoy the game.

I wandered into *Obruni* Castle just as Auntie Gifty was bringing over a pot of boiled yams. Yams are similar to potatoes, although heavier on the stomach. I was starting the long process of learning to like them. Fried, they look and taste like overcooked, dry roasties; boiled, it is best to mash them with a fork and cover them with an ample quantity of tomato-based stew. That evening, I had not yet worked this out. Over dinner, I chatted away to Merel, Martin, Chris and a new volunteer called Hanneke, who had arrived on a few months' leave from her post in the Dutch army. With a small amount of yam remaining on my plate, I felt a sharp tummy pain. When it did not go away, I casually dropped it into conversation.

Merel was considerably more experienced in Ghanaian cuisine, and offered her advice. It amounted to there being nothing I could do about it now, but in future I should bear in mind that since yam is a heavy root vegetable, it should be eaten slowly.

Chris averted the possibility of her launching into too detailed an analysis of the consequences to the digestive system of eating yam too quickly. His interruption was particularly timely, as it also solved the problem of where to watch the football.

"Isaac has invited us all to his house for the match," he announced. Isaac was the Rev's second son who, among other things, drove the Holy Hills School minibus, ferrying the children to and from school each day. A bear of a man, he, his wife Dora, and their two young children, Samson and Caroline, lived just across from the chief.

Shortly before kick-off we crowded into Isaac's house. At least six others from outside his immediate family had plonked themselves down on chairs, the bed or the floor. I had not quite finished positioning myself on a small wooden stool when Yaw jumped onto my lap. He landed rather heavily on my still-recovering stomach, and nestled his back into my shoulder and arm. The room was filling up.

Kofi Bosh lay sprawled on the floor next to three massive speakers. A long extension cable that had seen better days connected them to the TV. Dora lifted three-month-old Caroline onto her back. She secured the baby girl with a piece of fabric the size of a tablecloth, wrapping it around her own and her daughter's body. Samson had been charging around causing the sort of mayhem that only four-year-old boys can get away with. Now, though, he found, to his disappointment, that there was much less space to run into. He solved the problem by jumping onto his dad's knee, where he fell asleep.

As the game began, Ghana had some early chances. Optimistic remarks from my companions, that made Daniel's comments on the tro sound like the unbiased voice of reason, evolved into even louder excitement. This gave way to disappointment as Mali took the lead. In the second half, there was a surge of new hope, for the Black Stars had restarted strongly. Yaw could not keep still, despite my various protests; it seemed that yam and boy had teamed up to mount a joint attack on my stomach. Most people in the room offered various words of advice and encouragement directed at the screen. Sadly, it was to no avail. The rest of the room, and the ever-bouncing Yaw, were becalmed by Mali's second goal a few minutes before the end. Luckily, my sigh of relief now that Yaw had settled was taken to be an expression of disappointment at the scoreline.

Collins, who had been sharing a chair with Ishmael, was inconsolable at the final whistle. As we filed out of Isaac's house at the end, he wiped the tears from his eyes and sat on a tree stump. I thought I should say something to the lad. I remembered how I felt when, at roughly his age and watching on TV, I was powerless to stop Ronaldinho's free kick for Brazil from looping over David Seaman's ponytail and knocking England out of the 2002 World Cup. Nothing inspirational sprang to mind, however, and so I took myself off to bed. Making a trip to the toilet twenty minutes later, I noticed that Collins was still perched glumly on his stump.

I wondered what a Sunday would be like, with all of its religious connotations. Had I been a betting man, I would have put money on 'noisy'.

Chapter 4 – A new arrival

'Noisy' was only half of it. Prior to the Church service, I had been lulled into a false sense that there would not be too much going on. Around breakfast time, the Rev slouched in his chair wearing, of all things, a Liverpool football shirt. Bosh and the rest of the complex pottered around doing their daily doings. I could not see any of the children, which at least meant that Collins had, at some point after I had seen him on my toilet trip the previous evening, realised that football is only a game, and taken himself off to bed.

Church, Merel explained to Chris and me, started early for the children. They had a two-hour or so session of what roughly equated to Sunday school, which started at the rather ungodly time of seven o'clock. That explained their absence, then.

At that moment, a great cacophony of drums, bells and singing erupted from the previously quiet chapel; Sunday school had changed gear. Taking it in her stride, Merel continued her explanation: the library building next to the chapel doubled up as the church. The main service began in there at nine o'clock, she said.

"Oh right. What's it like?" I asked.

Chris was highly interested. He had a pretty strong faith, and was keen to go to some of the services on future Sundays once he had adjusted to life in the complex. Today, though, lesson planning for the following week awaited us both.

Merel – an agnostic – pulled a face at my question. "Wait and see."

What lay in store?

Solemn members of the congregation made their way in dribs and drabs to the library entrance. The women were wearing their finest and most ornate dresses; the men dressed suavely in shirts, ties and pressed trousers. Clearly the main service was a very important part of village life. The Rev was one of the last in, having replaced his football shirt with a white and black toga-like affair which covered most of his body.

What followed sounded more like a celebration than a service. There were, of course, the drums, singing and general hubbub of the daily morning Church. However, everything carried on for longer, and was louder by virtue of there being far more people present. Sunday mornings became quite a spectacle. The complex would be virtually deserted except for one or two of the women, either looking after young children or cooking something over a fire. The only significant sound from anywhere was the incessant din of the service. When the music was not playing, Pastor Robert or another churchman preached loudly and insistently. Pastor Robert really did not need the microphone that he used; everyone in the complex could hear him, never mind those attending his service.

One Sunday at the start of Lent I was quietly washing clothes in a basin of water, joking with the volunteers. Pastor Robert's sermon was carrying on about something or other. His tone rose and fell dramatically, but no more so than usual. Then, out of nowhere, he went up several notches. It was as if an ecclesiastical firecracker had been set off next to him.

"You must-a come and pray-a! You must-a come and pray-a! You must-a pray-a to God-a! You must-a pray-a to God-a! You must-a pray-a every day-a! You must-a never stop your prayer!"

The conversation stopped. We foreigners looked at each other, amazed not really by what he had said, but by the increased urgency (Pastor's sermons were always urgent, but this was unheard of) and feeling in it. Martin broke the silence.

"He means it, doesn't he? This is Intensive Church."

The Pastor Robert who preached so aggressively was a complete contrast to the mild mannered, softy-spoken man outside Church life. A foreigner to Ghana, he had left his native Nigeria and completed his theological training in Koforidua eight years previously. He moved to Kwamoso after chatting to the Rev during a meeting, somewhere or other, of the various branches of the Church.

Pastor was married to a lady called Ruth. She was a colourful character. The hairdresser, her favourite style was tight braids, and she would often be repairing or replacing the locks of Kwamoso's women. Oddly enough, Ghanaian women, particularly the younger ones, rarely display their own hair. The fashion is for extensions to be waxed onto their short, natural hair. The women of Kwamoso could be pretty image-conscious; at times Ruth was a busy woman.

Pastor was the secretary, later headteacher, of Holy Hills School; roles that he performed with quiet brilliance, and balanced with teaching occasional RME lessons. Especially when he became head at the start of the following academic year, he dealt with any problem with a few well-judged words or actions. The way he spoke to the children, especially the younger ones, was right on their level, whatever age they might have been. Even more endearingly, his dress sense was one of the nattiest imaginable. He had a selection of multi-coloured shirts which took the term 'eye-catching' to a new level. His favourite was a scarlet button-up, which he often wore with a pair of identically-coloured shoes.

After my first experience of a Sunday service, I went to have a chat to the Rev, who was once again slouching in his chair. I had been meaning to ask over the previous few days about his running the school. I hoped he may be able to accommodate my plan to stay in Ghana, possibly until Christmas, after I had finished with the volunteering company. When I mentioned this, he got all excited.

"When will you start?" he asked, wriggling himself in his chair to an upright position in a manner which was thoroughly un-chieflike.

I explained that I would be working at Wonderful Love until the start of May, almost three months hence. Since other volunteers would probably replace me, I reckoned I would not be needed there after that.

"The Form 3 students in JHS have tests in some weeks' time, I think that you will help out," continued the Rev, seemingly oblivious to what I had just said.

This was a little delicate. I was keen to work in one of his schools, Holy Hills or Mount Zion Primary, after I had finished at Wonderful Love. However, I had no intention of leaving Class 2 after just three days. Yet here was the village chief, my effective landlord to boot, telling me that he wanted me to work for him.

What to do? I had never upset a village chief before.

I tried my best to explain that whilst I was dead keen to help his school in whatever way I could, I could not actually begin teaching there for some time. It must have been good enough, as a broad grin broke out across the Rev's face.

"*A-heeeeeeh!*" he exclaimed, which is a common term of agreement. "No problem." The words jiggled themselves merrily around my grateful ears. I could breathe easy again. The Rev was still happy, since he had by now allowed his body to slide back into its customary slouching position.

Over the course of a conversation punctuated by outbreaks of laughter and the odd finger-clicking handshake, we agreed that I would begin teaching at Holy Hills in May. I would give the JHS pupils their English and Maths lessons. In passing, the school's provision of French cropped up.

"You speak the language?" he asked.

"*Le français?!* Yes, reasonably well," I replied. I thought back, on my wave of enthusiasm, to the good A-Level grade I possessed.

The Rev sat himself bolt upright again. "And you've been to France?"

"Of course. Quite a few times. It's a fantastic country."

The Rev began talking, about the school needing a French teacher badly. There had not been one in the school for just over a year, he said. Learning French was important because Ghana is surrounded by Francophone nations. I was nodding in agreement and periodically chipping in.

"So you will be our French teacher," he concluded.

"Of course!" I agreed, unsure if this was a statement or a request. I would be delighted, I said, to teach the JHS students, and the primary classes as well, if the Rev would like.

The Rev's manner suggested that he *would* like. He nodded and waved his arms. His words came out at a fantastic rate: "Very good, very good! The children will be most happy! They will be learning French again!" He thrust his hand into mine once more, greatly excited, and sent me on my way. I wandered over to *Obruni Castle*, feeling just as thrilled as my future boss appeared to be. Sitting down, I began to wonder whether I may have led the Rev up the garden path a little. It had been the best part of ten years since I had done my A-Level, and I had only very rarely used the language since then. The memory of a recent holiday to Bayeux returned to me. In the hotel's foyer, I had launched into a detailed explanation of where my friends and I had parked the car, in response to a question from the receptionist. A look of bemusement had crossed her face; it turned out she was asking me for the room key.

I would certainly need to do some homework. Finding *une dictionnaire* moved to the top of the list of Things To Do.

At Wonderful Love, Daniel took me by the shoulder over Monday's Second Break. He wore his storytelling expression; clearly he was not about to quiz me about the pictures that Class 2 had drawn to express their weekend in my Creative Art lesson.

"I was telling you about Ghana's independence."

We pulled a chair each out of Class 2's room and sat on the shaded concrete patio outside it. Lesson Two on Ghana's history was about to begin.

"Do you know the meaning of the word 'Ghana'?"

I did not. Doubtless I was about to find out.

"It means the 'warrior king'," Daniel explained.

Ancient Ghana had been a powerful nation. In using the old name for the new, post-independence Ghana, Kwame Nkrumah looked to create a strong national spirit of pan-Africanism. It was borne of Nkrumah's determination to fight for and uphold the rights of all African peoples, which the British had ignored through their colonial governance. He saw Ghanaian independence as "an inspiration for the future", and was keen for other colonies to follow Ghana's lead in winning its sovereignty.

Nkrumah's pan-African sentiment, continued Daniel, was expressed through his co-founding of what became the African Union. He decided to allow its headquarters to be based in Egypt. This was based as much on his pan-Africanism as it was on his pragmatism – he was married to the sister of Gamst Abdel Nasser, and reckoned his brother-in-law would do him a few diplomatic favours by way of thanks. Unfortunately for Nkrumah, family connections counted for little in Nasser's eyes, and Ghana benefitted little whilst surrendering a good deal of its clout in the new organisation.

Nkrumah's sense of pan-Africanism also saw him gave sums of money, frequently greater than Ghana could afford, to other newly independent African nations and to various anti-colonial movements. At the same time, he also invested heavily in developing his new nation. There was little thought among the politicians of the debt that was being created, and on the surface it all looked healthy. Education and healthcare were prioritised, and there was much improvement in Ghana's literacy rate and life expectancy. A huge dam was built at Akosombo, as a hydro-electric power station, putting the country on the way to energy self-sufficiency.

"That's quite close; you'll probably want to see it," Daniel enthused. "Building the dam created Lake Volta. It is the biggest artificial lake in the whole world[2]. Do you know how long it takes to get from one end of it to the other in a boat? Thirty-six hours! You should try it."

That was one thing that I had no intention of doing. One hour bobbing up and down on water is quite long enough for me, never mind thirty-six of them. Before I could ask Daniel what had been on this patch of land before Nkrumah had decided to put the biggest artificial lake in the whole world there instead, he had resumed the story.

Cocoa production doubled and exports rocketed. The nation appeared to be going places. Unfortunately, the President seemed to have forgotten those sentiments of freedom and justice which had been proclaimed with sovereignty. The cocoa farmers wondered why they were seeing little of the monies that had been generated by all their hard work. The answer did not satisfy them. The government was using the cocoa revenues to try to pay for all the lovely new infrastructure. The farmers hardly saw a pesewa of it.

The working masses were unhappy too. They were not seeing the improvement that they thought they would, particularly with those two things that employees everywhere are concerned with: pay and hours. They had heard Nkrumah's anger, twenty years before, towards the colonial government. Workers also remembered that his solution to the problems had been to strike. They followed suit. Nkrumah was incensed, and banned all strikes. Some railway workers defied him, and were jailed.

Nkrumah's next steps were even more contrary to his earlier sentiments. A little shamefacedly, Daniel elucidated the events which massively destabilised the nation.

In response to the strikes and growing complaints of his economic mismanagement, Nkrumah made Ghana a one-party state. He banned opposition parties and threw his election rival, Joseph Boakye Danquah, into jail, where he died

---

[2] The term 'biggest' can be interpreted differently. Lake Volta has the largest surface area of any man-made lake in the world: 3,283 square miles (or 8,502 square kilometres). In terms of volume of water held, Lake Volta is only fourth on the list of biggest artificial lakes, at 36 cubic miles (or 148 cubic kilometres). Lake Kariba, between Zimbabwe and Zambia, is the artificial lake which contains the greatest volume of water – 43 cubic miles (or 180 cubic kilometres).

soon after. Danquah was one of nearly three thousand political prisoners. This was the last straw for the military, which was already hacked off about the economic shenanigans, and when Nkrumah was visiting Hanoi in 1966, the generals staged a *coup* and replaced him with a military council.

Nkrumah went into exile in Bucharest, never to return to Ghana. In his place, the temporary military government released political prisoners and legalised opposition parties. In 1969, elections were held as promised. Dr Kofi Busia was elected president, and led Ghana as a democracy. Yet after a few years Busia's petty dislike of Nkrumah, who had forced the new president into exile earlier in life, irritated people. The public had forgiven Nkrumah – now dead – for his failings by this stage, and respected him as the bringer of independence. Busia made it illegal even to mention the former president's name.

Daniel looked glum. Busia made the economic problems worse by devaluing the cedi, which led to rampant inflation. The military sent him packing from Osu Castle, and replaced him with one of their own, General Ignatius Acheampong. His loudly stated intention to make Ghana's economy strong again proved to be another false dawn. Instead of knuckling down, the General spent most of the next six years ignoring his advisors and arresting people who, rightly or wrongly, he thought opposed his rule. When the military tired of his antics, they sacked him. General Frederick Akuffo replaced Acheampong, and set a date of June 1979 for more civilian elections.

As I was processing this, Daniel changed tack. He began talking about an army officer who had been bold enough to attempt a *coup* against Akuffo. It having failed, Flight Lieutenant Jerry John Rawlings was awaiting his execution. He must have been pleasantly surprised, I mused to myself, to find himself being sprung from his jail cell by a group of soldiers. Like Rawlings, they did not think much of the government's corruption and incompetence.

Rawlings was a powerful-looking and charismatic sort of chap, the son of a Scottish chemist and his Ghanaian wife. Undeterred by what had happened to him the first time, he organised another *coup*. This time he was successful. Once in power, Rawlings committed to the elections and civilian rule that Akuffo had promised. Dr

Hilla Limann was elected president, but Rawlings made him wait four months before taking over. The Flight Lieutenant used that time to make sure that the bureaucracy's days of diverting national revenues into their own back pockets were over. Rawlings sacked dishonest civil servants and made tax cheats pay up. More dramatically, he sent powerful members of the military to the fate – a firing squad – that had earlier been arranged for Rawlings himself. The former national leaders Acheampong and Akuffo were at the top of the list.

As promised, President Limann's government took over on time. Were things looking up again?

No.

Daniel reverted to his serious expression. The corruption and economic problems quickly took hold once more. Rawlings despaired. I was unsure whether the phrase, 'If you want something doing, do it yourself' exists in Ghana, but the Flight Lieutenant decided that the principle needed to be applied. In 1982, he seized the presidency.

I sighed at this point. Was Ghana heading for another round of broken pledges and the excesses of military rule? Initially it was. Rawlings arrested anyone whom he felt disliked his leadership, sent Parliament packing and banned the opposition parties that had been in it. However, he subsequently oversaw huge economic growth.

Despite this, explained Daniel, life for ordinary people was not improving in line with their expectations. Strikes continued through the 1980s, along with pro-democracy protests and *coup* attempts. When, in 1989, the jailed leader of one of these *coups* was found hanged in his cell, the world pointed accusing fingers in Rawlings' direction. This looked every bit the blatant, messy and immoral murder that it (almost certainly) was.

Rawlings response was perhaps surprising. He freed opponents, lifted the ban on political parties and called elections for 1992. Electoral monitors were happy that the election was free and fair. When results were counted, it turned out that 58% of Ghanaians had chosen Rawlings to be their president. Complaints over a new VAT (which sounded a familiar concept) led to its scrapping, and four years later Rawlings won another term as president.

Daniel's face had brightened significantly by this point, since Ghana's journey to the democracy that it is today was almost complete. Rawlings stuck to the terms of the constitution and stepped down after his second term ended in 2000. The following election was won by the opposition, John Kuffour's New Patriotic Party. Rawlings and Kuffour managed the handover of power, and Ghana has never looked back.

"And in December, I'm going to vote again," Daniel concluded, his face radiant with pride. He went on to give me a little run-down of the electoral registration process. It would open in a few weeks' time, and he, like most Ghanaians, would treasure his voting card dearly over the period until the election.

I had many questions for Daniel, which he took great pleasure in answering. When he was sure that my curiosity was satisfied, he called Collins to ring the bell. It was far later than it should have been, but no-one seemed to mind.

Least of all me. After listening to Daniel, I realised that I had not stopped doing things all day.

I had been given a new job at First Break. Either Dorothy or Diana had noticed that a growing number of children were suffering from ringworm. Dorothy had managed to get hold of some anti-fungal cream to treat it, and asked me if I fancied helping out. I was happy to: it gave me something useful to do and I could still have a chat to the Three Ds whilst I was at it.

Dorothy rounded up a selection of children with ringworm, and showed me the circular marks on the head and face of each child. Some looked pretty nasty; others were fairly recent cases and were not too bad.

Although general methodology to treat the ringworm marks is simple, application of anti-fungal cream, Dorothy and Diana had different ideas on the subtler points. Dorothy thought that hydrogen peroxide needed to be rubbed onto the infected area first, before the anti-fungal cream. No, said Diana, the cream alone was fine. It was usually best to use the method of whichever of them was paying most attention to me at the time. After a couple of days of treating each child, Dorothy seemed to be right. Her stern exterior cracked into a broad smile when I sided with her in yet another debate against Diana.

The children despised the ringworm treatment, leaving as it did white smears on the treated area. It was working, though. They had to lump it. The children's grudging acceptance of anti-fungal cream speeded up considerably after Dorothy had given a few of them a piece of her mind when she spotted them wiping it off. One poor girl in Class 1, Rosamond, virtually had a white face by the time I had finished with her after the first few days, so severe was her ringworm. After about a fortnight, though, hers was gone too.

Dorothy soon decided that 'Dr Lawrie' – as Diana had dubbed me fairly quickly – enjoyed applying hydrogen peroxide to the children, and thus should have the chance to apply some more. One breaktime, after a shift of ringworm treatment, I was about to have a little snooze on one of the benches before my English lesson started: Pastor Robert had overseen a particularly noisy Church service that morning.

Dorothy put paid to my plans. She presented me with a collection of children bearing various cuts on assorted parts of their anatomy. She gestured to the hydrogen peroxide and plasters; since I was kitted out as the doctor, she reasoned, I might as well treat children's cuts and scrapes as well. I sighed and poured out another measure of the chemical – the lovely idea of a powernap remained just that.

Most 'wounds', as Dorothy termed them, looked fairly innocuous. They were usually on the toes, feet or shins as a result of one type of football injury or other. Wisdom often had several, usually quite large ones. In contrast to the ringworm, the kids loved having their wounds patched up with a plaster. Morgan and Bentil treated them as medals testifying to their on-pitch bravery. Most children had a genuine cut, but there would always be a few hangers-on who just wanted a bit of attention. I moved them on amidst great protest, and not just from the child either. Dorothy didn't like it; she thought that every little scrape needed attention. "Look at this one, Dr Lawrie! Just look at it!" she would frequently implore, pointing at a graze on someone's knee that was scabbing over nicely.

"That's not a real wound," I would counter, giving her stubborn expression short-shrift. These disagreements sometimes went on for a while, depending on how passionately I felt the need to express my discord.

One Monday there was a huge crowd: there always was after the weekend, since two days' worth of football injuries had to be seen to. Jennifer proudly presented a huge, deep cut on her knee from some mishap or other.

"Have a look at this one Dorothy," I called. "This one's a proper wound."

As if to prove the point, Jennifer howled when I dabbed the hydrogen peroxide onto her flesh to clean it of dirt.

"The chemical only hurts them if the skin is broken," I explained. "If they don't feel anything, they're fine, because the skin is healing: it's a scab, not a proper wound." It was true – when raw flesh was not exposed, the children neither felt pain from the hydrogen peroxide, nor needed a plaster. Explaining this to Dorothy took a while, but eventually it paid off. Shortly before I finished working at Wonderful Love, I wandered past her when she was inspecting Collins' elbow. She looked up at me and broke into a smile as she told him to go back outside so that she could treat the next, "proper", wound.

The early morning sun was struggling mightily to push its way through the Harmattan clouds as the volunteers sat at the breakfast table one Thursday morning, nattering away. Dennis was walking towards the Rev's house with a gigantic bucket of water on his head, and the goats were meandering around the compound looking for scraps of anything to eat. The Rev was chatting to Pastor Robert. It was, in short, not the sort of day where anything out of the ordinary could be expected to happen, let alone a meeting which would become a significant moment in my life.

A taxi drew up, which was entirely normal since people commonly came to see the Rev. On this occasion, it was Augustine who climbed out of the car and headed for the chief. Seeing him in conversation, Augustine instead made for *Obruni* Castle. He was accompanied by two foreign women. A slightly large, distinctly plain brunette walked alongside him. An elegant blonde lady followed a couple of steps behind them, and casually stood herself just behind the brunette, out of my line of sight.

Augustine shook everyone's hand as part of his usual greeting. "These are two volunteers," he commented. "One is going to Koforidua, one will live with you." We were left unenlightened; Augustine ushered both of them away to meet the Rev, who by now had finished with Pastor. The elegant blonde moved gracefully over the dust of the complex. Her hips swayed rhythmically, and her hair, tied loosely on the crown of her head, bobbed gently up and down. Conversation picked up again around the table, I think. I was miles away, silently hoping that it would be the brunette who was going to live in Koforidua.

The two new volunteers both returned shortly after, and the large brunette said goodbye before turning around to return to the taxi. The elegant blonde glided towards the table and flicked a stray hair from her shining eyes. She took everyone's hand in a confident, yet very feminine, manner, and looked each of us in the eye in turn.

"I'm Lene", she said. It came out something between '*Lee-ne*' and '*Lair-ne*', with equal emphasis on each syllable. Her face curved gently down from her eyes, which twinkled with vitality. Her wide smile exuded charm. Her voice carried her words as if they were on wings.

We asked her the standard questions: where she came from, how long she would stay for and what she would do. Her answers were to-the-point, yet delivered with a zeal and sparkle. She came from Denmark, she would stay three months, and teach in a school called Mount Zion Primary – and she was sorry, but she had to run now, because Augustine was going to show her around Koforidua. She would be back later to chat properly. With that, my first encounter with Lene Poulsen ended, as she spirited herself over to the taxi where Augustine and the large brunette were waiting.

At some point over the previous minute and a half, I realised as the taxi pulled off, my eyes must have fallen out of my head. Once I had put them back in, I helped to clear the table. Chris collared me soon after.

"What do you think of the new volunteer?" he asked. I wanted to tell him that, in truth, she was the most beautiful-looking woman I had ever set eyes on. I reined myself in. It seemed the wiser thing to do.

"Seems nice enough."

He gave me a knowing look.

Over the course of the day, I discovered that many of Class 2 did not know their birthdays. I was surprised, and mildly irritated. It had kyboshed an idea that had germinated a few days before, to have an English lesson on dates of birth and where each child's birthday fell over the year in relation to their friends'.

Despite this, I had the sort of 'average' day with Class 2 that I loved, not only teaching them, but getting to grips with the characters within it. Their strengths and weaknesses became clearer to me each day. In any class, there are children who are brilliant at everything, like Sakyi and Abigail; and those who struggle with some topics and prosper in others. With their English being so limited, many of them had difficulties with lessons taught in their second language. Jennifer, for example, had a good mathematical brain but struggled with English and Creative Art. On the other hand, getting Gideon to add numbers together was an almost Herculean task, yet his grasp of English was – in comparison with that of the others – very good.

A couple of the pupils could not, no matter how hard they tried, make sense of schoolwork. Wisdom, the youngest as far as I could tell, never complained, but always struggled to get his head around what the lessons were about. He would ask and ask, but explanations and help would usually leave him with more questions.

Then there were the characters. Morgan and Bentil were 'the lads'; Israel brought his footballing personality into the classroom. On the pitch, despite his short stature and skinny frame, he was the clogger. He stood in defence and kicked anything that came near him, irrespective of whether or not it was spherical. Numerous plasters commonly adorned his skinny legs, as reminders of tackles that he had executed. One lesson I asked him to subtract nine from sixteen.

"Eight", he fired back.

I encouraged him to have another go, and got the same response. Twice I got him to count it on his fingers, and twice he came back to be, as determined as ever, that eight was the right answer. By this stage, Israel and I had the rest of Class 2 as a curious audience. Only when Ansah came to write all the numbers from one to nineteen on the board, and we counted nine of them off together did Israel concede that the answer was actually seven. Even then, it was reluctant, as though someone had rearranged the sequence of numbers in a deliberate act of subterfuge.

I called Victoria 'The Fighter'. I made a secret bet with myself most days as to how long it would take her to bash one of her friends on the arm. Usually it was before assembly, and always before the end of 'news time'. There was nothing malicious about it: when her friends ribbed her, she just swung her arm at the offender out of habit. It was play-fighting really, nothing out of the ordinary and certainly nothing to worry about.

Ghanaian children are a lot more physical than British ones. 'Violent' is the wrong word. Although they like to give each other a good swipe, they never knock heck out of each other, nor aim for the head. I had noticed, soon after arriving in the complex, that Peace and the other kids gave each other lusty bashes to the body or arms. To begin with I felt moved to reproach them for it, only to be told by the recipient of a solid thwack that it was all OK; only once did I see anything of the ill-natured variety.

I had liked Class 2 from the start, but it was in the following weeks, with my lessons happening day in, day out, that I got to find out what made each of them tick. Bernard, for example, loved playing football in goal. He proudly wore a pair of goalkeeping gloves that an uncle had given to him. Abigail was the unofficial authority among the children: the teachers asked her to lead Worship, and the marching songs after assemblies. Her maturity came from looking after her four younger siblings after school until fairly late in the evening. Only one was school age, the others she collected from a neighbour every day. Abigail's afternoons were spent bathing the children and cooking for her soon-to-return parents.

I had been mulling over another comparison with Britain when I got back to *Obruni* Castle much later: the litter that was strewn in many places around the complex and the roadside. I had been for a walk through the fields and paths that surrounded Kwamoso. The conclusion that I had reached was that, despite appearances, Ghanaians are very tidy people. There were, outside Accra, no bin collections; these would have had to have been funded by higher taxes, which wealthier people would have grumbled about, and poorer people would have struggled or been unable to pay. However, there was never any rubbish left inside houses, classrooms or tros. People treated the inside as 'their' space, to be kept spotless. The outside, in contrast, was less important. Although the immediate vicinities of living or working areas were kept tidy by sweeping and periodically burning the collected litter, the roadsides were not, since no-one had a personal need to keep them tidy.

That evening was spent in *Obruni* Castle laughing and joking with Lene (to a disproportionate extent), Bosh and the other volunteers. After the women had disappeared to bed, Chris and I were quizzing Bosh about all things Ghanaian. Peace and Ishmael were sitting slightly away from us, doing some homework.

Eunice breezed in to join us all. Characteristically, she wasted little time getting to the point.

"You like Lene." I guessed she was addressing me.

I nodded, and hoped that it would come across as non-committal and casual enough for her to leave it at that. It did not.

"Lawrie likes Lene," she chirped, happily, to no-one in particular. Of course, Peace and Ishmael got in on it as well, kids being kids. They busily gossiped among themselves in Twi, the words 'Lawrie' and 'Lene' being mentioned frequently. My saying nothing by way of denial was taken by everyone as confirmation that Eunice's theory was correct. Eunice, meanwhile, had commandeered the pen that I had been half-toying with and half-using in order to scribble a few notes in the diary that I was keeping. She amused herself, Bosh, Chris, and to a fair extent me, by writing a slogan professing my feelings for Lene. These had shifted now, in her teenage mind, from a simple 'like' to 'love', and the message was enclosed by what looked vaguely like a heart. It was all fairly sweet, really, although I suspected that she would have let everyone else in the complex know about by the morning.

Yet it was not mentioned. The way that the children had been brought up was not to chatter about other people, at least not in a place where any adult had the slightest chance of hearing them. It surprised me a bit though, since matchmaking would have been something of a novelty. Kofi Bosh was the only single adult living in the complex. He possessed a very un-Ghanaian determination to remain that way. Most others were part of the Rev's extended family; only Yaw's family, Pastor Robert and Ruth were totally unrelated. Other than BraKofi and Paulina, there were no romantic dalliances in this little community. I had been expecting the children to chat about this little revelation in a way that would have made the columnists of gossip magazines look reticent.

Chapter 5 – Independence Day

Slosh!

The sound grabbed my attention as the tro rattled through one of the villages approaching Koforidua. A woman had emptied a huge bucket full of lord-knows-what into the gutter by the side of the road, just as we passed her. Its greenish-brown colour gave it the appearance and consistency of a curry sauce that I had once been served at a rather dubious takeout in Reading.

This was my lasting memory of the journey to Boti Falls, a waterfall popular with the Koff-Town middle class which lies a short ride north of the regional capital. Another week had gone by, over the course of which I had told the volunteers and adults of the complex that, come the weekend, I planned to go to see what the waterfall was like. I also quite fancied a swim in the plunge pool, and a walk up a woodland path to see something with the curious name of the 'Umbrella Stone'. I was rather hoping that Lene would be up for this little adventure. Bosh and BraKofi had been before and did not want to go. That notwithstanding, on Saturday morning, Merel, Martin, Hanneke and a British volunteer called Jane, who lived across the main road in Habitat, made the journey. To my delight, Lene had also put her shoes on and joined us. Chris, however, did not. He was laid low by a particularly violent stomach bug, the effects of which do not bear mentioning.

Jane's slightly advancing years and fairly worldly knowledge of life in general earned her the nickname 'Auntie Jane' from Merel, who grew very close to her. I enjoyed Jane's company; she was the sort who got to the point quickly. She said what she liked and liked what she said. Even better, she wasn't remotely bothered when people disagreed with her, which they frequently did. Her job in Britain, tucked somewhere in one of the layers of the bureaucracy of the education service, gave us something almost in common. I usually found her bluntness and sardonic wit quite endearing.

The waterfall was different to what I had expected, largely because there was very little water around, and none of it was falling. It was, with hindsight, a mistake to go in the latter half of the dry season. The plunge pool was filled with green-tinged stagnant water which looked only moderately less appealing than the substance, whatever it was, that had entered the roadside gutter earlier on. There would certainly be no swimming today.

Despite the lack of a waterfall, the Boti Falls still provided a spectacular view that morning. The rock face, which is usually masked by the cascades of water that plunge alongside it, bears the scars of various types of erosion. After a while marvelling at its form, I gave in to a gnawing temptation. A climb looked an agreeable challenge; it was, at least until the moss and general slipperiness made it rather less agreeable, and somewhat too challenging.

Unbeknown to me, Lene had taken the opportunity to take a few pictures during one of the hairier parts of my scramble. Her eyes sparkled with mischievous glee as she showed me the photographs. Most showed my arms at jaunty angles as I bent over, just about managing to keep my balance some metres above the water. She playful teased me, something about how I was too far from anywhere with a hospital to be falling down into a pool of slime, and how, in any case, she was not going to be carrying me back to the main road to wait for a passing car to take me to a surgeon.

An impatient cough betrayed the fact that Merel, Martin and Hanneke were ready to find out just what on earth the Umbrella Stone might be. Jane, on the other hand, was quite enjoying herself sitting on the sand which formed a little beach by the unsavoury-looking water.

"You just going to sit there then?" someone chivvied her buoyantly.

"Yep," came the reply, in a typically matter-of-fact tone. "It's too blooming far. I'll see you walkers later when you're done." That was that.

The walk up to the Umbrella Stone was very pleasant. Mostly flat, we were able to stroll along, joking and chit-chatting. Then we arrived at the foot of a very, very, steep slope. The girls rolled their eyes at this sting in the tail, but took a deep breath and plodded up to the top.

When we arrived there, having climbed hand over hand for the final few meters, we were greeted by the most amazing sight. The Umbrella Stone has the appearance of a giant rocky mushroom. On this dull day, the final throes of the Harmattan, I could not help feeling that the rock bore not the slightest resemblance to an umbrella. Only later in the year did the meaning become apparent. On my second visit in June, a crowd of visiting schoolchildren was sitting underneath it. In the shade of the 'umbrella', they mopped their brows and drank sachets of pure water. The woman who sold them clearly knew a thing or two about locating a business.

School visits to the waterfall and Umbrella Stone occur almost every weekend. Whilst Martin paid sixty pesewas for the pleasure of climbing to the top of the rock, I had a chat to one of the teachers leading a group of JHS students. This particular bunch had come all the way from Cape Coast, a four hour drive – at least – away. After the usual questions – "What is your name?", "Where do you come from?", "How long have you been in Ghana?" – he explained that the waterfall is a sacred site. He informed me that there is a festival there every year on the first of July, and recommended that I go to it. In fact, he spent so long chatting away about it that I had to tell him twice that the sixty or so adolescents that he was accompanying were being led back down the steep path by their other teachers. He laughed, carried on chatting, and then eased himself down the slope several minutes after them.

The Umbrella Stone looks out over lush countryside, which seems to roll on forever. Sitting next to the stone and looking out, especially after the Harmattan season had ended and the view had grown substantially, gave a feeling of complete freedom and peace. This was no mean feat, given the noise generated by the crowd of children and other visitors. The hills and general greenery were quite strongly reminiscent of Britain's rural landscape, albeit with a couple of palm trees thrown in. It was an odd comparison in the humidity of the equatorial dry season.

I left the others at Koforidua's tro station, in order to have another look around the town whilst they returned home to get ready for the evening. Jane had invited us over to the house where she was living, for a chat and a quiet drink with the volunteers who lived with her. I had seen them a few times before. Eva was a Dutch girl of nineteen, her countrywomen Anna was about five years older. There were two German lads as well, although they were rarely seen around the house. Apparently they enjoyed the company of the television more than that of other people.

Jane had rather grandly explained to me some days earlier that her house had a roof terrace that her host family never used, which offered a fantastic view of the night sky. My mind had begun to explore the idea of this starlit facility, but just as thoroughly unrealistic visions of a recliner seat, with a cocktail in hand, gazing up at the constellations, were getting to the stage where the possibility of a small swimming pool seemed just about plausible, Merel had interjected.

"You like to exaggerate," she grinned, shooting a look towards Jane. "This 'roof terrace' is only the top floor of the house, which is still half-built. It's just a concrete floor and some breeze-block walls. And if many from *Obruni* Castle come over, we won't even have enough chairs!"

As if sensing my dampened spirits, Merel had continued: "She's right about the stars though, you can see everything. It's amazing in a power cut."

Power cuts were a feature of village life. They were barely noticeable during the day, since the electricity was not greatly used. In the evenings, though, they were a source of great frustration for the people of Kwamoso. Power cuts reminded them of the constant evening darkness that they had endured before electricity had been introduced to the village only a few months previously. They were referred to as 'light off', rather than 'electricity off' or anything else. The villagers loved the light; it was seen as the most important yardstick of local development.

It was a measure of how proud the locals were that they had electricity, when neighbouring villages such as Saforo still did not, that the lights stayed burning all night. They were often on in rooms where people were asleep. I would get up in the middle of the night for a toilet trip, and see the complex lit up. I found it slightly disconcerting to begin with, coming from a society where we are told to turn things off when they are not in use.

When there was a spell of 'light off' in the evenings, which was once or twice a week, everyone used torches to see their way around the complex. The locals went to bed if there were an extended period of darkness. In contrast, I loved the power cuts. With all the light pollution, the skies were less clear than I had thought they would be before I arrived in the country. Of course, they were far clearer than from most places in Britain; gazing up during cloudless nights, I often lost track of the time that passed. Evenings where there was 'light off' took on an added aura, each star was defined so sharply. The darkness added a feeling of mystery to the quietness of the complex at night.

Until August, when it fell below the horizon, the Southern Cross was visible. I loved looking at it, partly as I had seen it in South Africa and liked its simple form. Moreover, I had once been told in quite forceful tones by a rather brash Aussie that it can only be seen from the Antipodes. My protests, that anyone in the southern hemisphere should be able to see it, were initially met with a fair degree of hostility and scepticism. Consequently, it was quite a *coup* that he later, grudgingly, conceded that it was actually visible from anywhere south of the equator, "But nowhere from the north." Seeing it from Ghana, just about in the northern hemisphere, was a totally unexpected pleasure.

That Saturday evening, four of the five who had been to Boti trooped off to Jane's house. Chris was still feeling fragile, and Martin had developed a similar complaint. Bosh was doing something complicated with the music files on his computer, and BraKofi was nowhere to be found. At least it meant that we would all have a chair on the roof terrace.

We didn't.

Jane had forgotten that the family that she lived with had invited over some guests that evening, and so all bar three of the chairs were being sat on already. It was no problem; sitting on the ground, against the wall, was actually a lot more pleasant than I thought it would have been. One of the Germans had come up to begin with, but must have decided that the sofa in the television room downstairs was more comfortable. Eva and Anna had given their chairs to Merel and Hanneke when we arrived, and I had done the gentlemanly thing and let Jane take the third one. This chivalry also gave me a convenient pretext to sit down beside Lene on the concrete. The seven off us were chatting and laughing away, a bottle of tipple keeping each of us going.

A number of times Lene and I went off on a tangent from the main conversation. After a chat, debate or joke we returned to see what the others had moved on to talking about. At one point, we diverted from a discussion about a temperamental fourteen-year-old boy by the name of Yarro, whom a number of the volunteers knew from working at the Rev's Mount Zion children's home, and whom Lene taught at the school.

I asked Lene about Yarro and the things that she had seen him get up to. In return, she asked me about the children I had taught in Britain, and how they compared to those at Wonderful Love. Somehow we got on to chatting about some of the things in our daily lives that we had left behind. Sitting next to her and talking about this and that, I became aware of two things. Firstly, it had been quite a while since either of us had spoken to anyone else. Secondly, as well as being stunningly beautiful and highly intelligent, Lene's company was akin to that of an old friend, even though we had met so recently. I looked at her as she spoke to me, feeling an overwhelming desire to put an arm around her and hear her carry on talking all night. Of course, that would have been a crazy idea. Instead, I asked her another question about something trivial. Yet there seemed to be something different now – was it affection? – in her eyes.

I'm not sure whether I had imagined it or not, but a decision had to be made. It was now, or quite likely never. Near the end of her answer I slid my hand casually over the top of hers. I was about to pull it back again when she flicked her wrist around, and her hand held on to mine, giving it a just-perceptible squeeze.

Never had I been so content to be sitting on a concrete floor with a long-empty beer bottle.

We carried on chatting, smiling as we gazed at each other, and laughing at this and that which had come into our conversation.

This idyllic little scene was never going to last long though, with five others in such proximity. I suspect that they had grown a little suspicious when we had failed, after several minutes, to re-engage with their conversation. I heard Jane whisper to Merel: "Are they holding hands?" It may have come out far less subtly than she had intended, although with it being Jane, the question may equally have been deliberately indiscreet.

We glanced up to see five faces quickly turning away, and nonchalantly carried on talking.

Goodness knows how long we spent chatting away in *Obruni* Castle after we had walked, hand in hand, back to the Rev's house along with Hanneke and Merel. I learned my first Danish word, *dejlig*. It means lovely. "This is *dejlig*," Lene added, raising the hand that was holding mine, as further explanation. I was in full agreement.

Word spread quite quickly amongst the volunteers in the Rev's house. Walking out to breakfast in the morning, Chris grinned at me. As he tested his stomach's resilience with a piece of bread and jam, he asked me whether I had enjoyed my evening on the rooftop, whilst Merel looked on with an 'I-knew-it-all-along' expression on her face. I was quite glad that Lene was still in the process of getting up. Martin quickly found out too, after he had emerged from his sick-bed later in the morning.

As Intensive Church started up, Lene and I smiled about the surrealism of it all. I felt as happy as a pig in muck doing my laundry. She was busying herself preparing Yarro's class an English lesson at one of the tables in *Obruni* Castle. She seemed to have an extra sprightliness about her as she made a set of flashcards.

We were a touch worried about what the Rev and Florence would make of it all, although not for long. A small frown brushed across the Rev's face as he saw me brush a hand down her arm at some point in the afternoon. For an instant, my mind flickered with the feeling that I had still never seen a village chief in a bad mood. An instant later the trepidation passed, as the frown quickly turned into an open-mouthed smile of happiness.

Later, Merel, Hanneke, Lene and I went for a walk along one of the paths which led out into the fantastic countryside around Kwamoso. We asked Chris if he fancied it as well, but his stomach had evidently failed its earlier test with the bread and jam. He was lying down reading his book in *Obruni* Castle, his face distinctly pale. Martin was in a similarly sorry state, and blanched at the thought of any type of movement.

Contrary to what Lene and I had hoped, although perhaps inevitably, two conversations carried on for much of the walk. The Dutch girls reverted to their own language and left Lene and me to chatter away. Not that they seemed to mind the separate discussions in any way, but Lene and I resolved not to let a split develop between us and the other volunteers. In *Obruni* Castle that evening, a fantastic game of poker involving the four of us and the slightly healthier Chris (and, for a very short time Bosh, before he bluffed all his pieces of coloured paper that served as chips away, and retired to bed cursing his luck) seemed a good early indicator that no such division would happen.

Indeed, I was more concerned about my own tendency to do daft things. For a few evenings, after she had gone to bed, for a short time I worried that I would somehow put my foot in it, and ruin our friendship. After a couple of days that nervousness passed, as we realised that we had a great deal in common. It was fortunate, too, that the Rev, Florence and Auntie Gifty saw us as quite a sweet pair, and looked on happily whenever we sat or stood together in their presence. The children, too, got over their initial giggles and accepted the situation for what it was.

What excitement!

Dressed immaculately in their school uniform, Peace and Eunice marched out of the Rev's house as the early morning sun struggled to peep through the low cloud. Their pace was remarkable; at least twice as fast as anything I had previously seen them reach. They strode towards the school buildings, where there was a great unseen commotion on the grass behind the infants' section. Drums were being banged and tambourines shaken with great ebullience. Some commands were shouted, followed by an order of "Left, right, left, right, left, right, left, right, left, right!"

Suddenly the teenagers of the Junior High section marched out from behind Class 2's room and into view. They were a fanfare of flags, banners and percussion as they looped around the area where school assemblies took place and disappeared from view once more. More orders were barked, whereupon the children made a second lap and then a third. We volunteers – now numbering seven with the addition of another Danish woman, Pil, who would work on the volunteering company's building site – looked on at this remarkable, as yet unexplained, event.

Auntie Gifty strolled over to the breakfast table, with a flask of newly boiled water for tea or coffee. She must have noticed us all gawping at the unconventional, and early, start to the school day.

"Next week we are having Independence Day," she told us. "The children are practicing for their parade in the town. They will do it every morning until next week Tuesday."

Independence Day. How quickly that had come round.

The marching certainly looked spectacular, from what we could see from the table, and if practice made perfect then we were in for a treat come 6th March.

Peace and Eunice returned to the Rev's house, having reverted to their usual snail's pace, to get ready for the school day proper. Ishmael followed behind them. He was retrieving his Maths book from Eunice, who informed us that she had "Borrowed it to copy homework." They didn't beat around the bush, these kids. Peace excitedly told us all about the parade, how they would go to "the town" and march alongside the other schools. A prize would be awarded to the school with the best march.

"Mr Maxwell is not happy with us," she explained in her thunderous tones. "He says we are too slow." There was a long drawn out emphasis on the 'too', which I had come to realise was just another feature of Ghanaian English. "So we have to start at six-thirty every morning."

This seemed a less severe start time than it would have done when I first arrived, but still exceptionally early for school to begin. Clearly Mr Maxwell, whoever he was, meant business with this parade.

So it passed that, for the rest of the week, the JHS pupils practiced and re-practiced their marches each morning. The still unseen Mr Maxwell relentlessly exhorted the pupils to ever greater improvement from behind the infants' building. The cacophony of drums and shouting made an impressive spectacle all week. Walking down one day gave a picture of a pretty well-drilled bunch of youngsters. Pastor Robert was in charge that morning, though, so the identity of Mr Maxwell remained a mystery. He, too, mentioned with great pride the march in "the town". Would I and the other volunteers go?

"Of course," I replied. We would be delighted.

A couple of mornings before the parade, six-thirty had rolled on to quarter to seven. Practice had still not begun. The sky was turning a darker and darker shade of grey as the volunteers breakfasted, and the wind was picking up. Dennis strolled over to pick up a palm oil container, which had been cut off near the top so that it could be used to sweep rubbish into.

"Big rain is coming," he warned as gravely as he could manage whilst smiling a huge smile at us.

He was right. The sky was by now almost black. Less than a minute later, rain lashed down across the complex. We vainly attempted to keep the contents of the table dry. The din that the drops made on the tin roof of *Obruni* Castle was incredible; it was difficult to hear anyone speak. As with all Ghanaian storms, there was no gentle build-up of steadily increasing rain. One minute there was nothing, the next it was bucketing down. We knew when a storm was coming, but there was no telling whether it would hit in five minutes or thirty seconds.

Huddled in the middle of *Obruni* Castle, all we could do was laugh at the position we found ourselves in. That laughter increased when someone pointed out that my window was open – as it usually was, for ventilation purposes – and that the rain was slanting straight into the room.

I had a gloomy sensation that it was landing right onto the area of the spare bed where I had placed my flashcards for the day's Maths and English lessons.

Bother.

Perhaps there was a chance that they could still be saved. I jumped over the bench backrest and ran the few metres to the window. Pushing the shutter closed, I turned, ran and jumped back into *Obruni* Castle. The whole operation took around ten seconds, I would guess, yet it looked as if I had forgotten to undress before having my morning bath.

It did not matter, in fact, that my flashcards had gone all floppy and the ink had run. When the deluge had eased off to a heavy drizzle, I made my way to Wonderful Love and arrived at around the time that assembly was usually starting. I found only a handful of children who, to my horror, were running around and jumping full length into the mud of the football pitch. They were having a whale of a time, their green and white uniforms now predominantly brown, and festooned with the odd clump of grass. Wisdom appeared to have grown a miniature Afro. On closer inspection, it turned out to be a clod of sticky, wet earth which covered most of his head.

There was nothing to be done except wait. In the warm air of the open classroom, the flashcards dried out fairly quickly; outside, the ground, which had earlier had streams flowing across it, soon showed no sign of any adverse weather.

Daniel was the first teacher to arrive, and a look of wondrous bemusement crossed his face when he saw me.

"What are you doing here?" he asked.

I was not quite certain what to say to this, so I answered with the obvious. "It's a school day, Daniel. I've come to work."

I felt my hand being vigorously shaken. "We never come to school in the rain!" he exclaimed. "No-one does!"

With the ferocity of the downpour, I could understand why this was so. I tried to imagine the same happening in Britain. We would get hardly any teaching done.

Daniel and I chatted about the celebration for Independence Day, and he told me about a massive parade in Koforidua. Representatives of all the public services would form ranks and march, followed shortly after by children from the local Junior and Senior High schools. It would take place in the main square, he said, and would begin early. Many people would come to watch, as it is the most important event of the year. Of course, it would be a public holiday, which meant that all schools would close.

"Will you go?" he finished.

Obviously, 'The town' that everyone in the complex had been referring to was Koforidua. 'The town'. Koff-Town. Of course.

"Yes," I replied. "I'm going to watch the children that I live with in Kwamoso. They will be marching."

Dorothy and Diana trickled into school a while later, and when a large enough number of children had arrived we began teaching. It was just before the time when First Break would have ended, and so there would be only one lesson today.

It was a little frustrating, since by eleven o'clock the weather was hot and humid once more, to teach a greatly diminished class, but another lesson in the culture of the country. It was simply what it was. On rainy days, school would be severely disrupted.

Among the volunteers, an elaborate plan was hatched for the parade. Lene, Pil, Merel, Hanneke and I would go with Jane, Eva and two (more) Dutch volunteers who had moved into their house – Marieke and Catharina – to Koforidua. Chris had gone with the volunteering company to Cape Coast for a few days; Martin had returned to his landscaping job in Switzerland. We would watch the parade, and then spend a bit more time in Koff-Town. A visit to a hotel with a swimming pool was mentioned. It all sounded very nice.

I felt a degree of shock, therefore, a day or so before Independence Day when I overheard a conversation involving the Rev, about getting ready for the parade *in Adawso*. It transpired that I had been very wrong about 'The town'. It was a rather awkward situation when I was asked whether I still intended to go to watch the Holy Hills children marching. A quick decision had to be made, and I gave an answer which I still regret.

"I'm going with the volunteers to Koforidua, we're going to watch the parade there and then have a look around afterwards," I began. I added, as if it would make a difference, that the volunteers had thought that the children were parading in Koforidua. I felt guilty, that I had let the Rev, and the kids, down. I wanted to see the children marching, greatly, yet had put a jolly with the other volunteers before them. I wish, now, that I had either suggested to the volunteers that we change plans, or gone to Adawso without them. At least to have done something. The worst thing was that with Adawso being on the same route as Koforidua, it would have been easy to have taken a tro from the parade that the Holy Hills schoolchildren had participated in, to the regional capital. Our entertainments would not have suffered in the slightest.

The Rev's response was kind, although I think that, deep down, he was disappointed. "Oh, no problem, no problem," he said. "The Koforidua parade will be bigger anyway; you'll enjoy it more." Perhaps it was in light of this that I said nothing to the volunteers about changing plans once I had told them of the situation. Perhaps not.

I still felt uncomfortable about the whole business as Merel, Lene, Pil, Hanneke and I waved goodbye to the Rev, and crossed the complex. Isaac had started the engine of the school minibus, and Eunice, Peace and their classmates were going through the final run-throughs of their marching routines, led by Pastor Robert. We had told those children who lived in the complex that we were going to Koforidua, and not to Adawso. They had not batted an eyelid, although I suspect that they, too, were disappointed that we were not going to see their parade. We waved at them, and they smiled back at us.

Jane and the Habitat volunteers met us at Quarters Junction. We waited, as tro after tro flashed its lights at us. It was to be expected, of course, since the parades were such big events, and it was Adawso's market day as well. Eventually, we got on separate tros in dribs and drabs, and agreed to meet back up at one of the infamous numbered traffic lights in Koff-Town. Jane was typically jovial as she boarded her tro along with Eva: "I don't know which lights are blooming which, see you at the ones closest to the station," she called through the window, whilst the mate hauled the door closed.

Lene, Pil and I were the last to leave the Junction. In Koforidua, we met up with the others near to what were either the third or fourth lights. There were huge numbers of police officers out in force. Carrying guns over their shoulders, it was clear that they meant business. This was confirmed when we crossed the street without waiting for the lights to turn green.

"*Heh!* You people! You use the lights!" one of them barked sternly, as we reached the other side, where he was standing. His gun wobbled on its strap as he spoke. "You wait!"

It did not seem to matter that there had been no traffic coming. We put this to him, which drew a sharp rebuke. The gun's wobbling intensified.

"I said you wait for the lights! You wait!"

We apologised, and, taking the lack of any further gun-wobbling riposte as a sign that he was sufficiently pacified, carried on to the central square where the parade was to take place.

With the delay caused by waiting for tros at Quarters Junction, and then being told off by the constabulary, we arrived at the square slightly after the parade was due to begin. It did not matter; a few of the local dignitaries, including the head of the army division, were late as well. Someone was talking, most officiously, into a loudspeaker, to keep the crowd informed of what was going on. The parade, we were promised, would start "Very soon."

It was getting seriously hot. Standing around was becoming hard work, and it had only been ten minutes or so. I felt sympathy for the members of the various services, who had been standing in their ranks since well before we arrived. Clad in their uniforms of various colours, complete with gloves as white as the new fallen snow, several of them were feeling the sun's intensity as well. More than a couple regularly mopped their brow with a handkerchief. More dramatically, one army cadet, a lad of around twenty who wore a huge drum strapped around his body, had to be helped away by the medical people after the heat proved too much for him.

Spectators milled around and wandered around the edge of the parade area trying to find a better viewing spot. Suddenly, the loudspeaker crackled into action again.

"Stop walking around the edge of the parade ground!" it warned in a loud, purposeful voice. "If you do not stop you will be arrested!"

That seemed a touch disproportionate.

It did the trick though: for a few minutes people stayed more or less static. Before too long, however, there was movement again, but nobody seemed to mind. Besides, it was hard to tell who had a legitimate business to be walking around. Many people were selling water, and doing a roaring trade with the thirsty crowd. The usual snacks and phone credit were being sold, and there were also a number of people handing out small national flags made from paper. Adults and children alike waved them feverishly.

A whistle drew attention to a car pulling up near the square. Some official-looking people got out. They must have been the delayed dignitaries, because pretty soon after that, the parade got underway. There were all sorts of songs played by the military band, which marched along the width of the square in perfect formation. One trumpeteer blew with such exuberance it looked as if his face might explode at any moment. His lips, even as they pressed the mouthpiece of his gleaming instrument, had formed a giant smile, and his wide eyes shone with delight. The sense of enjoyment was everywhere.

Meanwhile, a group of kids had found a new vantage point, and had been joined by Merel, Marieke and Catherina. They were perched on the roof of a 4x4, which at some point during the band's performance must have arrived and been parked next to the crowd. There were probably twenty others squashed in next to them, and periodically more would scramble up to take advantage of the elevated view.

They had the best seat in the house as the parade got going, with all the services marching in their ranks around the square. The nurses in particular looked the part, their strides perfectly synchronised, and their standard being carried with supreme steadiness.

Most spectacular, though, were the school parades. Dressed in their finest marching apparel, of various different and often quite exotic colours, the children of each school marched past us. Each youngster's face was a picture of concentration, on what he or she had surely been practicing for days on end. The colours were a sight in themselves. There were some uniforms in shades of yellows or blues that were pretty eye-catching, and one school wore an electric pink. The Koforidua Islamic Girls' School outdid them all, however; its students were kitted out in dresses a remarkable shade of lime green. Had it been night, they could probably have illuminated the entire event by themselves.

Refreshingly, some way behind the schoolchildren, came a group of protesters carrying banners. Openly critical of the government, their slogans demanded free healthcare and better management of the economy. The image of Eunice's knee, riddled with infection that first evening in Kwamoso, came back to me, along with a great feeling of Ghana's continuing development. In how many other countries on the continent would something like this demonstration have been allowed?

A shout from behind the crowd next to me momentarily diverted attention from the proceedings. The 4x4's owner had returned and was less than thrilled to see that his vehicle had been transformed into the viewing gallery. The fun up there was over, but out in the square it carried on in full swing. Countless laps were marched, and the singing and beating of drums were relentless.

Eventually, either the requisite number of laps had been reached, or a conclusion had been mutually drawn that it really was far too hot to be worth carrying on. The parade ended, and I was left pondering contentedly the immense national pride that had shone through from everyone who had been there. The spectators waving their flags and cheering had done so wholeheartedly and passionately. A general feel-good factor permeated the square. This was truly a celebration.

The following day had been declared a public holiday as well. The government had a lovely way of occasionally announcing an additional public holiday at short notice, sometimes for no apparent reason. Either way, it was a bonus to have a free day in which to do a little more exploring of the local area.

Kofi Bosh viewed the day off as an opportunity to do a bit of tour guiding for the volunteers. During our breakfast natter, he dropped in the existence of a waterfall in Akropong. There was a raised eyebrow or two, but Bosh assured us that this one, unlike Boti, would actually be falling. He chattered energetically about how we would be able to have a good swim, and how there was no need to bring towels because the sun would dry us very quickly. As ever with Bosh, it was punctuated with his laughter at one thing or another. Once he was happy that we would all go that afternoon, he gave us a quick "*Me quaaba, wie*," or "I'm coming soon, OK," and disappeared.

Bosh often used that turn of phrase. 'Soon', in this part of the world, can mean anything from a few minutes to several hours. A better equivalent might be 'when I feel like it'. This time, around six hours passed, which was one of his longer efforts. We had just begun to wonder where on earth he had got to, when he re-appeared. One of the many things that he had been doing was to collect a group of the children to come too. Fifteen of us made our way off to Quarters Junction to flag a tro, or several tros, to take us up to Akropong.

I wondered how many of our party would manage to get onto the ten passenger vehicle (twelve people in total with the mate and driver) which drew up. Two passengers were already on board, and I was fifth or sixth in our little queue. It was, therefore, rather startling to look out of the window from the back seat and see that nobody was still waiting. With Peace having plonked herself heavily on my lap, the view forward was limited to the back of her head, and so I had not seen who else had scrambled on.

"How many people are on here?" I asked her. Surely some of our party must have found a taxi or another tro from somewhere.

As she counted past twelve, I began to wonder what number she would stop at. Fourteen was followed by fifteen and sixteen, and eventually she turned and said in a triumphant voice, "Nineteen!"

Hanneke eased Yaw to one side of her lap and tapped on Bosh's shoulder.

"What's this about 'overload'?" she asked, a tiny trace of apprehension just audible over her Army-trained coolness in the face of new situations.

Bosh looked about as concerned as a kid in a sweetshop. "It's OK," he reassured her. "Overload is only with adults. The children don't count; they're sitting on someone's knee."

Hanneke was not in the least bit reassured. She carried on, which seemed somewhat pointless since we were by now well into the journey. "But this is a twelve person tro. Twelve is twelve. Nineteen is too many."

"But the children are not taking up seats, so they don't count. Overload is only when the adults are sharing seats."

Bosh's logic seemed flawed, but was yet another example of how Ghana is simply different to the West. Strictly speaking, a twelve person tro is actually a twelve seat tro; theoretically, people pay for a seat, not for themselves. Since the children were sitting on someone else's knee, they were not taking up a seat and so there was no overload.

More practically, it also means that children do not have to pay a fare, which in daily life, when families travel, saves the sort of money that is the difference between being able to afford to make the journey or not. Whatever people feel about overload, and there were many complaints from Ghanaians about it, there was never argument about children making a tro too crowded and heavy. Indeed, there would likely be uproar if the rules were to be changed; sensibly, the police only challenge tros with more adults than seats.

We piled out at Akropong, and Bosh led the way down to the waterfall. It sounded like there were plenty of people down there already, which was unsurprising with it being a public holiday. It would be a good chance to have a chat with some other people, I thought.

How wrong I would be.

Unfortunately, what followed formed my first real negative experience in the country.

The waterfall is a small affair set in a wood, with a pretty strong torrent flowing over a jagged rock face, into a waist-deep plunge pool. We approached along a path running alongside the noisily gurgling river.

It was not noisy enough, however, to prevent our footsteps and chatter being heard when we were about fifty metres away. A mass cry of *Obruni!* went up from a group of youngish men splashing around in the pool. As one, they left the water and descended upon us. It quickly became apparent that the eight of them intended to say more than just 'Hello'.

"*What is your name?*", "*Which country are you from?*" These were the questions that I had grown used to hearing, and had no problem with giving an answer which may or may not have lead on to a conversation. The trouble was that this bunch were less interested in hearing the answer than asking the next question, most of which were directed at the white women. Bosh, a German teenager called Florian (who had only very recently arrived at the complex), and I were the only men; Lene, Pil, Hanneke, Merel, Jane and Eva outnumbered us.

"*Can I come back to your country with you?*", "*Will you give me your phone number?*", "*Will you come to eat with me tonight?*" These had been heard before and could be made light of, the 'No's' delivered with a smile and a joke.

The real problems started when our new acquaintances leeringly carried on, and on. "*Will you give me your number?*" became "*Give me your number.*" Similarly, the invitation to a meal had been turned into a command.

Bosh had gestured for Peace, Yaw, Eunice, Sandra, Ishmael and Dennis to make themselves scarce, which was good; this had the potential to turn unpleasant. There was little bother for Jane, she didn't exactly fit the profile that these eight prats had in mind for their next sexual encounter. The lad who did half-heartedly try his luck seemed only too glad to be sent packing by her no-nonsense rebuttal. The twenty-something ladies, though, were in varying states of agitation.

Bosh seemed to be having a bit of success in saying something to calm down one of the lads. Florian and I tried the same tactic of negotiation, although coming from *Obrunis* it had next to no effect. I glanced over at Lene, who looked to be holding her own against a skinny guy who was wearing what looked to be a very old tea-cosy on his head.

Another was explaining to Merel about how he played football for Liverpool and how he would cook her fufu, the *best* fufu, in his house. Once my joke about his transfer (a few minutes earlier he had been telling me how he played for Chelsea) had drawn a brief hoot of derision, he carried on telling Merel how he would be her husband when she took him to Holland. Unsurprisingly, Merel's face bore a look which should have told him that she wouldn't have taken him across the street.

It was time to be a touch more forceful.

My tone, as I pointed out to him that Merel had no interest in him whatsoever, was assertive enough. It was quickly clear that the idiot was not paying the blindest bit of attention. I was beginning to get a little irritated. One or two four-letter words probably passed my lips in the process of telling Idiot to find someone, somewhere else, who *was* remotely attracted to him, but I had not come close to 'angry' yet. That changed when his eyes turned to Lene. By the look on her face, she had nearly finished convincing her suitor that, in contrast to whatever he might have thought, she was in fact *not* the love of his life.

Whilst Idiot's weight was shifting from one foot to the other in readiness to make his approach, I jabbed a finger into his arm. "And if you even think of saying anything to her, I'll fucking kill you," I snarled. This was not the most intelligent thing to say, since Idiot was a bit bigger than me and probably a lot stronger. Blinded by the red mist, however, these thoughts did not enter my head, nor did notions of pacification. A torrent of Anglo-Saxon flowed out of my mouth as fast as the waterfall, and by a huge stroke of luck had some sort of effect. I am unsure exactly how it happened, but by the time that Bosh had come over to see what the heightened level of fuss was about, our voices had returned to a normal volume.

I was, and remain, grateful to him for taking over my side of the debate at this point, and started to make my way over to where most of the women had gathered. There was a tap on my shoulder. One of the others, who had seemed the least offensive of the lot of them at the start, began apologising to me. I likewise expressed regret for my part in the ugly little scene.

It turned out to be a fairly pleasant conversation, under the circumstances. His "brothers" were celebrating a birthday party, he expounded, and had maybe drunk a touch too much. In Ghana, he continued, it is common for lads to try their luck and talk to white women, partly because they are uncommon and exotic, and partly because many Ghanaians want to move to the West.

I thought it would be best to reciprocate in explaining cultural norms. I expressed how the way that they had courted the women was different from how it is done in western society, and that their conduct had come across as quite intimidating. Thankfully, everything ended peaceably, and I joined Bosh and the rest of our party in walking up a path to the top of the waterfall and by the river for a while.

The women were OK: Lene, Jane and Hanneke were smiling; Pil, Eva and Merel, looking slightly tenser, exchanged a few words about something. Young Florian looked thoroughly bemused more than anything else; Bosh and the kids were embarrassed. Hand in hand with Lene, I don't remember too much being said by anyone, although that may be because I was still pretty brassed off by the whole affair. It was a lesson, I supposed, as much in Ghanaian culture as my own need to not react aggressively to these sorts of situations. Bosh was brilliant, of course. Walking back to the roadside to return home later, he told us that these things occasionally happened, but that very rarely was it so lecherous.

Bosh, Florian and Merel took the children back to the complex, and Jane and Eva took the next tro to Habitat. Lene, Pil, Hanneke and I contemplated the afternoon's excitement. The conclusion was that a stop-off at Palm Hill for a bottle of beer was in order. It was most welcome.

Chapter 6 – Church comes to us!

Walking down the dirt road from Wonderful Love to the roadside after school one afternoon a few weeks after Independence Day, Diana and I were chatting about life in general.

"How do you see Ghana?" she asked.

"Very different, but I like it," I answered. There was clearly more to be said than that, but where to begin?

I decided. "Like the tro-tro. We don't have them in Britain. We have to catch a bus, which runs on a timetable. If you miss it, you're late for work. Here, if you miss a tro-tro, it doesn't matter, because another one is on its way."

Diana nodded, but said nothing, so I carried on. "And when we get to school, it's so easy. You can just arrive and teach the lessons you've planned, and then go home at the end of the day. I wish it could be like that in Britain."

Diana's face turned ever so slightly into a frown. "What do you mean?"

"It's brilliant here. There's no paperwork, no meetings, no rubbish. You can just teach." I cast my mind back to my previous school. A passionate soliloquy was forming. It was going to slam the interminable meetings led by a senior teacher whose voice was audible sandpaper. It was going to tell of how the teachers were told at unnecessary length of new whole-school initiatives, which made 'official policy' out of what we already did in lessons to stimulate children's interest. It was going to conclude with a lament of the numerous forms which were required to be filled in to 'evidence our good practice' – whatever that phrase meant – and had to be sought out from the deepest inner reaches of the school's computer network.

Before those thoughts could be expressed, however, Diana had turned to me, incredulous.

"But we want to have meetings, and we need paperwork. We should be doing that sort of thing to improve our school."

Diana's surprised reaction continued. It probably came from hearing about how much differently things happen in the West, and associating this difference with being 'better'. Therefore, by this logic, the western method must be the 'right' way to operate a school. Sadly, this was a common misconception among Ghanaians, and not one limited to education.

"Anyway Diana, we have at least two meetings every day, usually." In the broadest sense, we did. Over both breaktimes, the Three Ds and I would have a chat about all sorts (quite often Diana would be light-heartedly matchmaking for me), but school matters were normally discussed first. A few days earlier, for example, we had put a timetable in place for the approaching end of term tests. Most afternoons, too, we walked to the roadside to wait for the tro together, chatting away.

"We also take the register every day and record the children's test scores. We have schemes of work. What other paperwork do you want?" My question was intended as a rhetorical one, but nevertheless Diana appeared to search for an answer before giving up. Conversation returned to more humdrum matters.

It bothered me a little, though, that Diana wanted to see schools in Ghana develop the 'procedures' that we have in Britain. It was true that Wonderful Love could have been better organised. First Break could have ended when the timetable said that it should do, and the school day could have been longer. These, however, were not issues that would have been solved by ticking boxes and making life generally over-complicated with audits and pen-pushing. I made a mental note to one day drop into conversation the stress that British teachers in some cases suffer. Obviously, the paper trail and meetings are not the sole causes of this stress; but it's fair to say that without this administrative work, the profession would be less sapping. Maybe, I thought for a brief, mischievous moment, I should throw League Tables into the mix as well; although that, I fancied, would be a cultural clash too far.

The number of volunteers in the complex had risen again by this time. A chubby Canadian called Sasha, on two-month holiday from his job in a medical research lab, and a British gap year student called Charlotte had joined our number. She and Pil shared the room next to mine, which I now shared with Chris. The four of us developed a morning ritual of chatting through the wall that separated our rooms as the music and singing of the Church service got into full swing.

Charlotte had made everyone in the complex chuckle with a couple of slapstick episodes in her first few days. One evening she came into *Obruni* Castle with her tail between her legs.

"I can't believe it," she sighed. "I've just dropped my phone down the toilet." Before anyone had asked her how on earth she had managed to do it, somebody had jumped up and made their way over to the toilet block. For some reason, probably sheer curiosity, the rest followed. We peered down. There was nothing visible.

"I know," someone piped up. "I'll call it."

From the dark depths of the toilet, a muffled ringtone began and a dim light from the screen projected itself upwards. It was intriguing to see how deep the toilet's cesspit was: at least ten feet.

The phone was pretty quickly written off as a lost cause, but next morning Ishmael breezed into *Obruni* Castle. With a triumphant flourish, he handed Charlotte a slightly smelly, but dry and clean, mobile. He and Eunice, he recounted proudly, had fished it out at some point around dawn using sticks and an old rag.

"It works, too," Ishmael added. He was thrilled.

It was another example of the kindness and spirit of the kids in the complex that they would have even attempted something like it, and a measure of their ingenuity that they had actually managed it. The children's efforts, sadly, were to little avail. Later on in the week Charlotte left her recovered phone on a tro coming home from the Mount Zion children's home. Pil, Chris and I took the Mickey out her remorselessly for it during the next few mornings' through-the-wall chats.

Sasha was a nice enough guy, but had displayed a tendency to attempt to blind us with his knowledge of events past and present. This habit earned him the nickname 'The world's leading authority on everything'. It was an ironic moniker. There were usually inconsistencies, shall we say, between his understanding of certain facts and everyone else's. Fifteen minutes of conversation with him, I reckoned, was the limit.

Late one afternoon most of the volunteers had gone for a walk into the countryside. I had given Sasha his quarter of an hour and was chatting away with Chris and Lene, when from behind us we heard the word 'beach'.

Merel was telling Pil about one of the places that she had been to with Jane and Eva a while before, somewhere called Dzita, in the Volta Region. The '*Dz*' sound is pronounced similarly to 'je', as in 'jeans', so the name approximated to '*Jeeta*'. After we had found out a bit more about the sand, clear sea and lagoon, Lene turned to me with a very sensible idea.

"Let's go to Dzita this weekend."

I don't think I've agreed to anything as quickly.

That Friday afternoon, the tro that Lene and I were sitting in crossed the River Volta and rolled up to join the queue of traffic at the police checkpoint at Sogakope, the first town in the Volta Region. A scene unfolded that was truly breath-taking.

Although hawkers sell snacks, essentials and phone credit at almost all 'stopping' places, this was an unprecedented onslaught of traders. At least two dozen of them rushed to crowd around the tro before it had even stopped.

Arms were thrust through the open windows proffering bread, dried fish, plantain, water, phone credit and heaven-knows-what-else to everybody on board. Money changed hands at a furious rate, and things were quickly handed to those who had bought them. Passengers by the windows served as intermediaries between buyers and sellers. They passed payment from, and goods and change to, those sitting in the middle of the tro, who could not reach the windows themselves.

A barging match had developed between two bread sellers over who was going to have the middle window on the driver's side. It ended in disappointment for both; a third trader dodged past them and pushed a couple of his loaves through the window first. Then, just as quickly as it had begun, the whole scene ended when our driver fired the engine up again. As we accelerated down the road, a cedi note was thrown out of a window by way of belated payment.

Once we had got our breath back after this encounter, Lene and I caught a shared taxi[3] from the nearby junction town of Dabala, and another one at a village called Savietula. Presently, we stopped at a wooden building next at the roadside. A

---

[3] Taxis fall into two categories. A shared taxi runs on the same basis as a tro-tro, leaving a taxi station when it is full and plying a set route. A dropping taxi operates as 'black' taxis in Britain do, picking up a party of passengers and taking them to a destination of their choice. Dropping taxis are significantly more expensive.

sign on its gate announced that we had arrived at the *Meet Me There* Guesthouse. It was around half a mile from anything more substantial than a few houses. Lene opened the door, and we almost fell out of the back seat that we had been sharing with two other people.

We were quickly greeted by a jovial Zimbabwean-British ex-pat called Hugh. With his suntan, beard and beach attire, Hugh looked as though he was on permanent holiday. Hugh chuckled at our account of the journey, before he left us in the hands of a chap called Kojo, who would, Hugh assured us, take care of everything.

Kojo was quite something. Almost completely deaf and dumb, he took helpfulness to new levels. He insisted on taking both of our bags, and beckoned us to his canoe, which sat at the edge of a lagoon separating the guesthouse from the beach. Through a mixture of gesture and grunting he established that he would take us across the water, and put up a tent for us on the beach.

I was less than enthusiastic about the prospect of this little voyage. Doubtless Kojo was an expert boatman, but I have never been a fan of these sorts of ventures. It did not help that the canoe looked rather rocky; especially when our bags had been loaded into it. I wondered how I could communicate my pretty strong desire to walk the few hundred metres around the lagoon, and meet him and Lene on the beach. My eventual walking motion, looking a bit like the green man at a pelican crossing, was countered with an insistent rowing motion from Kojo. Just to remove any possible doubt, he pointed at Lene, who had climbed on board and was grinning excitedly.

It was the canoe, then.

Waking up in our tent on Saturday morning, I willed time to stop. Of course, it did not, as it never does, and the weekend passed all too quickly. Put simply, Dzita remains the most naturally beautiful place I have been to. Its palm tree-lined beach ran all the way to the mouth of the River Volta to the west, and eastwards into Togo. The waves that broke and rushed up over the sand came from a sea clearer than I had thought possible. There was nothing like it, even when I was able to compare it to other beaches in the country, many less than sixty miles away. The sea was so clean that neither of us used soap across the weekend. Swimming in the saltwater was as good as any bath, and far more invigorating.

I do not usually enjoy lazing around and doing nothing, yet that weekend I was in my element, mostly doing just that. We sat on the beach – with periodic interludes jumping into the incoming waves and swimming – and watched life go by.

We also had the odd walk along the sand, ankle deep in the tide, and on Saturday afternoon ran along the road that passes through Dzita village. Local people waved happily at us and gave us greetings, but there were none of the cries of *Obruni* (or *Yavoo*, its translation in the Ewe language of the Volta Region) that we had become accustomed to. We were left in complete peace. The village was totally at one with its surroundings. Most houses were constructed from wooden posts, with dried palm tree branches cross-weaved together and attached to them, to make a pretty solid wall. Roofs were made either in the same manner, or out of reeds. The villagers had an electricity supply and were protected from the Gulf of Guinea's strong waves by a thick concrete sea wall.

On the beach were wooden fishing boats, painted with fantastic multi-coloured designs, and big enough to fit four or five people. The fishermen, as in most of the coastal settlements, provided the backbone of the local economy, setting out most mornings and returning with the catch.

We were just about to walk back around the lagoon after a delicious dinner at the guesthouse's bar, when Lene got all excited. Far more excited, indeed, than I had been a while before, when I had managed to persuade Kojo that neither of us, or Lene, would suffer too much if we gave his canoe a miss.

A baby sea-turtle was making its way along the sand, jerkily pushing itself along on its flippers. As Lene squealed with delight, pointed at it, and jumped up and down in exhilaration, we failed to realise that we were not the only ones to see the hatchling. The guesthouse dog had spotted it too. Unfortunately, whilst we were busy taking a photograph of our little friend, the dog was sneaking up un-noticed. The poor baby turtle's last act before being scooped up in the dog's mouth was to unwittingly pose for us.

We related this tragic tale to Hugh. He became ever so worked up.

"It's time!" he gasped.

"Time? For what?"

"Hatching time!" he cried. He explained that there was a vast colony of the sea turtles, which laid their eggs in the calmer water of the lagoon. Periodically, there are mass hatchings of offspring; this was one such occasion. Hugh rounded up a few of the staff and two other guests, and raced down to the edge of the lagoon. Lene and I followed. Sure enough, tens of newly-hatched sea-turtles were scrabbling around on the sand.

How fabulous!

Whilst everyone else either looked on or cooed at the little reptiles, Hugh sprang into action. Forming his hands into a cup, he picked up as many of them as he could carry, and called Kojo for the canoe. Everyone else gathered up a fistful of sea-turtles, then stepped into the canoe to carry them out towards their natural habitat. Kojo must have thought it was Christmas as he paddled back and forth over the lagoon. There was a workmanlike feel to the job; nobody seemed to be saying much as the task was completed. Around half an hour later, we were finished. Those that were staying in the guesthouse itself crossed back over the lagoon in Kojo's canoe. Lene and I were left sitting on the starlit beach, gazing up at the Milky Way. It was perfect.

The following day we saw another function of the sea. Crab nets had been laid out beyond the shore. Groups of men and boys from the village were hauling them in. Old and young, they dragged in the lines attached to each of the nets, emptied the contents into buckets, and then moved on the next one further down the beach.

Happily, the sea-turtles were too small to have been caught up in the nets. Hugh, though, sombrely explained at breakfast time how very few would have been strong enough to survive their first night in the sea, regardless of the nets. It is all part of nature, I suppose.

Dragging the crab lines in looked like pretty onerous work, each one taking around half an hour. The fishermen must have had fantastic upper-body strength, honed through years of performing the same task: not one of them showed any sign of flagging. As they walked along the beach to the next line, we exchanged cheerful 'Hellos' and 'How are yous?' with many of them.

Meet Me There is run partly as a volunteering organisation, as well as a guesthouse. It has a mixture of local staff and westerners. Lene and I had a chat with Dougal, a Brit who was in charge of the volunteering side. He told us that the guesthouse arranged for westerners to go into the local school and help out with classes. The main thrust of volunteer work, though, was to provide the local community in the village with compost toilets. These, Dougal expounded, are far more hygienic than the cesspits which are dotted around the village in the ratio of roughly one for every five hundred people.

There was passion in Dougal's voice, which mixed with pride when he told us about the gratitude that he had been shown over the two years that he had worked there. The most rewarding part, he explained animatedly, is the opening of a finished toilet. Villagers throw a little party for such occasions.

Dougal also explained to us, as we were leaving that afternoon, how the fishermen hauling in the crab lines perform this same task every Sunday morning. The same process happens on beaches right along the coastline, in Ghana and its neighbouring countries. Enormous quantities of crab are transported to all the markets within travelling distance of these coastal villages.

I pondered on the way back to Kwamoso whether I might be able to get involved with Dougal's work at some point. The August school holiday sprang to mind. The idea of living and working with a bloke who got so excited about a loo was rather appealing, and he had been good for a laugh throughout the weekend. More importantly, the programmes that he was leading directly benefited the local people.

In the end, I decided not to, for purely selfish reasons. As with any type of work, there would be good days and bad days. I did not want to be fed up after one of the odd bad ones, in a setting as perfect as Dzita. Besides, living day-to-day in such a glorious place would lead me to take it for granted.

No, Lene and I would come again just before she returned to Denmark at the end of May, and that would be that.

Dong, dong- dong- dong, dong- dong- dong, dong!
Church had once again broken off sleep long before I thought it had any right to. I peered out of my bedroom window. It was pitch black.

It shouldn't have been.

By the end of March, the sky had begun to lighten by the time one of the children had rung the bell. Something, I reasoned, was up.

Chris had clearly been woken up by the din as well; his outline was moving on what used to be the spare bed.

"What time is it, mate?" I asked him rather sleepily. It was a Thursday morning; the volunteers usually spent a few hours of Wednesday evenings in the Blue Bar in Mamfe, meaning a slightly later night than the rest of the week.

Similarly drowsily, he said something in German by way of reply. Clearly it was too early for his English to be working.

"What?!"

"Oh, erm, sorry," he murmured. He reached over for his alarm clock (the alarm function was thoroughly redundant) and knocked it on the floor. His scrabbling around for it succeeded only in pushing it under his bed.

"*Scheiße!*"

I understood that well enough.

Eventually, he managed to retrieve it. He illuminated the screen.

"It's four-o-three."

Four o'clock in the blooming morning. What the blazes was going on?

Suddenly, I remembered. There was going to be the Mount Zion Church revival over the coming weekend. It was held annually over the weekend before Easter. It was the most important event of the year for the complex, but this year's, BraKofi had explained, was to be even more celebrated. It marked the twenty-fifth anniversary of the foundation of Kwamoso's branch of the Church.

The volunteers had been given a very official-looking invitation from the Rev earlier in the week, requesting our presence at the main service on Palm Sunday. Since it would last for most of the day, it was clearly a very big deal. Our invitation looked to be more of an instruction to go to at least part of it.

However, these recollections did nothing to account for why a Church service was starting at this hour.

Chris and I sunk back down into our beds, and closed our eyes. I managed to doze, or half-doze, for around ten minutes, before the most dreadful tuneless singing got going. Accompanied by the irregular banging of a drum, it brought us both wide awake.

Since this had obliterated any hope of getting back to sleep, we began our morning chinwag. It fairly quickly descended into a moaning session, even on Chris's part as a churchgoer. It grew more animated when there was a sudden upturn in the volume of the singing.

It was almost as if somebody had hooked up a loudhailer.

"No! They can't have!" Chris's words were far more hopeful than realistic.

Some seconds passed. This was unquestionably a loudhailer.

By now Chris and I could hear Pil and Charlotte in the next room having a similarly incredulous discussion. One of our through-the-wall chats started which, once we had accepted that we could not do anything about the racket, grew calmer. As our customary jokes lightened the air of annoyance, our thoughts turned to the revival, and what else might be going on early in the mornings. How much noise could one church make?

We got up at six, having gone some way towards putting the world, or at least the complex, to rights. I found the Rev talking to Pastor Robert by the front door. His tone of voice, indeed his general manner, was conspicuously lacking his customary charm. Evidently, something had got his back up; it turned out that he, too, was miffed about the noise that had been generated. Pastor Robert, it emerged, had not been in charge of the service. He had left it instead to a rather zealous trainee pastor called Emmanuel, who had come to stay in the complex for a few months to complete his instruction.

It was a little disappointing that, now I *had* finally seen a village chief angry, it was less spectacular than I originally thought it might have been. That little anti-climax, however, was more than compensated for by the Rev explaining, later on, that Church the following day would begin at the usual hour. It would also be conducted, he assured me, at the normal volume. The loudhailers, thankfully, would only be used for the main Sunday service.

That afternoon, returning from Wonderful Love, I found that the complex had almost finished sprucing itself up for the revival. Blue and red bunting had been hung up from the lampposts and trees in the complex, and a number of awnings were being assembled. These would serve as the covering for the Church seating area, which was based around the circular platform in the centre of the complex. The platform had been re-painted, its new white surface looking most splendid, if a little dazzling in the afternoon sunshine.

Slightly more oddly, Collins and his classmate Bismark were busy painting the bottom eighteen inches of the tree trunks in the same white as the platform. I asked BraKofi why this was. He replied casually that it looked neat. His brother Isaac gave a more practical answer when Chris asked him later. There would be many people coming, and if they drove through the complex in the evening, they may not be able to see the trees. The last thing that the Rev wanted, I mused later, was to have a visiting branch of the Church remember its twenty-fifth birthday party for the loss of a wing-mirror on an unseen tree during a parking job.

Guests began to arrive on the Friday morning. By the time I had returned from school, the complex was alive with visitors. Most of them had set up blankets on which to sleep, on various classroom floors in Holy Hills School. It was a pretty Spartan setting for a night's kip. Some, presumably the more important dignitaries, had been invited into the homes of some of the villagers. Peace's mum – a strapping lady called Cynthia – was looking after at least three of them, and Auntie Gifty had cleared a couple of rooms in her house. That was a most generous act, for it left her, Esther, Collins and Little Mabena with just one room for themselves.

By Saturday, the complex represented a market as much as part of a village. There were women and children selling the usual snacks, and coming to and fro carrying fresh supplies of everything on their heads. An increasing number of Church members sat, stood or walked around in conversation with each other.

Pastor Emmanuel was still trying to redeem himself after the loudhailer debacle the previous morning, wholeheartedly trying to be both the chaperone and host for every new face that he could find. Robert, altogether more collected, indulged in jovial discussions involving much arm-waving and laughter with those that had endured Emmanuel's whirlwind introduction. The Rev's third son, a gangly nineteen-year-old called Solomon, had made the journey from his university course in Accra to join the festivities. Solomon had adopted BraKofi's fashion sense at some point during his upbringing. He drifted around the complex in a vest, and trousers that hung from somewhere below his bottom.

Friday afternoon and Saturday saw a couple of services each; Friday's second was curtailed by a rainstorm which sprang up from almost nothing. Hurriedly, everyone moved the electrical equipment and percussion instruments under the awnings, and threw tarpaulin sheets over anything that was not sufficiently under cover. I felt particularly sorry for Florence, who looked like a drowned rat – as did everyone else – after completing that task, only to discover that no-one had arranged buckets under the roof of the Rev's house to catch the water running off it. By the time she had made a couple of journeys to fetch enough buckets from various parts of the complex, and set them up underneath the best run-off areas, she looked thoroughly bedraggled.

Palm Sunday dawned lovely and bright. There was much interest among the volunteers as to what the Church service would be like. Bosh had explained on the Friday that we needed to be attired in our smartest clothes, after which Chris took it upon himself to remind us all of this as often as he could.

"You must dress *very* properly," he chided at every possible opportunity, most notably on the Saturday evening when we were having a natter about what might happen the following morning.

"That," he gestured dismissively towards my t-shirt, which bore an almost-witty slogan, "Will not do. We're all going to be sitting on the platform, with the Reverend and the important people of the Church, you know. You must look *very* smart."

Just to wind him up, I strolled out for breakfast on Sunday morning wearing the same shirt, and watched his face fold into a wonderfully irritated expression. His seething had just about eased to the point where he could form a telling off in English, when I could keep a straight face no longer.

"It's alright, mate, I'll change it after breakfast," I managed, when I had finished laughing.

To his credit, he saw the funny side of it as well.

Eunice strode over to where the volunteers were sitting, in our Sunday best, shortly after half past eight. We needed to go, she informed us, to the library. The procession out towards the platform for the start of the service would shortly be starting. Eunice looked incredible, clad shoulder to toe in a deep-purple gown, with a matching mortarboard covering her head. She led the way to the library, and stood aside as we walked in. The other teenagers, those of the complex and visiting, were dressed identically to Eunice. They wore solemn expressions as they clutched their prayer books and order of service, awaiting the off. Someone hurriedly passed all the volunteers one of each.

In the brief passages of time just before an important event starts, tension always seems to take hold of everyone. This was one such occasion. Faces everywhere carried an expression which smacked of determination not to let anything go wrong, along with a trace of nervousness that something still might. The adults made last-minute adjustments to their suits and dresses; even BraKofi and Solomon had scrubbed up well.

It was something of a relief to everyone when Pastor Emmanuel finally opened the door of the library. He beckoned the children to lead the way out to the makeshift church. I wondered what would happen if it rained, but judged it best, under the circumstances, not to ask. I followed everyone out, past the awnings where the congregation would be seated, and up to the platform. I felt just a little awkward sitting right behind the Rev, particularly when a grumpy-looking visiting pastor turned around and asked one of the other volunteers what role we had in the Church.

The service itself began with a lengthy opening speech of introduction and thanks from the Rev, followed by a series of slightly shorter speeches from the visiting churchmen. Thereafter, it was full of the songs and percussion that we had all heard so many times, either first thing in the morning or during Intensive Church on Sundays. As each hymn reached its conclusion, the singing grew ever more joyful and raucous. It would almost certainly have raised the roof, if there had been one.

After a while, the celebratory nature of the service really started. The congregation came to the centre of the space which served as the church. The musicians restarted, and most people began dancing, waving long strips of purple or yellow cloth around as they did so. A procession not dissimilar to the Conga began. It snaked up and down the church, with the cloth being flailed in all directions. Eventually, it broke up into an unscripted display of bodily movement, singing and percussion. The coloured strips continued to be waved heartily, in some sort of rhythm to the various sounds that were generated. All earlier seriousness had been well and truly cast aside. At one point, somebody walked, or stumbled, into a pair of huge ceremonial drums called gong-gongs. They fell onto their sides with a crash and rolled several feet. It was greeted with laughter from all on the platform, a significant amount of which came from the Rev.

This colourful spectacle eventually drew itself to a conclusion. Everyone returned to their seat, and a few more hymns were sung. These preceded a number of recitals from the Bible and Book of Psalms which Pastor Robert, his wife Ruth and various members of the complex community delivered zealously. A number of cries of 'Hallelujah' and 'Amen' from the congregation accompanied the more significant lines.

Pastor Robert brought everyone to a hush, which was no easy task given the ebullience of the assembled group. He introduced a burly pastor from one of the other branches of the Church, who was clad in a gown that made his substantial size look even greater. In an unexpectedly low and measured voice, he began a long sermon about the duties of every Christian, which meandered along, between various topics, as if it were a gentle rural river on a summer's day.

The Rev turned around to the volunteers and looked as if he might be about to say something profound. He didn't. Instead he suggested that we go and get ready for lunch, which Auntie Gifty was on the point of serving. After a quick chat about what we thought of the event, he finished off with a comment that was most unexpected.

"I know that you people don't have the same types of service in your countries. You may find this a bit too much. So if you've had enough, don't feel that you have to come back."

That made it sound as though we could, if we so chose, sit down and get some peace and quiet. It was not quite as straightforward as that; *Obruni* Castle and the Rev's house were less than ten metres from the platform. There was no need to go to Church, I had once joked, or half-joked, to BraKofi; rather, Church came to us. This

Sunday was an extension of that general principal. Nevertheless, parts of the service had been quite heavy-going. Only Merel and I – ironically enough, the two biggest unbelievers among us – returned to the platform for any significant length of time.

By the evening, it would be fair to say that the complex was 'Churched out'. There was due to be a brief evening service which closed the revival. Bosh, for one, said that he would give it a miss. As for the volunteers, we too felt that we had experienced enough Christianity for the weekend. The women intended to go to bed early; Sasha, Florian, Chris and I made plans for a trip to Palm Hill, the bar on the other side of Mamfe, for a bottle or two of the local *Club* or *Gulder* beers. This was partly a bit of light relief after the four days of religious fervour, and partly to say farewell to Chris. In the middle of the next week, he would be flying back to Germany.

Shortly before we made our way over to Quarters Junction for the tro, Debra asked us what we planned to do, instead of going to the closing service. When we told her, a look of surprise passed over her face.

"You are going for hard drink?!" she asked.

"Yes," came our reply. It was hard to think what to add on to that by way of elaboration.

Debra grunted: "*Ah!*" a sound which is used variously to reflect anger, surprise or confusion. Debra's probably conveyed the former. Possibly she thought that we were going out for a skin-full: apparently some past volunteers had overindulged, much to the consternation of the Rev and his family.

Getting drunk, with the bizarre exception of during funerals, is frowned upon by most of Ghanaian society. Funerals are a special case, a weekend-long celebration of the deceased's life. They involve a heck of a lot of music, played at a heck of a loud volume, over a heck of a lot of speakers. Effectively, they are a Friday-night-to-Sunday-evening party, with dancing and singing creating a distinctly African flavour.

Otherwise, drinking on a large scale simply is not done; indeed, the vast majority of the complex's adults were teetotal. BraKofi enjoyed a beer or two, and Bosh would sometimes join us in Club 29 or the Blue Bar. He would drink two *Smirnoff Ices* and become totally silly. Even for the westerners, a couple of bottles of beer were enough anyway. Their volume (significantly more than a pint) was larger, and with the heat and humidity their effect kicked in more quickly.

Only once did I have more than I could handle, and that was completely by mistake. One evening the volunteers had gone to the Blue Bar on a Friday night. After a few *Gulders*, someone brought to my attention the existence of a local spirit called *Akpateshie*, and spoke very highly of it. At fifty pesewas a shot, it was worth a pop. Kwasi, the barman, opened a bottle and poured a most unappealing brown liquid into a tumbler. It was a very generous measure of what resembled, pretty closely, something that I had once found leaking from the engine of my car.

To my great, and pleasant, surprise, it tasted fantastic. Since I had experienced no ill effects, over the next half an hour or so, I drank three more. This stuff was not only delicious, but seemingly completely non-intoxicating.

Sitting in a taxi a while later, a peculiar feeling hit me at around the same time that I began to see two bends in the road, and two signs warning of the hazards of excessive speed, at a place where there had only ever been one of each before.

The hangover the next morning was one of immense proportions. There would definitely be no heavy drinking this Sunday night.

We actually had a terrific evening, once we had got out of the taxi at Palm Hill. Before we got in it at Mamfe Circle, Sasha had suddenly begun bargaining with the driver, offering one cedi per person, for a ride that cost sixty pesewas as a fixed fee. Unsurprisingly, it was a deal which the driver swiftly accepted, and it would not have been the done thing to go back on the 'deal'.

We sat looking out over the Akwapim hills, dotted with lights in the darkness, and laughed about the weekend's entertainment. I had a flash of inspiration for my *bête-noire*, the following morning's dreaded Creative Art lesson. The children would take their chairs outside and sketch the landscape. Bingo.

Class 2 brought their chairs and little sketchbooks out onto the football field at Wonderful Love. They listened attentively, on the whole, as I explained what they were going to do. The only one that did not have the first idea what was being asked of her was Patience. This was no surprise; she had wandered off half-way through my little pep talk. She thought that she had seen an animal, she explained once Regina and Jennifer had brought her back, and wanted to find out what it was. It was a stick.

As Class 2 got down to their drawings, I was also unsure whether Bentil had fully understood the task. He had taken a few paces from the group and relieved himself near to the penalty area just as I was getting to a crucial part of the instructions. Wisdom, however, way-laid me on the way to Bentil's seat. Could I please help him part two pages of his book, which he had managed to glue together the week before?

By the time I got to Bentil, he had already drawn a reasonably accurate representation of the foreground, complete with a scribble of yellow, green and brown which represented the plantain field just beyond the touchline.

Over Second Break, Suzy made an appearance as I was looking through the pictures that Class 2 had produced. The children were good little artists.

"I've been talking with the Reverend," she said after we had exchanged pleasantries and had a bit of a natter. "He's agreed to the volunteers running a two-week holiday school for the Holy Hills primary section over the Spring Break. He says that we can teach them whatever we like. The Holy Hills teachers will come and help as well. We'll have a chat about it later in the week."

The chance to see what the likes of Yaw, Dennis, Debra and the two Mabenas would be like in school sounded interesting. I readily agreed to it. The only downside, I realised later, was that it meant that the Holy Hills children would have only a very short break.

They didn't seem to mind too much though, when Lene and I told them all about it. We had spent an hour and a half with Suzy and another volunteer who lived in Mamfe. Mischa was a Scottish gap year student who had been working with Yaw's class at Holy Hills.

Over that ninety minutes, we had come up with a plan. The women pronounced it foolproof, and I suspected it was shot full of holes.

We would start some time into the Spring Break and only have lessons in the mornings, so that the children would still get some holiday time. The Holy Hills teachers would come into school, and we would split the classes between us all. The full-time teachers would run catch-up sessions to revise topics that they had covered in earlier lessons. Lene, Mischa and I would teach them one topic per week each, away from the syllabus, bringing in a variety of cross-curricular aspects.

I decided that my first topic would simply be called 'Football'. It would be instantly appealing, and would include Maths problems, an English lesson of reading and writing, and at least one Art lesson, in which the children would create a football stadium from cardboard, paper and cut up drinking straws.

There would be, in this idealistic timetable, an 'Activity' session for the last hour of each day. A football tournament seemed easy enough, but I had less confidence about a Holy Hills Olympics. Rather optimistically, this would incorporate such makeshift events as the shot put, using a rock as an improved shot, and a tug of war – "We're bound to find some rope somewhere in the village" – between groups of children. Once that had all been agreed upon, we had a good chinwag. Suzy by this stage had revealed herself not just to have a personality, but also to be quite good fun.

I didn't want to sound like a killjoy, but the Rev and Suzy's plan seemed to me to depend quite heavily on the school's full-time teachers and children turning up, out of term-time. I reckoned the likelihood of the former was dependent on the open question of whether the Rev would be paying them for this little venture.

I had quite a busy time, then, in the last week of the term. Daniel had asked me to write the end of term English, Maths and Creative Art exams for Class 2, and I wanted to get ready for these themed lessons at Holy Hills.

In the end, I had to write the exams again, after Daniel looked through them and declared them too hard for Class 2. I remember being moderately annoyed at this, since I was attempting to test all abilities in the class. Daniel seemed to want me to create a set of questions where even the likes of Patience and Wisdom would be able to get full marks. Try as I might, and did, I could not convince Daniel that children such as these two, lovely as they were, would never get full marks in any test.

"We're a completely mixed ability group, Daniel. We have a top end; the likes of Abigail, Sakyi and Morgan, who always do better in class than anyone else, the middle group, and then the weaker two or three."

I knew that the children were being asked to write, which, due to the nature of their English lessons they were not used to doing. Despite this, I pointed out that the children were all familiar with the words that they would need to use.

"No, no, these are too difficult," Daniel persisted. He pointed at sentences with the verb missing, like 'I [am] happy'. "You need to give them choices so that they know what word to use."

"They know it!" I exclaimed. "They've done it hundreds of times in class. They should be able to do it!"

"Lawrie, I'm asking you, please change it." His tone was earnest, he had placed a hand on my shoulder, and his eyes had taken on a look that spoke of his sadness if he saw the children struggling.

It was no use. I took the test home and made it easier. Daniel was thrilled with my amendments, and couldn't thank me enough. In hindsight, too, he was quite right about the difficulty which the children would have experienced with the original.

It was a pleasant surprise when he later told me that I did not need to be in school for the exam week. Madam Vera, the headteacher at Mount Zion, had told Lene the same the previous day. Suddenly, we found ourselves with a two-week break, and a guidebook-full of places to explore over the country.

Chapter 7 – Travelling the country

Two thoughts dominated as I stood by the water's edge: Lake Bosumtwi is remarkably beautiful, and the journey to arrive there, via the Immigration Office in Koforidua, had been unexpectedly straightforward.

Lene and I had heard stories of how it could take hours to log an application for a visa extension. In the worst cases – after they had waited an age to be seen – applicants had had the letter of application scrutinised to the nth degree, and had been made to fill in endless forms. All this was followed by news that there would be a ten-day wait before their passport could be picked up again.

That morning, though, it took all of ten minutes to complete the application process. Such was my surprise, it slipped my mind to ask quite why I was there at all, after only two months of my stay in Ghana. I had paid for a three-month visa from the Ghanaian High Commission in London before leaving Britain, yet I was already having to pay again to extend the visa. Lene was in a similar position. Months later, Suzy told me that she had arrived in Accra with a twelve-month visa, and had to pay for ten of those months again.

Lene had planned, before she arrived in the country, to have two weeks at the end of her time teaching to go travelling. One afternoon she had invited me to come with her, which I had swiftly agreed to. Among other places, she wanted to go across the eastern border to Togo, to see how it compared with Ghana.

"Can we cross the border and come back with these extensions?" we asked the Immigration Officer. He was a youngish man who was built like a mountain.

"Of course, you can go and come. It's no problem," the Man-Mountain replied jovially.

We each filled a form in, paid, and waited slightly nervously to hear how long it would take to process the applications.

The Man-Mountain smiled. "You collect the passports in three days."

That meant Thursday!

"Make sure you are there then, though, because we will close on Thursday evening for Easter."

Hardly believing our luck, we thanked him and said goodbye before he changed his mind. I hoped it would be that simple for the visits I would have to make in the future, to re-extend my visa when I had started working for the Rev.

Deep in the Ashanti region, twenty miles or so from Ghana's second city, Kumasi, Lake Bosumtwi is a holy site for the Ashanti people. The spirits of the dead come there to visit the god Twi, who apparently lives in the lake, on their way to eternity. If that is the case, then old Twi has picked the right spot to set up house.

The area was hit by a meteorite many moons ago. At some point over time, the resulting twenty-five square kilometre crater filled with water, forming the lake. Fast forward to the twenty-first century and its backdrop of densely forested hills provided the perfect spot for Lene and me to begin our Spring Break holiday.

We lay on the beach for a while nattering away, and then had a swim in the clear, warm lake. Since the water was so pleasant, and we were on our holidays after all, this was something that we did a number of times over the following couple of days.

It was a bit of a shame, therefore, when the time came to prise ourselves away from Bosumtwi's blissfulness a couple of days later. Part two of our holiday was to visit the forest and butterfly sanctuary at Bobiri Forestry Reserve, just off the main road between Kumasi and Koforidua. On the way, Lene reckoned, the village of Besease, with a traditional Ashanti shrine, was worth a look as well. I was less keen, but having heard her talk about how we would be able to see a traditional fetish priest, I had also become enthusiastic. The fetish priests, where they still exist, are still regarded as second only in the villages to the chief. They give spiritual advice and herbal remedies, as wanted or needed, to people who come to consult them.

Lene and I required directional, rather than spiritual, advice, that afternoon. We had a mix-up over which tro to catch at one of the junction villages, Kuntanase. Whilst we 'only' spent an hour faffing around, the delay meant that we would not be able to see the shrine and still have time for a look around Bobiri before the light faded. After writing the shrine off, a tro and taxi journey took us to a dirt track off the main Kumasi road, a few miles' walk from the rest-house at Bobiri's Forest Reserve.

We knew that the rest-house did not serve food without prior notice, so we bought bread and a couple of hard-boiled eggs at the roadside before setting off. The possibility of the place being full also crossed our minds, since scientists frequently conduct research trips to the forest and stay overnight. We reckoned such an outcome was unlikely, though, and pressed on.

It looked less than promising when we saw a dark green 4x4 parked adjacent to the rest-house. It bore the name of some institution or other which I suspected would conduct research trips to places such as this. A small, energetic-looking man appeared from around the other side of the vehicle and greeted us warmly.

A chat with him revealed that his name was Eric and that he was, indeed, a researcher. He and some colleagues had been measuring the carbon dioxide levels in the forest. They had a day remaining of a short field visit to survey the area, before they returned to their lab in Accra, to do whatever researchers do with their surveys in order to draw conclusions.

Interesting as Eric's tones made everything sound, it looked as though Lene and I would have to move on.

As if sensing my thoughts, Eric paused and changed tack.

"There are still some rooms left, though. You'll be fine to stay. And even if all the rooms were full, they'd sort something out for you here."

That was a relief. Eric finished explaining his theory that the level of carbon dioxide in the forest was rising, and led us into the reception area so that we could check in.

There was just about enough daylight left for Lene and me to have a walk along a road that led into part of the forest. Exotically-coloured butterflies were everywhere, in clusters of up to fifty in some areas. They zipped across the path as we strolled along, wondrous at the beauty of nature. It seemed inconsequential at the time, but we also commented upon the huge amounts of bamboo that grew in a fairly small area close to the rest-house.

"Which of the walks do you fancy?" Lene asked me the next morning.

We were standing at the start of a path leading into another part of the forest. A map showed four or five different routes around the forest. They all ended back at the rest-house, and none looked particularly long or demanding.

"Doesn't matter to me. We'll get round and out of here in plenty of time to get back to Koforidua for our visas."

With that, we agreed to do the four-mile route. It would allow us to explore the greatest area of forest, and, who knew, perhaps encounter something of Mother Nature's creation that we had not seen yet. And if not, then there would be plenty of butterflies to look at. With hindsight, it was a mistake to assume that there would be similar maps placed in the forest at strategic locations; there weren't even signs telling us where to turn. We also should not, the previous evening, have eaten almost all of the provisions we had brought. We shared the small remaining chunk of bread for breakfast.

The walk through the forest seemed simple, despite the lack of signs, as we negotiated roughly three quarters of the route from memory. We knew we were on the right track. We had crossed a bridge over a fairly big stream where the map had indicated that we would find one, and passed a resting spot that had also been marked. After another mile, and a left turn also prescribed by the map, we came to a crossroads.

Neither of us remembered seeing a crossroads marked on the map, on any of the routes.

Judging by the distance that we had come, and our general sense of direction, we agreed that it was likely that we needed to turn left. Off we went, until we met, after half a mile, a stream.

"Good, we crossed this earlier," Lene smiled as we approached.

"Shame we won't cross it here then," I replied once we had arrived at its bank. There was no bridge at this spot, and none of the conveniently placed rocks to use as stepping stones that are always there at these points in stories or films.

"Maybe straight ahead was better," she said.

We made our way back and took what was now a left turn at the crossroads. The track, much to our consternation, petered out shortly after.

Back we turned, and decided to give the final path a go. It was unlikely to be right, we knew, but we reasoned that since the routes had been advertised on the board by the rest-house, there must be a walkable way back. More in hope than expectation, we set off along it. We had not gone far when a mutual decision was reached. It just felt wrong. We were heading in completely the opposite direction to the rest-house.

Any other day, we could have done as every traveller has done since travel began, and used the sun as a navigational tool. Trust this to have been the only dull morning for weeks.

We agreed that it would be best to cut our losses, and walk out the same way that we had come in. Of course, that would mean another hour added on to the time, which in turn meant an hour off the time that we had to see the Man-Mountain at the Immigration Office for our visas. It was still early though. It would be easy.

I mused to Lene, idly, that some people would consider this situation, deep in a forest with no mobile phone signal, as gravely problematic.

Finding ourselves at the crossroads again, we headed back along the path that we had earlier walked down. We set our eyes to the right to spot the junction with the path that had led us to this one. I was attempting to explain the rules of cricket, and had recounted a couple of my more memorable matches of the previous season at my club. It was not much use, however. Lene thought it a daft game.

"You mean a match lasts *all day*?" was the summary of her views.

An interestingly-shaped tree stump brought a premature end to my latest tale of a poor umpiring decision.

"Do you remember seeing this on the way earlier?" I asked, since I did not.

"Yeah."

I shrugged at this breezy response and followed her. A moment or so later, we passed a small and particularly craggy-looking tree, with thin grey branches protruding diagonally outwards. Its trunk bent and grew outwards near the top, giving it a gnarled, hunch-backed impression. It reminded me of an elderly Roald Dahl villain. Had I seen it earlier, that would not have been a newly formed impression.

"Do you remember this tree?" I asked. "Because I don't."

Slightly hesitatingly, Lene assured me that it was alright.

Her opinion changed as we rounded the next bend and met a steep slope heading downwards. It was the first non-flat path we had encountered. She lit a contemplative cigarette as we sat on a fallen tree trunk and pondered the circumstances. Now that we were unquestionably lost, I regretted my earlier musing about problematic situations.

"If you were on your own," she asked thoughtfully, "What would you do?"

"Before or after hitting the panic button?"

She smiled weakly and looked up at me, a trace of uneasiness having formed on her face.

"I'd go back to the crossroads, and find a way to get across that stream," I replied, decisively.

"So would I."

We did. The stream appeared a bit narrower than it had done earlier, when we still had other options. I took a run-up and just about managed to land on the other side of it. Lene threw our bag over and then made a colossal leap over the water. She landed with her hands in mine, and her feet scrabbling on the edge of the bank. A high pitched squeal of delight and excitement signalled that she had regained her balance.

The first bit was done. As we made our way through the trees, we joked, almost tempting fate, about how this stream may have been a different one to that which we had crossed earlier. This path felt right though, just as the right turn from the crossroads earlier had felt wrong.

Even better, after few hundred metres more, we noticed bamboo growing up amongst the trees. This, we remembered with excitement, had grown near the rest-house!

There was a sudden noise. At least, I thought I heard one.

"Did you hear that?!"

"What?"

She paused. The noise, coming slightly louder now, sounded like a group of people, possibly even a group of researchers.

"We're there!" she cried.

The relief was terrific. We hugged each other, then ran along the last few hundred metres of the path and up to the rest-house.

Walking back to the main road, to catch the tro back to Koforidua, Lene was starting to flag. A proper breakfast was long overdue; adrenaline alone had until that point kept the pair of us going. She struggled, exhausted, along the last mile and a half, saying very little to conserve her energy, except for giving me a ticking off for trying to start a conversation. It dawned on me that she had guts in bucketloads. I could think of no-one with whom I would rather get lost.

We collected our passports from one of the Man-Mountain's colleagues that evening. Roadworks on the main road to Koforidua had seen our tro take a brief detour, passing through a small town with an unexpectedly large traffic jam on its main street. As we jerked forward periodically, I noticed a woman buying two live chickens at one of the many wooden stalls. Once she had been handed her change, she stuffed the squawking, protesting creatures into another of the black carrier bags that the other shoppers were using for the more mundane, inanimate purchases. Only Lene and I seemed remotely surprised.

The next day, Good Friday, we relaxed before our next little expedition. Merel, Pil, Hanneke, Marieke, Catharina and Jane would accompany us to the Volta Region over the Easter weekend. In their company, we would see a small town – whose name I had not caught when we had agreed to it sometime before – where something called *kente* weaving was done, and then go on to nearby Wli. Pronounced 'Vlee', this large village is home to the largest waterfall in West Africa.

I had been half tempted to set off later than the women and meet them on the way to Wli. The prospect of seeing some cloth being stitched sounded as interesting as a wet weekend in Wigan.

"Don't be so blooming narrow minded," teased Jane as I mentioned this on the tro. "You might even learn something."

The small town turned out to be called Kpetoe Agatime ('Kpetoe' is pronounced with the 'k' silent, and with emphasis on the 'pe'). Its *kente* workshop was highly interesting, a huge room with numerous weaving looms abandoned by most workers for the Easter celebrations. Three or four weavers were at work, however; one of whom keenly chatted to us about the principles of *kente* weaving, and showed us how the cloth was stitched with its intricate designs.

We had gathered around his loom, and looked on as he manipulated what in effect were two gigantic knitting needles. He worked at a ferocious pace. As the needles moved along, they made a loud 'click-click-clicking' noise. The sound far outdid that created by even the most enthusiastic grandmother's bid to churn out scarves for an oncoming winter. The result was that the yellow thread raced its way along the cloth, turning left, then right, then left again. It left a complex pattern which would later be complemented by all sorts of other colours.

Our new friend's skill would have been amazing enough as it was, but he was all the time chatting to us. He answered our questions and explained how each foot-long strip of cloth takes up to six hours to weave. The completed strip is then stitched to as many others as is required to make a garment. Dresses and robes for all sorts of celebrations are made in this way. They are worn by the local chiefs and their families. Fabrics are also produced, along with all sorts of souvenirs such as bags, purses and strips of cloth weaved with a greeting message.

He performed his last few 'click-click-clicks' and brought the loom to a halt. He led us over to the wall, where a vast range of different patterns had been weaved onto the fabric and left to flatten out. We were welcome, he assured us, to touch, feel and pick up anything that we fancied, and he would make sure that he gave us a "good price" for anything we wanted to buy. He showed us the other parts of the workshop, enthusiastically explaining about a couple of the different looms used for more specialist stitching jobs, and then let us wander about the place on our own. Partly as a result of his kindness, not to mention knowledge, he did a good trade that afternoon with some of the ladies in the party.

I went and had a chat with a weaver on another loom, who was having a bit of a rest from his work and tenderly rubbing his back. He, too, was happy to answer my questions. His name was John. At thirty-six, he reckoned, he was getting old for the weaving industry. I suspected that being bent over his machine for hours on end might be the reason for this, not to mention his aching back.

"Most leave around thirty-five," he said. "It's not good for the body." I well believed him.

John continued, and gave me a brief history of his craft. Although *kente* is mainly associated with the villages – close to where Lene and I had passed the previous week – around Kumasi, it originated in the area around Kpetoe: apparently, the Ashanti people copied the technique from the Ewes of the Volta Region. This is probably the locally-spun version of the story, although it would have been highly impolite to have made that suggestion[4]. Most of the finished cloth, John explained, is made to the order of local clients. The rest is sold at markets in the capital of the Volta Region, Ho, or local towns like Kpando and Hohoe. He smiled, and finished: "Anything that we have left over, we sell to merchants in Kumasi. They like the original weavers' work."

Merel came over after a while.

"We're all ready to go. Jane's getting a bit impatient, she's hungry."

I grinned mischievously at her. John and I had a natter about his Easter celebrations with his family. It wouldn't hurt Jane to wait a bit longer, particularly if it meant that I could give this thoroughly nice bloke the thanks that he deserved for his insight.

A thoroughly picturesque view unfolded as the tro wound its way along the dirt road covering the last few miles towards Wli. Lush greenery, as in the rest of the country, surrounded the road and offered terrific views. The hills straight ahead and to the left were even more breath-taking. The light brown rock-faces were lit up by the evening sun; they almost shone themselves.

Only a few hundred metres from the Togolese border, this was the sort of sight that I had come to see over the Easter weekend. We got out of the tro at Wli and marvelled, again, at the beautiful Ghanaian landscape. The village itself looked very similar to Kwamoso. Dirt roads led in three directions away from the centre, and everywhere the dusty earth had the familiar reddy-brown tinge to it.

---

[4] Historians and archaeologists have traced the origins of narrow-strip weaving to various West African kingdoms in the 11th century A.D. Elsewhere in Africa, archaeological finds of spindles and looms have been dated to 3200 B.C.

Children played football in the open spaces around the small clay brick houses, whilst women crouched over cooking pots. Goats and sheep roamed the streets and were only marginally less numerous than people. Children ran along, using sticks to guide what initially looked like hoops, as youngsters in a Dickens novel might have done. On closer inspection, these kids were improvising, rolling the rims of bicycle wheels instead.

We found a tiny spot bar to have a drink and a chat, in which the eight of us agreed that it would be best to walk up to the waterfalls – there are actually two, the Upper and Lower Falls – as early as we could, before the heat of the day kicked in. Alarms would be set for half past five.

That being the case, it was soon time for an early night. This was made slightly later by a brief stop-off at the church, to watch an enormous bonfire blazing away as part of the Easter festivities.

Five-thirty was comfortably the earliest that I had ever got up on Easter Sunday, but well worth it. Breakfasting at our hotel, the waitress informed us that we needed to go to the local visitors' centre before we hiked up to the falls, in order to pay an entry fee and get a guide. The guide was strictly necessary, she said, as the distance was "far" and the terrain "dangerous".

I had discovered by this time that 'far' is the default description for any distance that is more than a few minutes' walk away. To get a slightly more specific measurement, it was necessary to listen for the pronunciation and watch the facial expression. The further away something lay, the greater emphasis was placed on the word, and the more the face was scrunched up as the word was delivered. Today, 'far' was emphasised strongly, with much facial scrunching.

'Dangerous' is slightly different. I noticed that it was generally assumed that westerners are a lot less tough than Ghanaians. Combined with a concern for foreigners' wellbeing, it meant that people were cautious in their assessment of hazards.

I considered the walk to the Upper Fall to fit neither of these criteria. Granted, in terms of distance it was a good solid walk along uneven dirt paths, but there was no danger whatsoever. These are moot points, however, since they are made with hindsight. In any case, the guide was compulsory.

Ours set off at a lively pace, which slowed down neither to allow for photographs to be taken, nor for the steepening of the path. Consequently, he began to fall out with us. He stomped up the hill and periodically waited for us to catch up at our own relatively leisurely pace, as we *oohed* and *aahed* at various views, flowers and trees. It seemed a bit unreasonable, since we had each paid ten cedis for the walk. There was nothing too tense, however, until he turned to Pil and explained that we each had to cough up another five cedis as a private guide fee.

Production of the receipt showed that this was definitely not the case. After a brief discussion, he capitulated rather too easily for someone who was not just trying it on. We checked later, at the tourist office, and had it confirmed that the guides receive a proportion of the original fee. It was a great shame that this had taken place, for there was a complete breakdown in trust thereafter. If he had been taciturn before we denied his request, he was sullenly silent afterwards. Undoubtedly, he knew far more than the little that he chose to tell us about the waterfalls and the area in general.

All bar Jane and Catharina continued from the Lower Fall to the Upper. Jane's age and physical condition were such that she always intended to curtail the walk. Catharina, a keen amateur sportswoman, was still feeling the effects of the last of a string of operations on a damaged cartilage in her knee. She deemed it wiser to pass up the forty-five minute ascent to the Upper Fall.

They missed out: the Upper Fall was exhilarating. Much narrower than I expected, the water falls roughly a hundred metres. I ran into the crystal clear plunge pool, and was delighted to discover that it was deep enough to swim in: the cool, refreshing water reached shoulder height at its greatest depth. Even more exciting, though, was the waterfall itself.

"This is the world's best power shower!" I yelled at Lene and the four others from underneath it.

They shouted something back from the edge of the pool, which I could not hear over the crescendo. Huge drops of water crashed down on my head, shoulders, and outstretched arms, with bursts of ferocious force as the torrent occasionally grew stronger. A couple of minutes underneath it were enough, before the weight of the water became too great to bear. I let myself fall forwards into the pool, and swam over to its middle, where the ladies had gathered.

"Come and have a go of that," I cajoled them.

It took a bit of persuasion, and a repeat of the earlier power shower comparison, but eventually the ladies went and had a go under the waterfall as well. They came out thrilled.

We dried off in no time. The water evaporated; the heat of the day had started, even though it could not have been much past nine o'clock. Walking back to the Lower Fall, we took in the stunning views of Wli village and the surrounding hills unburdened by the effort of climbing the slope. Bidding farewell to our guide at the Lower Fall – by now he was slightly less sulky, even managing a smile as we parted – we joined Jane and Catharina sitting on the rocks near the plunge pool.

If anything, the Lower Fall is slightly more impressive than its counterpart. The water seemed to cascade with even greater velocity than at the Upper Fall. Standing under it saw 'the world's best power shower's' status relegated.

A colony of bats lived somewhere near the Lower Fall, we discovered at one point, when, despite the bright sunshine, many of its number came out to play. They flew around the top of the waterfall for a while, circling and turning this way and that, as we craned our necks to watch.

"Hey Jane", I teased. "Some of your family are up there. Why don't you go and say hello to them?"

The old bat wasn't impressed, and gave me a gigantic splash of water.

And so we whiled away the rest of the day. Later on, I went and had another look around the village, whilst the ladies sat in the hotel's garden gossiping about the things that ladies gossip about on Sunday afternoons. Much too soon, evening arrived, and then night.

Lene and I hoped to make a speedy getaway the next morning, for whilst a return to work awaited the others, we still had a week of holiday before Suzy's Spring Break School at Holy Hills began.

Our next ports of call were to be the historic coastal towns of Elmina and Cape Coast. To break the journey, we would make a stop-off in the coastal town of Winneba that evening, and have a look around its old-fashioned fishing port.

A speedy getaway, on Easter Monday, proved a tad optimistic. Standing at the roadside, there was a notable lack of tros. Or vehicles of any other type. A man strode up to us.

"Where are you going?" he asked, as everyone in Ghana seemed to.

Lene explained that we were looking to get to Hohoe, the nearest town, from where we would continue our journey.

"You won't get a tro now."

That was clear; we had been waiting over twenty minutes.

"No, there will be no tros today. I am in charge of the tros in Wli. They will not be running today. But I have a taxi, my brother will take you."

Lene and I looked at each other. This bloke was probably an opportunist, looking for a chance to make a bit of money. He certainly looked unlikely to be anything to do with the tros. Whether they would run at some point was an open question, but they were conspicuous by their absence thus far. We were also being offered a ride.

"OK," we began. Prices were bandied about, and after a few exclamations of the flat '*Ah!*' sound, from both sides, a fare was agreed.

The Opportunist called his "brother" – the Ghanaian meaning of the word applied, it was his friend – over, and said something to him in Ewe. He turned back to us.

"Wait small, small," he said.

The Brother disappeared, although a few minutes later returned driving a clapped out wreck of a car. It looked as though it might have been around on the original Easter Monday.

"This is your taxi," the Opportunist, for that is what he now certainly was, announced proudly.

Missing the distinctive orange panels, it most definitely was *not* a taxi. We put our bags in the boot and hopped in anyway.

After two or three aborted attempts to start the thing on the gentle incline, the two of them pushed the car to turn it around. The Brother got behind the wheel, and the Opportunist gave it a good shove down the slope. We freewheeled towards the roundabout, and mercifully the engine fired itself into life as the Brother turned the steering wheel.

Two jump starts later, the engine having cut out after ten miles or so and again a few miles later, we made it into Hohoe. What would the rest of the journey be like?

Perfect, actually, more or less. Changing in Accra, we had a taxi ride to Kaneshie tro station, which serves the routes west, with a smashing bloke. He worked part-time for the Church in a youth project. His taxi driving was a second job, when he was not guiding the teenagers through their journey into adulthood.

Having climbed aboard a huge tro bound for Winneba, the last space was taken by a youngish chap with black-framed glasses. His shockingly luminous pink shirt looked one size, at least, too big for him. It also made an ugly clash with the skinny black tie that hung three-quarters of the way down his chest.

"Why do you think he is facing the back?" Lene asked me. It was an excellent question, and one to which I had no answer.

We found out soon enough. He opened a battered brown briefcase, and pulled out an equally battered brown leather-bound book. Opening it seemingly arbitrarily, he began preaching from what turned out to be the Twi Bible. The passengers fell silent as he continued to read, with great passion, a number of verses. As the tro crept out of Kaneshie station, amidst a mass of other vehicles, a question formed in my mind. How long would this go on for?

We rattled down the main road, the sound of the tro's engine merging with the Bible reading, and its periodic echoes of 'Hallelujah' and 'Amen' from the mobile congregation. By the time he had stopped, we were approaching Winneba.

This small town provided quite a culture shock as we explored it the following morning. We saw a stark difference between the newer, slightly wealthier area of town, and the poor fishing port known as the Old Town. The division between them could have been mapped with a pencil and ruler, such is the immediacy between one and the other.

Walking through the Old Town, Lene and I felt pangs of guilt. A quarter of an hour earlier we had bought bread and hard-boiled eggs for breakfast at a stall near to the hotel where we had stayed, in the New Town. Yet on either side of us were numerous street traders who needed our custom far more than those we had bought from. One old man in particular, manning a rickety wooden stall, was dreadfully frail. His ribs and shoulder bones almost came through his skin, and his eyes stared out into the middle distance. Of course, it would have been impossible for us to change anything, for any of them. In hindsight, though, we really should have bought a bread roll or two from him, and saved them for later in the day.

We felt terribly out of place in this little community, especially at the fishing harbour itself. Here, rather than cries of *Obruni*, we met faces etched with puzzlement at what two westerners could possibly be doing in such a wretched setting. The beach was truly a working one. Fishing boats in varying states of repair were being readied for the next sail, and nets were transferred from person to person. As with any workplace, there was a toilet – a large section of the beach was pockmarked with human waste. There was nowhere else, after all.

As we looked out to the sea, watching some more of the boats at work, Lene and I chatted. Some of these things that we had seen over the hour since we had left the hotel represented a raw and hard-hitting view of reality in the poorer areas of the country. Not for the first time, and certainly not for the last, Lene and I were reminded of the fact that when the vast majority of people in the west complain, we actually have little to complain about. It was another eye-opening experience; one, moreover, that we struggled to come to terms with.

Elmina later that day presented a totally different feel, one that we were more used to. A former centre of colonial trade, the town was once very wealthy, as the grand old architecture showed. Buildings were decorated with columns and clock faces. Although the town has declined since its days at the centre of various European trades, there is still a degree of prosperity.

After a tro ride to Elmina's outskirts, we had taken a shared taxi into the town centre. The driver held the door for Lene as she climbed out. "Is she your sister or your wife?" he asked me. It threw me for a moment, and I decided to semi-feign ignorance. The traditional meaning of 'sister' made its use a little inappropriate, and I was unsure as yet whether the term 'wife' was similarly flexible in Ghanaian English.

"Oh, she's my friend," I replied. The driver grinned and re-started the engine.

The first thing that we noticed once the taxi had gone was the smell. Elmina's fish market spanned a significant area adjacent to our stopping place. It hummed!

Walking through the streets we passed, amongst the stalls and conventional shops, a pretty Methodist church. Five bizarrely decorated buildings, the *posuban* shrines, were dotted along two of the bigger streets. These are a common feature of towns in the Fante area of Ghana, which lies in the South-Western area of the country. The *posuban* shrines were built by companies of local people, known as *asafo* companies. Centuries ago, the *asafo* were responsible for the defence of the town. Elmina's shrines are incredibly ornate, with all sorts of murals and designs decorating their two or three storeys.

As evening approached, Lene and I went to the beach. We walked arm in arm. It was the first time we had done so. In that moment, in that delightful setting, with the sun beginning to go down, it felt right. Not a lot was spoken; it did not need to be.

The palm trees which lined the beach hid the sunset, but that mattered not a jot as we sat and looked at the white St. George's Castle and the sky behind it. Both changed colour as the sun dropped further and finally disappeared. In contrast to that morning, we felt totally at one with the surroundings. And with each other.

There was plenty of time for a proper look around the town the following day. The obvious starting point was the castle, which stands next to the beach and River Benya.

The castle was originally Portuguese, for it was they who were the first Europeans to come here in 1471. The town got its modern name, in all likelihood, from shortening the Portuguese phrase for the whole area. *Da Costa de el Mina de Ouro* meant 'The Coast of the Gold Mines', which was probably felt to be a bit of a mouthful.

One of the first Portuguese settlers, a chap called Diogo de Azambuja, got in touch with one of his compatriots, who was familiar with the local practices. The wily Azambuja asked his friend to arrange and interpret a meeting with the local chief, Kwamin Ansah, who the Portuguese called 'Caramansa'. Azambuja persuaded Kwamin Ansah to allow him to build a fort. He dangled the carrot, of the King of Portugal's favour, but also waved the stick, of goodness-knows-what if permission were declined. Probably against his better judgment, Kwamin Ansah allowed the Portuguese their castle.

Named after the patron saint that Portugal shares with England, *Sao Jorge* was originally a small wooden affair, built as a centre from which to trade gold with the Fante. It was successful enough that the Dutch wanted to add it to their little commercial portfolio. In 1637 they seized St. Jago Hill, in the middle of the town, which the Portuguese had rather stupidly left too-lightly fortified. It was easy for the Dutch to then attack the undefended landward side of the castle, and send the Portuguese packing. Just to make sure that the same thing did not happen to them, the Dutch built a little fort, Coenraadsburg, at the summit of the hill.

Looking around St. George's, we saw for ourselves the Dutch modifications to it, and the grim motivations which drove their construction. A distinctly un-Jolly Rogerish skull and crossbones adorned one doorway. This was the entrance to the large, dank, male dungeon where captives were held before they were transported on the middle passage to the Americas. They walked from the dungeons to the waiting boats, stooping and still chained, through a tunnel less than four feet high. The low roof eliminated what little possibility there was of a last stand against the castle guards.

A similarly sombre picture came to mind when we passed through to the female dungeons, which were based around a number of smaller rooms. These, like the male dungeons, were illuminated only by slits in the walls which served as windows. I thought back to what Daniel had told me on the tro back from Accra two months previously. It was truly horrific to think that humans had been kept in such a setting. A dungeon not too much bigger than a large living room contained over two hundred people, many of whom were sick and had nowhere to vomit (or perform any of the other necessary functions) but the space next to them.

Almost as dreadful was the lavishness of the Governor's Quarters. Adding insult to injury, he would select a number of the captive women whom he wanted to use to satisfy his own whims. They were escorted up to the governor by the guards, and returned when they had served their purpose.

What was notable, looking at the information boards which were displayed in the central building which the Portuguese had used as a chapel and the Dutch as a trading hall, was the commentary. Heavily critical of the Europeans, as it should have been, it neglected to mention anything of the Ashanti and Fante tribes' – albeit significantly lesser – contribution to this suffering. Nor was there any mention of the fact that Arab slave traders had raided parts of West Africa for centuries before the Europeans came along. Although this, too, was on a far smaller scale, the principal of enslaving innocent people was the same. It rankled, although not enough to mention it to the castle staff.

That evening, Lene and I sat in our hotel room and played a Danish card game called Five Hundred. Based loosely on rummy, I was still in the formative stages of learning its technique. We were about to mooch through town to a street stall, to buy an egg sandwich[5] for dinner, when the lights went off.

Walking through the dark was incredible. We had noticed the previous evening how the town came alive after dark. Couples courted, people sang and danced on the streets, and there was a general feeling that the town had let its hair down after the rigours of the day. In the power cut, this atmosphere was significantly more low-key. It was as though there was something missing; not just the music and light, but a more fundamental *je ne sais quoi*.

We ate our sandwiches down by the castle, looking over at the fish market – whose smell we no longer noticed – and the River Benya. We talked of our families back in Europe. Lene's face lit up as she told me how proud she was of her younger sister, who was finishing college and was about to move into a house with her boyfriend of several years.

---

[5] This is an omelette, which is fried in oil and placed in a circular bun. The whole sandwich is then pressed into the frying pan to soak up any remaining oil. Egg sandwiches are made at street stalls throughout the country, and were one of my favourite Ghanaian foods.

It was another reminder, I suppose, of our foreign-ness to Ghana. Not just that we were talking about such things, but that we were sitting leisurely in the middle of the port and harbour. A couple of people gave us sideways glances as they walked past. What we saw as a beautiful – quite romantic – setting, everyone else in the town saw as ordinary, humdrum and essential; a working environment.

The lights were still off, and remained so until we were nearly back at our hotel. As the power flashed itself back into life, a collective cheer went up from everyone on the streets. It was not just the lights that brightened, but the entire mood of the town as the almost party-like atmosphere got back into its swing.

What a contrast Cape Coast provided with Elmina!

The town was a maelstrom of people coming and going from the market. What was really striking, though, was the amount of taxis: they outnumbered cars by at least ten to one. Passing through the narrow streets on the way to the tro station, there was a relentless cacophony of honking horns. Drivers were impatient, either for a space to open up for them to drive into, or – in the cases of those with empty taxis – for a customer to ferry somewhere. One of the latter spotted Lene and me, and made his way over, loudly enquiring as to where we were going, and offering us a "good price" of several times what it should have been to take us there. He was a determined fellow, who was not in the slightest bit put off by our pleas of self-sufficiency. It took quite an effort to persuade him that we were not looking for a ride.

We had been a little wary of Cape Coast on the way, since Chris had said a while before that he had found a slightly intimidating edge to it. This initial in-your-face encounter, especially after the relative serenity of Elmina, seemed to bear his view out. Yet once we had gained our bearings, we realised that this was a thoroughly unfair assessment of the town. Sitting on the beach that afternoon, gazing at the huge castle to our left and the sea in front of us, people were friendly and unobtrusive. Some children sat down beside us. Ostensibly they were trying to sell water sachets, but were far more interested in casually chatting to us. Their friendly curiosity towards people who looked different to them came out in their innocent and childish questions. In addition to the usual ones, they asked why our hair was longer than theirs, and why we had different colour eyes.

Whilst three of them took it upon themselves to braid Lene's long blonde hair, a not inconsiderable task, I nipped off for a swim. The Gulf of Guinea was just as warm as it had been in Dzita a month earlier, although far more choppy. It was good fun to dive through the waves and swim across the current, although like all good things, too much proved unwise. When a gigantic wave crashed over me with greater force than anything yet, I had an unexpected drink. Enough was enough; it was time to explore around the back of the castle instead.

The sand ends at the rocks on which the castle is built, and resumes again around a corner as a small cove, before the working section of the beach begins. I caught a bit of a whiff as I neared the cove; it smelt suspiciously like droppings.

It couldn't have been, though, since a football match was in full flow there. A convenient break in play – the ball had been kicked into the sea – allowed me to jog across the impromptu pitch, and onwards to have a look at the fishing boats being readied a hundred metres ahead of me. Standing looking at the fishermen, I pondered how different a scene this was from Winneba at the beginning of the week. Cape Coast, as the regional capital, was more prosperous, and though none of the fishermen appeared to be wealthy, they certainly looked considerably better off than their colleagues along the coast.

Having taken it in, I turned back. The whiff was still present around the cove. Perhaps it was droppings after all. Approaching the football match, I discovered this was indeed the case. One of the players, a lad of around twenty, received the ball. He took a few strides forward, passed it to his mate, and then jogged off to have a squat by the rocks. No-one batted an eyelid. Clearly this was the accepted toilet. The normality of it all seemed extraordinary.

Cape Coast Castle provided an interesting reference point to St. George's in Elmina. The British constructed it in 1665, on the site of a wooden Swedish fort that had stood for eleven years. The biggest in the Gold Coast, it had administrative functions as well as slave handling ones. Indeed, it continued to be a crucial part of Gold Coast governance long after the ending of the slave trade which made it notorious.

Lene and I were in a guided group of twenty or so other people, mainly, but not totally, foreigners. In the castle's courtyard, we were shown three graves which lay on the stone-lined ground. One was for Governor MacLean, who ran the British Gold Coast throughout the 1830s with a respect for African customs that governors before and after did not display. When he died in 1847, the Fante chiefs spontaneously declared a period of mourning.

MacLean was buried next to his wife, Lady Elizabeth Langdon, who had died, heartbroken, sometime earlier. Having come over from England, she discovered that her husband was having an affair with a local woman, who had borne him a child. Shocked by his infidelity, she is said to have poisoned herself. (Other stories, however, say that she died of malaria, TB or alcohol poisoning.)

The last of the three graves was that of a Philip Quaqua. He was an African churchman who taught European schoolchildren in a room above the male dungeon, teaching them how to lead a moral life for the greater benefit of humanity. If that sounds rather hypocritical, part of the justification of the slave trade was that the captives were ungodly, since they followed traditional religions, and therefore savages. It was thus seen as perfectly acceptable that they should be used to advance the prosperity of Christians.

Quaqua was far from the only African working for the British in the castle. Many of the castle guards were also African – as they were up and down the coast – and worked to propagate the misery of thousands of other Africans. Tribal differences meant that the guards did not look on the captives with any more compassion than did the Europeans.

The scale of the castle was staggering, particularly the dungeons. Seeing those in Elmina had been humbling enough, but a second viewing of dingy, dark prisons rammed it home that Elmina's were far from a one-off. Indeed, there were in excess of twenty slave castles along the Gold Coast at the end of the trade.

Just as sombre was the 'Door of No Return', which led the slaves from the tunnel out of the dungeon, through the eastern wall, and onto the waiting boats. The name was a callous reminder to those captives who could understand English – as if one were needed – that they would never come back. On the other side of it is a symbolic modern plaque, erected when two descendants of Cape Coast captives visited the castle and entered the way that their ancestors had departed. It bears the legend 'The Door of Return'. It is no more than a gesture of course, albeit a poignant one. If only the history could be undone.

Three other anecdotes from the guide revealed just how horrendous that history is. Most of the group were shocked to hear how captives were fed a gruel-like substance. This was supposed to be passed around to each person by the guards. Whilst this was often the case, the less scrupulous guards simply threw it through the narrow slits in the wall (as in Elmina, they are so small that 'window' is the wrong word), and allowed a free-for-all to develop as to who would get to eat it.

In the female dungeon, it was explained to the group that the slave captains did not like to have new mothers on the ships, for they would fetch a lesser price on the auction blocks. When they, or pregnant women, were discovered, they were thrown into the sea; either from the castle or the ship.

The final unpleasant tale was related in a tiny cell located just off the courtyard. Not much longer, or wider, than an under-the-stairs cupboard, this was the punishment cell. Captives who had caused trouble for the guards on more than two occasions were locked in there up to six at a time. The door was only re-opened when lack of food and water had killed the last one.

This was the end point of the tour. Walking out of the punishment cell, a discussion had started between a group of Canadians and the guide. The guide was telling of how the castle is preserved as a reminder of what happened.

"And to make sure that things like this never happen again," added one of the Canadians.

The guide rolled his eyes, ever so slightly. I understood him: the 'Never again' factor is rolled into many places such as this, where horrendous events have unfolded. Yet horrendous events have continued to unfold around the world; on this continent in particular.

I thought that the guide did a great job in moving the conversation on. One of the problems, he expounded, is that the slave trade is not taught in many Ghanaian schools, and so young people get an unbalanced impression of it. Two Ghanaian teachers who were in the party nodded vigorously. They took up the narrative: people blame the Europeans, without understanding the full picture of local tribes' complicity. The guide agreed. One of his final statements left a great impression.

"Someone famous once said: you cannot play a piano with only the white keys – for the music to be played properly, you need to use the black keys as well."

Much later, Lene and I sat on the beach again. It was Saturday evening. The waves were still visible in the rapidly increasing dark. They made wondrously rhythmic and natural crashing sounds as they crested and then washed up onto the beach. To us, hearing them represented calmness and relaxation. How contradictory the sea is, we mused. Those captives would have heard it too, yet to them it would doubtless have sounded completely different. Its constant presence must have been soul-destroying noise. For those who work on it, depend on it – and how many of those must there be across the world? – or are just lucky enough to be able to look at it, as we were doing that glorious evening, the sea is variously beautiful, dangerous, strong, calming, and so much more.

Sitting back in *Obruni* Castle twenty-four hours later, I looked over at Lene again as we ate our dinner. Now that the holiday was over, and we had the Spring Break school to look forward to, I felt a little wistful. In just six short weeks she would be on the plane back to Denmark. The end for 'us' was beginning to close in.

Chapter 8 – The joys of Spring Break

I don't like to say "I told you so." It usually comes across as unconstructive. The two-week Spring Break school, though, was one example of when it would have been totally justified.

The teachers at Holy Hills had been working for over three months, save for a mid-term break of two days – which I felt was rather short. More seriously, they had been paid (I found out later) only sporadically. As a result, the Rev's assurance that they would be working with Lene, the Scottish volunteer Mischa, and me proved to be the pie in the sky that I had felt it to have been after the initial meeting before Easter, where Suzy had sat down with the three of us to plan the fortnight. Not that I remember the fortnight negatively; indeed, except for one day, overall I felt quite the opposite. I learned a great deal about the school, which stood me in good stead for when I started working there full-time at the end of May. I got to know the children a lot better too. Names that I had occasionally heard matched up with faces I had once or twice seen. The everyday pleasantries that I had exchanged with the children who lived outside the vicinity of the Rev's house transformed into more meaningful relationships. And the wealth of hilarious moments unwittingly provided by the kids was priceless.

We westerners undoubtedly made mistakes, for which the presence of the Holy Hills teachers would not have fully compensated. The most fundamental was that we allowed the children to come in their own clothes, rather than school uniform. We neglected to carry out the assembly which started the regular school day. Finally, we closed school at noon each day. With the latter, we had the children's interests at heart; they had had only the two-day break from learning since the beginning of January. The unintended consequence of these decisions was that the youngsters were freed from the routine and discipline of their normal school day. To them, it did not feel like 'proper' school. Like children everywhere when let off the leash, most looked to see what they could get away with.

The one Holy Hills teacher I was annoyed with was BraKofi. He had promised Lene and me that he would be around if we needed anything. Yet we saw him a grand total of five times during school hours over the two weeks. Twice he was spotted walking to Quarters Junction to catch a tro to Koforidua, and twice he arrived to my lesson uninvited and told the children off when they had settled to work. On the other occasion, he had stuck his head through the door frame over breaktime, to tell us that he would be away in Accra for a few days.

Another problem was that Lene and I were teaching alone in the first week – Mischa had, very thoughtfully, gone travelling. Consequently, we had to split the year groups between the two of us, rather than three ways. We had planned lessons on the basis of there only being the six primary school classes attending. It was something of a surprise on the Monday morning to see the likes of Peace, Ishmael and some of their friends in the JHS section turn up as well.

Since there were more of the younger children present, we kept to our plans of splitting Classes 1, 2 and 3 from the others. Lene loved working with the younger ones and was keen to take them as often as possible, which I was only too happy to agree to. I had been looking forward to having a class of older children since the initial meeting with Suzy.

Talking with the older class, whose ages ranged from nine to sixteen, was instructive. We kicked off the football theme that I had planned weeks before with an English lesson, on the rules of the game. The Ghanaian sense of fairness and respect came through almost immediately. We covered the most basic principles of kicking and heading the ball, and then I asked the class what else was important.

"You must respect the referee," chirped a bright lad in Class 6 by the name of Adjei.

"You must respect the other players," someone else offered.

"You must respect the coaches."

"And the crowd."

This was dynamite. We were writing a code of conduct more than a rulebook, but that mattered little. It was a shame that the professional sportsmen of the moment were not there to witness it, I pondered, as the children carried on making leaflets about the rights and wrongs of the game. Some of those so-called sporting heroes who grace, or disgrace, our television screens would have found it most instructive.

At the appointed time, Takyi, one of the sprightlier boys in Class 6, went to find the bell to signal breaktime. He returned empty handed. The bell was locked in the school office. BraKofi had the keys. He was nowhere to be found.

The lack of a bell was a major hindrance to starting the lesson after break on time. The children were used to wandering around the village at breaktimes. Unsurprisingly, they saw no reason why they should not continue to do so, taking as long as they fancied whilst they were at it. After all, their regular teachers were not present to enforce punctuality, and these *Obrunis* could not even muster a bell between them.

Although the vast majority did come back, eventually, for the second lesson, we had lost around half our teaching time. Lene and I swapped classes after break. I stepped into the younger class and, once order had been restored (those that *had* come back when they should have had grown understandably restless), addressed the latecomers. In my strictest tones, I explained that their timekeeping simply had to improve. Lene did the same with the older ones.

Would it have any effect come the following day?

Would it heck. The bell had still not been found, and even if it had, it would probably have made little difference. According to Eunice, Mr Livingstone, Holy Hills' headteacher, summoned the bellboy to ring the bell for the end of breaktimes when the children had drifted back into school of their own accord, rather than as the signal that the time had arrived when they should drift back.

"Alright everyone, today's 'Activity' session is about making sandwiches. Move into four groups, and I'll give you a chunk of bread, some tuna, a quarter of an onion, a blob of mayonnaise and a knife to cut and spread everything…."

It was Wednesday or Thursday; this was one of Suzy's final-lesson ideas that we had for some reason agreed on. Suzy's assurance during our initial meeting that she had done this successfully with children before – "They loved it, you'll have a great lesson" – ignored the fact that Ghanaians don't go in for sandwiches, except the omelette variety cooked on the street. It was an even bet whether any of the children had seen any other type of sandwich before.

Lene had asked me which class I wanted to take. I briefly considered the likelihood of a mishap involving either a bread knife or the jagged edge of a can of tuna. It seemed more probable with small children.

"I'll take the older ones. You prefer the younger ones in any case."

In the classroom, I had not long finished handing out the ingredients when Dennis appeared at my side and announced that his group had finished. I glanced up and saw Ishmael, Collins and their mate Bismark standing somewhat aimlessly around their table.

This was rather soon to have finished making four sandwiches.

"What do you mean?" I asked. Surprise rather than curiosity probably came through in my voice.

"It's finished."

"So you've made your four sandwiches, with tuna, onion and mayonnaise?"

"It's finished," Dennis repeated. He looked just a little sheepish. "Come."

I followed him over to his group's table. Confusion was running through my mind as to what Dennis might have meant. It presented a dilemma too: what on earth they could constructively do for the next fifteen minutes, if indeed their sandwiches were completed?

"See it."

Ishmael, Collins, Bismark and – less so – Dennis, looked on proudly as I surveyed their table. A few crumbs of bread lay on their plate, along with a patch of brine where the tuna had once been. The onion lay discarded on the table a short distance away from it, a bite-sized chunk missing from it. The mayo had not been touched.

"It's finished," Dennis confirmed, no longer looking so bashful now he was back in the company of his pals.

It certainly was finished, as much of it as was going to be.

I was briefly nonplussed.

"Erm, was it tasty?" It was the best I could muster.

"I ate most of the tuna", said Bismark. "It was good."

"The bread was nice too," piped up Ishmael. "But we don't want any more onion."

I declined to enquire about the mayo. Plan B had formed in my mind.

"Right then lads, why don't you see if Madam Lene wants any help next door?"

Madam Lene did not want any help next door.

The four returned, tails between legs, around a minute after leaving. They had become most apologetic, Lene must have put a flea in their ear. I let them have a chat; they could do the least harm that way.

In the meantime, the rest of the class carried on. Gordon Ramsey wouldn't have thought much of their culinary achievements, but after a while there were four sandwiches on each group's plate. A good deal of the fillings were smeared on the tables, mind, and most slices of bread were of significantly different widths at either end. Nevertheless, the butties had been made. Agnes, a fair-skinned girl in Class 6, held up a creation which resembled a cross-section of a valley as much as a sandwich. The top piece of bread had been cut diagonally, virtually into nothing, before a sharp change of direction had rescued a slice.

The children munched on their sandwiches in the last few minutes before closing. Yaw in particular was wolfing his down as if he had not eaten for quite a long time. The reason, I supposed, was that he hadn't. There was a decent amount of bread left unused at the end of the loaf; as the children filed out to go home I called him over and slid it into his hand.

"Thank you," he breathed as he looked up at me. He needed not have; his eyes said it far more effectively.

The boys eating the food, instead of making sandwiches, was not wholly unexpected, I mused later that day. Lene and I had seen over the week how all but the most conscientious had become more lax in their own clothes and the absence of their regular teachers. As with children everywhere who are given even a fraction of an inch, they had taken a mile.

Adjei summed it up neatly one morning. Yarro, from the Rev's Mount Zion Primary School in Tinkong, was blowing up an empty water sachet so that he could burst it with a satisfying bang.

"Sir Lawrie, they are fooling!" he complained to me as I moved over to confiscate the soon-to-be-popped sachet.

It was true. The older children were not making a great deal of effort. In the first few days too, the younger children struggled with the changed school routine. Although on the whole they worked hard, getting them to settle at the start of the lessons could be a struggle. The ringleader was a particularly headstrong youngster called John. He had begun school late, and at ten years old was still in Class 3, when most of that age group were two year groups above. John was in Lene's principal class at Mount Zion, and she had warned me about him.

"He just doesn't sit still," she sighed. "He wants to be the centre of attention. Once you get to know him, though, he's a really nice boy."

The first two statements were immediately accurate. I went through my repertoire of strategies for dealing with children diagnosed with ADHD, to little avail. For some reason, he took a disliking to me throughout those two weeks, which remained for some time after. Only much later did Lene's final point also prove true.

Lene and I closed school earlier on the Friday. Suzy had told us of a blood donation session at the hospital in Mampong, the small town a few miles south of Mamfe where, many moons ago, Bob Marley's grandmother had lived in a house on the main street. We were keen to attend, but it ended at noon.

The hospital was a sprawling compound of buildings. Luckily, signposts guided visitors to where they needed to be. We met made our way into a little room where there was a desk, a few chairs, and a doorway to the ward where blood was to be donated.

It was near to the end of the donation session. We heard Suzy's voice drift faintly from somewhere below us and to our left.

"Hi guys."

Her usually pale face was as white as a sheet, and she lay over three chairs. Once it was established that this was her normal reaction to giving blood and that she would be OK, we wasted no time in taking the Mickey out of her. Behind it, however, we had great respect for her doing what she had done, knowing how she would react.

Hanneke tapped Lene on the shoulder, and pointed over to the desk. It was our turn to register.

I began a process that was utterly reassuring. We were weighed, and for some reason Lene stepped off the scales looking a little relieved. Paperwork had to be filled in, and nurses asked the standard questions. Rather amusingly, some questions on the form bizarrely linked quite unrelated issues. One asked if donors had, in the last year, either had more than one sexual partner *or* had given or received money or drugs for sex. There was no further question as to which of these two scenarios a potential 'Yes' answer referred. This little ambiguity, and the use of an incredibly large needle for the initial blood test, aside, though, the registration procedure was virtually identical to the British one.

Lene followed me into the donation ward, to see what being hooked up to a blood bag looked like. She had forgotten what went on, she explained, since it had been a while since she had given blood.

"Oh, right," I mumbled, focusing on the needle that was about to be jabbed into my arm. Did it *really* need to be so long? And so thick?

"Yes", Lene went on. "They don't let me do it because I'm a kilogram too light for it back home. I was right on the limit just now."

She had kept that quiet, I thought.

It turned out that she had become increasingly nervous of giving blood since we arrived. Considering that, along with Danish medical advice, she had to take into account Suzy's state, our discovery that a whole pint is taken rather than the 470 millilitres in Europe, and the size of the needle that was almost ready to be stuck into me, this reticence was understandable. It was typical of her determination that despite these misgivings – it wouldn't be too harsh to say that she was crapping herself – she carried on nonetheless.

Waiting for a tro at Mamfe on the way back from the hospital, the Blue Bar's entrance sign up the road caught my eye.

"Fancy a beer?"

It seemed like a nice idea. Neither of us was feeling any ill-effects of having lost a pint of blood, and it was, after all, Friday afternoon. A bottle of *Club* later, we caught a tro to Kwamoso.

All was still well a few hours later. Auntie Gifty had kindly left us some of the rice and tomato-based stew that she had cooked for lunch, and we tucked into it. Sometime after, Lene was giving me another thrashing at her card game Five Hundred. As she nipped off to powder her nose, I joined in a chat that Merel was having with Jane, who had come over to *Obruni* Castle for the afternoon.

"Lawrie, come!" Auntie Gifty's raised voice pierced the air. It originated at the far end of the Rev's house.

"What have I done?!" I joked to the other two.

I strolled out of *Obruni* Castle and past the front of the Rev's house. This turned into a sprint when I saw what Gifty was calling me for.

Lene was lying where she had collapsed a few moments before, her face a similar colour to that which Suzy's had been in the hospital. She was talking, though, and a weak smile confirmed that she was alright.

I was not much use, since I had no idea what to do other than talk to her. Luckily, Auntie Gifty and Florence were far more clued up, and instructed me to fetch a bag for Lene to be sick into. They had already brought her a cushion, and given her a water sachet to drink.

The water was certainly better for her than the beer we had drunk in the Blue Bar. It was a fact not lost on Lene when she was sitting back in *Obruni* Castle a while later.

"You have some good ideas, don't you?"

Her sense of humour was unaffected, at least.

It knocked her off kilter for a few days. I suppose it goes to show just why it is recommended not to drink anything alcoholic after giving blood, and why there is a minimum weight limit for donors.

At school on Monday morning, we explained to Mischa the ups and downs of the previous week. She was horrified, particularly at the news that the children were not working as hard as they should have been. In term-time, she frowned, they knuckled down.

It would be OK this week, we assured her, since there were now three teachers, so the classes could be split up into three age groups, rather than two. Lene and I had also spoken to the Rev about our concerns. He had in turn spoken to BraKofi, who assured us that he would be on hand to make sure that everything was running smoothly. Lene and I had thought up a new 'Activity' session, to replace the awful 'Olympics' hour that we had talked about with Suzy. We would instead take the children on a walk around Kwamoso, to create a land-use map of the village. As a Geography lesson, it was only a set of colouring pencils away from being an outstanding plan.

We read the Riot Act to the children on the Monday morning, and began lessons. My second topic was about the road. Similarly to the previous week with football, I started with a lesson on the various 'dos' and 'don'ts' for motorists and pedestrians. The aim was to make a code of conduct, since that had gone down well seven days earlier.

What, I asked the oldest class, did they think were the most important things for road users to do? The answers I got were fantastic; the children were interested and motivated.

"You must not drink and drive," offered Eunice.

"You must not use your phone when you drive."

"You must not shout on the tro."

This started another lengthy discussion about the etiquette of being a passenger on the tro; our conversation was having its desired effect. Generally, people sit on the tro stony-faced and largely silent; it is one of the few places where it is possible to find Ghanaians who are not making a noise.

Adjei raised his hand, which meant that another highly intelligent answer was surely on the way.

"You must not shit on the tro."

Had I heard him right?!

"Yes," said Adjei's best friend, a tiny wisp of a lad called Samuel, who went by his somewhat odd nickname 'Blackie'. "You must never shit on the tro."

This was not as rude as it sounded: 'Shit' does not have the taboo status that it does in Britain; indeed, it is used in rather the same way as we use 'Poo'. Nevertheless, it seemed to me to be an outlandish statement.

Being in a minority of one, I let it go. The discussion carried on as it had done before, and the children made their ensuing code of conduct working as hard as I had seen.

It was too good to last the entire week though. Once the children realised that BraKofi's presence was not going to be felt (which was not long after Lene, Mischa and I had come to the same conclusion), most were just as half-arsed as before.

One day, lessons were in progress when the sky began to turn first dark grey, then an angry black. Ishmael raised his hand.

"Sir Lawrie, big rain is coming." His tone was grave.

It was hard to argue; the clouds meant that the classroom was darkening pretty rapidly.

It soon became obvious why school did not happen when it was raining, a couple of months after the wet morning at Wonderful Love. When the first drops of rain turned into something rather heavier, the children closed the shutters over the windows to keep themselves, their work, and the room, dry. The resulting gloom meant that they could not see the sums I had written on the chalkboard.

"It's no problem. I'll tell you what it says," I reassured them. It was somewhat optimistic; my voice had to be raised to overcome the banging of the downpour on the corrugated tin roof.

About two seconds later, it was clear that this was a futile exercise. In the ever-increasing downpour, the children had no chance of hearing my voice – I could barely hear it myself.

The rain continued to smack down on the roof. I let the children chat among themselves; there was little else to do. Since they were sitting happily enough, after a few minutes I splashed my way over first to Mischa's class, where the children were also chattering away, and then on to Lene's.

There, the most amazing scene awaited me. Lene's lesson with Classes 3 and 4 was on the Biblical flood. It seemed highly appropriate, I mused. The children were having a whale of a time, acting out the story. John, playing Noah, carefully shepherded the animals two by two onto the tables that had been put together to represent the Arc. The little tearaway had a strong bond with Lene, who cut him a little more slack with his lesser indiscretions.

Debra, playing the dove, was dispatched from the Arc. She returned with a twig that, having leant out of the door, she had plucked from a soaking wet bush outside. John cautiously piloted the Arc to the safety of dry land and ushered the rest animals off, whereupon they returned to their homes, dotted around the classroom.

Although Lene's flood was over, it seemed, with the rain hammering down more heavily than ever, as though a more general one was impending.

The ladies concurred. We closed school for the day.

Things came to a head on the Thursday. Lene had been distinctly unimpressed with Classes 3 and 4, Yarro in particular. She looked fairly grumpy when she had finished telling the troublemakers off at breaktime.

"Are you sure about this walk around the village?" she asked pointedly, looking at the paper which I had brought for the children to produce their land-use maps on.

"Nope," I answered. "But can you think of anything better without a football?"

She couldn't. Nor could Mischa.

The three of us gathered the children together and explained what we wanted them to do. We made a point of emphasising that they should not wander off or lag behind.

We may as well have been talking to a brick wall. We sent John home after he had kicked one of Class 2, a little chap called Eric, in the stomach. Thereafter, ignoring his marching orders, John made as much a nuisance of himself as he could. He loitered just beyond the back of the group as we trailed around the village, mapping the locations of the various facilities.

In one way, it was a worthwhile activity. Adjei in particular contributed a number of perceptive comments, particularly about why Olivia's chop bar had moved from the centre of the village to Quarters Junction. 'Chop' is a lovely Ghanaian-English word, meaning either 'eating' or 'food'.

"People, when they are driving, they like to chop, so they stop and go to Olivia's," he volunteered. "Olivia's, they have moved so that people can chop banku and fufu on the road."

Unfortunately, the number of children completing the activity diminished steadily as we made our way round. Many of them ducked into the small paths that led off the larger ones that we were walking down, and made their way home. Even conscientious Eunice briefly disappeared – she had stopped at a stall to buy credit for her mum's mobile. Only seven children were still there at the end when we called it a day on the approach back to school. It was six really, since one of them was John, who had still not gone home, and had now begun irritating some of the younger ones. I took him to one side and advised him that it would be better if he stayed off the next day. It would be an unofficial suspension. The whole business was thoroughly dispiriting.

Never before had I given up on a school day; but on the Thursday evening I could have taken or left the Friday.

We actually had a super morning to end the fortnight.

It felt as though the pressure that the three of us had applied on ourselves, to deliver quality lessons, had been lifted. After the mayhem of the day before, it could get no worse. Lene and I met Mischa at the entrance to one of the classrooms and cracked a joke or two as we waited for the children to arrive.

How to fit a road into a classroom?

That was my dilemma as I began my lesson with the youngest of the three classes. An easy solution presented itself. Taking a piece of chalk, I simply drew two parallel lines down the middle of the concrete floor, about a metre and a half away from each other. This would form the road; a third, dotted line gave it added authenticity.

I had watched some of the smaller children as they crossed the real Mamfe-Koforidua road at or near Quarters Junction. They often either looked only as an afterthought, or not at all. Somebody, I decided, better teach them how to do it properly.

So it came to pass that over the following forty minutes, the children of Classes 1 and 2 learned and practiced the old maxims of stopping, looking right, left and right again (I remembered that Ghanaians drive on the other side of the road just in time to swap the order around) and listening for traffic. In turn, they approached the side of the road, and crossed it carefully. Once they had all successfully crossed it once, I decided have a little fun with them. They were to move "Back across the road," to the other side of the room. Only Yaw's sister Mabena, who may have seen the glint in my eye, treated the 'road' as a road. Whilst the others ran back as fast as they could, she crossed the road safely.

"You are lucky there are no cars coming," I teased them, as they crossed back over the road, safely, and then back again, safely. Practice makes perfect, after all.

It got a bit more competitive after a few more goes when I introduced myself as a car, driving along the road. The children had to wait for me to cruise past before they crossed. When I brought in a number of other passing vehicles, in the form of the other children, the friendly rivalry intensified. Eric turned into a racing car and sped along the road trying to overtake all the others. I had to gently remind him to stick to the speed limit before he caused an accident.

At breaktime, I watched as Mabena and a couple of her friends toddled off to the Junction. Would they, I wondered, have remembered anything that we had just practiced in the lesson?

They surpassed themselves, crossing the road displaying vigilance that made them look like ambassadors for the Green Cross Code.

I abandoned my plans for Classes 3 and 4 after break; they could do this too.

After the Spring Break, there was a week for me left at Wonderful Love, before my time with the volunteering company finished and I began working for the Rev. Daniel and I gave the children the results of the tests that they had done whilst Lene and I had relaxed beside Lake Bosumtwi. As I had expected, they reflected the wide range of abilities in Class 2. Morgan had come top, which surprised me. I knew he was an intelligent boy, but there was even more behind the 'Jack the Lad' exterior than I had thought.

Only around a third of the children had returned to school in the first few days; indeed, even on Friday we still had around a third missing. That was normal, Dorothy assured me; many of the parents had got used to their children helping them with the family work over the holiday. They either forgot that school was re-starting or simply wanted to keep their children on, helping with the family's work for a few extra days.

I mentioned to Daniel about the road safety activity, and how I could repeat it with Class 2. He eagerly agreed. He was concerned for the children's safety on the road, as were Diana and Dorothy. Another teacher delivering the message would be a good thing, he said. Traffic was rare in Akokoa. When the youngsters went to the market at Adawso with their parents, they were unused to the hazards presented by the road. I would save this lesson until Friday, my last day, when more of the children would be back in school.

It went well: even Patience stopped, looked and listened. At First Break, I sat with Diana and Dorothy, and told them all about it. We had run out of supplies to treat ringworm and wounds, so there was nothing left to do except have a natter. As I was finishing, Daniel came jogging into the room, shouting for me most animatedly.

"Lawrie, come! The children are playing football!"

This was no surprise at all. In fact, it would have been most unusual had they not been doing so.

"Let's join them," he exhorted.

What a good idea!

The game was a fantastic, hell-for-leather affair. I had imagined that, whilst the children played as competitively as ever, Daniel would go easy on the youngsters.

I was wrong.

Pretty quickly he upended Bentil and took the ball from him, before sending a lovely pass through to Abigail. A fine save from Bernard stopped her from opening the scoring.

We finished one-all, around forty-five minutes later. Morgan scored a screamer, which rebounded off Diana's classroom door. The bang that it made terrified her and Dorothy; it was almost worth falling behind to. I equalised after Bentil had put in a cross worthy of the Black Stars' team, never mind that of Classes 1 and 2.

Beginning my final lesson, English, I felt distinctly un-teacher-like. Sweat poured from every orifice, as I stood in front of the class and re-capped words to describe the weather with them. No amount of excitement on behalf of the children when they were given a clap for a correct answer could do anything to make me feel fresher.

I was flattered and proud when, at the end of this last lesson, the children each came and took my hand, and said 'Thank you' to me for teaching them. Flattered because I did not think that I had done anything out of the ordinary with them, that other, better, teachers may have done. Proud because the children's words of gratitude were delivered with a far greater fluency than they had been capable of when I had met them three months before.

Dorothy and Diana were complementary as well. Daniel made a little speech which really pulled on my heartstrings. The impact I had made, he said, was far greater than any other volunteer teacher that the Three Ds had worked with. I was thinking of asking why, but he continued.

"Lawrie, you're not afraid to tell them that they have made mistakes with their work, that it is wrong." This was true. "But then you tell them what they must do to make it better, and you let them know that they *are* able to improve. Then in your next lessons you always start with a reminder of the right way of doing what some got wrong the last time."

Although this seemed to me to be fundamental to teaching, part of the job that has to be done to allow children to progress, it was touching nonetheless. The warmth in Daniel's face cheered me even more than his words, and continued to until we got to the roadside and boarded the tro.

Turning to me as we sat, he smiled again. "I've learned a lot about teaching from you. Thank you once more."

I was quite unsure what to say, and more than a little bowled over by his comments. For want of something better, I explained to him that I would take on board a lot of the things that I had seen from him in the classroom, and that of course I would visit Wonderful Love when time at Holy Hills permitted me to. In what felt like an instant, we had reached Quarters Junction, and I was waving goodbye as the Three Ds moved off around the corner.

Before I began at Holy Hills, however, there was to be a week at Mount Zion Primary School in Tinkong. I would work there for a week with Lene, before she and I went travelling for her final two weeks in Ghana.

As expected, the young children at Mount Zion possessed far more English than did the youngsters at Wonderful Love. Living in a larger settlement on a main road, Tinkong's population came into far greater contact with English speakers than did those in out-of-the-way Akokoa. Just as importantly, the Mount Zion children had been at school for a longer period of time.

Lene had warned me that the children in her classes displayed a greater willingness to challenge the rules than Morgan, Bentil and their friends. She had done so, in fact, several times since she had come to Wonderful Love for a morning in March. Mount Zion had had the same two-day mid-term break as Holy Hills had enjoyed, and Lene had wanted to see what 'my' school was like. She reminded me of it again as we walked the few hundred yards from the roadside to school this Monday morning.

Her caution seemed totally at odds, however, with what I saw as we rounded the corner of Mount Zion's block of classrooms. Several immaculately dressed children, sweeping and preparing the school for lessons, greeted us most politely. Lene introduced me to the headteacher, Madam Vera. In the course of our chat, Vera asked me to teach Mathematics to Class 4, followed by giving the amalgamation that was Lene's main class – Classes 1, 2 and 3 – their English lesson. I had followed Lene's lead in coming prepared for having both these groups; the Rev had explained that Madam Vera always taught the joint Class 5 and 6.

The sense of order remained during assembly. Madam Vera stressed the importance of the children keeping their uniform looking smart at all times, of wearing closed shoes rather than casual flip-flops, and of the need to work hard in class. A few swishes of her cane through the air left me in no doubt as to how she dealt with anyone who stepped out of line, and ensured silence throughout the delivery of her message. She dismissed all classes to their lessons, and followed Class 5 and 6 into their room.

So far, so good.

What on earth had Lene been talking about?

I was still none the wiser ten minutes into my Maths lesson with the two children in Class 4. Yarro had had his moments in the Spring Break School, but he and his mate Chandrak listened attentively as I set them an exercise on the chalkboard. Next door, Lene had mentioned John's name a couple of times, in the tones that teachers use when a child is beginning to push their luck, but that was to be expected. There was nothing out of the ordinary.

A sudden bang took my attention, not to mention that of Yarro and Chandrak. It was followed by the sound of a couple of pairs of feet running across and out of the classroom next door. I peered out of the window. Two boys were climbing up a bank of earth behind the classrooms. One was instantly recognisable as John, the other turned out to be called Rami, also in Class 3.

As I opened my mouth to ask them where they *should* be, and what they *should* be doing there, Lene appeared. Her feathers looked a little ruffled by this interlude, particularly as the rest of her class had been distracted by the commotion, and were now growing louder. It took a good deal of encouragement from both of us to get the boys back into Lene's room.

"I'd probably send those two to Vera for that," I suggested. "She can have a chat to them when you've finished."

Lene rolled her eyes at me and breezed back into her room. What did that mean?

Curiosity got the better of me. Once I had helped Yarro with a complex bit of a sum, I popped out of the room and headed towards Vera's door. The sight of her stopped me in my tracks. The fearsome-looking and authoritative figure of assembly was now sprawled over a table just outside Class 5 and 6's room. The rhythmic up-and-down movement of her shoulders and back was confirmation that she was enjoying a deep sleep, whilst her class wrote answers into their books in silence.

I was gobsmacked.

Order, however, had been restored in Lene's room. It largely remained there, save for the occasional word of gentle admonition, until the ringing of the bell for First Break by one of Vera's class an hour later disturbed it.

Lene and I dismissed our classes and joined Vera at her table. By now the headteacher was fully conscious, and tucking into a plate of tilapia and rice. I dropped into conversation how there had been a misdemeanour during Lene's lesson, which had disturbed my class as well. The upshot was that John and Rami were brought before her, and received almighty swishes of the cane until they apologised. It was something, I sensed, that would not be a lasting solution. Why, I wondered, did it have to be like that? An assertive word in the boys' ear in the immediate aftermath of the event would have had far greater effect.

During my own lesson with John and Rami's class, it became clear just how good a job Lene had been doing with the three different year groups. The children had vastly different levels of understanding of English, not to mention a wide range of general learning abilities. Rami and the sole member of Class 2, a splendid little boy called Odei, were the most gifted. It was easy to see why the children sometimes caused trouble. They frequently had to wait a while to be set work as the teacher explained different tasks to the others, and ensured that the weaker ones – Theresa in Class 3 and a tiny boy called Nanayaw in Class 1 – understood the foreign language in which their instructions were given.

I felt exhausted after just a ninety-minute lesson with them.

"How do you do that?" I asked Lene that afternoon.

"I just do. I have to," she shrugged.

Mount Zion needed a bit more help. I made a mental note to have a chat to the Rev about it that evening. Perhaps it would be a better idea for me to replace Lene there than work with Peace *et. al.* at Holy Hills.

The Rev seemed open to the idea and told me to leave it with him. He knew of some of the problems at Mount Zion and was in the process of appointing a new teacher, although I doubted that he was aware that Madam Vera used lesson times to get her head down for a kip.

As there was nothing else that I could do, I returned to *Obruni* Castle. Lene was shuffling the deck of cards once more, anticipating another victory at Five Hundred. I was beginning to run her close, however, and secretly fancied my chances. The game was relatively even until I absent-mindedly put down a card that I should have known not to. In frustration, and almost as a reflex, I jumped in the air and landed sitting back on the bench. It failed to take my weight. A gigantic splintering sound rang out. The Rev and Florence, sitting outside the house, broke off their conversation and stared in my direction.

Oops.

I inspected the damage. A crack ran the width of the bench and almost right through its depth. It was distinctly wobbly.

I walked shamefacedly over to the Rev, apologised profusely, and nervously awaited his reaction.

"Don't worry," he chuckled. "These things happen. It can be fixed."

Phew.

I found Bosh later and guiltily explained what I had done to *Obruni* Castle, his beloved creation. Wanting to fix the damage myself, I asked if he knew where I could find wood, nails and a hammer. He didn't, off the top of his head.

I felt all the more ashamed a few mornings later, when I looked out of my bedroom window and found Bosh mending the bench to the rhythm of the early Church service. I rushed outside and tried to persuade him that it should be me, not him, doing the repair job. He wouldn't hear of it, and only reluctantly allowed me to stay, and watch him do me yet another favour.

There was little change over the rest of the week at Mount Zion. I met the other full-time teacher, Mr Daniel, on the Wednesday; he arrived at school half-way through the morning. The following day, he turned up only slightly earlier – just in time to see me getting stuck into a lesson that I ended up being pretty proud of. Lene and I had arrived that morning and asked Vera, as usual, what she wanted to happen with the mixture that was Classes 1, 2 and 3, and with Yarro and Chandrak in Class 4.

"You can teach Classes 5 and 6."

This was unexpected, but I tried to take it in my stride.

"OK, Vera. What would you like me to teach them?"

"English."

Mmm. I had been hoping for something more specific than this broad subject area. I quizzed her again.

"They are learning adjectives," she explained. "You can continue with them."

That seemed alright. A quick think about what activities I could come up with and I would be fine. I had brought some paper with me, so flashcards could be made to introduce each word, I reckoned. Ten minutes would be enough.

"What time do you want me to start?"

"You can begin now, until First Break."

Armed with a few pieces of chalk, I had about four paces' worth of space between Vera's desk and the classroom door to think of how to keep a new class occupied for over an hour and a half.

The easy place to start was with the children's names. It would buy me some thinking time. As they introduced themselves and I created a seating plan, I came up with the first few learning activities.

Over the next eighty-five minutes or so, I enjoyed the rollercoaster ride of the off-the-cuff lesson. Ofsted requirements that I adhered to in Britain, of having a clear focus for each stage of the lesson and sharing these with the children at the beginning, flew out of the window. As pupils worked through one activity, I racked my brain to think of the next. First, we had a competition to see who could find the most adjectives, then the children worked out the opposite of each, and grouped clusters of those which were synonyms. These tasks culminated in the writing of a descriptive story, using as many adjectives as was feasible. A quiz to identify adjectives from a list of words ended the lesson. It was quite a come-down when a tall, thick-set lad called Elias, who was the bell-boy, raised his hand to tell me that it was time for him to signal First Break. Part of me wanted to carry on teaching; I even had a few more activities lined up.

All too quickly, the week ended. Lene bade her farewells to Madam Vera and Mr Daniel, and I told them that I might well see them soon. Although he was an appalling timekeeper, there was something immensely likeable about Daniel; and despite Vera's faults as a teacher she too was a well-meaning woman. She lived with the boys at the Mont Zion orphanage, and had the substantial job of caring for them in the afternoons and evenings. As if that were not enough, the younger children often woke her in the middle of the night needing a bit of T.L.C. – I understood why she needed to catch up with a bit of sleep at school.

I was positive about the possibility of working at Mount Zion; there was clearly a lot that I could do there to relieve the burden of short-staffing on the other two.

First in my thoughts right then, though, was my last two weeks with Lene.

Chapter 9 – Goodbye my friend

Perhaps, in some parallel universe, John Milton visited Dzita, and used it, rather than the temptation of Christ, as his inspiration to write *Paradise Regained*. Sitting on the beach in the Saturday afternoon sunshine was just as perfect as it had been two months earlier.

Lene had said her goodbyes to the Rev and his family, Kofi Bosh, the volunteers and everyone else in the complex. For me, too, it would be the last time that I would see several of the westerners. Only Florian and a Danish bloke called Mikkel, who had arrived a week earlier, would still be there when I returned to start work at Holy Hills.

Just before Lene and I left, the pleasant smell of goat being cooked on a grill began wafting over *Obruni* Castle. The meat was definitely sourced locally; I had seen the animal being led away on a rope to have its throat slit the previous evening.

Dennis had been delighted when I told him that we would go to Togo after Dzita, for he had been born there, and moved to Ghana as a young child. The Rev had adopted him after his parents died when he was ten.

"You can bring me something," he suggested hopefully. We laughed, and I promised to find him something either in Togo's capital Lomé, or in the hills further north.

Sitting on the tro, I had mixed emotions. I was looking forward to the trip, particularly the Togolese leg; yet ever mindful that these would be the last sixteen days Lene and I had before we said goodbye at Accra's airport. We rattled along the road towards Mamfe. I felt happiness that I would be coming back to this beautiful part of the world, yet it was tainted by the reality of coming back to it without Lene.

At Dzita, however, all that seemed far away. We spent another wonderful weekend together. The natural beauty amazed us just as it had on our first visit; the Gulf of Guinea was just as clear and warm, the sand of the palm tree-lined beach as soft. Just as he had been in March, Kojo was charmingly insistent that he paddle us over the lagoon in his canoe every time he had the opportunity to do so. Our hardest decision in those three days came when Kojo was busy with something else. How would we get from the beach to the *Meet Me There* Guesthouse bar: walk around the lagoon or swim across it?

"Swim," was Lene's verdict.

"Walk," I said simultaneously.

"We'll race then. You go round, I'll swim it. Loser buys."

This was a good little challenge that Lene had set down. She was a strong swimmer; the roughly nine-mile round trip from the Rev's house to Wonderful Love and back had become more or less a weekly run.

"Game on."

She won. She also won on the way back when I suggested a double-or-quits deal.

There was a hint of sadness when the time came for us to move on. We would take a tro to the small town of Keta, where the Danes had built a slave-trading outpost in 1784 named Fort Prinzenstein. After a quick look around, we would go on to Aflao, on the Togolese border, and hence to Lomé.

As we set off, I looked wistfully out of the window. Lene had read my thoughts.

"You really won't ever come here again, will you?"

"No." I left it at that. I could have gushed about how I could never go somewhere so incredible without her, about how she was part of the fondness I had for the setting... but that would only have got both of us thinking again about what was going to happen in just under two weeks. It went unspoken, but we were both steeling ourselves for that final embrace before she walked through the departure gate.

A remarkable piece of graffiti adorned the tiny dungeon at Fort Prinzenstein. Judging by the sharpness of the white lettering on the dirty wall, it must have been written fairly recently. It concerned the historiography of the African men, women and children who spent their final days on their continent cramped and immobile in the squalor. "Until the lion has his historian, the hunter will always be the hero", it read. A set of shackles lay preserved on the dusty floor. Otherwise, the lack of attention that is given to this fort makes it even more of a stark reminder of the horrors of the trade then the renovated Cape Coast and Elmina castles.

A sign reading "*Bienvenue au Togo*" adorned a gigantic brick gatehouse just along from Aflao's busy eastern market. The gatehouse served as the official border crossing. Our pulses quickened: we were nearly there! Dodging the currency traders, who apparently quote wildly inflated exchange rates of cedis to cefas in the hope of making an already fast buck even faster, we entered the Immigration Office. We filled in our form for leaving Ghana, and queued at the desk to hand it in. I had taken my passport back after a young man had stamped it with the word 'Embarked', when I felt a tap on the shoulder. It drew my attention from admiring the crisp green lettering imprinted on the passport page.

"Listen to this."

Lene's voice was grave. So was the expression on her face. A slightly-built immigration officer with round glasses had pointed something out to her. He had a calm, studious and slightly apologetic manner, which told of his disappointment in having to break an uncomfortable piece of news.

"Leaving Ghana is no problem for you," he began. "But you will have to get a new visa when you come back. The visas that you have will expire when you leave. It will cost a hundred and fifty US dollars."

Neither of us had that money spare.

"But-" I began my protest.

Lene cut me off. "He explained to me. Our extensions from Koforidua don't cover leaving the country and coming back."

I looked into her eyes. How could this be true? In my case, I was not that surprised, since my original visa had been a single-entry one. Lene's, however, was the multi-entry type.

The immigration officer was sympathetic, but there was nothing that he could do. If we wanted to go to Togo, we would have to pay a hefty fee to get back into Ghana. We could "go and come," he said, later on or even the next day, if we wanted to think about whether we still wanted to cross the border or not. He was sorry for the misunderstanding.

I felt sorry for Lene more than anything. She had been so keen and passionate about going to Togo, whereas I was happy to be there with her wherever we ended up.

It was in those circumstances that we made our third and final beach-stop of the day. We strolled onto the sand and heard a moderately irritated voice come from just behind us. It asked the inevitable question.

"Where are you going?"

Turning around, we discovered that the voice belonged to an armed policeman.

"Just along the beach. Is that OK?" we replied, anxious not to offend.

A slight grimace crossed his face, but he nodded his consent, so we thought nothing of it.

It was a touch odd then, we thought, when the same question was asked a few moments later. This time it was a soldier, sitting in what looked like a fortified beach hut. His tone betrayed a hint of surprise. When we explained, he somewhat reluctantly allowed us to proceed, as long as we stayed within his sight.

The conversation between Lene and I that unfolded on the sand led to a pragmatic decision. Togo sounded fascinating, but it was more money than Lene could afford. I, too, would likely run out of money some time earlier than expected if we crossed the border. Instead, we could see some more of Ghana before heading into Accra for her last few days. We would sleep on it, and see if we felt the same in the morning.

Decision reached, we smiled at the soldier as we made our way back to the road. Out of the corner of my eye, I noticed a sign that we had not seen earlier. It read "Access to beach strictly prohibited."

That explained a lot.

The silver lining of not going on to Togo straight away was that we had some time in Aflao to have a look around. The currency hawkers plied their wares across the town, not just near the border. I was tempted to be mischievous, and ask one of them for a rate for exchanging one currency to another, and then asking for the opposite exchange, just to see what would happen. Lene's reaction would probably have been disproving, though, so I didn't bother.

In many ways, we found Aflao to be unique amongst towns that we had been to. For a start, there was a Gallic taste to the street stalls, most of which sold crusty French baguettes. We bought a couple of the breads, and discovered that they were warm. *Fantastique!* Or was it just the result of the heat of the sun, which was beating down furiously, and not that of the oven as we had concluded in our excitement? Either way, it was not quite as delicious as real French *pain*, but came close enough.

Taxis did not exist in the same way as in all other towns we had been to. Instead of orange-panelled cars, motorbikes gave lifts to one person at a time. Indeed, most private vehicles were motorbikes rather than cars. As was customary across Ghana, most riders and passengers did not wear helmets. I had always thought that this was a violation of the law, to which the police turned a blind eye. In Aflao, I was proved wrong. Policemen periodically whizzed by on their own motorbikes, minus headgear.

After dark, Aflao really came alive. Markets were picking up, and on the streets people set up frying pans and little stoves on which to cook omelettes. There were numerous cries of *Yavoo*, the Ewe equivalent of *Obruni*. Rather disconcertingly, another frequent cry – 'Hey, Whiteman!' – was sometimes shortened to 'White!' Not for the first time, I pondered the consequences of shouting "Hey! Foreigner!" – or "Blackman!" – at people on the streets of Britain.

Passing moto-taxis rushed through the streets, ferrying people from place to place. Horns beeping, they weaved through the crowds of people that milled around the streets. Some of the unluckier pedestrians were used as apexes, as corners were negotiated at the maximum possible speed. It was quite an adrenaline rush just to watch it.

By the morning, all this had gone. It felt as if we were walking through a different town as we picked up a baguette and a rather un-French-looking *Niçoise* salad to breakfast on during our next tro-tro ride.

We were not going to cross the border. Dennis would have to be disappointed when I got back to the complex, short on Togo memorabilia. Instead, our next destination was the highest mountain in Ghana, Mount Afadjato. It was not too far from the waterfall at Wli where we had spent Easter Sunday. Our journey took on a familiar route as the tro wound its way along the steep and twisty roads of the Volta Region. After a change of vehicle at a tiny junction town called Golakuati, Lene and I found ourselves dropped off on a remote piece of country road. A bumpy track made a junction just ahead of us. It looked unpromising, to say the least.

We were about to begin the slightly daunting task of pondering our next move when a solution presented itself. It always seemed to do so in Ghana, often at the timeliest moments. A motorbike drew up, whereupon its rider asked us – of course – where we were going.

"Oh, the mountain! You'll need to stay at Liati Wote. Do you know that place?"

We had heard of the village, but it would have been stretching it a bit to say that we "knew it".

"I am the caretaker of the rest-house there. It's very close to the mountain. I'll call my brother, he will help me to take you. Wait small."

I wondered whether, like the chap we had met in Wli who said he was in charge of tros, this was just another helpful bloke looking to make a few bob. Many Ghanaians, either because they are eager to help or because they think that they can make a quick profit, claimed to be all sorts of things. Through chatting to this man, though, it became clear that he actually was the rest-house's caretaker. My doubtfulness looked doubly silly when his brother arrived – from their facial features and mannerisms, it was pretty clear that they were siblings. I climbed onto the back of the caretaker's motorbike, Lene settled down onto the other machine, and we zoomed off down the (now much less unpromising) track.

"Do you see that mountain there?" he yelled, pointing towards the peaks ahead of us. I could just about hear him over the engine and the noise of the tyres on the path's loose surface.

"Yes."

"That is Afadjato, the highest mountain in Ghana."

I adjusted my position on the pillion to look straight down the line of his arm. The summit of the mountain that he was pointing at looked quite a bit lower than the summit of the one just to the right of it.

"That one?" I asked quizzically, pointing.

"That's right," he replied. "It's eight hundred and eighty-five metres high from sea level. You will go there tomorrow."

I let the little disparity pass, however, and had forgotten about it by the time the caretaker had stopped his motorbike and I had got off. Quite by chance, he happened to mention it again as Lene and I followed him into the rest-house. It turned out that although the larger mountain, Aduado, stood at more than nine hundred metres, it was in fact just on the Togolese side of the national border.

You know it's humid when you leave a sweaty shirt to dry on a rock, and it is still damp after forty-five minutes in the sun.

This was despite an easier than expected walk, bearing in mind that we were scaling Ghana's highest mountain. Following a single path, it took well under an hour to reach the summit. To be fair, the official height is largely irrelevant to walkers: Liati Wote itself is at least three hundred, and probably nearer to four hundred, metres above sea level.

With the sun beating down on the summit, Lene and I took in the incredible landscape. In front of us, Liati Wote sat nestled in the thick woodland scrub which extended as far as the eye could see in all directions. To the left, we gazed slightly upwards to look at the summit of Mount Aduado. To the right, the hills that reached into the distance hid several villages, including Wli and its magnificent waterfalls, in their formations. I turned around, and took in the forest which concealed Togo's border; beyond it, uplands extended towards the towns in the centre of Ghana's neighbouring country. We had harboured hopes of seeing these on the way to a more mountainous area further north.

"Take a look at Togo's hills, Lene," I jested. "This is the closest we'll get to them."

I received a playful punch in the arm for my trouble.

We sat down on a rock, chatting about this and that as we always did. It was nothing groundbreaking, but again I felt an immense contentedness swim over me. Here we were, just the two of us, sitting in this spectacular setting. It was perfect. At that moment, the knowledge that this sort of thing would not last much longer only made the tranquillity greater.

The second city of Ghana was the antithesis of this. A stop-start line of vehicles jerked past Kumasi's endless crowd of sellers and pedestrians, all of whom looked to be blissfully uncaring of the perils of traffic. In fact, they could well have been walking, trading and dodging the traffic in time to the beat of music and honking of horns which provided the auditory backdrop to the scene. Roads and pavements blurred into one; the informal boundary usually created by a kerb did not exist.

Despite our view of Kumasi's central streets through the tro window, stepping into the maelstrom of the sprawling Kajetia station was still a major assault on the senses. Five water sellers rushed over when Lene still had one foot in the tro, and thrust their wares at us. Thirsty after the journey, I fumbled some coins and bought myself and Lene a few sachets each off at least three of them. This was not through any thought of dividing revenues fairly, but because sellers' hands dropped sachets into mine more quickly than I could work out whom they belonged to. If any of them were paid the correct amount, it was through their judgment rather than mine.

We had phoned a hotel hours earlier, now came the trickier task of finding it. The guidebook's map would only be of use in helping our navigation once we were out of the mass of humanity and vehicles that was the tro station.

In the event, the book was of no use whatsoever, being as our hotel was not located on the street that the author claimed it was. Once we had phoned for directions, trudging through Kumasi on a Friday night provided greater excitement than it needed to. Amongst other things, taxi drove so close to me that I received a hefty clatter on the arm from its wing mirror. Lene decided that she needed to relax a bit, and lit a cigarette. A passing man then let off a tirade at me. The gist of it was that Lene had no right to be smoking on the street.

Although smoking is generally frowned upon in Ghanaian society, we had both seen other people – Ghanaian and foreign – having a smoke in public, untroubled by hassle. That his ire – "You are failing to control your wife!" – was directed at me, was more than a little bothersome. Why did I have to "control" my female friend, I asked him. Why, also, did he not have the courtesy to address her, or both of us, rather than simply me? Poor Lene looked highly embarrassed at the scene that had been created. The word 'prostitute' was mentioned over the course of his rant as well, which to Lene's credit she shrugged off. In order not to make a difficult situation worse, we turned and walked away. My parting shot of "Mind your own business" was in hindsight rather petty. It was, however, less inflammatory than my true thoughts, which were that the bloke was a sexist, arrogant and rude blankety-blank.

It was something that we could brush off and laugh about later though, when we were sitting on our hotel bed after dinner, engaged in a game of Five Hundred. I was finally starting to get the hang of the card game and had actually managed to win a few hands over the course of our holiday.

Very excitingly, we had found that the hotel's restaurant served steak. This represented the luxury of luxuries, which could not be passed up. Lene did not quite manage to finish hers; I wrapped up the remainder in a serviette. I would have it for breakfast the next day. It seemed a terrific idea.

Looking around Kumasi the following morning, we noticed how it was only fractionally less busy than it had been the previous evening. The streets possessed a different air to other towns. People looked, or glared, at us, and there were none of the *Obruni* catcalls that there had been almost everywhere else. Yet whilst that was welcome in one way, for we did not have to constantly respond to greetings or '*Where are you goings?*', at first it came over as being quite oppressive; almost malevolent. In such a busy, bustling environment, we felt we needed to keep an eye over our shoulders. Fortunately, despite the tension that neither of us ever truly shed, there were no further misadventures. More cheerfully, we noticed a number of intricate statues and sculptures dotted about. Most were carved from wood; the Lion Statue in the middle of one roundabout looked particularly spectacular.

On the other side of town, we took a deep breath and headed into Kajetia market. This is a mass of stalls which originally occupied a large square. Over time, it has thrown itself out over twelve hectares, spreading across the tro-tro station (with which it shares a name) at one end, and eventually petering out some way into a series of backstreets at the other. A wonderful, if slightly frenzied, atmosphere is created by, apparently, ten thousand traders over this area. Although we did not count, it was a statistic that I could well believe, as we stepped over various boxes which lay in the spaces between stalls that passed for aisles, and dodged past sellers and customers. At one point, a couple of women stood over some great metal basins, and stirred a concoction which bubbled ferociously. It had the consistency of custard, the colour of chocolate and the smell of – well, let's just say that it was pungent.

Various skinned animals were piled up on the meat stalls on one edge of the market. Chunks were being separated from one of the carcasses of beef – or could it have been goatmeat? – by forceful applications of some of the largest meat cleavers in Ghana. A few metres (although a great number of tentative paces) further down were the fish stands. Various salted and dried fish stared up at us, with their ever beady eyes, from wooden tables.

The greatest surprise of all, though, was seeing a section of the market that had spilled over onto the disused railway line. Traders sat or stood on the rails selling their goods, whilst others stepped delicately over the wooden sleepers. Most of these had gigantic baskets on their heads, which carried all sorts of things from one place to another.

"It's easy to see," Lene mused thoughtfully, "How a small fire would devastate somewhere like this."

I was slightly taken aback by this statement. Was she a closet pyromaniac? She didn't seem like one.

Then I recalled reading in the guidebook, as we were planning this leg of our trip in Aflao, how the whole place had been gutted in 1995, 2001 and 2009 by fires. They began very small, but found constant fuel over the vast expanse to consume the greater part of the market. The cost to people's livelihoods must have been huge.

Another benefit of Kumasi, in addition to being a highly interesting city to walk around, was its proximity to the Ashanti shrine in Besease, and a smaller one nearer to Ejisu. Lene reminded me how keen she had been to visit one of them during the Spring Break, when we had been around the area but not had time to pay a visit before going to Bobiri. Now that we had a second chance, I agreed, it seemed daft not to make the journey out there to have a look.

Arriving at Besease, however, we found that the shrine was not just closed, but also more or less derelict. The shrine closer to Ejisu was similarly inaccessible and run-down. Their neglect must have been fairly recent, and was a great pity; the guidebook told us that they were well-maintained and popular with tourists.

Slightly dispirited, we trudged back to the roadside to wait for a tro. Our disappointment stemmed not only from having missed out on seeing the shrines, but also because of the sight of such culturally significant buildings in such disrepair. On a more urgent note, my stomach was beginning to complain; I guessed that its beef with me was the breakfast sandwich which I had made from the previous night's leftover steak. It seemed pointless to mention it, since we were heading back to the hotel in any case. By the time we reached the centre of Kumasi, and were inching, painfully (literally in my case), through the traffic, my stomach's complaint had turned into a full-scale rebellion. I broke it to Lene that we could do with getting back to the hotel reasonably quickly. She only really understood the gravity of the situation, though, once we were off the tro: I set off on as close to a headlong dash through the streets as was possible.

That evening, as my stomach continued its revolt against steak butties, and Lene looked after me and read her book, Chelsea played Bayern Munich in football's European Cup final. It drew a large TV audience. Efforts to sleep the stomach ache off were hampered by *oohs* and *aahs*, a groan as Bayern took the lead and a wild cheer as Chelsea equalised. There was pandemonium when Ghana's favourite club won the resulting penalty shoot-out; that night, the party went on and noisily on.

The following morning a reality hit me. We were about to make a trip to the last area of Ghana where we would stay before heading into Accra. Our first stop was the village of Akwidaa, which lies near the most southerly point of Ghana. It boasts little other than a stunning and deserted beach. Of course I was excited about it, but the fact that we were heading there meant that Lene and I had just one week left.

A mile or so outside the village, a delightful place with the equally charming name *Green Turtle Lodge* awaited us. After a journey lasting all day, with three changes of tro, we finally made it shortly after dusk. On the second leg of the journey, a grey tro had overtaken ours, which itself was travelling at a decent lick. The manoeuvre, executed with the customary recklessness, carried a wonderful irony. As the grey tro sped away, a message on its rear windscreen advised, "Don't hurry."

The *Green Turtle* was certainly not a place at which to hurry. Though not quite as beautiful as Dzita, it was the perfect antidote to what had been a slightly stressful experience amidst the hustle and bustle of Kumasi. Swimming, walking up and down the beach in either direction, reading on the sand or playing Five Hundred, we felt a contentedness there. A bar set into the sand, and carved in the shape of a boat, served delicious food and drinks. Three beautiful sunsets later, though, it was again time to move on. It would be a short hop, around ten miles up the coast to the village of Busua. There, said the guidebook, a lagoon and two former slave castles would keep us occupied just in case we fancied a break from the beach and sea.

We walked into Akwidaa for the last time, and waited on the beach, adjacent to what amounted to the tro station, for a ride. After half an hour had passed, a tro pulled up, and some people got out. We ambled over, and found the driver and mate chuckling away in a most relaxed manner.

"Are you going to Agona?" We asked of the junction town where we would change for Busua.

"No, not today. Tomorrow though."

Blimey. It had only just turned noon.

It was no problem, though. It was a nice day. We sat back down on the beach. Another would come soon.

Helpfully, a young lad came over to us just over an hour later, and explained to us that there was a second, bigger station on the other side of the village. "You can get a tro from there any time," he called cheerfully as he waved us off down the path that he had pointed out.

Akwidaa was far bigger than we had anticipated. Small houses built of either cement blocks or clay bricks and reeds backed onto tiny streets, which all led to the central area. A church and a school complex dominated the scene. However, there did not seem to be any sign of a tro.

We were definitely in the right place, though. A number of people came and had a chat to us. They all reassured us that, yes, this was the place to wait for a ride to Agona.

At long last, a tro pulled up. Everyone got off, which was expected, since the next destination in that direction was the Gulf of Guinea. The driver revved the engine once more, but instead of turning around, he pulled over to the roadside. There, he got out his sponge, and prepared to give his pride and joy a wash down.

"Erm, are you going to Agona?"

"Not today," came the happy reply. "But a tro is coming."

"But lots of people are waiting." That was a slight exaggeration; a mother with two children had joined Lene and me under the shade of a tree at the roadside.

"Yes, but one is coming, one is coming right now."

As Ghanaian-English phrases went, that was one of my favourites, although also one of the most infuriating. It was a perfect reflection of the easy-going Ghanaian lifestyle. 'One is coming' meant that, at some point, one would eventually turn up. 'One is coming *right now*,' by extension, was recognition that the person asking the question was anxious to get going. He or she would still have to wait until one turned up, though, however long that would be.

He was proved right, though: one *was* coming. The shadows had begun to lengthen when a tro spluttered to a halt in the road near where we were sitting. The mother rounded her children up, and we followed her onto the tro. A large crowd of people had gathered by now, and everyone piled on. Lene and I managed to get a seat on the back row, cramming our bags in with us. I sat next to the window, Lene to my left. Two well-built men took up the rest of a back seat designed for three. Overload? Who cared?

Certainly not the driver, nor the mate. None of the passengers regarded it as a problem either, and we moved off, bouncing along the bumpy track that led to Agona. After a few miles, the tro stopped. People would be getting off here, I thought; we would have a bit more space.

How naïve. More people got on.

With Lene's backpack rising to head height from my lap (we had swapped, since hers was heavier), I couldn't see a thing in front of me. I realised that opening my window would solve this little problem – I could put my right arm out and hold on to the edge of the roof, trucker style. This would free up enough space to tilt Lene's bag diagonally, allowing me to see at least some of the road ahead. It worked a treat. The view was far from brilliant, but I could see.

We bounced along for several minutes into, and out of, what from my restricted viewpoint looked to be a pretty little area of managed woodland. Lene said something that was muffled by the backpack on her lap, but sounded as if it might have been about Busua. I was about to reply when a peculiar tilting sensation overtook me. It was almost as if we were flying. We weren't, of course; the tro had lurched onto just its two left-side wheels. The thought occurred that it was out of control. No, I reassured myself in the same instant: other people have crashes, not me or my friends. Next thing I knew, we had banged back down onto four wheels.

And up again. The added weight of the overcrowded vehicle meant that the momentum of falling back onto four wheels carried us over to the other side. The left wheels were now off the ground. I just about had time to realise that it was, actually, real. This time, gravity would not be strong enough to right the tro. It continued its inevitable fall, and hit the ground with a dull thud.

Looking down through the window, which was now underneath me, I could see two things. Mainly the ground, with its little pebbles and red earth. I could also see most of my forearm, though not the two or three inch section near the wrist. That was still out of the window, wedged between the tro and the ground. After a couple of seconds, I realised that it was far less painful than I thought it probably should have been. I glanced up at Lene, who was now above me.

"Are you OK?" I asked, with no little concern.

"I'm fine. Are you?"

That was a relief. People near the front were by now beginning to climb out through what had been, until a few moments ago, the windscreen.

"I'm alright," I answered. "It's just that-"

"Good. We need to get out."

"I can't, I'm stuck."

"Don't be daft, come on."

I explained to her what the matter was. Horrified, she peered over at me. I could sense that she might be about to panic, since my prone position looked significantly worse that it was. "It's OK. You need to get out," was the best I could manage, as she began scraping a little dip in the earth for me to wriggle my wrist free.

"You need to get out," I repeated when she and I had finished. I ought to have explained that having a little more space would provide me with extra leverage to extricate my hand. She and the two well-built men who had been next to her climbed over the seat in front. I grinned up at them to let them know I was alright. Either Lene or one of these two signalled for the passengers to lift the tro up fractionally, and I snatched my arm out through the dip that Lene had created. I crawled out of the tro, and into the open. After the driver and several passengers had checked that I was OK, which I was, save for a cut on the arm, I helped the other men to push the tro upright again. Predictably, it was in a sorry state. Its left front tyre was punctured; this was probably the cause of the accident. The driver had done well, I reckoned, to correct the initial lurch leftwards.

As I hugged Lene, I expressed my amazement that everyone had just got off, without any commotion. She looked quizzically at me. Reality had been totally different, she explained, remarkably coolly. There had been a fair amount of panic among the other passengers. Parents, themselves distressed, had had to soothe the cries of their frightened children. I had been so wrapped up in events that I had not noticed.

Gradually, people began to escape the scene, hitching rides in passing vehicles. An argument had developed between the tro driver and two of the male passengers. A taxi stopped to pick Lene and me up. On the way to Agona, we told the driver what had happened. We tried to brush aside the fact that we were pretty shaken. On reflection, we should have asked the taxi driver what might become of the tro's driver and mate, and the vehicle itself. It just did not come to our minds.

In Agona, we looked for a taxi to Busua. It was getting late, and there were not as many as there probably had been earlier. A voice called from our left.

"Busua, one cedi twenty pesewas!"

That sounded good. We made a beeline towards the driver that had called.

"And a cedi extra for each of the bags," he said, almost as an afterthought, as we were sitting down.

That was highly irregular.

"We'll go with one of your mates then," Lene replied. We moved away, and decided that a little break was in order.

In a little alley between two stalls, having asked permission from both of their owners after the little incident in Kumasi, Lene lit a contemplative cigarette. How would I feel, she wondered, about cutting Busua out and stopping a night somewhere half-way to Accra, such as Cape Coast?

It made sense. We would not have had long in Busua anyway by this time, and it would have meant a heck of a long journey from there to Accra. I had the school holiday in August to go back there if I wanted. More importantly, Lene looked, and sounded, as if she had seen enough of the dirt tracks.

In a strange sort of way, we were both totally relaxed by the time we sat down on our bed in Cape Coast. Months later, Lene told me that the accident stopped her being uptight about leaving, and made her enjoy every second of the remaining days. Looking back, it was possibly something which helped to secure our lasting friendship. You don't go through that with someone and then lose touch.

And so it was on to Accra, for a weekend in the capital before Lene made the long journey home and I made the substantially shorter one back to the Rev's house. Her flight would take off on the Monday evening, and I would stay the night in the city. I had made a decision. I was not going to stay at the airport to watch the plane take off. Some people want to do things like that. For me, though, it would only have been more painful to wait, knowing what was going to happen and being unable to do anything about it. I wanted my last impression of her to be walking away, her figure, in the flesh. Not of an aeroplane taking off.

The last days passed ever so quickly, as we looked around the city once more. We took in the delights of the large Tettah Quarshie art market, named after a pioneer of the cocoa industry. Tettah Quarshie had lived in the area as an apprentice blacksmith, and later set up a cocoa farm not too far from Kwamoso. Beautiful paintings and craft-work adorned the numerous stalls, which were manned by friendly, and witty, tradesmen and women.

"*Obruni!* Come into my shop. I'll give you a good price!" they called as we approached, before ushering us in and quoting astronomical starting prices. The negotiating game thus began at every stall. A laugh, joke and compliments on the fine examples of handiwork led up to an equally preposterous counter-offer. From this, a fair price would either be agreed upon or not. Whatever the outcome, there was always a laugh and a wave as we moved on to the next stall, where the same process would unfold again.

Across an enormous roundabout, also bearing Tettah Quarshie's name, lay Accra Mall. Stepping inside was like stepping back into Britain, into any one of the shopping centres in our cities. It felt distinctly odd, yet at the same time totally familiar. Shops bearing various global, European or South African high street brands fitted themselves neatly alongside each other. The Mall was the preserve of the monied proportion of the city, with as many foreign customers as Ghanaian ones. We strolled around enjoying the air-conditioning for just long enough to almost imagine we were in Europe. Then we walked through the automatic exit doors, and were knocked back by a heat that was unquestionably African.

We had also intended to look around a fantastically interesting place by the name of *Trashy Bags*. This is a factory, run by an NGO, which recycles used water sachets and makes bags, computer mouse-mats and other accessories out of what otherwise becomes litter. From *Trashy Bags'* leaflet, the products looked pretty swish, too; they would make ideal presents for more than a few friends. Supporting the initiative appealed greatly. A shocking statistic, that we had seen somewhere, was that approximately forty million water sachets are discarded every day in the capital alone. Often they simply lie in the streets or the gutters that run parallel to them. Most of the rest are burned, creating different environmental problems.

We had seen on the leaflet the name of the district of Accra, Dzorwula, in which the workshop was located. Unfortunately, neither Lene nor I knew its proper pronunciation, or remembered its spelling. The upshot was that the taxi drivers shook their heads as we tried to communicate the district: *"Djorzula?"*, *"Drowuza?"*; "Trashy Bags?" This too was unfamiliar – *Trashy Bags* was still a new enterprise and had not managed to get itself into the consciousness of ordinary people. One driver was incredulous that such a place could even exist. Sadly, the same probably applied to the overwhelming majority of the population, who had thrown to the ground or burned sachets for years because that was the way that they had always disposed of them. At the moment, there is little action from authorities to change people's minds, although this may well change in the coming years. I hope so.

On our last night, we walked around the city arm in arm, as we had done in so many places over the previous weeks. Amongst the usual sights of traffic, and candles signifying places to buy cooked food, we noticed a number of people sleeping rough on the pavements. We had not seen that in other towns, although later in my stay in Ghana I would. It provided sharp perspective.

We missed a turn in the darkness, and ended up walking along a street roughly parallel to that which we should have taken. A tall metal fence bore graffiti betraying the hostility which some local people felt towards economic migrants from Nigeria. One prominent message declared "Ghana for Ghanaians"; others were considerably more vitriolic. Clearly these sorts of problems are by no means limited to the West.

We pottered around on our last day together. We chatted, laughed and generally enjoyed each other's company, just as we had done on all the other days since we had met. In an internet café, Lene checked that her flight had not been cancelled or pushed back for any reason; it had not. It brought home, again, the reality of us parting in an ever decreasing amount of time, yet in a strange way it would also have felt wrong if she had been delayed. We had prepared ourselves for it to be that evening, said the previous night the sorts of things that had to be said on a 'last night', and had made our respective plans for the next day. It would have taken a good deal of mental energy to push everything back twenty-four hours.

The end of the afternoon signalled the start of the final countdown. I reckoned on a bed in a dormitory for that night. Our journey to the airport began with a trek along the city ring road to the *Salvation Army* hostel, which lay on a side street.

We arrived at a bleak building. This was it; cheap and, on other days I'm sure, cheerful. A few young western lads milled around outside one of the dorms, before their mate joined them and they left. Lene sat down on a bench whilst I crossed the courtyard to check in. A youngish bloke wearing a basketball vest and baggy tracksuit bottoms raised himself from a lying position to a sitting one as I approached.

I explained that I was after a bed in a dorm.

"She can't stay in the same room," he replied.

Was it a smirk that briefly came over his features as he said this? Maybe it was a figment of my imagination, or a trick of the light. Perhaps I was just irritated that he had referred to Lene simply as a dismissive "She", without even raising his eyes in her direction to acknowledge her presence. Either way, I took a disliking to him. I answered through gritted teeth.

"My friend's not staying."

I paid, took the key, and left my backpack on an unclaimed bed.

Lene and I walked back to the main road. We were almost there, when I realised that I had left my wallet in the dorm. She waited whilst I jogged back to fetch it.

Jogging back, Lene's distant figure looked a little hunched. As I got a little closer, it looked as if she had been crying. I understood; I had shed my own tears the previous night, after she had fallen asleep.

Nothing needed to be said. We just held each other in our arms.

Some minutes later, we found a taxi. We got to the airport. Lene checked her bag in. She had to go through the gate at quarter past eight. It was all very clinical. We had around an hour left.

We had around half an hour left. Then ten minutes. We were sitting on a kerb outside, looking out at the lights of Accra, talking about the past three months and the future; her course re-starting back at Aarhus University, my work starting in one of the Rev's schools. We had been laughing, reminiscing, speaking about meeting again one day, in different circumstances, as friends.

"What's the time?" I asked.

"Ten past. You really are my five minute darling."

We carried on chatting. Then it was time.

We stood up, and embraced for the final time. She turned and walked across the tarmac to the door marked "Departures". I watched her go. She turned back one last time, and we waved at each other. Part of me wanted to run after her and take her in my arms one, final, time. I stayed where I was. It would only have meant more goodbyes. She turned again, and was gone.

I turned and walked along the airport drive to the main road. I considered carrying on the five or so miles to the *Salvation Army*, but I had a sneaking suspicion that they locked the gates around half past nine. I flagged a tro. It stopped, and I got on.

The hostel seemed quiet. I stood in the dimly-lit courtyard and rang a friend in Britain; I needed to talk to someone. Not long into the call there was a loud whooshing noise from above.

Typical. The hostel was directly under the flight path from the airport.

A small jet raced across the sky low above me, banked, and headed eastwards. I remembered from the departure screens that a flight to Lomé left shortly before Lene's.

Hanging up soon after, I had come to the conclusion that had I gone to bed, I would only have been waiting for the noise of Lene's plane taking off. Hearing but not seeing it was the worst of all options. I stayed in the courtyard and thought back to my earlier decision, briefly amused; I was going to watch the take-off after all. Black humour.

Another whoosh signalled that, slightly later than it should have been, Lene's plane was airborne. It soared past the front of the hostel and south over the sea. Moments later it arced gracefully, as befitted the lady on board for whom I had stayed outside to watch it, and began its journey north. As it roared through the night, getting smaller and quieter with every second, I thought once again of the wonderful times we had shared, and smiled at her. The plane became a bright dot in the distance, and then disappeared.

And then reappeared from behind a cloud. Only for a second, though, before it disappeared again. I stood and watched a few moments longer, just in case this, too, was just a cloud. It was not. This time, Lene's plane had gone for good.

I dragged myself away from the hostel courtyard. I could not be bothered to have a shower; that could wait until the morning.

The dorm light remained on as I lay in bed. It was no problem; half past nine could not be considered late. A couple of blokes were plugged into headphones, and another was watching something on his laptop. Despite everything, I felt strangely at peace. Relaxed, even. Lene was safely up in the air, and I was about to start work again.

The rest of my time in Ghana, I realised, was about to start.

Chapter 10 – Mr Loren

After a fitful sleep, I got up at half past six. Although the main light had been turned off at half past eleven, the laptop had continued to illuminate the dorm with its blue glow for a few hours after. Long before it was light, the memory of Lene's plane re-appearing momentarily from behind the cloud woke me; it refused to go away. So did the tears which were welling in my eyes. The tranquillity that my mind had enjoyed the previous evening was gone.

I picked up my untouched backpack, ignoring my recollection that I had left showering until the morning, and walked out of the hostel. Whilst rainclouds were set in over my head, Accra's sky was a beautiful azure blue; the air was warm even though the sun was visible only over the lowest rooftops. It had been my intention, over the previous days, to have a stroll through Accra before I returned to Kwamoso. This morning, though, I didn't feel like it.

The complex was quiet when I got back shortly after ten. The Rev was holding one of his meetings of the village chiefs outside his house. It was the sort of gathering which it looked best not to disturb. There was a new face in *Obruni* Castle, partially hidden behind a thick book. An introduction revealed that it belonged to a French gap year student called Manol, who was temporarily incapacitated with a stomach bug. She had been parachuted into Lene's classes at Mount Zion. Chatting away with her about John, Rami and their friends in Classes 1, 2 and 3, I noticed that the Rev had adjourned his meeting and was making his way over to his office in the school library.

I excused myself, and jogged to catch him up. He seemed to be moving a little less freely than I remembered. A great smile crossed his face as we shook hands.

"My son has returned!" he exclaimed gleefully. "It is good to see you again."

The feeling was mutual. It was a relief to see a familiar face.

"How was your travel?"

"Wonderful." I swallowed hard, managing to nip in the bud the lump that was just beginning to form in my throat. "We had a fantastic time. Lene sends her best wishes, by the way."

The Rev's face lit up once more. "Good, good. She's a lovely girl."

That was certainly true. We walked and talked to his office. Inside, he beckoned me to take a seat. We got down to business.

"So you will be with us until December?"

"I'd love to be, hopefully until the end of term before Christmas." I replied.

"Which age group would you like to teach?"

We had agreed several weeks before that I would take the older children. Perhaps he wanted my confirmation.

"And which subjects would you like to teach?"

Again, I told him I was happy with what we had agreed, although if he wanted me to teach at Mount Zion I would do.

"Good," he replied. "Because I want you to teach English, French and Maths at Holy Hills, to JHS." He paused, before continuing: "And when would you like to start?"

I had envisaged starting the following day. As much as anything this would give me time to look over schemes of work and get something prepared.

"Erm, whenever you like, Reverend."

"Good, you can start now. Pastor Robert will show you around."

So that was that. My backpack remained in *Obruni* Castle as I met some of my new colleagues, Madam Lydia and Mr Sam, and the teenagers who comprised Form 1. Peace's face was one amongst five others.

A voice came again in my ear.

"You can teach them English."

Clad in the same shorts and T-shirt as I had been for the previous twenty-six hours, I was unsure whether Pastor's utterance was an instruction, a suggestion, or a question. I glanced at the timetable that was written on a large chalkboard at the back of the room. According to that, after First Break today, a Twi lesson followed something called BDT. There was no mention of English whatsoever.

"OK," I agreed, with a trace of reluctance. "Until what time?"

"Second Break is at one-twenty."

One-twenty. That left... two hours and ten minutes.

Having nothing but chalk to teach with, I put the same lesson into action as I had done in similar circumstances at Mount Zion. I had no idea whether adjectives were on the scheme of work, and at that moment, frankly, I didn't care. Fortunately, Form 1 appeared sufficiently unfamiliar with the term for it to be a worthwhile topic.

Once the lesson got going, I forgot everything that had gone on before. For those two hours, going with Lene to the airport the previous evening – and waking up with the memory of her plane flying in and out of clouds – had never happened. I had entered a zone where I was with the children in a little bubble, inside which nothing else mattered, or even existed.

The bell rang, and the children went outside for Second Break. My bubble had been popped. Back in reality, I found myself wandering out of Form 1's room and over the grass towards the shade of a tree where the other teachers had congregated. BraKofi made more introductions, giving my full name – Lawrence – before I greeted everyone and shortened it to the normal 'Lawrie'. As I exchanged vigorous handshakes with an assortment of men and women whose names I had not taken in, I noticed, too late, that they had misheard the shortened version of my name. Someone asked one of the others, in Twi, something including the words 'Loren', 'Maths' and 'French'.

Before I could say anything, BraKofi had placed his hand on my shoulder. "You look tired," he said kindly. "Go and eat, and have this afternoon off."

Those words reminded me that, in addition to not washing or changing, I had also not eaten since noon the previous day. All three were quickly rectified back at the Rev's house.

Spots of rain were turning into something much heavier as I jogged back across the complex after washing my plate next to Auntie Gifty's stove. The place was deserted. I had hoped to find someone to talk to; clearly this was not going to happen.

I reckoned that re-arranging my room was the next best thing. I had emptied it before leaving, in case the Rev wanted to use it for another volunteer. Most of what I had had been put into a cardboard box and left at the end of the corridor. Unpacking was going to have to be done at some stage anyway, and it would give me something with which to occupy myself.

It was a task which I completed almost mechanically, completely devoid of enthusiasm. I did not pay attention to how far along with the job I was getting, as my backpack and box emptied, and the shelves filled. It was something of a surprise when I finished. A dilemma presented itself: what the heck was I going to do now?

I had forgotten all about schemes of work, and school was now over. In the absence of anything more constructive, I drifted to the fridge by the entrance of the house and picked up a water sachet. The house was still silent save for the steady drumming of rain on the metal roof. I guessed that Manol was in bed with her stomach bug; the Rev's family and the other volunteers could have been anywhere. As I walked aimlessly back to my room, I noticed the door of what had recently been Pil and Charlotte's room, next to mine, was wide open. My eyes were drawn into the space behind it; except for two bare beds and an empty shelf, there was nothing.

After the night before, this morning, and then the high of teaching, followed by the come-down of returning in the rain to the empty house, for some reason this was the straw that broke the camel's back. I sat down on the spare bed with my head in my hands and allowed myself to fall apart.

When I had pulled myself together, the rain had begun to ease. I put my shoes on and went for a walk. I had an overwhelming feeling of nothingness; mentally I was almost numb. Only later did I work out the underlying cause of this hour-long breakdown. I had spent so long getting ready to say goodbye to Lene, and watch her walk out of my sight for the final time, that I had given no thought at all to how I might feel on returning to the Rev's house. Nothing about what I found had surprised me, but I was totally unprepared for its impact.

That evening, my phone rang, interrupting the conversation in *Obruni* Castle. I had been chatting with Bosh, BraKofi, Mikkel, Manol, Debra, Yaw, and a group of the JHS children, who were doing their best to make it look as if they were busy with homework. I crossed my fingers that it would be Lene. It was: she had got home safely, and hoped that I had too. Sitting on the side of the circular platform chatting to her, the feeling – of *feeling* – that I had been missing most of the day gradually returned. Several minutes later, Debra and Yaw heard my laughter, and called over to enquire as to whom I was speaking. I answered and they came running over. I explained to Lene how it looked as though the rainy season was starting, and joked that she had left at the right time.

All too soon, we said our goodbyes again. She promised to call soon, and we hung up.

"Where is Lene?" asked Debra.

A lump built up in my throat again. I looked at her young, winsome face, and let her innocent question swirl around in my mind. Next to her, Yaw's eyes looked into mine, as if searching for the answer on my behalf, so that I would not have to think it all through again.

"She's back in her country now," I replied.

A solitary tear rolled down my cheek. I wish that it had not, but it did. "But she's OK," I added. There was silence, and two more tears made their journey down my face. Debra and Yaw stood, motionless, for an awkward moment. Understandably, they looked as though they had no idea what to do. Then, simultaneously, they swung themselves up and around so that they were on either side of me, and put a friendly hand each on my leg. I wrapped an arm around each of their shoulders, and they moved theirs around my back. We sat there, not saying much at all. We did not need to; their actions spoke more loudly to me than words ever could.

Although I still missed her, life returned to something like normal over the next few days. Chatting to the likes of the Rev, Pastor Robert and Kofi Bosh helped. Undoubtedly, getting into the thick of it at school also refocused my mind. I met, finally, Mr Maxwell. He was entirely different from the mental image which had been conjured in the instant of hearing his name several weeks ago. Inexplicably, this had been of a shortish middle-aged chap with greying hair.

The real Mr Maxwell who stood in front of me was a tall, wiry man wearing a long-sleeved grey shirt, a size too large for him. Short strands of hair, protruding from his upper lip and chin, could only with extreme generosity be called stubble. Heaven knew why, but dark glasses covered his eyes (someone told me later that they were for glaucoma).

"Loren, Loren!" he cried, by way of greeting.

"Mr Maxwell? Hi. How are you? It's Lawrie."

Maxwell laughed a deep, hearty laugh, slapped me on the back and laughed joyously again. He seemed a loud, expressive and fun-loving character. When he was satisfied, he thrust me eagerly towards the other teachers. In his excitement, although his introductions started off referring to me as 'Lawrie', he quickly reverted back to 'Loren'. The name seemed to be sticking.

That I had shaken hands with most of them the previous lunchtime mattered little, if at all. Lusty handshakes were shared with the two whom I already knew: Mr Sam, who taught RME and Social Science, and Madam Lydia. Lydia told me that BDT stood for Basic Design and Technology, and that, along with Twi, this was her subject. During our brief chat, I found out that BDT was the equivalent of Graphic Design and what used to be called Home Economics, but learned nothing of why she had taught neither of her subjects to Form 1 as timetabled the previous day.

Equally hearty handshakes were exchanged with the other teachers. These were Mr Seth, who taught Science to JHS; Madams Esther, Regina and Rebecca who taught the infants; Madam Paulina who had Class 3 and Madam Pat of Class 5. Maxwell explained that he was Class 6's teacher. He seemed to be in overall charge of the school as well. I put it to him that I had once heard mention of a Mr Livingstone, who had been described as the headteacher.

"*A-heeeh!* Livo, yes!" Maxwell rejoined noisily. "His wife is having a baby; he will be back in school soon." I awaited further comments from Maxwell, since he looked, and sounded, like a good talker. Instead, he turned and shouted for Takyi, the bellboy, to call the children to assembly.

Each class had swiftly formed their lines following Takyi's cry of "Assembly *pleeeaase!*" Maxwell began talking to them about the importance of looking smart and of having neat fingernails and short hair. He then instructed the children to "Bring a cutlass" to school the next morning.

Cutlass?

The revelation that the children were indeed being instructed to bring cutlasses, or machetes, to school provided a surprise, although not nearly as much as what happened next. Maxwell had called for a cane some minutes earlier and had been swishing it through the air during the last part of his address. Out of nowhere, he called a number of pupils forward, from all age groups bar Nursery and Class 1, and was now administering thrashings to the backside or hand of each of them. Many of them recoiled from the shock of being hit with this thin strip of wood. Eunice was virtually in tears.

It looked barbaric. In fact, I thought to myself as I stood there and watched it take place, it *was* barbaric. Maxwell had probably made clear what the reason for it was whilst I had been daydreaming, with no little amusement, about the possible uses for a machete in school. Surely, though, there was no justification for this. I felt sick being part of it, which, as part of the teaching staff, I most definitely was.

Yet this was the reality of teaching in a Ghanaian school. I had been sheltered from it at Wonderful Love. Since it was run by the volunteering company, the Three Ds were bound by the western sensibilities of the organisation and were not allowed to cane the children, even if they had wanted to – which I doubted. Dorothy had carried one, and occasionally feathered children's hands with it when their nails were dirty. I was never sure whether Diana or Daniel approved even of that.

I faced a massive moral dilemma. I found this caning deplorable. I knew that it went on, a few of the children had mentioned it long before, and I had seen it with Rami and John at Mount Zion. It was mainly used for lateness or incorrect school uniform, and sometimes for poor test results. Its use to enforce discipline was much rarer, since behaviour, in terms of not causing disruption during lessons, is on the whole very good.

Knowing about it or not, seeing it happening in front of me, and for no apparent reason, with the consequent pain that it inflicted on the children, was another thing altogether. I wanted no part in it.

I came to realise that it was not as simple as that, though. Despite my contempt for the cane, the reality was that I was now a teacher in the school, and teachers in the school used it whenever they deemed it necessary. The children also knew that caning was a standard punishment if they stepped out of line in any way. Kids are kids; they will always do what they feel they can get away with. It spoke volumes that, over the

Spring Break School, the children were less attentive. Yes, they were working without their regular teachers, and in their own clothes, but they were also in an environment that did not contain the threat of corporal punishment. A group mentality pervaded amongst the children – we can act as we please, *Obruni* won't cane us – which accounted for several of the problems that Lene, Mischa and I had faced. Dennis had casually told me, before the two weeks had finished, that to him it was not 'real' school. Peace, Eunice and even Yarro all said the same over time.

This is not to say that everything would have been perfect if we had waved canes around at all times, far from it. There is far more to promoting children's good behaviour than the warning – or actuality – of hitting them with sticks until they step back into line. A suitable routine and a sense of humour are but two essentials. Indeed, the only real trouble we had with really 'bad' and disrespectful behaviour, rather than just childish silliness, was when we took them for the land-use walk around Kwamoso, and most had wandered off.

To tell the children that I would not use the cane would have triggered thoughts that my lessons were neither serious nor important. They would thus have had *carte blanche* to muck around. *Obruni* doesn't cane. We'll do what we like.

Even giving the impression to the children that I disagreed with the cane would have sent out the wrong impression. Not of me, but of the school. Whether I liked it or not, caning was a legitimate punishment. Expressing criticism of this fact would have undermined the discipline policy of the school. If the children came out with statements along the lines of '*Obruni* thinks you shouldn't cane us,' it would have made everyone's position difficult.

One morning a few weeks later, after I had got to know everyone better, I sought out Mr Maxwell and Mr Livingstone over First Break; the headteacher had returned to Holy Hills a few days after I started, with news of a baby boy called Jesse. I put it to them that they should consider other ways of disciplining children. They were nonplussed. Madam Lydia was sitting with them, equally bemused, along with another young chap called Mr Enoch. Enoch taught ICT. I considered it a rather daunting job, since his only resource remotely related to computing was a rather dog-eared old textbook.

"But Lawrie!" Maxwell by this time had finally got to grips with my name. "What do you mean?"

"Well, in Britain, we keep children behind at break. Or after school if they've been really bad."

The four of them looked at me as if I had presented them with a ticking bomb. Their counter-argument was two-fold. The second part of it was entirely logical and sensible. Firstly, though, I had to disagree with their protests that they or another teacher should not have to stay in the classroom looking after children who had been late for school or committed some other misdemeanour.

"It's part of the job," I answered. "It's our responsibility as teachers to punish children proportionately." That seemed straightforward enough.

It was, though, another difference between Ghanaian schools and what I had been used to. If I felt that they had missed my point, which was that in Britain, teachers' job descriptions included the overseeing of detentions, they felt that I had missed theirs – that in Ghana this was not the case. 'Break' was a time for the teachers to relax as much as for the children to do the same. And after school? That, judging by the look on the teachers' faces, was way beyond the Pale.

We had to agree to disagree on the issue of duty. I did not push it too far in any case. I was working in the school only temporarily, so any unpopular changes made as a result of my encouragement could easily be changed back when I had gone. Nor was I in charge of running the school, the Rev had asked me to be a teacher: no more, no less. Most importantly, I was a foreigner in their country, where the use of the cane was national. Who was I to say what should or should not happen, regardless of what I thought of the practice?

The teachers' second point in favour of caning concerned life's practicalities. The children at Holy Hills, in many cases, worked with their parents after school in one role or another; there was no way that they could be held behind after closing. I cast my mind back to Peter and Thompson at Wonderful Love, who had not even been able to come to school in the first place, and felt a little silly.

There was a touch of comedy as well. I had dropped into conversation a few days earlier that during the British winter, it is dark by four o'clock, when the detentions in my previous school finished.

Maxwell was horrified. "You make them walk home along the road, in the dark?"

"Yes. Although some get a lift-"

"*Ah*!" The grunt of disproval emerged from all four Ghanaian mouths. They continued voicing their disbelief, not to mention outrage, at the peril that this must cause children, and the callousness of schools to allow it.

They had undoubtedly imagined the detained children having to walk home along something like the twisty, unlit Mamfe-Koforidua road, which has no footpath except for a small section towards the next village. I left it a few days before telling them about pavements and streetlights, not to mention the lengthier twilight in Britain, but they were only marginally less appalled. A few strokes of the cane, they argued, was far less cruel.

Different perspectives.

Over time, as I hardened myself to seeing caning taking place at assemblies on a daily basis, I reached a middle ground. It remained, to me, an abhorrent and out-dated practice. Yet, when done proportionately, that is to say without inflicting extremes of pain on the students, it had its positives. It was a quick, simple punishment. It was over and done with in less than a minute.

The children also knew the consequences of a misdemeanour. If they had not washed their shirt, it was because they had made the decision not to do so. Similarly, when they were late for roll-call, which could be as early as half past six, in most cases this was because they had chosen not to come in at that hour. They did not all fancy helping to prepare the school for the day's lessons by sweeping and tidying up. Other children arrived for roll-call, then went back home if anything urgent needed to be arranged for their parents' stall.

Finally, some of the children, the JHS boys especially, looked upon their and their peers' ability to take a caning as a badge of honour. Collins, in particular, knew when he deserved a caning. He would stand, arms folded, looking almost bored whilst the teacher on duty gave him his required amount of strokes. The afternoon before I left Kwamoso in December, Collins told me – no longer his teacher – how much this kudos mattered. Dennis, too, quite enjoyed watching his mates look on whilst he stood there and nonchalantly took his beating. On the other hand, those in JHS that made a fuss were gently ribbed by their year group after assembly.

None of this ever sat well with me, but over time it came to sit less badly. And, though I would have if left with no choice through applying the school rules, I never caned a child myself.

On my second day at Holy Hills, the children began lining up for assembly. As per their instructions of the previous day, they were clutching their machetes. Mr Maxwell turned to me. "Loren, Loren!" he cried.

I quizzed him as to the machetes.

"Today they will do weeding," he replied.

"Weeding?"

"*A-heeeh!* The school compound is too bushy, so they must weed it."

By this, he meant that they would be cutting the grass. Again, to me with my western sentiments, this seemed like a waste of learning time for the children. They had exams coming up at the end of term. However, someone had to cut the grass: the school did not have the money to pay for a lawnmower, let alone a caretaker, and so the task fell to the children. It was another seemingly inappropriate practice which also had its upsides. A comparison with Britain, about the students not taking things for granted, is not really valid, since the Holy Hills children never had the chance to experience the professionally maintained facilities which British schoolchildren do. Yet they never damaged anything around the school area. The only problem was litter (mainly discarded water sachets), which was picked up every morning following roll-call. Yet dropping rubbish to the ground was a normal feature of society.

Children from Class 3 upwards bent over and hacked at the grass with their machetes during the morning. It was humid, and sweat glistened on their brows despite the leaden sky blocking the sunshine. I thought back, once again, to my old classes in Britain. What would their reaction have been to doing this task every six weeks or so? I chuckled at the thought.

Despite caning them and making them labour with their machetes, the children liked and respected Maxwell. He had a charm about him, and he would always laugh with the children and enquire as to their welfare and family. He was also a good teacher; his Class 6 could do Maths and written activities at a standard similar to, and sometimes higher than, the JHS classes.

Maxwell decided that the area was sufficiently less bushy after a shade under two hours' toil. Takyi rang the bell and called for "Breaktime *pleeeaase!*"

When he had been summoned for "Break over *pleeeaase!*" sometime later, I had Form 1 and then Form 2 for French. In the absence of a French teacher since the previous July, no schemes of work had been collected from the Ghana Education Service's office in Akropong. In any case, if there had been one, there would have been little point in following it. The Rev agreed with me that since the children had not used the language for so long, even taking it from the beginning, and teaching September's topics, would have been unsuitable.

I had prepared myself shortly before Lene and I had gone away, collaring a few of the JHS children individually to see what they understood. Eunice had displayed a reasonable grasp of her *ça va tres bièns* and her *je m'appelles*, and could just about manage a conversation. Others were, erm, less proficient. Going over body parts, most of them could not tell their *derrière* from their *coude*.

Putting arses and elbows aside, I decided that I would teach the two JHS classes the numbers for their first lesson. It would be confidence boosting for the children if they remembered them; useful learning if they did not. For me, it would be a convenient start before I got my head around what else I could teach them that would be both useful and accessible.

There were more immediately pressing matters, however, at the closing of school on my first Friday afternoon. Ghana had a qualifying match for the next football World Cup to play against Lesotho, in Kumasi. The game would be shown on television, and would kick off a few hours later. I had been invited by Mr Seth to watch it, in the unlikely location of Bismark's house, just outside the complex. He assured me that there would be no problem with simply turning up at the house of one of our students. Sure enough, Bismark and his dad were only too happy for us, along with Yaw and several others of the children, to join them in the huddle around their TV.

The game was an easy win for the Black Stars, who put seven unanswered goals past the hapless visitors and were cheered all the way by everyone in the room. The football itself was only part of what held my attention. I was amazed by the TV commentators. They sounded as much like Ghanaian fans as broadcasters, shouting their team on to even greater efforts. Then, at half-time, an electricity company's advert lasted for almost the whole of the scheduled break in the coverage. It called on people to invest in the firm, and explained the numerous benefits of light. It struck me as a little odd that the latter point was so extensively laboured, since surely anyone watching on television had an electricity supply already. It also gave an irony to an hour-long floodlight failure which interrupted the second half, and caused the two other adults to vent great frustration at the national infrastructure.

More revealingly, I got a taste of how Ghanaians take the Mickey out of other countries, as, for example, the Brits do with the Irish. After a Lesotho player had trodden on the ball instead of passing it, with the result of falling on his bottom and gifting one of the Ghanaian players a shot on goal, Bismark cracked a huge grin and pointed at the screen.

"Look at that!" he chortled. "Hey, Lesotho! You don't even have transport! You have to walk from that place to that place!" It was a slur on Lesotho, yes, but also recognition of Ghana's development, in comparison to other countries with lesser infrastructure. At least I thought so. Perhaps he was just being triumphalist.

Bismark's phrase, 'That place', is a widely-used catch-all piece of Ghanaian English. It describes any location, from a country – "You come from Britain? What is the weather like in that place?" – to parts of a town – "The Immigration Office is in Koff-Town, you must go to that place for your visa." I thought for a while that geographical locations were the limit to the term; I was wrong. One afternoon, during Second Break, Yaw sat on the window of Form 2's classroom, and looked suspiciously as though he was planning to climb through it. Bismark apprehended him thus: "*Heh!* You must not pass through that place!" A few days later, during an English lesson, a delightful girl called Belinda asked for some help with sentence structure. My advice that she should insert a comma was initially met with confusion.

"Where must I write a comma? This place? *A-heeeh! That* place!"

Belinda was a real character. She was slightly short of stature and massively short of sight; she sat at the front of her classroom and would move her table as close as possible to whichever part of the chalkboard she was squinting at. She was a wholehearted student, asking questions when she needed a bit of help, and grunting periodically as she tried to process my answers. It was always clear when she had come to comprehend whatever she was working on. Her grunts of thought-processing would turn into a longer and higher-pitched '*A-heeeh!*' of understanding.

Over the course of my first weekend back, I digested the English and Maths schemes of work and flicked through the relevant parts of the textbooks. I found, amongst other things, that Form 1 would be learning how to give directions as part of their English studies. I found a huge piece of card somewhere, and set about creating a street-plan of a fictional town, with numbered buildings. I hoped that practical application of finding the tro station, pharmacy and others would broaden the children's vocabulary to more than, 'Pass through that place', and, 'That place is far', which was about as specific as they got.

Not having a scheme of work for French turned into a bonus, in that it gave me great freedom to teach what I wanted. My street-plan, I realised, could also be used as the basis of French lessons on directions and the names of facilities in town. Moreover, French topics could be the same for both JHS classes (Form 3 had left after exams in March), since we were starting from such a low baseline.

Looking through the Maths schemes of work was less pleasurable. Re-learning topics that I had last grappled with in my own school days was expected, and I was unsurprised to find that I also needed to learn some concepts which were totally new to me. What I did not expect was that the demands of the curriculum would be so rigorous. Some of Form 2's work was as challenging as GCSE work in Britain. Although all of the class were of what in Britain is GCSE-age, fifteen or sixteen, they were the equivalent school level of the end of Year 8.

As I grappled with the algebra section of the textbook, I – predictably – discovered that children were still having to find x ("Do you mean no-one has found it yet? Where's it hidden?!" I joked to BraKofi). I remembered how much, in my own school days, I had disliked the topic, and struggled to understand exactly how $2a^2 - b$

equalled *2(c+d) divided by 3*, not to mention why they need to be equal in the first place. BraKofi tried, and failed, to convince me of the necessity of the topic, although he did manage to remind me of its fundamentals. After a great deal of effort and a fair amount of frustration, I finally had my *Eureka* moment as I successfully tackled the harder of the equations that I was going to have to set Form 2 over the next few days.

Coming to school to begin my first full week, then, I was well prepared and looking forward to getting going. Standing in the shade of a tree, I listened as Mr Maxwell started the assembly.

"School fees-*oh*!" he began. "If you are still owing school fees, I will sack you!" He swished the air enthusiastically with his cane as if to give further clarity that a good deal of the children would be sent home.

It was another dilemma. I was a bit peeved at not being able to be in the classroom doing my job. Over and above that, though, was a concern that the children were being denied an education. Only Peace remained of the Form 1s; I allowed her to copy up some notes that she had missed from Mr Sam's Social Science lesson the previous week. There seemed little point in teaching her the lesson I had planned whilst the other five were not there. Most of the other teachers had done the same with their significantly reduced classes.

On the other hand, Holy Hills was a private school, in that it was run by the Rev and not the Government, whose schools are free. The Rev's levying of fees was not done for profit; they were used to pay the teachers' salaries, in addition to buying the chalk and stationary which the school needed. Nor were fees excessively high: they were set at between twenty-five and forty cedis a term depending on whether the child was in the infants, upper primary or JHS. For most families, this was affordable, particularly since they could be paid in instalments. The Rev recognised that a few *were* unable to pay. Yaw and Mabena, for example, were exempt from all school fees, and in return Yaw's dad did a bit of labour for the Rev. There was, too, a Government school in the village. Parents who for whatever reason did not want to pay for their children's education always had the option of sending them there.

More to the point, there had to be some action taken when school fees remained unpaid. It would have made a mockery of the whole system if non-payment were allowed to slide.

In the time that we had, largely idling around, I got to know the staff for more than just their names and subjects. Madam Paulina had strong religious convictions – even stronger than everyone else's – and was appalled to learn that I did not. A thoroughly interesting discussion ensued, during which we dissected the meaning of the Bible, and Paulina invited me to the following Sunday's service at her Church in Akropong. It ended with her promising to give me a copy of the Bible to read and me promising, over her laughter, to give it straight back to her.

Mr Maxwell, meanwhile, demonstrated his great gift for the gab. His expressive voice was invariably that which was leading the breaktime chatter between other teachers. One morning, I had walked back to the Rev's house to put my street-plan away. As I returned to Class 5's room, where we had been sitting, Maxwell was audible long before he was visible. He looked not the slightest bit bashful when I told him so.

The school term rattled on, and fairly soon I felt as if I had been teaching at Holy Hills for years. Each of the children demonstrated a friendliness and sense of humour that livened up lessons and made them a pleasure to teach. Ishmael created mirth in Form 2 when writing a description of a standard weekday, which ended: "And when I am tired I go to bird." Eunice proved herself highly proficient at French but a dreadful mathematician. Bismark, in addition to a knack for arithmetic (although, through not having calculators – even for pi, which was simplified to twenty-two over seven – almost all the children had become proficient at one-off sums), enjoyed regaling tall tales about exploits he wished were true. He would begin convincingly enough, such as his story of a visit to Accra. A simple visit to relatives was disrupted by a series of twists and turns, which led to him boarding, and then having to fly, a plane to Ivory Coast, where he became a fluent French speaker. After the climactic moment, or when he had run out of ideas to prolong his adventure, a grin would break out and illuminate his entire face.

"Yes, Sir Loren!" – he still used the name that Maxwell had introduced me by – "That's a small lie," he would concede. "A small, small one!"

Whilst Bismark's 'small ones' were keeping Form 2 entertained, Form 1 were ticking along nicely as well. I was also teaching a lesson a week of French to Classes 3, 4 and 5, and two for Class 6. Class 5 in particular were lovely. There were only four children; Yaw's classmates were two girls – Abigail and Gifty – who looked identical, and a boy called Dixon. By contrast, Class 6 was the biggest in the school, with ten pupils. They had remembered a great deal of the French that they had been taught the previous year. Unlike the other classes, it was possible to have conversational lessons with them fairly soon: when, that is, they were not being sent by the Rev or Maxwell to run errands such as fetching water from the pump.

Outside school, the Rev had developed great faith in me. One afternoon, a new volunteer asked me if I knew of any good walks around the area. Elizabeth was an American trainee teacher, who was working at Ebenezer Primary, another school in Kwamoso.

"Plenty," I replied matter-of-factly. "Put your shoes on and I'll show you one."

Debra overheard. She fancied coming herself.

"Ask your dad," I advised. I reckoned it may have been a little awkward to have broached the subject with him myself.

The Rev was delighted, and waved us all off, telling us that he knew that Elizabeth and I would look after his daughter, and that we should have a good time.

I was surprised that Debra had wanted to come, since she had displayed no interest whatsoever in going walking in the past. Indeed, most locals never walked for pleasure, and considered it quite bizarre that I did. It was a sentiment I could understand: their walking was functional, it was necessary to fetch water or firewood. Moreover, the beautiful countryside was for many people the workplace, and so they did not look at it in the same way. I had seen it before with the fishermen in Dzita and Elmina, the gorgeous settings were part of the fabric of their existence.

I was enjoying life. There was only one thing that was bothering me. Since Lene had called that first night after we had returned to our respective homes, three weeks before, I had heard nothing. Still, I was planning to go to Koforidua to pick up my latest visa extension, so I could drop into the internet café on the way back from the Immigration Office. Lene would have emailed to let me know how she was getting on.

Not a dickey bird.

Out of sight, out of mind, it seemed. After all that we had been through, she had dropped our friendship, as easily as coins are dropped into a wishing well.

Close your eyes, Lawrie. What do you want?

She did not have to get in touch at all. Maybe it would be better if we never spoke again. She lived a long way away, and we both had our own lives to lead. I would get over it, with the passage of time. Alternatively, she could send a message saying that, for one reason or another, she wanted all contact to end. At least then I would know.

No, of course those things were not what I wanted. The intimate side of the relationship was over, but we had had far more than that over the time that we had spent together. No matter how much I tried to pretend over the next few days that it was all of no consequence, that the time that we had enjoyed in each other's company was all in the past and meant nothing now, what I wanted was to talk to her again. Not to hold her in my arms or walk hand in hand with her; those days *had* gone. I just wanted to chat to her, disagree and joke with her, imagine her face widen with delight at some amusing comment or circumstance that we would tell each other about. Just to hear her, someone I knew – really knew. A friend.

Over the subsequent days, being in the classroom from eight until three was a relief. It took my mind off everything else, gave me something to focus on. I could place myself back in the bubble that I had created for myself in that first lesson with Peace's class.

It was when I got time to myself after school that I would begin to think of her again, miss her again, and wonder why she had not got in touch. Walks through the fields and along the paths, rather than providing the distraction that they were meant to, provided the encouragement for the doubts and uncertainties to creep back into my mind. They would lurk there, multiplying like bacteria. I would often come back to *Obruni* Castle more uptight than I had left it.

One evening, as Bosh, Yaw, Debra, Mikkel, Elizabeth and I were playing cards, she rang me out of the blue. As I threw my hand down and jumped up from my section of the bench, Bosh broke off from blagging about the unbeatable cards which he assured us that he was holding. He looked slightly surprised that I had folded so quickly, until he saw the look of release that must have formed over my face.

I skipped out to sit on the platform, leaving it to the others to call Bosh's bluff. She was sorry that she had not called, but she had been busy lately. How was I doing? How were the village, the Rev, the family, the kids?

My answers fell out after each other. Everything was perfect, fantastic and wonderful, because it was now; now that she had called and we were chatting again. Only later, when we had spoken on the phone many more times, about many different things, did I realise what she had meant by having "been busy lately". A difficult move of house and a separate ending of a previously close friendship had only been the start of it.

I am glad now that I did not know all that then. It would have made my little anxieties seem childish; she had more important, real, things to deal with.

Chapter 11 – Auntie Gifty's house

Bosh had puffed his chest out and was walking towards *Obruni* Castle one morning after breakfast. He held a bunch of plantains in his right hand.

"These are from my garden," he announced proudly.

"Get off it, your garden is a disgrace," I sneered. "You've bought those from the Junction."

If that sounds a little harsh, it should not do. Bosh was a good joker and I had, along with Merel and some of the previous volunteers, seen his garden some time before. It was a patch of ground which he had taken over, just behind Isaac and Dora's house. There was nothing in it but litter, and broken sheets of corrugated iron. Bosh would have had more chance of growing plantain on the moon.

He brushed my criticism aside with his customary high-pitched laugh. "No, Lawrie, it is true! I took them from my garden this morning. Come and see."

I followed him across the complex. Bosh was in full flow about the maize and plantain that he was about to harvest, and his garden eggs that would soon be ready. I began to have less confidence in my earlier assessment: why would he be showing me around if there were not something impressive to be seen?

As I rounded the corner behind Isaac's, a most impressive sight met my eyes. A corrugated metal sheet served as a fence around a fertile area a few metres square. At the back, bamboo canes had been tied together to provide support for climbing plants. One section even had a roof over it to protect Bosh's saplings from the rainy season's occasional downpours[6]. Towards the front, maize plants and plantain trees stood proudly upright, ready to surrender their yield to the cooking pots. The top sections of plastic bottles were being used as funnels to channel water towards the back section. Eat your heart out, *Gardeners' World*.

I was speechless for a few seconds. Bosh deserved a major apology. I turned to him, and I clapped him on the back.

---

[6] The rainy season begins at the end of May, and lasts until early-mid August (slightly later in the north). There is rain most days, yet unlike the torrential rain of dry seasons, it is usually a prolonged, heavy drizzle. There is a shorter 'second' rainy season in October. 2012's rainy seasons saw much less rainfall than average.

"This is brilliant," I enthused. "How did you get it looking like this so quickly?" I realised that it had actually been almost two months, just before Lene and I had left to go travelling, that Bosh had shown me his garden in its initial sorry state. The transformation, however, was still remarkable.

"Oh, Lawrie, I've tried my best!" laughed Bosh. He, with a little help from King David, had worked hard at it most of the time that Lene and I had been jollying around the country, and he had put an hour or so in most days after I had returned. The results were incredible. It looked like there was enough growing to keep Auntie Gifty busy until the end of time.

By this time, I had found myself in a new house. The Rev had been asked, by the volunteering company, to host a number of groups of teenage volunteers from the beginning of July. They would live in his house, and the back of Isaac and Dora's, for two weeks at a time. Bosh had been employed to help look after them, which I was pleased about. Elizabeth had returned to her teaching practice in Boston, Manol to France, and Mikkel had moved to Mamfe. I was to take up residence at Auntie Gifty's house in Habitat.

To my horror, I discovered that the space which Auntie Gifty had cleared for me consisted of two rooms. This left her, Esther, Collins and Little Mabena with only one room between them. I looked for Gifty straight away, and told her that she and her family had to have one of them back. She was insistent that she would not – there was no door between the rooms, and I had to, apparently, have my privacy.

"Lawrie, you are our guest," she added. "You must take both rooms. You have all of your teaching books, you need the extra space."

It was a typical example of Ghanaian hospitality. Gifty would not have my argument that four people had greater need for space than a couple of Maths and English textbooks. In any case, there was plenty of room for these next to my bed. Reluctantly, I gave in, and wandered back across the main road to unpack.

I still saw plenty of the Rev and the family. One Saturday morning, I sat in *Obruni* Castle munching my breakfast. The two-week teenagers had been taken for a weekend in Cape Coast by Bosh, Suzy and Augustine; I was enjoying the peace and quiet created by their absence. Outside the Rev's house, a meeting of the chiefs was starting up. Although this was a frequent event, a great hubbub was brewing around the Rev, Nana Addo – the King of Kwamoso – and the other chiefs. Cynthia (Peace's mother) and Auntie Gifty had gathered along with several other adults, some of whom I did not recognise. They were talking excitedly amongst themselves about something or other.

Little did I realise that what would unfold here would be an illustration of the power which the chiefs could wield in the village.

As the buzz of chatter intensified, an edge developed in the atmosphere, which I had never experienced before. There was an increasing tension.

Something was afoot.

I decided that it would be imprudent to stroll over and ask what was going on, such was the sense of strain in the air. Instead, I sat on the table and observed, with a mixture of curiosity and apprehension.

Suddenly, the chatter stopped. A man was being dragged towards the Rev by two, no three, others. His arms were bound to his sides with something quite thick and grey – was it some sort of coil? Whatever it was, it was wrapped around his waist, and his torso too. Despite this, he was struggling gamely for freedom, and the three burly men had to restrain him. They hauled him in front of the chiefs and dumped him to the ground on his backside. The chiefs began a fierce spate of shouting, in Twi, directed at the unfortunate bloke on the floor.

What was going on?

BraKofi sauntered over from the crowd into *Obruni* Castle. I was still sitting and looking on, now with feelings of awe and revulsion, at the dramatic scene that was unfolding in front of me.

"This man here is a robber," he announced. "Last night he stole a roll of electrical wire that was going to be installed near the middle of Kwamoso." He waved his hand towards the people who had gathered. "Some of these people are witnesses. Reverend and the chiefs are dealing with it."

They looked to be doing just that. Their words were spoken more calmly by now. Presumably they were going through the evidence. The robber remained on the ground, still bound by the stolen wire.

BraKofi wandered back to the centre of the action; I remained rooted to the table. The crowd of onlookers had multiplied, but had also stepped back from the chiefs, allowing them their space. Eventually, the robber was permitted to speak, his words punctuated by disproving '*Ah's*' from those watching. These, however, were silenced. The robber was allowed to say his piece, before the chiefs began talking again. BraKofi returned to me as a shouting match developed. Elements of the crowd briefly looked to get involved before being shooed away by the Rev, who looked to have taken charge of the case.

"This man is lying," BraKofi explained, translating the important bits of the argument. "Reverend is proving that what he is saying is wrong, and he doesn't like it."

A taxi pulled up next to the platform, and the burly men who had brought the robber lifted him up and frogmarched him, still protesting, over to the vehicle. The trial was over. The men pushed the felon into the back seat, and climbed in after him.

"They are going to the police station," BraKofi cut in. "Reverend has fined him. This is normal. The robber does not accept the judgment, and so the police will look into the case instead."

Apparently, the police are initially bypassed in such matters, with the village authority being the first point of contact. Only if, in cases such as this one, the accused does not accept the chiefs' ruling, is the case referred to the police. The Rev chuckled, later, when I asked him what would happen next.

"The man is guilty," he explained. "People caught him with the wire. He did not accept justice. The police will ask him the same questions and then make him pay my fine. If he refuses, he will go to the court, where the fine will be bigger. It's better for him to see sense."

The following evening, I saw the Rev again when I came over to *Obruni* Castle for Auntie Gifty's evening meal. The robber, the Rev smiled, had admitted his guilt to the police and accepted the chiefs' verdict.

"It's cold. Too, too cold." Mr Maxwell shivered and grumbled about the rainy season as he readied himself to begin assembly one morning. In their lines, the children stood tense and wrapped their arms around their chests. Belinda wore a hoodie which almost totally engulfed her. True, it had turned a touch cooler than usual over the previous days, but it was nothing like "cold". To be sure, I had on a short-sleeved shirt. It was a revealing sign, though, of the difference that a drop of a few degrees can make, when people are used to a fairly constant temperature across the year.

The exam season was approaching. School became quieter as the children spent a significant proportion of lessons with their heads down, beavering away at class tests in practice for the real exams. Meanwhile, the teachers grew, marginally, more tense. Every afternoon at the closing assembly Maxwell and Mr Livingstone exhorted the children: "Tomorrow-*o*, bring your Printing Fee." Maxwell light-heartedly appointed Dennis as his secretary. Dennis would be in charge of taking all of the collected money to Pastor Robert's office.

I asked what the printing fee was all about. Maxwell explained that the end of term exams had to be photocopied, for which the children had to foot the bill. The cost varied from class to class depending on how many exams the children would sit. It ranged from two cedis fifty pesewas for the younger ones to five cedis for the JHS classes. Generally payment of these was prompt; in some cases the instalment of what would usually have been school fees was processed by Pastor as the printing fee. This ensured that the children had paid for their exams, and thus could sit them. Despite this, a few of the children were still sent home to fetch the money. On the whole, kids being kids, they had either forgotten to bring it or, more likely, forgotten to mention it to their parents. As with their school fees, due to their poverty and their relationship with the Rev, Yaw and Mabena were exempted.

The teachers also gave frequent after-school reminders that the children should "go home and learn" their classnotes. Mr Sam had told me a good time earlier how "the children, they don't learn at home. They forget all."

It was true. I had noticed myself how the JHS students would listen in class and get all of their answers correct in their exercise books or when I asked them. Then, a few days later, they would have only vague recollections of how they had gone about the topic earlier in the week. They packed their books into their bag at the end of lessons and, usually, only took them out again at the beginning of the next lesson; the concept of revising was totally alien to them. To be fair, as Sam himself said, many of them had jobs to do after school and thus did not have the time to be re-reading classnotes. Belinda, for example, went straight from school, to either the roadside, helping her mother to sell fruit, or the water pump.

The business of confining schoolwork largely to school was nevertheless having a massive effect on the children's progress. Moreover, from what I had seen, when they did sit down in the evenings to do homework, often they did it together, and spent longer chatting than learning. Some sort of action had to be taken.

Probably better late than never, the Rev stepped in. Forms 1 and 2 were called to the library one afternoon. There, the Rev, Pastor Robert, Mr Livingstone, Mr Maxwell and I told the children quite bluntly how important it was that they studied. I told them how I had, year in, year out, had similar discussions with Year 11s approaching their GCSEs. Many of them had ignored the advice and had subsequently done poorly. I also related how in some cases there *had* been a response, and consequently a higher grade. The Rev laid out more immediate terms. If their exams were poor, they would lose three weeks of their August holiday. Our efforts shocked the teenagers sufficiently for them to nod their heads and promise to try harder. The five adults agreed that we would have to wait and see whether we had made any lasting impression.

Sitting in the library one Wednesday morning, I looked at the time as Worship carried noisily on around me. Eunice and her classmate Grace were leading the school in the singing of hymns. Bismark, Collins and Ishmael were geeing everyone along by walking around the room, whilst shaking or banging various percussion instruments like there was no tomorrow. Madam Paulina, meanwhile, was scanning her copy of the Twi Bible, preparing herself to preach to the assembled children. None of this was out of the ordinary, for it happened every week; what was different was the time. It was well after half past nine. According to the timetable, Worship should have finished over twenty minutes ago. Even going by precedent, we were a good few minutes past the usual wrapping up time.

I was moderately concerned, since I had a French class test planned for Form 1. Class tests were an informal measure of children's progress. Although the results were recorded on pupils' reports, they were less important than the end of term exams set by the Education Service. Still, I reflected, it was Wednesday. Worship would finish when it was ready to. My French test could be shortened in any case.

As the hands of the clock moved around, and the singing and dancing carried on, it became apparent that the French test would have to wait. I was pondering when I would next have the opportunity to set it, and coming to the slightly irritating realisation that it would be very close to their 'real' exam, when I noticed that there was something different to usual going on.

Everybody had moved their chairs to one side of the library, and now stood together in a circle. What, I wondered, could they be doing? My confusion grew deeper as Madam Paulina positioned herself in the middle of the circle, reading at a fantastic rate from the Bible. In full flow, Paulina's preaching was always a spectacle. Her voice rose and fell most dramatically whilst her hands whirled around like a dervish, to add greater weight – as if any were needed – to her sermon. Now, whatever her words meant, Paulina's address was having a powerful effect. Around her, the children and all the other teachers, bar Mr Enoch, stood hand in hand and began a low-pitched chant. Enoch stood in the corner with his back to the room. He looked upwards, arms outstretched, and spouted passionately in Twi: something about God and how his and Jesus' mercy would save us. His face, from what little I could see of it, was tense, and his arms twitched in slightly jerky movements as he spoke.

This was highly unusual.

A steadily rising crescendo built up eventually to a tremendous climax of percussion, singing and cheering. Children and teachers hugged each other and clapped their hands in delight. As quickly as it had begun, the bizarre little service finished.

By now, there were only a few minutes until breaktime. Takyi was sent off to ring the bell. All other children helped to pile the chairs and get the room looking like a library again. I turned to Madam Lydia.

"What was that in aid of?"

Her response almost defied belief: "There were bad spirits in the school," she replied, sounding rather relieved. "We chased them out."

"What do you mean?" the question fell out of my mouth involuntarily.

"Demons," she answered, now in a more level tone. "There were evil spirits and demons in the school. They want the children to follow the Devil. They will get inside the children, and then they will fail their exams."

I was unconvinced, to say the least. I was also massively curious. "How did you know about the demons?" I asked.

"You can just tell." Lydia paused, perhaps noticing my scepticism despite my best efforts not to show it. "The children are not doing well enough in class, their tests are too bad."

I struggled, greatly, to believe this. The children's tests were poor because of a general lack of application and hard work, not because of demons. Surely, doing some learning would be far more effective use of time than standing around in the library holding hands and making a hullabaloo. I decided it would be prudent to say nothing of this sort; I had no intention of coming across as condescending about the school's religious practices. Still, it seemed illogical, even if it did make everyone feel a bit better.

By hook or by crook, Forms 1 and 2 got through their class tests. I was pleasantly surprised to find that the children's not uncommon practice of copying work ceased totally in the tests. The children in JHS knew that the questions had to be done by themselves. It was a similar story with my French tests for Classes 3, 4 and 5; they too got on in silence. It was not all easy though: getting time to give Class 6 their class test proved a tough nut to crack.

According to the timetable, I saw them twice a week, on a Tuesday and Thursday. A series of mishaps, however, meant that in the three weeks prior to the Education Service's exams, I saw the class for a grand total of half an hour – long enough to set them only about half of the class test. First the Rev was speaking to them, something to do with moving on to JHS the following September. Then, next lesson, Mr Livingstone had either mis-read or (more likely) ignored the timetable, and was running through corrections to their Maths class test. Another time Mr Maxwell had sent them all to the library, to tidy its inside and cut the grass around its outside. Once they had been sent to the pump to fetch water.

On the Tuesday of the week before the exams, therefore, I had to make sure that they would have their test. To be sure, I double-checked with Maxwell.

"Your class must write their tests for me today," I smiled at him as I gently poked him in the arm. "Don't be sending them anywhere – weeding, fetching water, to the library, *anything!*"

He laughed his laconic laugh and shook my hand in all manner of directions. "Fine, yes, yes!"

"Period two," I reminded him as I turned to go to Form 1's room, where a Maths lesson awaited. "I'm coming!"

Half-way through Maths, I popped outside and peeped through Class 6's window, to check that nothing was amiss. On the way over, it sounded quiet. Too quiet. It soon became apparent why.

Dennis, Takyi, Blackie and Adjei were sitting on the tables having a natter. They were the only ones in the room.

"Erm, Dennis. Where are the girls?" I asked.

"Sir Lawrie, they have gone to fetch water."

The only surprising thing about his answer was that it did not surprise me. Still, I mused as I returned to Form 1, there was still half an hour left; the girls would be back in plenty of time.

With a few minutes of the first lesson left, I nipped out again to check up on Class 6. I propped myself up against their window frame and surveyed the scene. Agnes, Sandra, Benedicta, Gloria and Gifty occupied the places that the boys had been in earlier.

"Erm, Aggie. Where are the boys?" I enquired knowingly. I braced myself for the answer that I knew I was about to hear.

"Sir Maxwell has sent them to fetch water!"

Of course he had.

"Where is Mr Maxwell?" I asked.

"He is next door, talking to Madam Pat," they replied.

I glanced towards the adjoining wall. Maxwell's voice could be heard from Class 5's room. I strolled around to Pat's doorframe and saw Maxwell sitting on a desk, babbling away to her whilst Yaw and the rest of Class 5 diligently completed a Science test.

"What's this about not sending Class 6 anywhere?!"

"Please, Lawrie, they are coming right now!" Maxwell cried. His smile remained, as irrepressible as ever.

It was impossible to be cross with him, he was too lovable for that. I cracked.

"When are they going to do their tests for me?" I implored, holding his eyes.

"Oh, it's no problem, they will write them today," he answered, becoming aware that he was in my bad books, but also sensing that I seemed to be forgiving him.

He was right, though. The children did their tests later on, albeit in a truncated form. It was enough, though, for me to mark the papers and get a rough idea of how much they had learned.

The following week, the 'real' exams passed, in general, unspectacularly. Each exam paper bore the rather grandiose title, "Assessment for Improving Learning". As with the class tests, it was without any great difficulty at all that silence was enforced throughout the school; the area was quieter than I had ever heard it. Virtually the only noise emanated, unsurprisingly, from the mouth of Mr Maxwell, largely unseen as he sat with Class 6 and periodically wandered through the other three classrooms of the upper primary school. His cry of, "Primary school, start work!" at the beginning of each exam was followed by regular, loud announcements of how long each class had left. They unwittingly provided a useful gauge for the Form 1 and 2 students as they wrote their own papers.

I entertained myself whilst supervising the exams by browsing through spare copies of the respective papers for JHS. Questions came in two parts, with multiple-choice and open-answer sections. I had a direct interest in the Maths and English exams, and looked over them with a degree of concern at how well the children understood topics that they had covered before my arrival. The French papers I considered a write-off, since I had been teaching the subject – with the Rev's blessing – with no regard whatsoever as to what would be on the test. I translated the questions and hoped that the children would be able to work out at least basic answers to some of them. Predictably, they had done as much as they could way before the exam was due to finish. Common sense prevailed, and I let them out early.

Looking through spare copies of other subjects' papers was highly educational. The RME and Social Science papers especially gave me great insight into Ghanaian culture and customs. I learned that in Winneba, where Lene and I had been so moved by the poverty of the Old Town at the start of the Spring Break, there is a huge festival every year. During it, the chief orders an antelope to be hunted and brought back to the town for a feast. If the hunters are unsuccessful, it is a bad omen for the coming year.

As I flicked through the various papers, there were a couple of questions – or rather options in the multiple-choice sections – that were, to me as a westerner, hugely amusing. Form 2's ICT exam asked what actions one could take to prevent viruses harming computers. Various types of software were given as possible answers, along with the rather less plausible alternative to "Call the police".

Another question which made me smile was of a far more grave nature. Ghana, sadly, suffers multiple problems from the results of unplanned pregnancies, often those of teenagers. Whilst a wholly legitimate question in an RME exam, therefore, "Sex before marriage can be considered...", the presence of "superb" in amongst a host of more suitable options somewhat tickled me.

Not as much as the sight, and sound, of me marking Form 1 and 2's Maths exams tickled Auntie Gifty as she sat in *Obruni* Castle having a rest. She watched as I looked and looked again at the outlandish responses that were scribbled down on many of the test papers. To my gloom, the answers did not change between glances; they remained ugly defecations of the sheets that they were scrawled on. Comments all too familiar from an exasperated teacher poured from my mouth: "How could Peace not know this? She's had at least two lessons on it!"; "Ishmael knows that angles in a triangle add to 180 degrees, why has he written this answer?!"

After the meeting in the library with the JHS children a few weeks earlier, we teachers had appreciated the need to wait and see about their exam performances. Well, I had waited, and now I was seeing. The results were shocking. Peace had the highest mark in her class, which at forty percent was nothing to shout about. Bismark managed a moderately higher percentage to top Form 2. Most of the rest of his class were in the twenties, although a boy by the name of Kwasi Owusu did not make it into double figures. Even this, though, was better than the two lads in Form 1: Amu managed a score of three percent, Kennedy totalled two percent, including zero on the multiple-choice section. That had taken some doing, with each of the forty questions having only four possible answers.

As one disbelieving groan gave way to another, Auntie Gifty cleared her throat and turned to me.

"You sound annoyed with them," she began.

That was an understatement. I turned to her and smiled.

"Look at their other tests as well," she continued. "It's not your teaching, they won't have done well on their other exams either. They haven't done enough work."

I held her eyes. The words had been considered, and, delivered with Gifty's wisdom, struck a chord. I relaxed; I suspected that she was right. I felt significantly better, and we chuckled at teenage habits.

Looking at Madam Lydia's and Mr Sam's papers the following day it turned out that Auntie Gifty's assertion was indeed correct. Sam in particular was crestfallen that the children seemed not to have looked at their notes, let alone learned from them. We told the Rev. He was furious, if unsurprised, and therefore calmer than I expected. His response was simple. The children had been told that they would lose their school holiday if results did not improve, and they had not. They would be ordered before the Rev on the Monday of the final school week and given the news.

There were no exams on the Friday afternoon, and so I went up to Wonderful Love. I would see the Three Ds, and watch Class 2 play a football match against Ebenezer, the primary school on the other side of Kwamoso. Daniel had phoned me a few days earlier to tell me about the game, would I like to come and watch?

I was excited about seeing everyone's faces again as I walked up the dirt road to the school. Approaching the buildings, I saw the children tearing around, in what I presumed served as their warm up. A huge cry of '*Obruniii!*' turned into "Sir Lawrie!" as I came closer. Wisdom and his classmates sprinted up to me, and pulled me along to where Daniel and Dorothy were sitting. I dropped myself into a chair next to them. The 'Hellos' and 'How are yous?' quickly led on to a catch-up of how we had all been doing over the weeks since I had finished working with them. Diana soon appeared from her classroom, and established that I had still not found a wife; Daniel strode onto the football pitch to direct the children's practice.

The match kicked off and got going, with no little shouting from the crowd of onlookers that had gathered. There was a mixture of encouragement and rollickings given out from the touchline, as tackles and passes were attempted with varying degrees of success. Bernard, the goalkeeper, was given an almighty telling off from someone when he dropped the ball between the posts to concede the opening goal. Minutes later the same person gave him an equally lusty pat on the back when he atoned with a fine save. Morgan equalised in the second half with a powerful strike that deflected off the post, and almost scored again near the end. There was a penalty shoot-out to settle the match; Ebenezer won it, after Sakyi missed his spot-kick. The poor soul was devastated. It took a great deal of time, and several arms round the shoulder from the Three Ds, his dad, his team-mates, and me to cheer him up.

Forms 1 and 2 were summoned by the Rev on the Monday afternoon, and told in no uncertain terms what he thought of their lack of application. Thirteen guilty faces looked back at him as he said his piece; they could have no argument over what they were being told. Term would finish on Wednesday. As of the following Monday, whilst the Primary school remained closed, it would be business as usual for JHS.

The last days in the term were, for the teachers, all about writing end of year reports for the children and collecting any last remains of unpaid school fees. I suppose it is the equivalent of the final few days in British schools, where the children watch a DVD as a reward for their work over the course of the rest of the year. Since we did not have any DVDs to play, much less anything to play them on, the children were allowed to play football or entertain themselves by other means. If that seemed anticlimactic, though, the very last day of term was very special indeed.

'Our Day' is a school-wide celebration of the achievements of the previous year. Although the JHS pupils had not achieved a great deal at all, especially results-wise, it would have taken a very hard heart to exclude them from the proceedings.

Children brought in food that they or their parents had cooked, and shared it with their friends. Some brought rice, others kenkey (another stodgy cassava-based dish, similar to, but heavier than, banku), others still pieces of meat, or fruit. It was kept in the classrooms over the morning, as the children entertained themselves. Then, when the teachers were happy that they were ready, Takyi was called to ring the bell, and the celebration started. The children spread out on the grass and shared their food, eating it like a picnic, with their friends.

The teachers had also brought food in to share with their colleagues and the children. Most of it was home-cooked, although Madam Paulina and Madam Pat had cheated. Their pieces of chicken, salad and rice looked exquisite when they were opened: this seemed too good to be true. Sure enough, a bite of meat proved not only delicious but piping hot. They had been to a chop bar in Habitat, which had the slightly dramatic name, *The Limit*. A wonderful hour and a half passed by, where children and teachers laughed and joked among themselves and with each other. When all the food was gone, school was declared over for the year, and the children could enjoy five weeks off. Except for, of course, those in JHS.

At Auntie Gifty's, life was terrific. I still felt a bit awkward having two rooms to myself, whilst the other four who lived in the house shared one space. However, none of them cared a jot. Esther insisted on giving me a massive handclap every time that she saw me, and Collins grinned at me just as much as he did when he was sitting in his classroom. Little Mabena, meanwhile, carried on living her blissful little life in the manner of any other happy seven-year-old girl. For her, nothing had changed at all, except for having someone new to talk to.

When her work looking after the two-week teenagers allowed, Suzy and I would make an occasional Saturday evening trip to Palm Hill. There we would exchange our latest tales of life as an *Obruni* over a couple of bottles of beer. A great many laughs were shared, and we would always be the last to leave. The staff would frequently put the chairs on the tables with great emphasis, and give other subtle hints that it was closing time. Returning home from these evenings out often proved interesting. Taxis still ran to Mamfe after eleven, but it was the luck of the draw as to how I would find my way back to Kwamoso. Often it was a walk down the hill, which lasted just over an hour; sometimes I would manage to wave down a passing car. Once, a tro driver, making his way home after finishing work, wound down his window, told me that he recognised me from Kwamoso, where he also lived, and offered me a ride. It was gratefully accepted.

One of my first tasks in Gifty's house had been to fetch water. I had not done this since the initial effort few days after I arrived in the complex, when my bad shoulder had made it a mammoth task that I did not particularly want to repeat. I had had no need to, in any case: the adults in the Rev's family looked upon the trips to the pump as the kids' job. It would have been very strange for them to see me, or any other of the adults living in the Rev's house, troop down to the pump on a daily basis.

This, though, was different. Even though I was not relishing the prospect of hauling full containers up the paths, there was no way that I was going to allow Collins and Esther to fetch water for the five of us by themselves. The day after I moved in, I had a quick peak in the water cistern before I went for a run. It was nearly empty. The decision of when I would fetch water for the first time had been made for me.

I drew a series of surprised looks from the various people that I had passed on the way to the pump, most of whom had never seen me before, let alone witnessed an *Obruni* fetching water. Various comments flowed from their mouths. Most of these were incredulous, and incomprehensible, gasps containing the words '*Obruni*' and '*nsuo*', the Twi word for water. At the pump itself, there were many questions: "*Obruni, can you pump?*"; "*Obruni, can you carry?*" Whilst the first of these tasks was simple, my ability to perform the second was open to question.

The memory, from the previous ordeal at the pump, of failing miserably to carry the full container on my head, and struggling back to the Rev's house with it in my hands, had become fresh in my mind when it became clear that fetching water would become part of my daily life. I considered alternative methods of carrying a full container. The conclusion that I had reached was that on the shoulder would be best: it would provide a more stable base than my head.

When I had finished pumping, it was time to see whether this theory held water as well as the container did. I heaved it up and into position. The twenty-five litres were just as heavy as I had remembered. I put the thought of the next three or four minutes' struggle to the back of my mind, and plodded along the path. After a couple of breaks to swap shoulders, I staggered into Auntie Gifty's garden and emptied the load into the cistern.

I made a second journey, after which my arms were exhausted. Over time, though, the trip to the pump became not only easier, but also quite enjoyable. I would see the same faces down there, often those of the children at Holy Hills. Belinda and her friend Bernice from Form 1 were frequently there at the same time as I was, and we had a good giggle whilst we waited in what passed for a queue. After a few visits, I also grew quite friendly with the man who was in charge of the pump. I was initially surprised to hear him ask for ten pesewas on one of my first trips; I had never heard of any of the children being asked for it, nor had anyone mentioned it. I shrugged my shoulders, and told him that I would bring money when I returned for the next load in a few minutes' time; whereupon I handed over twenty pesewas, to cover two containers' worth.

I relayed this little tale back to Collins when I saw him a few hours later.

"Twenty pesewas, *Ah!*" was his shocked response.

I was bemused.

What I had not realised, until he subsequently explained it to me, was that the ten pesewa fee covers all of the visits that one person makes in a session of fetching water, which is typically two or three. The likes of Dennis, Collins, Peace and Eunice regularly went together, making three or four trips at a time. They threw in a couple of ten pesewa coins between them; in short, the enforcement of the payment was relaxed, to say the least. I became known to the man at the pump – whose name, strangely enough, I never found out – as 'the businessman'. I nicknamed him 'the taxman' in return. Ten pesewas became sufficient to cover up as many trips to his pump as were needed.

After my initial over-payment, Collins decided that, in light of my naïveté, he would come with me next time. I was amazed, again, by the ease with which he carried an open basin virtually full to the brim, balancing it almost perfectly on his head, with the support of his hands at the top of each side. Hardly a drop was spilled on the walk back to Auntie Gifty's, nor did Collins seem remotely exerted by the task.

"How do you do that so easily?" I asked in wonder.

"It's simple," was his casual reply.

It was probably the wrong question, since the children fetch water from a young age. Little Mabena would go to the pump with us from time to time, and totter back with a small basin still filled to the top. Collins had done it most days for twelve of the sixteen years of his life, so had Esther. It had become almost second nature to them, as easy as working a television or computer is for many small children in Britain. It was easy to understand why most Ghanaians, the men especially, were so muscular.

As time at Auntie Gifty's passed by, I too became increasingly adept at fetching water. I felt fitter for it too: after a while the trips from the pump were no longer a physical challenge, and fetching four or five containers' worth was usual. Esther would always ask in the first weeks, semi-teasing, "Are you tired?" when I had finished emptying a container; my face would invariably answer for me. By the end of July, when I had been living with her a month, she was telling me to slow down.

It was interesting to watch the two-week teenagers get stuck in to life in the complex. To their credit, they generally adapted very quickly, and enjoyed living in the Rev's house; the Rev and the family liked them too.

Only one of the three groups presented problems, acting as if they were on a package holiday. The others threw themselves into village life and interacted with everybody. One group loved the difference in culture to such an extent that one morning they went to the five o'clock Church service, to see what it was like. They were still raving about it when I joined them for breakfast.

Of course, they were still kids. Bosh occasionally related to me the exasperation that he occasionally felt in the course of his work supervising them. Yet his complaints were, in the grand scheme of things, to do with silly childish things that teenagers do. Bosh thought that they made too much noise in the evenings, were slow to get ready, and went to bed too late (although a few mornings of their being woken up by the Church bell at five saw to the latter problem).

I had my fun with them too. There were two main sources of pop music in the complex at this time. Kofi Bosh had always enjoyed his sound system – it was rare that there was not music coming from his house when he was around – and BraKofi had recently bought himself a CD player and amplifier.

"Why is it," a Scottish teenager called Alex asked me one morning shortly before the group flew home, "That only those two play music in the complex?"

"Well," I began. The truth was that Isaac and Dora's speakers had packed up some time before and, to my knowledge, no-one else possessed any. This, however, was rather prosaic. An idea had formed in my mind that was quickly taking on a life of its own. "It's to do with their names."

"What do you mean?"

"Only people called Kofi are allowed to play music. It's a village bylaw."

"Really?" she replied, astonished. Almost all of the fifteen or so present were now listening.

"Oh yes," I replied. "It's enforced most strongly. Who else do you know called Kofi here? That's why the others don't play music. Bosh and BraKofi play it for them so that everyone has something to listen to."

I explained that some of the meetings which the Rev held with the other local chiefs dealt with incidents of law and order, and kept a straight face long enough to expound that the punishment for playing music without a permit – issued only to people by the name Kofi – was banishment from Kwamoso. The teenagers were hooked. They had seen a couple of the meetings that were held outside the Rev's house; my explanation was thoroughly plausible.

I had fully intended to own up to my mischief before they left. Unfortunately, on their final morning I had finished breakfast and gone to Mamfe for a Sunday stroll with Mikkel before the teenagers got up. They had left for the airport by the time I had returned. I felt a pang of guilt, wondering how many of them would go back to their families and explain the gross musical unfairness that underpinned the society that they had been living in. I owned up to Bosh and Suzy when I saw them later.

Both thought it hilarious; Suzy lamented the fact that her job prevented her from playing such pranks herself.

Mr Maxwell's hearty laugh as I relayed the story to him told me that he too found it highly amusing. We were waiting for the JHS children to arrive for the first day of their extra three weeks of lessons. We agreed that everything should be exactly the same as in term-time, despite the absence of the Primary school. The only difference was that we would finish each day at twelve-thirty, just before Second Break. I was initially against this, remembering well what had happened over the Spring Break holiday school. Maxwell won me round, though, and to be fair I was probably being overly cautious. Besides, I reasoned, tongue wedged firmly in cheek, it would give the children more time to learn their classnotes at the end of each school day.

I felt slightly sorry for the Class 6 children, whom the Rev had instructed to come along as well. They found themselves beginning Form 1 early. Dennis, Blackie, Benedicta and co. had worked hardest of any of the year groups, I reckoned, over the seven weeks that I had been teaching at Holy Hills. Their exam results had been pretty good too. Perhaps the Rev wanted to make sure that they did not fall into bad habits. Whatever the reason, it meant that Peace's class were now Form 2, and Eunice, Ishmael and their mates had become Form 3.

I was pleasantly surprised that there was no dissent from the children whatsoever, no questioning of why they had to be in school in the holidays whilst everyone else was enjoying themselves – not even from the new Form 1. I had semi-prepared a fairly forceful riposte for Forms 2 and 3 that could be used if needed. It centred on exam results, and how percentage scores that averaged in the twenties and thirties across their subjects were quite unacceptable for a bunch of people of their, undoubted, ability. I was pleased that it was able to remain unused; the children carried on with school as normal.

Perhaps too much so. Despite the teachers' frequent urgings, signs were that the children would not apply themselves outside the classroom now any more than they had previously. This did not change even when it was pointed out that their lackadaisical approach had lost them their holiday in the first place. Hard as they worked in lessons, and much as they remained enthusiastic to learn – "Sir Lawrie, please teach us," Grace implored one day, when a couple of the Form 3s had arrived a few minutes early to class – from one day to the next, much of the newly-learned methodology used in completing their class work had been forgotten.

But then kids are kids!

I was washing my clothes one Sunday afternoon in Auntie Gifty's garden when I heard two vaguely familiar voices. They were coming from the dirt road the passed the house. I looked up and saw Yaw and John wandering towards me, smiling and waving prodigiously. John had moved out of the Rev's children's home in Tinkong and was now living back in the complex with his mother. He and Yaw wanted to know what I was getting up to, now that my appearances in *Obruni* Castle were much more limited.

We had a natter about this and that. Yaw told me how he had scored more goals than John in their latest game of football, and John protested that this was all nonsense. John climbed up the tree in Gifty's garden barefooted, and Yaw hid his flip-flops behind a pile of bricks. We play-fought and chased each other around. I was suddenly a child again, enjoying the larking around just as much as they were.

Gifty's kitchen was a little room at the end of the toilet and bathroom block. Yaw went inside it to have a nosy around, and John slid the bolt closed to lock him in. After a while he asked if I thought that he should let Yaw out. I shook my head, and we chuckled as Yaw banged on the door a little longer. A few minutes later John asked me again. I nodded my consent, then, as John opened the door, I pushed him in there too and flicked the bolt back into place. I joked through the door at them, and after a while opened it to free them. The room was empty. I stood momentarily in disbelief, until I noticed that the shutters over the window were open – the boys had climbed out.

A sudden shove in the backside knocked my off balance and into the kitchen. There was a bang and a click, as the door was pushed shut behind me, and then bolted. I scrambled out of the window and ran round the outhouse block, back into Gifty's garden, where they and I chased each other around a bit more. It was that sort of an afternoon. When the boys sensed, around the same time that I did, that I was getting a bit too tired for it all, they clapped my hand, laughed their goodbyes and ran back towards the complex. Feeling physically older, but mentally fifteen years younger, I returned to the basin of washing which, what with all that fun, I had forgotten about.

I found myself growing more and more fond of the children; these two, of course, but also the others with whom I lived and worked. Most of the JHS students I could easily relate to, they were old enough to be able to have all sorts of conversations with. I had quickly come to like Bismark, Belinda and their mates. Within the complex, I had always enjoyed the company of Peace, Eunice and Dennis. Now, though, I was starting to develop stronger bonds with the younger ones as well: Samson, for example. Isaac and Dora's little tearaway would run up to me for a high-five whenever he saw me walking back from school in the afternoons, and I began to feel great affection for his scraped knees and sense of excitement at virtually anything.

One Sunday morning, when Bosh had taken the latest group of two-week teenagers on their weekend trip, I had finished my breakfast and was writing a letter to Lene. Samson dashed into *Obruni* Castle at top speed, and jumped on the spot for a while as he pondered what to do next. Spotting a piece of bread, he decided that he fancied eating it with jam. I opened the pot that he had picked up and given to me, and handed him my knife. Very carefully and deliberately, Samson scooped out a blob of jam and moved it towards his waiting bread. He was nearly there, when most of it fell onto the table. Unperturbed, he scooped it back up, and spread it across his bread and the table, in roughly equal proportions. Next, he reached for the pot of peanut butter; he had a sweet tooth, Samson did. Delicately and deliberately scooping up a load on his knife, he smeared some of it over his hand and a little more onto his jam-covered slice of bread. Looking awfully proud of himself, he chomped away at his creation.

He flagged during the last few mouthfuls, and worked out that he needed a drink to wash it down with. There was no water on the table, except for Gifty's thermos flask, which was about half-full of hot water. A brief vision of Samson scalding his hand persuaded me to suggest that making his hot chocolate should be a team exercise. He heaped three of the largest teaspoons-full of chocolate powder imaginable into – mainly – his cup, and then stirred whilst I filled it with water.

Whilst he ate and drank, we played all sorts of word games. He had begun to learn the English names of things found on the table, and he had great fun demonstrating his progress, holding up jam, cutlery and my letter, and gleefully reeling off their names like a little expert.

A roaring noise behind us took the game into a new phase. Through the trees behind *Obruni* Castle, we could see a lorry being driven up the hill, its engine protesting vehemently at the gradient.

"Lorry!" Samson laughed as he pointed at it.

"Brum brum! Look! What's that coming?!" I was discovering an entirely new side to myself.

"Tro-tro!" cried Samson, blowing a huge raspberry to mimic the note of its engine as it whizzed down the hill in the opposite direction to the lorry.

Goodness knows how long we carried on for, until Dora's voice called Samson from across the complex. The little scamp jumped down from the bench, put his flip-flops back on his feet, and padded over towards his mother. He was nearly there when he realised that Dora wanted to give him his dreaded bath. He stopped dead in his tracks for a moment and tore off in the direction of Peace's house, with Dora in hot pursuit. She caught her runaway son next to Auntie Gifty's cooking pots and carried him, now bawling his opposition to becoming clean, back towards a bucket of water next to the front door. Once stripped, he made an ill-fated break for it again, before Dora caught hold of his arm and dragged him back to his soapy fate.

I returned to Lene's letter, which was now adorned with a smear of peanut butter, feeling almost broody.

Chapter 12 – Nana Kweku Fianko Bekoe

"Have you heard?"

Madam Lydia's voice was somehow different to normal, a little more urgent and ever so slightly flustered.

"Heard what? No!"

"The president is dead!"

Surely not. Lydia loved a joke; this must be a wind-up. Presidents don't just die, do they?!

"No," I smiled at her. "You're joking."

"No, really! He passed yesterday. Have you not heard the news?!"

I had not, but then that was nothing new: the Rev did not have a television in his house. Moreover, neither of the TV owners – Isaac and BraKofi – had mentioned anything, let alone the death of John Atta Mills, the head of state. It took Lydia quite a while, and the help of Mr Sam, to convince me that it was true.

It was a huge shock, they explained. Although it was common knowledge that President Mills had been treated for throat cancer in Europe some time previously, there was no panic. He was convalescing in Accra and was expected to return to full health reasonably soon. Out of the blue, he had taken ill and been rushed to the capital's Thirty-Seven military hospital, where he died a few hours later.

It all seemed very dramatic. Already, Lydia and Sam explained, the vice-president John Mahama had been sworn in. He would lead the nation in the run-up to the presidential election, which would go ahead as planned in December. There would be a period of mourning, before a state funeral in Accra in some days' time.

That evening, I called at BraKofi's house and watched the news. It consisted almost totally of tributes to Atta Mills. They came from all manner of people who had known him in one capacity or another, from his old teachers and school-friends to political allies and adversaries. Amongst other things, I learned that he had died just three days after his sixty-eighth birthday.

Over the next week, there was a massive outpouring of grief across the nation. Although President Mills' policies were not particularly popular in the Akwapim Hills – most people to whom I had spoken about the election said that they intended to vote for the opposition New Patriotic Party – the sense of loss was just as strong in this part of the Eastern Region as elsewhere. On the way to Koforidua one afternoon a few days after he died, the tro passed a roadside billboard which displayed a moving tribute ending, "You served us well". It remained up for weeks.

Other than BraKofi's and Isaac's televisions being more in-demand than usual, little changed in the village over the week following Atta Mills' passing. The chiefs still conducted their meetings outside the Rev's house, the extra lessons for the JHS children continued as normal, and life rolled on. The following Tuesday, though, there was a great hubbub near the stalls at Quarters Junction as I walked towards school. Red and black bunting – the funereal colours – was being erected in the middle of the village and a crowd was gathering around, jigging to the beat of two enormous drums.

"What's going on?" I asked Mr Maxwell, who was flicking through a book ready to give Form 1 a Maths lesson.

"Today is one week since President Mills died," he explained.

Of course. The penny dropped. I had not been watching as much of the television in the last few days, having become a little 'Atta Mills-ed out' after the virtually blanket coverage since the news broke.

"It's his funeral today then, is it?"

"Oh, no, just an event to mark one week. The funeral is next week, Friday."

This was like a little pre-funeral, then. Form 2 and I got stuck into a lesson about active and passive sentences. We were beginning to make headway with this somewhat dry topic, constructing compound sentences in various tenses, when the sound of Takyi ringing the bell drifted into the room. Maxwell burst through the doorway in a most animated manner.

"Stop everything! Stop, stop!" he cried.

What on earth was the matter to have got him so worked up?

"Today is a holiday!" he announced breathlessly. "It is a week since the President passed; they have announced a holiday for it. We must close school!"

So that was that. The children quickly lined up on the grass, and conducted the formalities of the closing assembly. It seemed rather incongruous singing the closing song, which commenced with the line, "Now the day is over, night is drawing in" and went on to mention the "shadows of the evening", whilst the sun blazed down, virtually from its highest point in the sky, at half past eleven.

On the Friday of the following week, John Atta Mills' funeral was held in Accra. It was a public holiday, of course. It would have been wholly impossible, not to mention totally insensitive, to keep the population at work whilst what I supposed would be the most lavish funeral in the nation's history went on. Acting on an impulse of the afternoon before, I went down to the capital to attend the funeral in Independence Square. I was astonished that no-one wanted to travel down to Accra with me, except for Chris, the German volunteer. He had returned to Kwamoso a few days earlier in order to begin the groundwork for some sort of foundation, in partnership with the Rev, for the benefit of the Mount Zion-affiliated schools and the children's home. He would be leaving relatively soon, but would come back again towards the end of the year as well.

Estimates for what time the funeral would begin varied greatly, so Chris and I agreed to set off for Accra early. BraKofi had reckoned on ten o'clock, Isaac as early as eight. Vaguest of all was Augustine, who had popped into the complex during the evening to speak to the two-week teenagers. "Oh, any time in the morning!" he replied cheerily when I asked him.

Many of the tro-tros and taxis that we passed on the way to the capital were adorned with red mourning ribbons. Some had images of the former president, in the form of transfers, on their sides or their rear windscreens. Around Mamfe Circle, the numerous Atta Mills tribute posters had been adorned with more red ribbons; this was truly an event of historical significance.

Through Madina and into Accra, the roads were jammed with mourners making their way to the funeral. For once, the traffic stuttered along in a reasonably orderly fashion; there was none of the jostling for position that I had grown accustomed to. The gravity of the moment was probably the main cause of this; someone on the tro joked to Chris and me how no-one wanted to cause a crash that blocked the roads on the day of the president's funeral. The presence of numerous police officers lining the streets doubtless served as extra encouragement for drivers to be careful. One lane was completely coned off, which puzzled me, considering that this might well have been the busiest day for incoming traffic that the capital had ever seen. The rationale became clear, however, as a limo with tinted windows and a police escort sped past us, followed at intervals by others. These were the visiting dignitaries: VIPs for whom it certainly would not do to be waiting in Accra's congestion. Hillary Clinton still managed to be late, apparently. Whatever her excuse was, it could not have been the traffic.

The tro inched forward and eventually reached Tema station. Chris and I hopped out and made our way down 28th February Avenue, the main street leading to Independence Square. It was, predictably, thronging with people: both mourners on their way to the funeral, and hawkers looking to cash in by selling water, red ribbons and the like. We relaxed a little, reasoning that we were not late, for there would have been greater urgency shown by the pedestrians if the start off the funeral were imminent.

The banks of seating around Independence Square were packed. Standing half-way up one, searching unsuccessfully for an empty space, Chris and I copied numerous other people by plonking ourselves down on the steps. We had a terrific view of the participants getting ready for the start of the ceremonies, either on horseback or marching, and the seemingly obligatory drums which were being moved into place and periodically beaten.

Disappointingly for us, although perhaps unsurprisingly given the weight of numbers, the group of people that had sat on the steps was barked at by a policeman, informing us that we were blocking an escape route and requesting quite firmly that we move. A shaded spot was duly exchanged for standing in the blazing sunshine. Suddenly, a mounted parade signalled the official start of the funeral, and the trumpeteers began to play a solemn tune. The atmosphere was electric. Impromptu drummers and dancers had gathered on a walkway in front of us. As they jigged and twisted their way past us, they obscured the view and drowned out much of the content of the speeches and hymns in memory of the former president. Yet it mattered little. As an unofficial sideshow, they were as spectacular in their own way as the main event.

As the public commemoration ended, and the funeral moved away from Independence Square to Osu Castle – in the grounds of which President Mills would be buried – Chris and I drifted back towards the main road. We bumped into two teachers from Kumasi, who had made the five-hour journey to watch the funeral. We got talking and had a natter about the ups and downs of the profession. Although I was unconcerned about working through the first part of the scheduled holidays, it was refreshing to hear other teachers describe their relief at having time off. It was a sentiment I and my former colleagues in Britain had frequently aired. Yet the teachers at Holy Hills had hardly broached the subject, and I had wondered whether Ghanaian teachers were somehow immune from the pressures of school life. Clearly not.

In Kwamoso late that afternoon, Bosh, Chris and I made a trip down to the football pitch in the centre of the village, to watch a friendly match between the local amateur team Akwapim United and a side that styled itself the 'John Atta Mills XI'. To the unknowing eye, it looked more like Aston Villa against Wales, since the respective kits were old strips from these teams: it was nice to see the results of these donations being put to good use. The football pitch had once again become the focal point of the afternoon, many people had come to cheer on one side or the other, or shout encouragement to their friends who were playing.

The time of year had rolled around where I needed to go back to the Immigration Office in Koforidua to extend my visa again, this third visit would cover me for the rest of the year. One day after school, I had an aborted trip: neither of the two cash machines in Koff-Town were functioning properly, so I could not withdraw the necessary money to pay for the extension (the only other local ATMs were in Akropong, in the opposite direction from Kwamoso). At least returning to the complex meant that the Rev could sign the letter that Pastor Robert had typed on my behalf. Since the school office did not have a printer, I had had to run it off in Koforidua. The following afternoon, flush with money from a now-functioning cashpoint, I swanned into the Immigration Office with my signed letter, handed over my passport, and filled in the application form. Looking around, I realised that the immigration officials have a nice life: of the eight on duty, one spoke to me, another did some typing on a computer, and the rest watched TV!

Pastor had seemed concerned before I left that he had forgotten to type my letter on paper headed with the Holy Hills school name. I brushed his worries aside. "It's been easy the other two times," I reassured him. "In and out, and pick it up a few days later." Pastor had remained sceptical.

The young official who spoke to me at the Immigration Office was just as unconcerned about the letter's presentation as I had been in Pastor's office. However, his easy demeanour changed when he asked me for my Residency Permit.

What was this?

"You have to have a Residency Permit to live in the country when you have been here as long as you have," the young official told me.

"Erm, I've never been told I needed one," I replied, a little unsteadily.

"You do." The stern reply seemed at odds with his youthful appearance.

I braced myself for bad news. How much would it cost? Or would I be in hot water for not having one already?

Luckily for me, the young official's face had brightened. "Don't worry," he said cheerily. You'll be OK without one. Collect your passport in three days."

I breathed a little sigh of relief, and pushed the whole visa business to the back of my mind, where it stayed until my phone rang the following evening. It was the chief of immigration, a bulky fellow whom I had met the time before, called Michael. Contrary to most Ghanaian conversations, this one began with no small-talk whatsoever: not even a 'Hello'. He cut brutally to the point.

"This is Lawrence? You need to bring another letter, tomorrow," he informed me, before I had finished confirming my name.

"OK," I replied gently. I was rather bewildered by the content of Michael's call, and the deadline he had imposed. "What's wrong with it?" I guessed that some crucial detail of my business in Ghana had been missed off.

"It's not on headed paper."

Pastor had been right after all.

I explained this a little ruefully to him at school the following morning, whereupon he pored through the documents on the computer, tutting and shaking his head in a most unpromising manner. Eventually, he found some old document on headed paper. He copied my letter over onto it, and saved it on his pen drive. Over breaktime, I took a tro to Akropong – thankfully the town was not in the midst of a power cut – so that the new letter could be printed. After school, the Rev signed it and persuaded me to stamp it with the school ink-stamp as well. Off I went back to the Immigration Office. After much reading and re-reading, Michael pronounced it up to scratch.

I cast my mind back to the day in April when Lene and I had been there for the first time, and spoken to the friendly Man-Mountain. It had been so much easier then.

Over breaktime a week later Michael called again. With the same lack of fanfare as his original call had contained, he instructed me to collect my extended visa immediately. Summoning all my diplomacy, I managed to persuade him that, since I was about to teach Form 2 a Maths lesson, nobody would be grievously harmed if I waited until that afternoon. Michael's grunt prior to hanging up suggested that a compromise had been reached.

It was with a good deal of relief, walking out of the immigration building clutching my passport, that I realised I never had to have anything to do with the place again.

Furthermore, school had that day finished for two and a half weeks – the JHS children had covered the topics that they had been required to over their additional lessons. It was time to do a little more exploring of the country before the new academic year began. I had not ventured far from Kwamoso, save for a weekend at a beach resort called Kokrobite, with Mikkel and a few of his mates from the volunteering project, since Lene had returned to Denmark two and a half months before.

I had been considering a trip to the north of Ghana for some time. There were a couple of reasons *not* to go, centring on the length of the round trip, and hours that would have to be spent crammed – in varying states of discomfort – on tro-tros.

Chatting to Maxwell one afternoon in his garden after school, he expressed his opinion that it was "Too, too far."

Yet my overwhelming feeling was that there would be such a lot that I would miss out on if I chose not to go, since I had heard that the north of the country was very different from the south. In the end, it was a no-brainer: when else was I going to be able to go to see the Muslim city of Tamale, the stunning countryside around Bolgatanga, and Mole National Park?

The evening before I set off, the Rev called me over. He was sitting at his table next to the front door of the house, eating a bowl of fufu.

"You're invited," he said, gesturing at his meal. I scooped up a handful, and dipped it in the spicy sauce.

"Tomorrow, you will travel," the Rev continued. "People will ask you your name. Tell them that you are Nana Kweku Fianko Bekoe."

I swallowed my mouthful of fufu and looked at him. What was he talking about? Just as I realised, the Rev spoke again.

"You have been here some time now, you are like family. And 'Nana' is the word for a respected person."

I looked at him for a moment, deeply touched. Yet it was entirely typical of his spirit that he should bestow such a name upon me. We had a chat about smaller matters, before Pastor Robert arrived to make an enquiry about church services.

Nana Kweku Fianko Bekoe.

Now that did sound grand.

As luck would have it, the next morning I hitched a lift to Koforidua. Isaac was driving Chris in the school minibus to the regional capital, to arrange the purchase of some new tables for Holy Hills School: they would be paid for with money that Chris had raised in Germany. Peace and Collins had clapped me merrily on the back before I left; Auntie Gifty had placed her hand on my shoulder.

"Travel safely," she implored. "We'll see you soon."

First stop was Kumasi. In the days before travelling, I had thought back to the fairly oppressive feel to Ghana's second city that Lene and I had experienced in May, and was slightly edgy about going back there.

How wrong could I have been?

This time, I felt completely at ease. Possibly it was the feel-good vibe of the school holiday, although I doubt it. Walking around with the benefit of knowing the layout of the city from the previous trip, the streets of Kumasi felt similar to those of Mamfe or Koforidua. The only difference was that, in Kumasi, these streets were significantly busier and more numerous. Kejetia Market, heaving as ever on a Saturday afternoon, was again exhilarating. So long did I spend mooching around the stalls, I almost forgot that I had intended to look inside Kumasi Fort. Built in 1897, it served as Britain's administrative centre once they had annexed the Ashanti lands to the Gold Coast colony.

Fairly hurriedly, I made my way along the thronging streets and arrived at a red-brick building. In fact, 'red-brick' does not really suffice; the blocks used to construct the fort were coloured a deep, almost burgundy, shade. Passing through the main gate, I was met by a group of the fort's custodians. Initially, they shook their heads when they heard what I wanted. I was a few minutes past the official last-entry time, they explained; it would be impossible for me to enter. Some good-natured haggling took place, during which I dropped in my history teaching background and a subtle reference to the Ashanti queen Yaa Asantewaa's imprisonment in one of the fort's cells at the turn of the twentieth century. Her crime was to have led an army against the British in a forlorn attempt to preserve her tribe's independence. Eventually, I managed to elicit suitable sympathy for them to let me sneak onto the back of the final tour.

Standing in the middle of the cell in which Yaa Asantewaa had been locked up, I was able to touch all four walls without having to move more than one pace. It was another lesson in the ill-treatment that the British Empire meted out to its African captives. Even more brutal, although not entirely unexpected, was the presence of another punishment cell, similar to that at Cape Coast Castle. Here, troublesome prisoners would be locked away, as a group, and left without food or water until the last one had become too weak to survive.

The fort's museum is dedicated Ghana's history post-independence. Equipment and arms used by Ghanaian peacekeepers in areas such as Rwanda, Lebanon and the former Yugoslavia were revealing insights into the role that Ghana played in dealing with the crises of the 1990s. The lamentable UN response to the Rwandan genocide in 1994 was highlighted, next to a particularly gruesome weapon used by the Hutu tribe against the Tutsis. Named 'The Headbanger', it was a lump of wood with nails knocked into it. No further explanation was needed to work out its grisly and terrible use.

That evening I met up with a couple of other tourists who were staying in the same hostel. A few French lads, a couple of groups of English graduates and two German sisters had got chatting and planned an evening drink in a bar. Since I had not yet had an end of term beer, I readily accepted the invitation to join them. Sitting around the table with our tipples, it turned out that the Germans, Mirjam and Hanna, were planning a trip reasonably similar to mine. We agreed that we would go as far as Tamale together, before they headed to Mole to see the wildlife, and I went to some of the villages near to Bolgatanga, in the far north.

I felt somehow out of place talking to a bunch of westerners who had been in Ghana for a week at most. Despite our shared 'European-ness', the conversations about daily life seemed far away from those to which I had grown accustomed.

"I can't believe that the Government is going to tax us so much when we start our jobs, what do they need it for?" one of the graduates was exclaiming.

"It's not like the health service actually does anything," another grumbled.

"Two hours I waited to get my finger seen to when I dislocated it last year," a third interjected.

"And the council's bin lorries wake us up before seven."

It went on. The bit of me that did not care that they were not yet worldly or mature enough to comprehend how lucky they were, that the facilities about which they were complaining so ardently actually existed in the first place, wanted to shake them until the thought that they might be taking one or two things for granted entered their heads. To keep the peace, I said nothing, and made a mental note to mention it subtly to them later on if the chance arose (it didn't). Gazing across the road, I wondered how much Government help the woman grilling sausages on the opposite pavement had received in her lifetime.

Presently, a Ghanaian bloke sat himself down next to us. After a pleasant introduction, he started talking at – rather than to – our group about how he wanted to marry a white woman, go with her to her country and live what he perceived would be the easy life with her. Casting his eyes around the table, he was not in the least bit concerned with the lowered heads and averted gazes that his comments had drawn from the female proportion of the gathering. Indeed, it only served to encourage him to expand upon his love of European and North American females.

Why, I wondered, did so many Ghanaian men hold such views? Mr Enoch and countless others had told me that they aspired to marry a westerner and emigrate, and that they held white women in higher regard than Ghanaian ladies. I thought back to the confrontation at the waterfall in Akropong the day after Independence Day. I understood the misconception that all white people have piles of money. Those that Ghanaians had ever encountered had been able to afford to travel to Ghana, and exchange rates mean that even fairly expensive commodities seem cheap to westerners. It was also understandable that they had no idea about the western cost of living. Yet the thought of having saved for a long period of time in order to pay for these luxuries was equally alien to them; as was, more importantly, the discretion that westerners expect when meeting members of the opposite sex.

If that were a rude awakening for Mirjam and Hanna, they saw another aspect of the different culture at Kejetia tro station the following morning on the way out of Kumasi. I had long become used to the odd tug on the arm by people selling at markets. However, it was a new and, understandably, quite unpleasant experience for the German sisters. They became quite agitated when the third or fourth trader took hold of one of their arms, attempting to interest them in some of his DVDs; it took a fair amount of negotiation to calm the two of them down. Yet, whilst it seems threatening because of our social etiquette, it is far from the intention of the stallholders to cause worry: they are simply trying to attract attention to their products. That it is commonly white people who are touched is logical – the rich *Obruni* can afford to buy. The decency of virtually every Ghanaian I met, regarding the personal safety and welfare of others, was first class.

Once we had boarded the tro, I did my best to explain this to Mirjam and Hanna. After a bit of persuasion, they came to understand, albeit disapprovingly, what I was telling them. The chat, along with the aid of spotting a sign on the pavement announcing that 'crocodile machetes' – whatever they were – could be purchased at a nearby shop, restored their nerves. Lighter-hearted conversation started. It concerned our destination, the Boabeng-Fiema monkey sanctuary. Run by local and foreign biologists, the area is home to the mona and colobus species of monkey. The sisters were confident that it would be possible to stay overnight in a lodge that was run by the sanctuary. The idea appealed: we would not have to faff around looking for a hotel, and we could have a second look around the place the following morning.

After a couple of changes of vehicle, at the town of Techiman and a small village named Nkoranza, a ride on a tiny tro took us close to the entrance of the monkey sanctuary. By the clanking of metal coming from the back of the vehicle, there were possibly more loose parts to its mechanics than fixed ones; one rattle turned out to be the floor hitting the inside of the wheel arch.

At the sanctuary, the three of us were met by a knowledgeable-looking white lady. Her thin-rimmed glasses, and hair neatly pulled back from a somewhat chiselled face, gave her the unmistakable air of a scientist.

Our first impressions were right; she was leading a group of Swiss biologists that had been observing the monkeys over the previous months. The presence of this research team, along with a group of European medical students visiting the sanctuary on a jolly, created a problem for the Germans and me – the boarding lodge was already at its official capacity. Sadly for us, neither the Swiss head scientist nor her Ghanaian counterpart was willing to be flexible with the rules.

Nevertheless, we were welcome to look around. Tagging on to the group of medical students, we were treated to the most spectacular tour. The brown and white colobus monkeys kept their distance; the monas, slightly smaller and more vivid in colour, were only too keen to come within inches of us. They proved to be very sociable little animals: especially when bits of banana were on offer. Although it was a bit touristy, I was nonetheless thrilled to watch the little darlings eat out of my hand, before jumping and swinging themselves, with all four limbs and their tail, from branch to branch in search of more snacks.

The monkeys are socialised not just through contact with the tourists, but also by their interaction with the people who live in the village backing onto the sanctuary. Both species are traditionally seen as sacred by the local people. The explanations vary depending on whom you believe, but a traditional god called Daworoh figures in all of the stories: in some, he promotes them as bringers of good fortune; in others, the original colobus and mona monkeys were his children. Either way, they are held in such high esteem by the villagers that they are not hunted; indeed, when one dies a funeral is held. We looked at a pretty extensive monkey graveyard, full of headstones marked with the species, gender and date of burial of each of the deceased.

At the end of the tour, Mirjam, Hanna and I remembered that we needed to find a way back to somewhere with a place to stay. By sheer chance, a group of teenagers from the Seventh Day Adventist Church in Kumasi had been to Fiema village, next to the sanctuary, and had pulled in at the sanctuary on the way home. One of the pastors leading the group kindly let us join their vehicle for a ride back to Techiman, where we would be able to find lodging. Our journey almost turned sour: two or three of the churchmen soon began declaring their love for Mirjam and Hanna. As the sisters shifted slightly in their seats, we managed to steer away from this subject, and good humour was restored. A fascinating conversation developed about Kejetia market. When it was opened in the early 1960s, the (possibly apocryphal) story goes, Nkrumah sent his deputy to conduct the official niceties. This man's command of English was less than brilliant. His speech amounted to, "I declare this market open. Buyers will buy, sellers will sell, and armed robbers will rob!"

The following morning we awoke in a hotel room which, despite having a bed plenty large enough for three to sleep on top of, and all the standard fittings, cost us the equivalent of just over a pound each.

It was time to move on, to Kintampo. This small town had once been the central point of the British Gold Coast, before the colony's expansions to the north and east. These days, its main attraction is a delightful waterfall.

To begin with, it looked as though we would not get there, at least not cheaply. At Techiman tro station, the mates all shook their heads.

"You can only go to that place with a taxi," they told us. "It will be three cedis fifty pesewas each."

We toddled off to the mass of taxis that waited next to the tro station. Incredibly, virtually all of them were tiny *Daewoos*, which looked like they would never in a million years seat the usual four passengers. It looked like even the three of us would be a bit of a squeeze.

"*Mma ache*," I greeted, the Twi for 'Good morning'. "We are going to Kintampo. How much will it cost?"

"Thirty-five," came the reply, instantaneously.

"*Ah!* No chance!" I fired back.

"Yes, yes, it's a good price!"

As I attempted a bit of haggling, some clarification revealed that this was an alternative method of expressing the price quoted by the tro mates. In 2007, the Government had re-denominated the currency. The old cedi, which had suffered massive inflation, was replaced with the current 'Ghana cedi'. In practice, the currency was simply rebranded, with the last four zeros knocked off the original denomination. Yet many people across the country still used the old numbers in conversation. I had become familiar with an egg sandwich, costing one cedi fifty pesewas, being referred to as 'Fifteen thousand'; it was simple enough to convert an old value to its new equivalent.

Very confusingly, it turned out that 'Thirty-five' was actually a shortened form of 'thirty-five thousand', or three cedis fifty pesewas. The driver explained this on the way, and that further alternatives were 'three point five' and 'three five'. One I had managed to get my head round that, we moved on to chat about our destination. Fifty or so kilometres from Techiman, Kintampo is approaching the Muslim north, the driver explained. There was a roughly even split in the town between Islam and Christianity as the religions of choice.

"In the morning, you will hear the call to prayers," he advised.

"Oh right," I answered, realising that it might be an early wake-up the next day. "What time does that start?"

"Oh it depends, around three o'clock going."

Three o'clock in the morning. Best have an early night.

First, though, the Germans and I would have a look at the waterfall. It had been given good reviews by the taxi driver, and did not disappoint, except for the plunge pool being too shallow for a swim. Water cascaded down three levels of rocks. Droplets of spray spattered every now and again over a boulder, and on to the small beach on which the three of us sat and chatted, in between forays into the pool to stand under the falling water. On the way back from one of these, we bumped into a chap who turned out to be a JHS teacher in Techiman called Emmanuel.

"What is your name?" he had asked.

"La-" I began, before catching myself just in time. "Nana Kweku Fianko Bekoe," I replied.

Emmanuel chuckled, and I explained myself. As I did so, the looks on Mirjam and Hanna's faces changed, gradually, from utter bewilderment to a milder state of incomprehension.

We had a pleasant chat with Emmanuel about Europe, and Britain in particular. He had studied for a while in London, and loved the Tower. "It's better than Osu Castle. You can go to look at it, no-one stops you!" he joked, and guffawed when I mentioned my ill-fated attempt back in February to take a picture of Accra's biggest castle.

Shortly before sunset, the sisters and I had a wander along Kintampo's main street. It dawned on me that the three o'clock call to prayers, which our taxi driver had told us about earlier on, would be a holiday substitute for Kwamoso's church bell, only rather noisier. Not only would it be broadcast through a loudhailer, but the mosque from which it would emanate was less than a hundred yards away from our hotel.

A reasonably elderly man greeted us as we strolled along, and asked where we came from. He had a kind manner, yet it was that of a man who had seen much of life's ups and downs.

"Oh, you are from Europe?" he enthused. "I worked in Holland some years ago." He asked us what we thought of life in Ghana. We told him our thoughts, of the calmer lifestyle, and the crowded markets. I mentioned that over the six previous months, I had changed my perception of a number of aspects of life.

"I have talked with many Europeans who have come to this country. Most are about your age, but few stay so long. One group who did stay for many months, two or three people, one of them said to me, 'When I came here, I thought I had all the answers. Now, I have only more questions.' They had seen things that they struggled to understand."

I suddenly felt some memories flood back to me. The camera at Osu castle that I had been laughing about hours earlier, with Emmanuel. The fishing beach at Winneba. The night-time street scenes in Accra, of rough sleepers and graffiti. I had thought I had known the causes and effects of these. Had I?

Little did I know then, that there was much more that I was yet to encounter. And probably more still of which I remain ignorant.

Chapter 13 – The Beautiful North

Bang on time, at three o'clock the next morning, the loudspeaker crackled into action. Good golly it was loud, and lengthy as well. On the bright side, the earliness meant that, once the call to prayers had finally finished, it was possible to doze off again until a more agreeable hour.

So it was that Mirjam, Hanna and I were fully rested up when we left Kintampo, to carry on to Tamale. This required another three-hour tro ride, this time right to the heart of the north of Ghana. Looking out of the window, I could see that the landscape was spectacular, and, just as I had been told, very different from the south. Gone were the palm trees that were so common everywhere else I had been, and in came fantastically tall specimens, with narrow, light grey trunks. More breath-taking still were the enormous termite mounds that were dotted around at the side of the road or in fields: some of them must have been at least fifteen feet tall.

Sitting in front of Hanna and me was a mother with a boy of two. They were off to visit relatives in Tamale, the lady said as she bounced her son on her knee. The little lad was just old enough to have developed a curiosity of the less usual things around him, a category into which a group of travelling *Obrunis* most certainly fitted. He stood on his mum's lap and stared in wide-eyed delight as we waved and made faces at him; he giggled and gurgled and eventually nodded off on his mother's shoulder.

Masses of bicycles wiggled down cycle paths separated from the streets by little strips of concrete as the tro entered Tamale. The little boy had woken up and faced a dilemma: which was more interesting, this new scene out of the window or the mysterious white people behind him. As if reaching a compromise with himself, he moved his head from side to side every so often, switching his concentration between the two competing attractions.

The Grand Mosque is prominent in the centre of Tamale; the city almost revolves around it. A huge cream-coloured building, each of its four corners bears a green dome just small enough not to take the onlooker's attention away from a much larger one in the centre of the roof. Entering town, it was a sight for sore eyes and – as I would later discover – a very clear landmark.

After a roadside snack of grilled plantain, our first stop was the tannery and leather market. In the backstreets of the city, a group of highly skilled men worked to wash and waterproof the goat skins – as well as those of cows, sheep, antelope and, oddly enough, crocodiles – before they were hung up to straighten out and dry. In due course, they are transformed into all manner of things: sandals and wallets were just the start of it a list which extended to souvenir 'Welcome to Tamale' signs.

Neither Mirjam nor Hanna fancied my suggestion to look at the football stadium built for the 2008 African Cup of Nations. Whilst I wandered off to find it, they paid a visit to the cultural centre to have a look at some of the artwork that it was home to. As I walked, I noticed that it was turning quite a bit cooler, and that the sky had darkened to a rather threatening shade of grey. I suspected that my two companions might have made the better decision. The wind was picking up to the extent that the traders on the streets felt it necessary to cover their stalls with heavy tarpaulin sheets. Further down the road, others of them tied their sheets down with great care. By this time, the sky was filled with low, black, thunderous-looking clouds: a fairly major storm was brewing.

The football stadium would have to wait: the shelter of our room at the *Al-Hassan* Guesthouse was a far more attractive option. I turned around and re-traced my steps. All was going well, until an unfortunate wrong turn saw me head away from the hotel, and begin a loop around the edge of the city centre. Where on earth was I going, I wondered, as the raindrops began to smack into the tarmac. I walked on, pondering my predicament. Suddenly, the Grand Mosque's domes appeared from behind a set of buildings. Relieved at no longer being lost, I made a beeline for it, through what had fast become a deluge of slanting rain.

Standing in the shelter created by the Grand Mosque's wall, an imam gestured towards me. I approached him, wondering what to say. He shepherded me inside, and pointed towards my shoes and then a prayer mat. I thanked him profusely before he went off to his business. Almost before I knew it, there I was sitting in the biggest place of Islamic worship in the country. There was silence, except for the rain on the pavement outside and the footsteps of the occasional imam walking through the mosque, its cavernous interior accentuating the tapping of their feet on the floor. I watched curiously as most people continued their private prayers, and a few others sat and watched. Perhaps, like me, it had been shelter rather than faith that had drawn them inside.

The peacefulness of the Grand mosque led me to stay there for several minutes after the rain had stopped. It was a well of tranquillity in the middle of the flurry of the city's activity.

The next morning, I bade my farewells to Mirjam and Hanna in one of the most memorable spots in Tamale. A crossroads led to the tro station to the left and the bus station to the right, where the sisters would later catch the bus to Mole National Park. The intersection stood adjacent to the meat market. On an old wooden table, cooked cows' heads and trotters, of all things, waited to be bought. I struggled to think of any possible uses for them, although I supposed that there must be some.

I boarded a tro headed for the wonderfully named junction town of Walewale. There, I reckoned, I would find some sort of transport to take me up to the beautiful Gambaga Escarpment, for a few days of walking and sightseeing in the hills. Walewale seemed to be one of the less common destinations out of Tamale; it took an hour for nine other passengers to take seats. Nevertheless, it was pleasant enough watching the tro station go about its business in the time that I sat waiting.

At Walewale, I was pointed further up the road and to the right, where a bus bound for somewhere called Nalerigu (a name which sounded familiar from numerous consultations of the guidebook) would be waiting. Sure enough, as I rounded the corner, a line of passengers was filing onto a waiting vehicle. Luggage was slung onto its roof and held down with thick ropes. 'Bus' was an incredibly loose description. It looked more like a cross between a truck and a 4x4. However, it was heading in the same direction as I was. Perfect.

I paid the driver, who handed me an object that resembled a wooden spoon. I looked quizzically at him. This served as the ticket, he explained; everyone holding one of these would be identified as a legitimate passenger. The seats at the sides of the bus filled up, as did some fold-down ones in the aisle. There were a couple of bangs on the roof, some of which sounded a bit too heavy to have been merely a suitcase, but no-one seemed alarmed. Pretty soon we were off. It was only after a few minutes of the journey, when I shifted my gaze fractionally, that I noticed a foot dangling down. It turned out that there were twenty or so extra passengers perched on top of the bus. They must have been clinging on to something or other that was fixed, for no-one fell off as the bus bounced up and down, and lurched from side to side, along the bumpy and pot-holed road.

Some incredible sights passed along the way. Lone farmers toiled away in the fields, spraying their crops against the backdrop of the open, rugged landscape. Villages were formed of kraals – little round houses arranged in rings of five or six, each building connected by a wall. Made from clay bricks and plastered using mud, they house the extended family, with people's nephews, nieces or cousins living 'next door'. I pondered the point that these types of settlements appear throughout Africa. These kraals had moved with the times, however. Almost all had wires supplying them with electricity, and many had television aerials attached to their roofs. A small number were also fitted with satellite dishes, which presented the most incongruous of sights as we rattled by.

Entering Nalerigu, it was time for a bit of a rest, and a sit down in the afternoon sun. A vast expanse of water that I caught a glimpse of through the opposite window seemed the perfect spot for this, and so from the bus station I followed the road back up to this incredible lake. An hour or so later, it was back to the bus station for the next leg of this magnificent journey. The road up to Nakpanduri, at the height of the Gambaga Escarpment, was a track through real wilderness. Except for one pick-up truck, I saw not a sign of human activity for almost an hour, save for the ruts created by previous traffic. Then, out of nothing, the onset of wooden stalls, animals and people indicated that the bus had reached its destination.

Firstly, I had to find somewhere to stay. The guidebook said that there was a Government-run rest-house nearby, favoured by the scientists that study the area. It was a small building tucked away just off the main road. The caretaker, Kwabena, hailed me as I looked for something resembling a reception. As Murphy's Law dictated, the scientists were in town, meaning that it was full. My pleas did not alter the fact that there was no space left, not even for Nana Kweku Fianko Bekoe.

However, Kwabena told me, there was a tiny lodge called the *Sillim* Guesthouse a few minutes' walk away. I would have passed it, he explained, on the way from the roundabout that served as the transport hub.

Kwabena and I struck up a chat about the area, and he led me to a rock at the side of the building which overlooked the landscape. The view was jaw-dropping.

"Those scientists know where's good for them," I laughed, as he pointed out various landmarks.

"This is where the scientists go," Kwabena explained, directing my eyes to what looked like a cliff face about a mile across from where we sat. "In this place there are many insects and trees that they study." He mentioned a few of them and told me a bit about them; he was clearly a knowledgeable biologist himself.

I tried to take in the amazing sights. An enormous plain extended out in front of us, on which, in the middle distance, a conical hill raised itself. The northern-most town in Ghana, Bawku, sat to the north-west of it, Kwabena said, beyond which lay Burkina Faso's border.

After Kwabena had finished his verbal tour, he wished me luck and returned to the repair of a doorway that he had been attending to before I arrived. I stayed where I was, absorbing as much as I could of what lay in front of me. It was some time before I remembered that I still had nowhere to sleep that night.

Fortunately, not only was the *Sillim* Guesthouse easy to find, it also had a vacant room. Its proprietor was a lovely lady called Diana. Short and squat in figure, her maternal attitude extended to her guests as well as her teenage boys, Richard and Bismark. These two acted as the translator for many of our conversations: Diana possessed only rudimentary English and I had picked up just the most basic of phrases in the Dagbani language.

The following morning, I bought bread and a couple of hard-boiled eggs from one of the street stalls, and began a day of walking along the main Bawku road and paths leading off it, across a patch of the vast landscape that Kwabena had shown me. The road was a mishmash of dust, stones, holes, and the odd piece of surviving tarmac. A lorry trundled its way most cautiously along it, bobbing and weaving as it strove to find the best passage. Otherwise, all was quiet. I took a path to the right and followed it through the fields, stopping every so often to gaze at the hills on top of which Nakpanduri stood. The odd solitary farmer tended to crops or hacked at weeds with a machete. From time to time, a man or women would come out of his or her kraal or pass me along the path. There was perfect peace to the area, as though everything was at one with nature. Presently, a young man wobbled towards me on a bicycle. "*Baatu!*" he smiled in greeting, the Dagbani word for *Obruni*, "Where are you going?"

"Just walking along," I answered him.

"Oh, cool, cool," he laughed. It transpired that he, like the vast majority of people in the area, was a farmer. He was on his way to get some wood, to burn on his family's cooking fire. It was, in other words, a conversation similar to the many that I had had with friendly strangers over the time that I had been in Ghana. It was exceptional, however, in that it put across to me how isolated this area is in comparison with the others that I had been to. "Everyone is a farmer here, man. We all depend on the land and the weather, we have nothing else." His English was excellent; unlike most people, he had been to Senior High School, the next step after JHS.

Much later in the afternoon I sat on the rock at the Government rest-house, taking in the view again. Presently, I heard Kwabena's voice offering his greetings. I told him about the enjoyment that I had experienced in the twenty-four hours since we had last spoken.

"You know," he said, turning to me, "You would like the caves on the road out of the other side of town."

I nodded, and he gave me some directions that would see me "walk small" down the road until an opening on the left.

Thanking him once again, I set off. After ten minutes or so, I felt a sudden weariness come over me. It was unsurprising, I supposed, since I had been walking most of the day. The "small" walk quickly came to feel quite the opposite as my heavy legs paced the tarmac. My knees ached. The onset of drizzle persuaded me that the caves could wait until the morning, before I moved on to have a look at Bolgatanga. I sheltered under a tree before making my way back into town and finding something to take to eat in the *Sillim* Guesthouse's garden. At a stall, I discovered an interesting fruit which looked like a crinkled crab-apple. I added one to the bread and tin of sardines that I had bought a few minutes earlier.

It tasted vile!

The following morning I awoke with an odd sensation in my stomach. I ran along the guesthouse's corridor to the toilet for the first of what turned out to be far too many occasions to keep tally of. The prospect of diarrhoea is never nice in any circumstance. This morning, coinciding as it did with a morning of travel along the bumpy roads around Nakpanduri, it took on an extra unpleasantness. Even keeping water down was proving impossible. Clearly I was in no fit state to explore Kwabena's caves; it was time to move on, and hopefully recover a little on the journey.

I made my mind up that, since there were two roughly equidistant routes to 'Bolga' (the way I had arrived, or via Bawku), I would board the first bus that was leaving. A Bawku-bound bus pulled up not long after I arrived at the roundabout, and I gingerly eased myself onto it. Over a two-hour journey, I battled my grumbling innards and gawped through the window at the fascinating kraals in the villages.

It should have been a momentous feeling, as I changed vehicle in Bawku, to be standing almost as far north in Ghana as was possible. Rather anti-climactically, instead of looking around the town and taking it in, I felt capable of nothing more than a slightly shaky walk, from the bus station to the tro-tro that was parked a short distance away beyond a crossroads.

Another two-hour journey, to Bolgatanga, began. I was squashed up with my bag in a way which, I mused, even the proverbial sardines would probably have considered a bit tight. Then the memory of the effects that the previous evening's tinned variety had had on me made the analogy turn my stomach; instead, I concentrated on the landscape once more.

Arriving in Bolga, I felt brave enough to drink a sachet of water. Luckily, it stayed down, and I could walk around the city in relative harmony. There was a spot of sightseeing – one or two ornate buildings stood out – but mainly I was looking for somewhere to stay. The Catholic Guesthouse was recommended by the guidebook as being nice and cheap; unfortunately, it was closed for refurbishment, and so could only be used as a (by then much-needed) toilet break. Next to it, statues of numerous saints and several of the apostles adorned the streets in what amounted to Bolgatanga's Catholic quarter. A bit more exploring revealed that for some reason – heaven knows why – Bolga is as much a Christian town as Muslim one. When my tummy began grumbling again, I made a beeline for another guidebook hit, the *Nsanmini* Guesthouse. After exchanging pleasantries with its owner that were, in the circumstances, rather too lengthy, I made another headlong dash to the toilet. Returning to my room, I lay down for what I intended to be a power-nap. I awoke three hours later.

Bolgatanga by evening was very pleasant. I mooched around looking for a light bite that would not offend my stomach too much. The 'No Food for the Lazy Man' takeaway tantalisingly offered a bowl of *waakye*, or bean stew. Tempted as I was, I decided that there would be a great risk of such a spicy meal leading to No Sleep for the Ill Man that night. I opted instead for a couple of boiled eggs and a banana.

The safe decision was vindicated the next morning when I awoke, feeling quite a bit better. In my healthier state, I even noticed, stuck to the wall opposite my bed, a sign bearing the instruction, "No spitting on the wall."

I reckoned I was well enough, therefore, to have a morning visit to the (horribly stereotypically named) village of Bongo, before heading back to Tamale. Here, in the middle of a stunning rocky landscape dotted with grazing livestock, a smallish hill rises, at the top of which lies Bongo Rock. I hoped to discover if the guidebook's claim, that it "emits a convincingly resonant vibrating boom when struck", stood up. For some reason, I doubted it would.

Although I could see the rock, I never got the chance to verify the guidebook's claim (when I got back to Kwamoso, however, the Rev chuckled and told me that it was rubbish). The hill seemed to be totally devoid of a footpath to its summit. After a scramble up about a third of the rocky slope, I decided that I was a terribly long way away from anywhere that set broken limbs. I eased myself back down, and plodded along a little further along the path before heading back towards Bongo village.

Back in Tamale at around half past three, I reckoned that I had an excellent chance of catching the two o'clock bus to Mole National Park. Stories from all manner of people who had used it or – like the chap at the *Al-Hassan* Guesthouse's reception to whom Mirjam and Hanna had spoken – were familiar with it, told of its notorious lateness. These tales looked inaccurate, however, when I arrived at the bus station and asked at the ticket office for Mole: the lady behind the counter shook her head. Not to worry, I thought. I could entertain myself over the afternoon looking for the football stadium that the rain had got in the way of a few days earlier.

Then she spoke: "I'll sell you a ticket when the bus arrives. Wait some."

Experience and local knowledge had won out again.

I milled around for a while in the bus station, watching the comings and goings of the various hulking orange buses of the state-run *MetroMass* Company. Most of them looked not only as if they had been running for the best part of forever, but that they could probably keep going forever more. Rain had fallen heavily in Tamale over the course of the day. Huge, dirty puddles had formed on the ground in places; a significant amount of the rest of it had been churned into slightly oily mud by the movement of the buses.

It was a while later that another of the orange monsters pulled up. The driver flicked over a sign in the windscreen so that it read 'Mole', which was a hopeful sign that he may get going again soon; then turned the engine off, which was not. Other people had seen this event, and a queue was rapidly building up at the ticket office. At the desk, I was presented with a ticket which had the number thirty-four scribbled on its back. I assumed that this was the thirty-fourth ticket that had been sold for the journey, and cheerily presented it to the conductor. He was a tall, slim man, whose *Sainsbury's* fleece seemed a touch out of place. He appeared rather brusque, which, I reckoned, on balance was not surprising. After all, he was working on what must have been the least prompt bus service in the whole of Ghana. I sat down on a seat fairly close to the front; there was no need to walk along the narrow aisle and put the rest of the passengers in danger of being inadvertently wiped out by my backpack.

The bus filled, the engine started, and the conductor boarded. He glared at me.

"Give me your ticket!"

I handed it over, slightly taken aback.

"This is number thirty-four!" he barked. "Go to the correct seat!"

"What do you mean-" I began.

"You must sit in seat thirty-four," he ordered. "Go to that place!"

I got up, still bewildered, and edged my way carefully through the packed bus. The conductor followed close behind, as if checking that I was obeying his instruction. If he had assumed that seat thirty-four would be empty, he was wrong. More orders were issued. This time they were directed at the middle-aged lady sitting there, for her to get up. I protested that she should remain seated, and I would stand or find somewhere else, like *her* designated seat, but the conductor would have none of it. She ended up (along with some others) sitting on the floor of the aisle some distance behind me. She appeared not in the least bit fussed at this, nor that there was a massive stem of someone else's plantains resting on her knees.

The bus eventually left shortly before five. Rattling down the main road which links the north to the middle and south of the country, my stomach began to rebel again. Not to worry, I thought, as we turned at a junction and passed a sign showing eighty-six kilometres to the national park. Even allowing for the bumpy nature of the dirt road, it would take less than two hours to get there, and I could have another lie down.

Three hours later the bus was still going, not yet having reached the villages of Damongo and Larabanga (which probably should be classed as a small town, considering its population of four thousand) that lie a few miles away from Mole. Rumbling along through the pitch black evening, we could have been absolutely anywhere in the world. Looking out of the window, there was no sign of light from the land whatsoever, and cloud cover meant that the sky, too, was completely dark. I realised that I had been on the move since shortly after midday; it was now approaching half past nine. I felt drained. Just as I was beginning to wonder if we would ever get to Mole, lights flickered on the horizon. This was Damongo: the end was, if not in sight, then at least not too far away.

The bus had emptied out almost totally by the time we were pulling away from Larabanga, the second of the two stopping points. Those that remained on board were employees of the national park, returning to begin another week-long shift. We drew up outside the visitor centre. As I was hauling myself along the car park to sign in at the office and get a dormitory sorted, I received a tap on the shoulder. It was the conductor.

"How are you?" he asked, in an unexpectedly friendly tone.

"Well, my stomach is paining me, but apart from that I'm fine," I replied.

We chatted away amiably about life in general as we walked to the only lit room that I could see, where we duly signed a form saying that we had arrived. The conductor was telling me that, after a day off, he would leave on the Monday morning, just as I planned to.

"Make sure that you are on time," he smiled as we ambled towards our respective dorms. "The bus leaves at four o'clock exactly."

I thanked him and said goodnight. I knew this, and had heard that the return bus service, unlike the journey out, always left promptly. Being reminded of the departure time in my exhausted state, though, only made the early hour seem more unpleasant.

I woke up to the sound of what I guessed were monkeys moving around and chattering, although it could have been any number of species of wildlife. I felt thoroughly refreshed. I had a slightly dickey tummy still, but it was nothing on what it had been the previous evening. Stepping out into the morning warmth, I strolled over to the visitor centre, to put my name down for the morning game walk, before heading to the bar for breakfast. With it being the European holiday season, there were plenty of foreigners around. As such, the kitchen staff had put together a smashing menu, which catered overwhelmingly to the western palate. I had forgotten quite how good fried egg on toast tastes, particularly when washed down with fresh orange juice: these home comforts were massive luxuries.

Bushbuck antelope stood around in the open savannah as the small party of western tourists walked along the pathways. We were being guided by a park ranger, who was clearly an expert on the park's flora and fauna, but who delivered his knowledge in a disappointingly humourless, matter-of-fact way. The animals that we could see, clustered together, were most certainly females, he explained; the males stay alone until they find a mate, and then disappear once the offspring had been born.

"Sounds familiar," a middle-aged woman, who had been clustered together with a group of other middle-aged women, chipped in, her timing impeccable. The tourists cracked a smile at that one, even the men, but the ranger gave her group a frosty stare and resumed his monologue. He talked about the tradition in Winneba, which I had seen on the exam paper at Holy Hills, of hunting antelope at the annual festival, and the various other species of antelope which the park contained.

Next, he pointed out a couple of different varieties of monkey that had congregated in the shade of some bushes, and then took us on to what he promised would be the highlight of the tour. This was the watering hole, where we would, in all probability, see some elephants. Sure enough, crossing a small wooden bridge over a stream, in the distance stood six of the magnificent creatures. They were in the water, drinking and washing themselves with their trunks. At other times of the year, the ranger elucidated, far greater numbers congregate here. In the rainy season, though, there are plenty of other sources of water, so the watering hole becomes less used.

These elephants looked to be a family. There were three adults, and a pair of what were probably the equivalent of teenagers. They were accompanied by a much younger calf that came up just past the knees of the three adults, and was the focus of a great many *coos* from the mouths of most of the tourists.

Great efforts had been made to raise awareness of the elephants in the local communities, the ranger told us. Over the previous two decades, hundreds had been shot by people in the local villages upset – understandably – at their fields, and therefore their livelihoods, being trampled by the explorative beasts. The park had also taken the measure of driving the elephants slightly further away from the settlements. Happily, he concluded, numbers in the park are now rising once more. With that he had, abruptly, finished his tour. Once everyone was satisfied that they had seen enough of the elephants, he led us back to the visitor centre.

Larabanga is the home of the oldest mosque in Ghana. After the guided walk, I hitched a lift on the back of a motorbike to have a look. The story goes that it was constructed in 1421 by an Islamic trader called Ayuba. Passing through the area on the way from Medina to the Atlantic coast, old Ayuba had a vision in which he was instructed to throw his spear as far as he could. Wherever it landed, he should construct a mosque from mud bricks and sticks. Awaking from sleep the next morning, Ayuba found that the foundations had already been laid. No doubt delighted that the groundwork had been mystically done for him, he built the rest himself.

The mud-and-stick mosques are common in the north of Ghana, although mainly in the Upper West Region, which I did not visit. They are white buildings with prongs sticking out of them in lines across the walls. It is a fascinating design. Larabanga's mud-and-stick mosque is a tiny affair, and is one of countless mosques in the exclusively Muslim village. It has an appearance that at first glance resembles a big white tank, being five or six metres in length and width, and no more than three metres high; a smallish tree near one of its corners hangs over its roof. It would have been interesting to have had a look inside, but my request was met with a 'No'; as a non-Muslim I was not allowed to enter.

That evening – after a thoroughly entertaining game drive on the roof of a *Jeep* with some not-quite-elderly Germans, the highlight of which was a monkey who sat in the middle of the path, engaging in a lengthy stare-out with our driver – I reflected on the days that I had enjoyed so much in the north. It seemed, in some ways, foreign from the rest of Ghana. People had been so open and welcoming, particularly Kwabena, and Diana and her children in Nakpanduri. The scenery had been just as stunning, although in a different way to the south, with a more rugged appearance.

I had considered, before I left Kwamoso, visiting the Upper West Region and seeing its capital Wa. According to the guidebook, it has much striking architecture – bigger mud-and-stick mosques and the palace of the Wa-Na, the local king – and picturesque surrounding countryside. I mulled it over again in bed. Wa was another gruelling set of bus rides away, and I still had not shaken off the last of this stomach bug. I had enjoyed ten super days; now was the time to go home.

At quarter to four the following morning, the *MetroMass* conductor walked past my dorm just as I was shutting the door. We shook hands and clicked fingers, and picked up our chat where we had left it two nights before. I told him of the fun I had had looking at the wildlife; he related how much he had enjoyed having a day off to rest. As we approached the bus, I handed him my fare and was given a ticket. I checked the seat number on its back, and climbed on board. Just in front of me, another foreigner plonked himself down where he fancied. As if he could sense this laxity, smell it even, the conductor launched himself up the steps, and began barking orders for the half-asleep tourist to find his correct seat. The transformation from his social side to his working one was incredible.

Chapter 14 – A faltering start to term

The Rev was terribly excited that I had made it to Bawku. He had worked throughout the north of Ghana as a younger man, on engineering and construction contracts. He expressed delight when I told him of the journey time from Bolgatanga to Tamale.

"Only three hours!" he repeated, astonished; in 1972, it had taken two and a half days.

I had moved back into the Rev's house now that the last of the groups of the two-week teenagers had gone, allowing Auntie Gifty her two rooms back. He quizzed me the morning after I returned about what Bawku was like, almost forty years after he had left for the final time. I hoped he would not feel too let down by my admission that, other than through windows, I had seen a junction and about a hundred yards of a street, due to my rather weakened state.

"Oh, you must be tired; you should rest and take it easy," he cautioned. There was something of an 'I mean it' in his tone of voice, as well as genuine care for my well-being. School would restart in less than a week; it would not do for one of his teachers to be incapacitated. I reassured him that I was fine, and that my stomach had now fully recovered. I proved my health by going for a run, to Wonderful Love and back. The Rev's moderately disproving look, as I returned to his house nearly an hour later, betrayed a degree of annoyance that I was neither resting nor taking it easy. Fortunately, the stern rebuke that I was expecting, and probably deserved, did not materialise.

Later in the afternoon, in the internet café in Koforidua, where I had gone to send some pictures from my trip to the north back to friends, a sudden chill gripped my body. It would be nothing, I reckoned. I finished off the final quarter of an hour of my session and told Chris, who still had ten minutes of his time left, that I would wait outside. The sunshine, after all, would inevitably warm me up again after this reaction to my first taste of air-conditioning since I-don't-know-when.

It did not.

If anything, as Chris met me outside and we strolled back to the tro station, I felt worse. Before too long, a most unpleasant sensation had come across my lower body. I had the sensation that my hips were seizing up; it was as if I were a robot, overdue a good oiling. To relieve the pain, I walked bent over, which did the trick for about a minute, before the ache kicked in again. Never had I been so relieved to squeeze onto a tro.

At Quarters Junction forty-five minutes later, walking was again a painful experience. I was totally worn out. Perhaps the Rev had been right after all, that run may not have been the best idea. A good sleep would sort me out. I went straight to bed. The next thing I was aware of was singing from the morning Church service. Eleven hours had passed.

The next few days went by without incident. The tables that Chris had ordered for school had arrived, and I helped him and Bosh to move them into classrooms. I noticed that I felt chilly in the evenings. Initially I put it down to cool weather, until I realised that I was the only one wearing a sweater, and still feeling shivery as I chatted to people clad in T-shirts. Over the next couple of nights, a headache developed as well. Still, during the days I was feeling perfectly healthy. These headaches would pass.

Term began, and I got stuck into the rigours of teaching once again. I had spent the evening before dreading it, just as many teachers in Britain often do at the end of a holiday. As ever, it was the thought of school restarting that was the problem. The first day passed as first days always pass. The children's brains were rusty, and there was a general sense of things being dusted down and used again. The Rev called a meeting on the first day, and reminded the teachers of the importance of their jobs; Madam Pat, Madam Rebecca and Madam Paulina had been late, and received a strong ticking off. Three girls, Leticia, Mabel and Raquel, had joined the ranks of Form 3, and within two days it seemed as if they had been in the class forever. As always at the start of term, the holiday quickly became a distant memory.

So everything was just as I had hoped that it would be, except for these nagging headaches. They persisted in the evenings, and were now beginning to make me feel a bit sluggish during the days too. On the second day of school, Augustine phoned me: his company's volunteers had arranged a football match for the following afternoon against Akwapim United, and were short. Did I fancy playing?

I certainly did, although I doubted that I was in the best shape. Somehow Form 3 got wind of the game, and spent most of their Maths lesson the next morning asking how many goals I thought I was going to score. It was all tongue in cheek, of course. United were a decent side, the volunteers were a mixed bag of men and some women, of massively varying ability, who had never played together before. I had not even met the vast majority of them. The exceptions were two new volunteers who had moved into the Rev's house now that the two-week teenagers had gone. A lad called Robin had arrived from Germany on his gap year, and a Dutch lady, Roelanda, was on a working holiday from her job running the computer network at her branch of *Ikea*.

Against my better judgment, I did not call Augustine back to cry off. Within a minute of the kick-off, I knew that I should not have been on the pitch. I was slow to everything and felt lethargic. In the centre of midfield, along with Bosh, who had been roped in as well, I don't remember winning a tackle. Ten minutes into the second half – having moved to left full-back, where I was out of the way – the inevitable happened. United's right-winger was a powerful seventeen-year-old called Isaac, whom I knew reasonably well. Going in for a tackle with him, I was as late as a mainline service to London Euston. I missed the ball completely and felt his full force crashing into my knee. We helped each other up and carried on with the game. Fluid quickly built up above my kneecap; I could feel it wobbling as I ran around, chasing the shadows of United's players. The game, a 4-1 defeat, could not end quickly enough.

The Rev and his family saw straight through my attempts to hide my hobble once I had returned home, and expressed their concern about my condition throughout the evening. Struggling around school the next day, I had to explain countless times what had happened as both teachers and children reminded me: "Sir Lawrie, your leg is paining you!"

Three who did not were Mr Seth, Madam Lydia and Mr Livingstone. Seth had moved to Accra, and the Rev had transferred Lydia to Mount Zion Primary School. The headteacher, meanwhile, had taken a job closer to his home near Koforidua. In their place, Mr Daniel had come over from Mount Zion to take on Seth's JHS Science classes. I was glad about this; I had liked him straight away in the couple of days I had spent with him in Tinkong. Maxwell had moved to JHS, to replace Lydia and also teach English: with there being three classes in JHS now, I would concentrate on French and Maths. A young and vivacious lady called Gifty had joined to teach Livo's old class in the primary school. Although so slight it looked like she might at any point snap in half, Madam Gifty certainly knew how to educate a class.

More significantly, Pastor Robert had been appointed headteacher. I was thrilled for him – and for the school too. Pastor would run a tighter ship than Livo had done; standards would be higher.

In the midst of another headache, Bosh, Chris and I were having a Friday night chat in *Obruni* Castle.

"Your knee is still swollen," he told me. "I am going to treat it for you."

I squirmed, just perceptibly, in my chair. There was no point denying that my knee was bad, but what was this about treatment?

"I'm going to stop the swelling," Bosh answered when I expressed my thoughts. "Hot water will make it better."

I wondered how exactly Bosh would do this. The gist of his reply was that he would place a cloth soaked in the hot water on my knee, and "apply small pressure." It was a method that Bosh had picked up from his uncle when he was much younger, living in the Western Region and working with the rest of his family on a big cocoa farm near their village. His uncle had done physiotherapy to soothe the aching joints of the cocoa workers, and passed on much of his knowledge to the young Bosh.

I was significantly happier with this news, until the treatment started. Bosh brought a bucket of water that he had gone off to heat, and a cloth. He dipped the cloth in the water and wrapped it around my knee, pressing so hard that it felt that the whole of Ghana was pushing down on the bulbous joint. I gripped hold of the arm of the chair and clenched my teeth.

"Don't worry, Lawrie, it will be better in the morning," he persuaded me in between squeezes.

"I'll chase after you if it's not!" I joked.

Bosh held my eyes, briefly shifted his gaze to my knee, and looked back up at my face. "Will you?" he chuckled.

The pain was excruciating, and got no easier to bear as I grew used to it. It was scant consolation that it had taken my mind off my headache. I howled in agony at one point, as Bosh dipped the cloth in the hot water and pressed it down on my swollen joint harder than ever. Finally, he uttered words which filled my heart with first relief and then dread: "It's finished. I'll do it again tomorrow."

Next morning, my knee was far less swollen, and walking was significantly more comfortable. Bosh ambled over, looking most pleased with the results of his efforts. Despite my protests that it really was not necessary, so good had his treatment been the previous night, the cloth and hot water soon came out again to renew their therapeutic assault.

Whilst my knee was getting better, the rest of me was deteriorating. I was fortunate that it was a weekend. With no school, I could bring a mattress into *Obruni* Castle and lie down in the shade. I passed the weekend having a laugh with the usual suspects in the complex, reading my book, and wandering around Kwamoso to test my knee out.

In the very small hours of Monday morning, I awoke sweating and feeling thoroughly dreadful. The bed sheet was soaking, as was my T-shirt. I fumbled around in the dark – it was 'light off' again – and exchanged my wet things for dry ones. The Rev appeared at my door.

"Are you alright?" he asked, sounding concerned.

"No," I answered flatly. "But I'm sure I'll be fine in the morning." This was a statement borne out of stubbornness, rather than an honest appraisal. I was beginning to wonder if something serious might be afoot.

"Do you need to go to hospital?"

"NO!" I replied, considerably more abruptly than intended. I have never liked the idea of going into hospitals. I had no intention of going anywhere near one unless it was a dire emergency, however grim I felt in that moment. "Thank you," I added, hoping that I had not inadvertently offended the Rev with my bluntness.

Sure enough, by the time that I had got up and had a bath after sleeping, a little, through the din of the Church service, I felt back to the condition that I had been in for the past few days: not good, but just about well enough to go to work. Over breakfast Chris, BraKofi, Bosh, Robin and Roelanda joked with me about how, now it was Monday, I would have to stop lying around. I made my way over to school. As Mr Maxwell began assembly, I found myself, for the first time since the previous Friday, having to stand upright.

I felt what remained of my energy fall from my system, and stepped over to the bench that Madam Paulina was sharing with Madam Gifty and Madam Pat. I realised that, to watch the rest of the assembly, I would have to support myself on its backrest. Maxwell caned those that had arrived late or untidily dressed, and then reminded them that they were not to go off the school site at breaktimes. This was a new rule that Pastor had introduced the week before. It had contributed greatly to lessons starting more or less on time.

When Maxwell had finished, and the last classes were marching to their respective rooms, I lumbered over to where he was standing, talking to Pastor.

"Max, Pastor, I'm ill. Do you mind if I go and have a lie down?"

"What is wrong?" they asked with great concern.

I explained the symptoms. They looked gravely at each other and then back at me.

"How long have you felt like it?"

"Ooh, just over a week. But it's only been really bad since Saturday."

Looks which mixed amazement with horror fixed themselves on their faces. "Get to the hospital. You have malaria! It's serious!" they answered. Deep down, I knew that they were right. The prospect of the disease had lurked in the back of my mind since I had arrived in Ghana, and I did not want to over-react to feeling poorly by prematurely claiming that malaria was the cause of it.

I made my way over to where the Rev was sitting on his chair outside the house. He looked concerned, yet unsurprised, to see me.

"Reverend," I began. "You were right. I think I need to go to the hospital, I can't stand up properly. Pastor and Maxwell think that I have malaria."

He sprang into action. "I'll call a taxi. Madam Paulina will go with you."

"What about her class?" I asked.

"He gave me a look which told me that there were more important things in life than keeping Class 3 occupied. "They can go in with Class 4. It's not a problem."

I got myself inside and gathered up my wallet to pay for the hospital treatment. By the time I had made it back outside, Paulina was striding across the complex. I thanked them both for looking after me, and the Rev waved away my question of how much I owed him for the taxi.

In the waiting room of Tettah Quarshie's hospital in Mampong, I felt infinitely weaker than I had done the only other time I had been there, to give blood in April. I was immensely grateful that Paulina was with me. She knew exactly which queue I needed to be in when we arrived, and exactly where we had to go next after I had signed in at one desk, and completed various registration forms at another.

The queue for treatment meandered around the waiting area. Periodically, Paulina and I shifted along from one side of a bench to the other, and then onto the next one as we progressed nearer to the front. She rebuked me most ardently for having carried on teaching the previous week without saying anything about feeling ropey. She explained that she had had malaria a few times, as had most people that she knew. With medical attention, she said, it is not serious. I presumed that she was trying to comfort me – without saying it, she viewed malaria in the same way as we in Britain see a heavy cold. We all get one every so often, and it is a real nuisance, but after a week or so of treatment we are back to normal. Whether or not comforting me was her intention, I certainly felt more relaxed.

Although I was utterly drained, I neither expected nor received preferential treatment from anyone in the hospital: my position was not truly serious, in that I was about to see a doctor. There were numerous people who looked to be in a far worse state than I was. I dreaded to think what their ailments were. Worst of all was a frail-looking woman. She looked middle-aged at first glance, but was almost certainly about as young as her twenty-something companion. Rashes and lesions covered most of her hands and face. Her clothes covered, I had no doubt, the full extent of her affliction.

It took less time than expected to progress to the front of the queue. Paulina and I were led down a corridor and into a room. I met Dr Mensah, who wore a kindly expression. Her words, those of an experienced old pro, reassured me that I would be fine. She, too, was incredulous that I had left it so long, and even more so that I had been about to begin teaching a few hours earlier. I opened my mouth to mention the football match, and quickly closed it again. I reckoned it would be easier for everyone if she did not find out about that one. Unfortunately, Paulina began relaying the tale just as I was biting my tongue.

Dr Mensah rolled her eyes, wrote a prescription, told me that I needed to rest, and sent Paulina and me on our way to the pharmacy.

"Make sure that you *do* rest as well," said added as we thanked her. If she had been wearing glasses, they would surely have been on the end of her nose as she delivered that comment, eyes peering over the rims at me in a 'Mother knows best' manner.

The hospital's pharmacy was closed; the staff were striking for a pay rise. Paulina, more clued up about it than me, reckoned they deserved one. We left the hospital and crossed the road to another pharmacy. I fished the prescription out of my pocket and tried to decipher the words that Dr Mensah had scrawled on it. That old chestnut about doctors having illegible handwriting, I reckoned, must be true the world over. I gave up and handed it to Paulina, who screwed her face up, shrugged, and passed it to the pharmacist when we arrived at the counter.

Perhaps doctors' writing is a sort of code, known only to those in the medical profession; perhaps the pharmacist had been working long enough to be able to match medicines to the relevant scribbles. Either way, he glanced at the prescription, and immediately reached into a drawer. He pulled out two boxes of pills. The smaller one contained something unpronounceable which I had to take twice a day; the tablets in the larger one were to follow meals. I thanked him and paid. As I nonchalantly handed the money over, it was slightly shocking that the tablets were, for me, so cheap: thirteen cedis, the equivalent of between four and five pounds. The consultation in the hospital had been less than half that price. Yet one of the reasons that malaria is such a killer is that some people cannot afford the treatment.

Not a great deal happened over the next three and a half days. Early one morning, as dawn was breaking, I got up and gently eased my way to the toilet, after spending a good few minutes gearing myself up to do so. Ruth, Pastor Robert's wife, was standing outside the house, waiting for the Rev.

"I heard that you have malaria," she said compassionately.

"Mmm, I do," I mumbled, desperate for the loo.

"I will bless you," she announced, and took hold of my hand. She began chanting something which, except for frequent mentions of "Jesus", I failed to process. It was typically kind of her, although at the time I was more concerned about my bladder. Ruth needed to complete her work as the conduit of Christ's healing powers reasonably quickly, I reckoned.

"You are healed!" she declared eventually.

"Thank you!" I breathed, thoroughly grateful. I strolled as nonchalantly as possible around the corner to the toilet block, making sure that Ruth would not see that my relief was more that I could get off to the lav than at the power of the Lord.

Lying on my mattress in *Obruni* Castle, the days assumed a pattern. I watched people go to school or work in the morning, and then noted the markers of the time: school's First Break, Second Break (over which the other volunteers returned), and finally school's closing. I periodically read a book which I had borrowed from the library, until my brain gave up processing the words – usually this was after about five pages. During the evenings, I would listen to, and occasionally summon the energy to contribute to, the conversations of whoever had gathered in *Obruni* Castle. One such evening, I shivered under a sheet that someone had kindly brought out for me, and curled myself up a little more. Yaw saw what was happening. He came around the table, tucked the sheet under the mattress and rested his hand on my head.

"You'll get better soon, Lawrie," the delightful little boy whispered to me.

It was most heart-warming.

By the Thursday morning, I was becoming bored. This was good news: I was getting better; previously I had been too shattered to do much more than observe the movement of people and the lengthening of shadows. I was beginning to seethe at the injustices of malaria. It was the worst illness that I had ever had, by far. The exhaustion was constant. I woke up every morning soaked with cold sweat. Yet I was lucky, for I was able to access treatment. The rest of the community, too, were in a similar position, albeit that the cost of the medicine hit harder for them than for me. Bosh and Florence came down with it later in the year; Auntie Gifty's grand-daughter, Little Mabena, had suffered from it in early August. The adults understood the symptoms, but for five or six days – and nights – Mabena would cry in pain and, I guessed, frustration at the constant ache that had taken hold of her. Gifty had comforted her wonderfully, sleeping hardly at all whilst she looked after the young girl. Yet Mabena too had been to the hospital, and recovered quickly.

In other parts of Ghana, particularly the more isolated north, there is not the same infrastructure or personal wealth. And Ghana is one of the more developed nations in the wide belt of tropical countries where malaria is a constant threat. Treatment is, therefore, often either very difficult to access or too expensive. All five strains of malaria can be fatal if the parasites overcome enough healthy blood cells, although falciparum (the most common strain to affect sub-Saharan Africa, and the one that I had) is particularly severe. In theory, the prevention of malaria is relatively simple. Mosquito nets, to us, are cheap – they cost £2 ($3 or €2.50) each. Thanks to the work of numerous charities they are donated to those in need of them. Just as importantly, advice is given about why it is so vital that they are used. However, in many areas there are not enough nets, and still too little awareness of their effectiveness: even in Kwamoso, far more people did not sleep under them than did.

Statistics prove that the nets work in preventing the transmission of malaria (averting 50% of cases, according to the WHO), as well as my own accidental findings: a couple of times I fell asleep without closing my net properly. In the morning, without fail, there would be red marks from mosquito bites on areas of exposed skin – luckily, the mosquito or mosquitoes that had caused them were not on those occasions carrying the malaria virus. Just as tellingly, my malarial episodes both followed hotel stays during which I had slept without sufficient netting.

Whilst the body can develop a small degree of resistance to malaria, it is impossible to become immune to it. Most Ghanaians who I spoke to about the disease had suffered from it at some point. In a strange sort of way, the fact that they had received treatment and recovered is part of the challenge of charities' awareness programmes on the importance of sleeping under nets. Bosh, for example (who did use one) later told me that Paulina's perception of malaria being the Ghanaian equivalent of a heavy cold was common. He reckoned that people felt, since they had got by well enough without a net in the past, that there is no need to suddenly start using one just because some visiting charity worker said that they should. This rather blasé attitude, I suppose, is borne of the conservatism and unwillingness to change habits that are parts of human nature, albeit ones that must be overcome. Maxwell's insistence that I must "Get to the hospital, it's serious", was likely at least in part an example of the Ghanaian concern for my wellbeing as the *Obruni*, who was not used to dealing with the disease.

To illustrate the severity of malaria, across the world it killed 584 000 people – 90% of who lived Africa – in 2013, the most recent year for which the WHO has statistics. Just under four-fifths of these were children under five, who have not developed any sort of natural antibodies to the disease. Although the mortality rate has fallen by about a third since 2000, during the same period the population at risk from malaria increased by 25% globally and by 43% in Africa[7]. Much more still needs to be done to reduce and eventually eliminate this terrible disease.

On Friday, I felt sufficiently strong to make a return to school. I was nothing like totally healthy, but there was a school trip to Akropong that I was desperate to participate in. If I am honest, I would not have made my comeback until the Monday had it been any other week. A number of the JHS students were going to the annual Yam Festival as part of their Social Science work. Armed with their exercise books and pens, they jumped on the school minibus and waited for Isaac (who was driving), Mr Maxwell, Mr Sam, Madam Pat and me to join them. Chris was also coming, having been invited by the Rev to join the school in watching this local extravaganza.

The Yam Festival celebrates the start of the yam season, when the root vegetables are harvested. It is one of the highlights of the regional calendar; indeed, President Mahama was due to make an appearance at some point in the day, although in the event, he only arrived after the school trip had left. The festival lasts the full week, but Friday is always the highlight. The chiefs and kings of local villages parade

---

[7] For a more detailed analysis, refer to the World Health Organisation's World Malaria Report 2014.

through the streets, before going to the palace of the King of Akropong for a more formal ceremony. The parade, Pat assured Chris and me, would be spectacular.

The days before Friday are spent building up to this climax, with events such as a ceremonial gathering of the yams to begin the celebrations and an official mourning of people who have died over the previous twelve months on the Wednesday. Come the evenings, the crowds begin parties on the streets which last, well, until they finish.

It shocked me, at the time, that neither Maxwell nor any of the other teachers had told the children anything about their behaving themselves on the streets of Akropong. Sam had told me that the town would be heaving with people. My mind flashed back to a school trip a few years previously. At the Albert Dock, our Year 8s had thrown their pencils and worksheets into the water and run amok, until my colleagues and I decided that enough was enough and it was time to make an early return to school.

When we got out of the minibus, however, it was immediately clear why there had been no stern words of warning about what was expected. Every one of the children conducted themselves in an exemplary fashion. It was not just the threat of the cane either; they were genuinely excited at seeing the festival. The thought of misbehaving had not entered anyone's head. We walked, in an orderly group, along the streets, watching the town ready itself for the parade. A woman carried her yams in a basket on her head – "*Ah!*" Maxwell lamented. "She should have brought them yesterday." Traditionally, he explained, they are not carried on the morning of the parade. Everywhere there was a fervent atmosphere. People bought plantain, water and other refreshments, or settled down in the shade of a shop entrance or overhanging roof to watch. Police officers maintained a close eye on the proceedings, just in case of any trouble.

Maxwell and Pat led the children back to the main street and sought out a place to stand, and wait for the chiefs' parade to begin. The children settled themselves down and nattered away to each other. I had felt myself flagging somewhat towards the end of our walk, and it was something of a relief to be able to find the shadow of an overhanging roof. The crowds continued to gather, and after a while a couple of gunshots from ceremonial rifles signalled that the parade was about to start.

What a spectacle it was! There was the occasional ear-splitting bang from one of the rifles being fired into the air, making me and several others jump. Musicians either banged gong-gongs (one of the big drums that are used during festivals), or blew into horns. They marched exuberantly up and down the high street, then gave way as the first of the chiefs came into view. Pat's prediction seemed to be spot on. A large group of men carried what looked like a sturdy wooden stretcher, on top of which was a chief on his throne. He looked incredibly grand, waving almost regally at the crowds with one hand and clutching a decorated golden cane in the other.

Over the course of the next hour or so, he and others (some of whom were women, known as the queen mothers) were carried through the streets. I thought I saw the King of Kwamoso, Nana Addo, nod at the school group as he passed. Music played, gong-gongs were beaten incessantly and were surpassed in loudness only by periodic gunfire. Some of the chiefs and queen mothers were carried along in bigger wooden structures resembling kayaks. They beamed with delight as they waved to the people who had gathered to witness the parade. Many of them had decorated their hair with golden braids, and almost all joyfully waved elaborate canes or ceremonial guns above their heads. Some of them were well into the party atmosphere, jigging up and down and side to side on their raised seat. I sympathised with those carrying them as the sun beat down; doubtless all this movement made an already arduous task even more punishing.

Just watching, in the heat of the midday sun, I was struggling. The shadow of the rooftop had slowly receded since we arrived, and I had sat myself down on the pavement some time earlier. A sachet of water failed to rouse me, and, with the noise reverberating in my ears, I reckoned I had seen enough. I hauled myself up and sidled over to where Isaac and Maxwell were fully in the spirit of the occasion, clapping and singing away like there was no tomorrow.

"Do you mind if I take the bus key?" I asked Isaac.

"No problem," he replied, and fished it out of his trouser pocket. "You rest small, we're coming!"

I laboured through the crowds of spectators and found the school minibus. Climbing on, I plonked myself onto a row of seats, opened the nearest windows, and lay down.

The excited chatter of children woke me. I don't know how long I had been asleep for, but I felt significantly better for it. The minibus filled up again, and we headed back to school to be in time for closing. Inching our way through the throng of people, we passed a big rally for the New Patriotic Party, the main opposition to President Mahama's National Democratic Congress. I had a chat to Peace and her mates. They had loved the festival, they said. It was the first time that they had been to it, and they wanted to go back to it later in the day – would I take them on a tro-tro?

Kids being kids, most of them had paid scant attention to their instruction to make notes about their experience. Benedicta in Form 1 was a notable exception. She had written down a lovely account of what went on, and how much she had enjoyed it. In contrast, one of her friends' notes were personal reflections of a different nature: "I was hungry and so I ate ice cream", was her summary of the day's activities.

I slipped my shoes on, and made my way through the Rev's front door and into the complex. It was my first day of school 'proper' since malaria had sent me to hospital. It was slightly chillier than normal, a mist had descended over the hills around Kwamoso. A sheet was draped over the Rev's chair and table, and Nana Addo looked to be having a conversation with it. That's odd, I thought, as I glanced at the scene. On closer inspection, however, two feet and a head were poking out of either end of the fabric. They belonged to the Rev, clearly he was feeling the cold.

There were two more new faces in Form 3, lads called Eric and Daniel. The latter was much older than the others at nineteen, and carried a more worldly air about him. To begin with, he was a bit of a nuisance: he had a smart, or not-so-smart, comment for most things I said. Once he was onside, though, he revealed himself to be a charming and quite witty young man. Just like the others, he worked hard in class and, just like the others, he displayed an unwillingness to knuckle down outside school.

Takyi had been replaced as the bellboy by a new member of Form 1, a little livewire called Caleb, who I remembered from Class 6 at Mount Zion. He was a cheeky chappie who had an excellent mathematical brain and a fondness for checking the time on his little red digital watch. This was his most cherished possession – towards the end of lessons, he would frequently look at it and point out how long remained until he had to ring the bell. One morning later in the term he looked crestfallen.

"Sir Lawrie, I have lost my watch," he told me at the start of the lesson before First Break.

He was a ball of nervous energy as the class started working, fidgeting constantly. In the end, I placed my phone – which, like the other teachers, I used as my timepiece – on his table in front of him so that he could monitor how long was left. Without it, I reckoned, he might well have cracked.

Later on, he was all smiles again. His watch had fallen into his bag earlier in the day. The world had righted itself.

Before I knew it, my 'first' week had slipped by. Although the malaria had gone, teaching – indeed standing up for more than ten minutes – was still incredibly tiring. School was closed on the Friday. It was the day when Nana Addo made his annual trip to pay homage, as King of Kwamoso, to the King of Akropong at his palace in the town. The village was having a day off.

The Rev had asked Bosh, BraKofi and Isaac to go, to represent the complex. Chris, Roelanda, Robin and I were also invited. A week after the Yam Festival, I found myself piling into Issac's minibus again. However, rather than sharing the bus with group of kids, we were (somewhat unexpectedly) sitting with the chiefs who, along with the Rev, governed the village. The Rev himself did not go. I never found out why, but I suspected that it might have been because of his health. He seemed to have slowed up over July and August, and walked around the complex ever more cautiously.

The king's palace was a surprisingly unspectacular affair. It was on Akropong's high street; I had been past it several times without realising what it was. Only the presence of some vaguely ornamental writing and symbols on the wall above the main door – these too I had not spotted until I walked through it – gave it away as something more than just a larger than average building. Inside, its plain corridors bore little resemblance to what I had imagined they would be.

Everyone filed into to a courtyard, with seats arranged for the guests. The chiefs then passed through another door, and re-emerged several minutes later, having changed into white robes. They took their places near the front. Nana Addo and his son, a slightly-built boy of around twelve, were seated amongst them. Bosh remembered that he had to present the King of Akropong with a bottle of Schnapps that we had clubbed together and bought. He excused himself and climbed somewhat awkwardly over another row of assembled guests.

A choir called the Revelation Youth Group had set itself up just in front of us, and opened the mini-festival with some lusty renditions of various hymns and other songs. Half-way through one of them, a goat wandered into the area where the ceremonial part of the event would occur, and bleated rather pathetically. It had clearly escaped from the clutches of its minder, who rapidly appeared and pulled it back towards the rear courtyard. Goat being a popular meat at events like this one, I did not rate its chances of prolonged survival very highly at all. At least everyone would have the peace of mind that comes with knowing that the food is fresh.

After a series of short speeches, welcoming people to the occasion, the paying of homage began. Nana Addo stood in front of a basin of water and said a short prayer. He was then given a large bottle of Schnapps, and poured a measure of the spirit into its cap. To my great surprise, he threw the contents of the lid into the water. To my greater surprise, he then began repeating the process whilst chanting something in Twi.

I hoped that it was not our Schnapps.

"The King is purifying the water," Bosh explained when I gave him a curious sideways glance. Perhaps, I thought, the next time I was pouring a measure of hard stuff into my mouth, back in Britain, I should expound that I was purifying myself; I suspected that no-one would believe me. Meanwhile, Nana Addo was carrying on – he must have tipped at least twenty lids' worth into the water. When he was satisfied that the water was sufficiently pure, Nana Addo picked up the basin and took a long swig from it. I was astounded by what happened next. He strode over to the area where the King of Akropong was sitting along with his entourage, and sprayed the contents of his mouth all over them.

Bosh turned towards me as the inevitable question was forming on my lips. "This is to show his respect for the King of Akropong," Bosh narrated with a glint in his eye – probably having predicted my surprise, and certainly hugely amused by it. "It is a blessing and a show of his appreciation for them."

Nana Addo had an unusual blessing for his son, too, albeit without a shower of spittle and alcohol. The boy stood in the middle of the courtyard whilst his father took an egg from a basket on the ground. He circled the egg three times, clockwise, around the boy's head, and then hurled it against the wall at the corner of the courtyard. Two more messy globules of shell and raw egg had been splattered on the brickwork by the time the ritual was completed. This seemed to mark the end of the formalities. The assembled people listened as the choir struck up a few more songs, then made their way down to the courtyard at the rear of the palace for lunch and drinks.

Just inside the courtyard lay another basin, with the gruesome sight of a skinned goat propped up rigidly inside it. A gaping cut to its neck grabbed the attention of some of us volunteers, unused to seeing such gore. At the opposite end, two more similarly ex-goats were being manhandled into basins by two women who were in charge of cooking them. Florence had arrived at some point, and was standing in the middle of the courtyard chatting to an elderly lady. I was sure I had never seen her before, yet her face looked familiar.

"Lawrie, this is my mother!" Florence beamed.

Of course! The face that looked back at me as I greeted her was a thinner, older version of Florence's. Doubtlessly, in the past Florence's mum had possessed exactly the same aura that the Rev's wife exuded in the present.

Food began to be served, and I was handed a plate of chicken and rice, with the tomato-based stew that accompanies a great many Ghanaian dishes. I had quite fancied the goatmeat, which some of the others in attendance were enjoying; Auntie Gifty never cooked it for the volunteers (I had built, over time, the impression that Ghanaians think that westerners dislike it), so I could only sample it occasionally. I decided it would be highly impolite, however, to ask to swap, and tucked in hungrily.

The afternoon was given over to music and dancing. The Revelation Youth did sterling service as the party kept going. Bosh took me and the other volunteers for a little walk along the backstreets of the town. We ended up at the house of one of the King of Akropong's advisors, who had gone home for a rest. We had a chat about the day's excitement, our respective jobs, and life in general over a glass of juice. After draining a second offering, we wandered back to the celebration, which was still in full swing. Smoke wafted over the palace garden's walls from three huge barbeques, on which the three skinned goats were being roasted for the evening meal.

Later on, I went to the pump with Dennis to help him fetch water. It was frightening to see the extent to which malaria had taken the strength from me. Carrying just one of the big containers back to the Rev's house was an epic struggle; a second had to be my last.

Cocoa. It is the second largest export from Ghana after gold. Numerous cocoa farms can be found across the country. The town of Mampong has one of the oldest, however. Covering just over a third of a hectare, Tettah Quarshie's Cocoa Farm has been harvesting the crop since 1879.

The Rev told me this one evening, and that it was open to visitors. The idea of a Saturday morning trip quickly germinated.

Chris, Roelanda and Robin were similarly interested in seeing what happened at a cocoa farm, and the next weekend we traipsed off to await a tro at Quarters Junction. Yaw caught us up on the way. "Can I come?" he asked, his eager little eyes yearning for an adventure.

The five of us knocked on the main gate of the cocoa farm sometime later. There was no answer. We knocked again, and then admitted defeat, retiring to sit in the shade of a tree before we headed back to the complex. Presently, a youngish man in a white shirt opened the gate. He looked around in the way that people do when they suspect that schoolchildren have knocked on their door and run away.

"*Mma ache*," we greeted him from across the road. "Please, is it possible to have a look around your cocoa farm?"

He burst into a smile. "Yes! Come, come," he enthused. We made our way in and were shown to a little wooden bandstand-like structure with a huge picture of Tettah Quarshie adorning a board next to it.

"*Akwaaba*," he grinned by way of more formal introduction. "Welcome. My name is Thomas. I am one of the workers on the farm." Thomas went on to tell us all about how Tettah Quarshie had grown bored of his work as a blacksmith in Accra. He had made a trip to Fernando Po – modern day Equatorial Guinea – and returned with cocoa beans in 1876. His initial farm in Accra was unsuccessful because of the levels of salt in the soil near the coast, so he came up to his native Akwapim Hills. In Mampong, he found land on which to start the current farm. The five of us listened, spellbound, as Thomas spoke. Yaw in particular was massively curious, and thoroughly enjoying his morning out.

"The cocoa pods grow all the way up the tree." Thomas explained, revelling in his guiding role as he showed us around the farm. All eyes lifted upwards, and we saw scores of pods hanging off the trees' branches and trunks, right the way to their tops.

Thomas held out a long stick with a rounded blade at the end of it. "This is a *go-to-Hell*," he explained. He lifted it up into one of the trees and hooked it over a cocoa pod. "This one is a ripe one, it is yellow," he continued. "You hook it with the *go-to-Hell* and it falls, like it is falling down to Hell."

That explained the bizarre name then.

A single tree can produce a hundred cocoa pods in a year, Thomas said, as he led us over to a table holding the pod that he had brought to the ground. He opened it; a white goo revealed itself, in which the cocoa beans lay. These are removed, Thomas explained, and left wrapped in a leaf from a plantain tree (each one is roughly a foot long, and several inches wide) for a week to ferment. After this time, the beans have dried out and turned brown. He handed us some each; we sampled the bitter, yet pleasant, taste of pure cocoa.

Nothing of the fruit is wasted, Thomas continued. The fresh pods are either fed to animals, or allowed to dry and then burned; the ash is mixed with water and used as the basis of a black soap. The beans are sent off to the processing company to be turned into various forms of chocolate.

Cocoa beans fetch two hundred and twenty cedis for a sack of sixty kilograms. This sounded good, until I converted it to sterling; it works out at about eighty pounds. Then Thomas explained that the average tree only produces fifteen kilos a year, and I realised that this price was, actually, very low.

Yaw was having a fantastic time, although understandably started to get a little restless as the adults discussed the economics of cocoa. Thomas had a little pop at Ghana's neighbour Ivory Coast, which recently overtook Ghana as the leading exporter of the product.

"Here in Ghana we produce the best cocoa. We ferment it by hand; in that place, they use machines instead. Their cocoa is mass-produced, it is not as good," he insisted. We took Thomas' word for it: he was clearly very passionate about his work, and he had been an outstanding source of information for us. We thanked him as he got back to work. Heading back to Kwamoso, I felt thoroughly educated.

That evening, Bosh, Robin, Roelanda and I had a little drink at Palm Hill to bid farewell to Chris, who would soon go back to Germany. I would see him again shortly; he was due to return before Christmas, to do some more preparation for his and the Rev's foundation. Chris had invited a couple of others as well: a woman called Gladys, who was a friend of Bosh, and young lady called Rose. A jolly good time was had by all; Gladys in particular was a good laugh.

The seven of us squashed into a taxi on the way home. The driver kept us entertained with some of his favourite local pop songs, which Bosh and Gladys jigged along to enthusiastically. It mattered little to Bosh, or anyone else for that matter, that his bottom kept hitting me in the face as he did his best, in the confined space, to throw some shapes to the catchy little jingles coming of out the taxi's speakers.

Chapter 15 – Back in the thick of teaching

Music woke me one morning. This meant that it was very early indeed, since the bell had not yet been rung for the Church service. I decided that it must be coming from Florence's radio, which was often turned on at times that would be deemed anti-social in Britain. The thought crossed my mind to ask her to turn it down, before I remembered that – as a guest of the family and a foreigner in the complex – it was not my place to make such a request.

Over the next few days, the same thing happened, starting at the painful hour of four o'clock. After a couple of mornings of it, I had resigned myself to the different attitudes towards noise that prevail in Ghana. I listened to the hymns and the DJ who, like the vast majority of his colleagues across radio stations, had that irritating habit of talking over the last verse of most songs. It seemed odd, though, that the radio was left on when the bell had been rung, and the Church service had started, and was turned off just before it ended.

One morning, with another hymn belting out, I went to the toilet block. It took me a moment, as I walked down the corridor, to realise that the noise was not coming from Florence's radio, or anywhere else in the house. I stepped outside, where it was even louder. The Rev was sitting on his chair in the dark.

"What is the music?" I enquired.

"Oh, it is coming from the new loudhailer in the village, he replied laconically. "It is the information centre."

"Loudhailer?!" I probed, involuntarily.

It transpired that the installation of electricity had made it possible to broadcast the local news, not to mention the word of God, to the village. The information centre was a building that lay somewhere – unseen, but most definitely heard – to the left of the Rev's front door. Up to that point, apparently, a couple of people had delivered the news by shouting it out as they rode around on bicycles.

The loudhailer was clearly here to stay, and so I would just have to get used to it. Waking up to its crackle, followed by its outburst of music, became part of the daily routine. The sound of the bell an hour later became a relief, for it signalled that we were more or less half-way through the hullabaloo of the information centre's music and announcements. These were broadcast loudly in Twi, by a voice as deep as the blue sea itself. There was a regularity to the, for want of a better word, programme. The first few songs each morning came in the same order. The final one was always a jolly little ditty with an uppy-downy rhythm, which, Bosh explained one day, was a hymn called *Safnat Panea*.

One Tuesday morning the loudhailer's volume had been turned up to another level. The noise reverberated around my head. '*TURN IT DOWN!*' a little voice shouted inside my mind, furious at the nutcase who had cranked the sound system up to such a ridiculous degree. I considered doing something about it for a moment, before deciding – as I had done the first time I had heard the amplified tunes – that this was really none of my business.

Sod it. I got out of bed and slid my flip-flops on. I strode out of the house and followed my ears. Walking down one of the paths through Kwamoso, the sensible part of my brain tried to assert that going to see whoever it was who was in charge of the loudhailer was not a good idea. However, having come this far, I was not about to turn around and slink back to bed with my tail between my legs. The noise was, after all, way louder than usual.

I arrived at its source. The information centre was a curious building. It looked like a deserted house, with, unlike most buildings in Kwamoso, a first floor. Music emanated from four metal loudhailers attached near the roof. A flight of steps to the upper level looked to offer the best way to find someone, so up I went. At the top of the steps was a door. I knocked. There was no answer.

In for a penny, in for a pound.

I pushed the door. It opened, and I stepped into a corridor. Along its right hand side were a couple more doors. The one closest had a light behind it. I knew I was way past the Point of No Return, so I took a deep breath and knocked.

A shortish, bald man of medium build opened the door, and looked at me curiously. A clock on the back wall of the room revealed the time to be eleven minutes past four.

"*Mma ache*," I began, in the customary manner, before getting straight to the point. "Your loudhailer is very noisy this morning. Please will you turn it down?"

The bald man looked slightly taken aback. "Who are you?" he asked, peering over his glasses. It was a fair question, I suppose, bearing in mind that he was looking at a grumpy-looking *Obruni* who had arrived uninvited. Furthermore, I had not given the slightest thought to my appearance. Clad in a T-shirt and boxers, I probably looked ridiculous.

I explained that I was living with the Rev and that I worked in his school. I had a full day of lessons and needed to be rested up so that I could teach them properly. My tone had softened considerably now that I had got the issue off my chest. We began as agreeable a conversation as was possible under the circumstances. His name was Nana, he said, and he was the information officer. His job was to spread the word of God and broadcast local messages to the villages.

Villages? Plural?

Nana went on. The information centre served Saforo and three villages on the other side of Kwamoso. The furthest of these, I realised, was about two miles away. That explained why it was so loud every morning.

"The people like to hear the hymns, they ring up and ask for their favourites."

Mollified, I made my way back to bed. Nana had agreed to turn the volume down just before I left, when I had asked him a second time, although I held little hope that he would do. Heading back along the paths, however, the loudhailers were certainly quieter than they had been, and remained so for the rest of the morning. Lying awake in bed as the music played at its usual level, I had a small feeling of exhilaration. Not only had I got away with visiting the information centre with my irregular request, I had actually been successful.

That afternoon, I wandered back across the complex after school had finished. The Rev, sitting in his chair outside the front door of his house, called me over.

"Lawrie, Nana informs me that you went to see him this morning."

Eek. Having complained about how I had heard the music, now I was surely to face it.

I took a deep breath. "Yes, Reverend, I did." I thought that I had best leave it at that.

"He says that you asked him to turn the loudhailer down," the Rev continued.

"I did. It was very, very noisy this morning and-"

"You did exactly the right thing," the Rev cut in with a smile. "This morning was too, too loud. It will not be so loud again."

A huge wave of relief coursed through my body.

News spread quickly. Bosh came around to *Obruni* Castle in the evening, full of his usual laughter. "I can't believe that you even went there," he chortled as I explained what had happened.

A couple of days later, the Rev called me over again. This time, his words rang less joyfully through my head. He wanted me, he explained, to go to Mount Zion School in Tinkong, and work there on a Thursday and Friday, teaching Maths and English. There was nothing wrong with this request; indeed, I had suggested to him a few months earlier that I could do some good there. It was just that I was well into my stride at Holy Hills. The children, despite their unwillingness to read over topics at home, were making reasonable progress in class. They had exams at the end of the term, a few months away. Who would take their Maths and French lessons whilst I was not there?

I had also got to know and like the teachers at Holy Hills, especially Maxwell, Paulina, Sam and Daniel. The latter two would sit in the shade of a tree next to the JHS buildings over breaktimes or in their odd free period. They would bring a table out, arrange chairs around it, and either get some marking done, or, if their work was finished, have a chat. Daniel's office, I called it, much to their amusement.

Much had changed at Mount Zion when I arrived there on my first Thursday morning. Madam Vera had left, as had Madam Lydia. These two buddies had gone to the college in Koforidua and enrolled on a business course. I did not blame them. Lydia had been upset by the Rev having transferred her at the start of term, and Vera had become fed up at not being paid on time.

In their place, a lady called Mavis, who had started shortly after Lene had finished in May, was the new headteacher. Alongside her, Peace's sister, Faustina, a lady called Selina and two blokes named Edwin and Daniel taught the youngsters their lessons. Like the teachers at Holy Hills, these four were all young. Daniel was twenty-three, the others either nineteen or twenty. Mavis, at twenty-eight, represented a wealth of experience. She taught Classes 1 and 2 all subjects bar French, with a maternal, but stern, manner. The others taught subjects rather than classes: Faustina taught English, Selina Citizenship and Religion. The women were likeable people. They were also very competent teachers who got along well with the children.

The men, on the other hand, I found quite difficult, unfortunately, to get along with as professionals. Daniel had a speech impediment and was generally quite slow-witted. His subject was French, although his command of the language made mine, even before I had started practicing in readiness for picking up classes at Holy Hills, look like that of *un Parisien*. Edwin seemed to do little other than tell the children off. He taught Twi and a little bit of Maths, although was frequently outside the classroom, lolling around in the shade of the terrace. The times when he was with the children, he was often swishing his cane around, with little effect other than intimidating and cowing them.

I was not to know their teaching styles, however, when I arrived that first day. Madam Mavis had started assembly, and was explaining to the children that school fees would be collected over the coming days. As the children were dismissed to sweep their classrooms before lessons started, she introduced me to the teachers and their subjects. The usual clapping handshakes and snapping finger-clicks were exchanged, along with some hearty banter about the differences between Ghana and Britain.

"What would you like me to teach today?" I asked Mavis. It seemed, from her earlier introductions, that most subjects had been covered.

"You can teach Maths," she began in response. I smiled, this was straightforward. "And Science," she finished.

I glanced at her; this was unexpected.

"It has been many years since I learned any Science," I said in a cautionary tone.

"Oh, it's no problem," Mavis replied. "You can teach Maths first if you like, or rest small."

"What about the timetable?" I asked.

"Our timetable is not good, we don't use it," Mavis replied casually.

I was shocked, although, unfortunately, not surprised.

"We are going to make a new one," she continued.

Slightly relieved, I offered to assist in any way that was needed.

I asked Mavis questions about what topic within Science to teach them, and where the relevant textbooks were kept. She played a straight bat. Her answers revealed that there was neither a scheme of work (it had not been collected from the Education Office in Akropong), nor any textbooks. The latter was simple to remedy, as I could borrow the relevant books from the Holy Hills library to prepare lessons with. However, I had no intention of going to Akropong to find the Education Office. Apart from it meaning that I would have to go through the rigmarole of explaining who I was, and quite why I needed a scheme of work after more than a month of term-time, this was the headteacher's job.

That first day I taught Classes 5 and 6. Exclusively boys, they had lessons together. It made sense: Class 5 numbered two – Yarro and Chandrak, whom I had met in May when they were Class 4. Class 6 had six in theory, although five in practice: one of them, a boy called Joseph, rarely attended. We did Maths after First Break; near the end of Second Break, Mavis asked me to go to their class again. I had spent an hour and a half on indices with them thirty minutes previously; I had no intention of subjecting them to more Maths. That left Science.

Good grief.

It helped me greatly that asking Mavis what topic I should teach had resulted in a shrug of the shoulders and the response, "Whatever you like". I had free rein.

In the minutes before the bell was rung, I remembered that I had been interested in astronomy as a youngster. This hobby had been satisfied by watching *Horizon* programmes until I virtually had space dust coming out of my ears. I reckoned that I had remembered enough to be able to cobble together a lesson on the solar system.

Even though they had met me before, Classes 5 and 6 had that morning wanted to see what they could get away with in the presence of an *Obruni* without a cane. Fundamentally, though, they were a nice bunch; once we had taken time to establish the ground rules, we were fine. The afternoon's lesson finished with the children on the field. A chubby boy called Bright represented the sun, since he was wearing his yellow school shirt (one of the more confusing of the Rev's schools' little foibles was that there were two uniforms – yellow shirts for Mondays, Tuesdays and Fridays; white ones for Wednesdays and Thursdays, as this day was). The others took the roles of some of the planets, and replicated cosmic forces by orbiting Bright. They were even spinning around on their axes – at least to begin with, until a gangly boy called James became dizzy and fell over. Perhaps we did not need to stick to the principles of physics quite so rigidly.

Fun as that had been, I had no intention of carrying on making Science lessons up off the top of my head. For a start, I would very rapidly run out of topics that I knew enough about. More importantly, I needed to teach them something that would appear on their end of term test. Faustina mentioned that she had taught Class 6 a little bit of Science earlier in the term. She knew that mosquitoes were on the scheme of work: they were for all classes, as part of a Government push to educate children about malaria prevention. She had taught that unit, though; and had as much understanding of the rest of the Science curriculum as any other English teacher could be expected to have.

Shortly before teatime, I collared Yaw when he had finished fetching water, and asked him to lend me his Maths and Science classnotes. I knew that he would have no problem with me looking through his work, but gave him a couple of bananas that I had bought on the roadside anyway, as a token of appreciation. The ever-hungry lad was delighted, and sprang off to find his exercise books.

Perusing Yaw's class work, I found that I had a lot to learn. I knew little about seeds, the major topic in Science. The Maths, about sets of numbers and the various operations that could be performed on them, was something that I had seen in the JHS Maths textbook in June. It had looked fiendishly complicated; I had crossed my fingers whenever I looked at a new scheme of work that sets would not appear. Now that they had, the saving grace was that I had a week in which to mug up on the topic, and those for Science – Mavis had told me to concentrate on the younger classes and their times tables over the course of Friday.

I also had put in place an evening class in the library for Form 2, who had lost a Maths lesson with me being at Mount Zion. I knew that not all of the children would turn up, since some of them lived in the next village, along the unlit main road. I did what I could by cajoling Peace into making sure that Belinda and Bernice, who did live in Kwamoso, would show up.

In the event, they were almost an hour late, but at least they came. Maxwell ran fairly regular evening classes for the JHS children, and so my session was not the shock to the system that it might have been had he not done so. Maxwell's were, theoretically, compulsory, so those that lived in Kwamoso almost always came. I doubted that they would have shown up so late to his lesson, and gave them a rollicking until they promised that they would not do it again. In truth, it mattered little to me; I had been spending the time in the library, waiting for Form 2, very usefully, swotting up on seeds.

The Education Service had given a training session for the Holy Hills teachers shortly before the end of the previous academic year. It had gone down well, and a follow-up to it had been planned. Unfortunately, for whatever reason, it never materialised. I had mentioned to the Rev in August that I could deliver part two. Since then, he had acknowledged a few gentle reminders that the offer was still open, but done little else. Out of the blue one morning, Pastor Robert ambled over during First Break, whilst I was sitting, along with the other teachers, listening to Maxwell.

"Lawrie, Proprietor is calling you," he said in his typically understated manner.

I followed Pastor over to the school office, where the Rev sat behind his desk wearing his football shirt. He invited me to sit down.

"You mentioned training for the teachers," he began. I nodded, and he continued.

"When will you be ready to do it?"

"Any time you like, Reverend."

Although I had nothing to show him, I knew exactly what I was going to tell the staff. To build on what we had heard in July, I would talk about planning more varied styles of teaching, and ensuring that lessons started and finished when they should have done. A number of teachers' lessons overran, meaning that time was lost from the subsequent lesson. Mr Daniel was terrible for it. Quite regularly, I was timetabled to teach classes following one of his Science lessons. I usually lost twenty minutes or more whilst the children copied his notes up from the chalkboard.

"Wonderful," he replied. "Then I think that Wednesday afternoon is best."

Wednesday afternoon turned into Wednesday morning. It made sense, since the children had been set off weeding some more of the school compound.

Beginning the meeting in the library, it struck me that Pastor was possibly the most mild-mannered man I had ever met. He was going through all the formalities – such as thanking God for granting us the time to have the session – when a voice from outside yelled, "Pastor, come." Two girls from Class 4, Aysha and Rebecca, rushed through the door. Maxwell stood up, whilst the other teachers remained rooted to their seats, slightly taken aback by the unseemly showing.

Pastor turned around, glanced at the pair, and paused. "Don't speak to Pastor like that," he said quietly, but firmly, as the two little faces looked up at him sheepishly. He then attended to the girls as if nothing had happened. It turned out that they wanted to know how far along a patch of grass they were to cut.

I had a few butterflies in my stomach as Pastor resumed his introduction. I had never formally advised anyone on teaching before. What if they thought I was talking rubbish? How would they respond to the idea of discussing their practice among themselves before feeding back to everyone else?

In the end, most of them listened attentively, to me and each other. Mr Enoch took studious notes, Mr Daniel and Mr Sam jotted down some of the more salient points. I was a bit irritated that Madam Rebecca and Madam Regina had a chat through bits of what I was saying, although it probably concerned their infant classes to a lesser extent than the other year groups.

After a relatively quiet afternoon, during which a few of the teachers asked follow-up questions about what I had told them during the training, Thursday arrived. It was time to go back to Mount Zion.

The first job was to sort the timetable out. The children were set to work weeding, and Mavis, Edwin, Faustina and I set about a piece of paper and drew up a schedule that we were all happy with. There were a few points of contention and several dissatisfied snorts of '*Ah!*' as various lessons were rescheduled. Once we had come to agreement, Faustina stuck the finished timetable up on a wall, Mavis rang the bell, and we gave the children a slightly early break.

Presently, it was time to put into effect the knowledge that I had acquired about seeds. Classes 5 and 6 had decided, as children do, that they were going to try me out again and see what they could get away with. I had almost finished winning them over to my pretence that the inside of a seed *was* in fact a thoroughly exciting subject, when a chicken ran into the classroom and clucked a few times. Despite this being a fairly regular occurrence, in Yarro and Bright's eyes it was something far more worthy of the description 'thoroughly exciting' than seeds would ever be. They decided to launch themselves across the classroom to try to catch it, whilst James jumped around in delight. I was back in the thick of teaching again.

"Unbelievable!" began my tirade, once the offending children were back in their seats, and the witless bird had escaped. A boy called David sniggered as Bright caught his eye. "And what you find funny I fail to understand! *Ah!*" It was the biggest telling off I had given since an unruly class in Britain just over a year before. A point, however, had to be made.

"Everybody go to Madam Mavis' table and line up!" I had noticed that she was not teaching and was instead marking books outside Class 1 and 2's room. A grim silence fell over the seven in the room, and they filed outside. I quietly told the three who had done no wrong that it was only the others who were really in trouble. In front of Mavis' table, I delivered a stern lecture about what I expected from the children. Once Mavis had chipped in her two-penn'orth, that should have been that.

Unfortunately, Edwin had heard the commotion. He marched out of Class 1 and 2's room, swishing his cane through the air. It was only with great effort that I was able to persuade him not to cane the innocents, which, for now, included David the sniggerer. They and I returned to the classroom. Much as I was annoyed with Edwin, I reckoned that Yarro, Bright and James deserved whatever came to them, and left them to their fate. If nothing else, it would make them think twice before getting up to similar antics in the future.

Once the three of them had returned a few minutes later, the rest of the lesson was conducted with no vibrancy whatsoever. The classroom was like a morgue. I felt quite uncomfortable, although knew that I could not do anything that would expose my feelings to the children; that would have shown me to be soft. Indeed, against my scruples, I made the three miscreants clean the toilet block over Second Break to leave them in no doubt of my disgust with their silliness.

Despite, or perhaps because of, this, over the following weeks, I struck up a superb relationship with the class. They were a hard-working and good-natured bunch, who liked a joke but knew exactly when to get down to business again.

It was getting to the point of the year now when I was beginning to have to consider returning to Britain: I had eight weeks left in Ghana. I began to really notice and savour the small things about life in the hills. In the Blue Bar one evening, I looked out across Mamfe Circle and over the coastal plain at the lights of Tema and Accra. It was peaceful, somehow. I felt totally at ease. I thought of Lene, and how happy I was that we had spoken numerous times since she had returned to Denmark that evening in May. At the little market by the Circle, people were busy buying and selling. On the streets, others walked along, going from place to place. Cars rounded the roundabout on their journeys, taxis and tros took people to various destinations. In the bar, people chatted and sipped drinks to a backdrop of music. Everything, it suddenly struck me, was the same as in Britain. Alright, the details were different, but the purpose of life, the *raison d'etre*, was just as it is in the West.

More small but memorable events happened one Saturday. Mid-morning, I had finished reading a chapter of a book that I had borrowed from the library, and felt restless. A short walk would do the trick, I reckoned. I put my shoes on and set off along one of the paths that led off towards the hills outside the village.

"Lawrie!"

The shouted voice caught my attention. I turned around and saw two heads looking through the undergrowth.

"Lawrie!" the voices repeated, "Wait small, we're coming!" Yaw and John were scampering down a slope by now, waving the machetes that they had been using to prune the vegetation around the back of the library and Yaw's house.

"Where are you going?" they asked breathlessly, once they had skidded to a halt by my side.

"To the end of the path," I replied, as John and I started a mini-playfight. Glancing up at a slightly gloomy sky, I added, "As long as it does not start to rain some."

Yaw laughed. "It is only small rain that is coming. Let's go!"

Off we went, chatting away about this and that, whilst the boys periodically took massive swipes at the grass with their machetes. Light drizzle began falling, and grew progressively heavier.

"Are you sure that this is 'small rain'?" I asked Yaw.

"Yes, yes, small rain!" he answered, totally unconcerned. I was sceptical, but we were all enjoying ourselves. We were by now so far from the complex that if the 'big rain' came, even if we had turned round and gone straight back, we would still have been soaked through.

The boys' local knowledge proved right, though. In the second, shorter, rainy season, this was 'small rain' after all. Before too long, it had eased to virtually nothing. The boys jumped around in the puddles and splashed each other. Out of nowhere, John apologised for having been naughty when Lene and I had taught him. I was momentarily overwhelmed by his maturity.

"You're a sensible boy," I told him, when he had finished explaining how much better he felt about school now he had transferred to Holy Hills.

Nearby, an orange tree had shed some of its fruit. Yaw and John used their machetes to peel an orange each, and laughed their delight at the taste of the sweet flavours. I politely declined their offer to peel me one; their stomachs were doubtlessly stronger than mine. I did not like the look of the remnants of undergrowth that were stuck to the machete blades, and were mixing with the flesh of the fruit.

The 'big rain' that Yaw, John and I had managed to avoid came that afternoon. It hammered on the roof of *Obruni* Castle whilst Robin, Roelanda and I looked on. Florence had waved away my offer to help set up buckets to catch the overflow of water from the roof, and instead tasked Dennis and Blackie with the job. Dennis made his way inside once the job was done, whilst Blackie danced around in the rain in his boxer shorts and rubbed the water into his skin. Yaw and John ran over and joined him, chasing each other around as the rain continued to lash down. A little rubber ball appeared from somewhere and a game of volleyball developed over the washing line, which was weighed down by someone's sodden bedsheet. It ended sometime later, when the rain had eased off again. Just in case they were not wet enough, Blackie emptied a small bucket of water over Yaw and was then himself drenched by John. Only Dennis, who had returned just as this began, was unamused – this was the water that he had got soaked setting up the buckets to catch. Before too long, though, he had entered the spirit, throwing a bit more of the water over Blackie as they transferred it to the Rev's main container.

I walked over from the library towards the school buildings at the end of First Break one morning. In one of the classrooms, Maxwell was talking. That was nothing new. From a distance, it sounded as though his voice was coming from either Class 4 or Class 5's room.

"Lawrie, Lawrie!" he called through Class 5's doorway, as I made my way to Class 6's room to drop off a set of flashcards for their French lesson. "I have important news!"

I stuck my head through the window and leaned on the outside wall. "Oh right, what's that?" I asked curiously.

"I am changing my name to Martinson Asare," he announced proudly.

I had learned not to be too surprised by Maxwell. "Why is that?"

It was something to do with how he had lost his birth certificate, and had been to Accra to sort out a duplicate. For some reason – I chose not to ask – he had signed his name as Martinson Asare on the new one. As a result, he was now required to change his name to follow suit. It all sounded rather bizarre.

A short while later, Maxwell popped into Class 6's lesson, just as I was explaining something complex about verb endings. He began writing on the board, as the rest of us looked on. Once he had left, presumably to do the same in the other classrooms, we could see "Maxwell Kwapong change to Martinson Asare" scrawled in chalk. Yaw and his three classmates looked at it, bemused. We broke off from '-er' verbs, and I did my best to explain to them what was going on.

The following day, the newly-named Martinson was setting up a laptop on the teacher's desk in Class 6's room as I strolled in over First Break. What he brought up shocked me to the core. They were pictures that his friend, a journalist, had taken. They showed the effects of a road accident, where a tro had ploughed into the front of one of the huge orange *MetroMass* buses. Apparently it had happened the previous afternoon, not too far away, on a road towards the Volta Region. The consequences were horrific. Most of the other teachers were present, tutting and shaking their heads at the grotesque images. There was a collective gasp at more than one severed arm lying near the ruined tro. As Martinson continued the slide show, we saw pictures of numerous people helping to carry away the bodies of those who had been killed. One man was lying on the roadside, his skull cracked so badly that his brains were oozing out onto the tarmac. Only one of those who had been on board the tro had survived.

That was distressing enough, since we all used the tro-tros, but worse was to follow. I did not find out until the end of the day, but two of Mr Sam's sisters and his infant nephew had been among the victims of the crash. Sam had not been in school that day; clearly this was the reason.

Over the rest of the day, various opinions were expressed about the reasons that accidents are tragically common on the roads in Ghana. Some blamed the state of a significant minority of the vehicles, whose lack of roadworthiness varied from being a bit clapped out, to an accident waiting to happen. Others felt that drivers' irresponsibility, particularly with speeding and overtaking, was the cause; others still felt that it was the fault of the authorities, for not doing enough to curb this imprudence. In truth, in all three views had some merit. Although recent safety awareness measures had led to road accidents becoming less frequent nationwide, their occurrence remained dreadfully high in most regions of the country.

I had a long tro journey to make at the end of the week. Suzy and I had agreed a few weeks previously to make a trip to Donkorkrom, the main town in the little-visited Afram Plains area. This part of the Eastern Region is cut off from much of the surrounding area by Lake Volta, which borders it on two sides.

I took my overnight bag to Mount Zion with me on Friday, and after school I met Suzy in Koforidua, where she had spent the afternoon working. We met a rainstorm – the last throes of the mini-rainy season – in Koff-Town, which set us back by an hour or so. It meant that we ended up staying the night in the busy little town of Nkawkaw, rather than Adawso, the port on the shore of the lake. Arriving in the dark, we nipped into a stall, and asked the people who ran it if they knew of anywhere to stay the night. As luck would have it, the stallholders were very friendly with the owner of a hotel who, they assured us, would give us a "good price" for a room. We chatted to, and laughed with, them, whilst a phone call was made on our behalf to their hotel-owning friend.

"He's coming," the caller announced happily as he put his phone back in his pocket.

The hotel owner was a big chap with glasses and the sort of wide, trustworthy face which would have eased the mind of even the most nervous traveller. His name was Samuel, he said cheerily as he shook first Suzy's hand then mine. He would drive us to his hotel and make sure that we got something to eat. Sure enough, once we had dropped bags our off in a tidy little room, Samuel whisked us off to a chop bar that he knew. Samuel had five children, he told us, two of whom were also called Samuel. The others also had names containing the Biblical prefix or suffix 'el-' or '-el'; he and his wife, he explained, had not considered any names without such religious significance.

Waking up and looking out of the window in the morning light, the stunning scenery of the range of hills leading to the Kwahu Plateau dominated the view. Suzy and I stepped onto the terrace at the side of the hotel and took in the incredible scenery. We had to be pretty quick about it, however, because we were not sure how long a tro journey to Adawso would take. We wanted to get there by ten o'clock, when the first of the twice-daily ferries left, since the second departed at five in the evening. Suzy and I made our way out of the hotel, in what we reckoned from Samuel's rather vague directions ("Go straight, it's not far") was the direction of the tro station. Parked on the roadside a way ahead of us was a *MetroMass* bus, its engine loudly ticking over. As we got closer, a sign reading "DONK RKROM" became visible on the inside of its windscreen. Hardly believing our luck, we bought two of the few remaining tickets and jumped aboard, without any consideration of what misfortune may have befallen the missing 'O'.

The journey up through the hills proved just as spectacular as we had hoped that it would be at six-thirty, when we had seen the landscape from Samuel's terrace. Arriving at Adawso, Suzy and I counted our lucky stars that we had overnighted in Nkawkaw. There was no sign of even the smallest place to stay. Boarding the ferry, we looked out over the spectacular sight of Lake Volta. It was hard to believe that this was part of a man-made lake, that with the largest surface area in the world no less, which had existed for less than fifty years.

The ferry filled up; the last vehicle that boarded was a truck with a gigantic load tied to its trailer. Among the bags of farm produce stood a sheep, balancing somehow on the top of the pile. As the ferry got going, ahead of us we could just about make out our destination across the lake, the port of Ekye. Pronounced 'E-chay', it had a similar small-town look to Adawso. The ubiquitous football pitch stood on the shore, and a joint called the 'Be Nice For Me' spot bar waited for thirsty travellers immediately beyond the port. Next to it, a crowd of hawkers had gathered, selling all sorts of refreshments to people stepping or driving off the ferry.

The bus rumbled forward, and along a series of twisty and bumpy roads. Eventually, we arrived at Donkorkrom. The first job was to find somewhere to stay. We had seen signs through the bus window pointing out two or three guesthouses. The first of these that we went to looked a lovely little place. It had a terrace to sit in, and, more excitingly, a tree which contained two colobus monkeys, which jumped around in its branches. These two little cuties were introduced to us by May, the receptionist, as Peace and Sammy; they looked down at us with the mildest of curiosity.

Suzy and I fancied a decent walk. I had been gradually building my strength back up in the weeks after recovering from malaria. Seven weeks after getting back to work, longish rambles no longer left me feeling totally shattered.

We set off down a little road out of town, and had a wonderful time walking past little settlements with wooden houses, and people who waved friendly greetings. Turning at a junction, we eventually encountered a village. The houses reminded me of the kraals in the northern regions, despite being neither round nor grouped together. In their size, colour and general feel, however, they could well have been in the beautiful north of the country.

Back at the hotel that evening, the owner was sitting on terrace watching the news on TV. He welcomed us, introduced himself as – another! – Samuel when Suzy and I greeted him, and invited us to join him. A report on the Afram Plains area was being aired.

Samuel explained to us that despite being known as the 'Breadbasket of Ghana', the Plains area receives little money from the Eastern Region, of which it is part. As a result, it is one of the poorer areas of the country. President Mahama's National Democratic Congress, however, had pledged in its election manifesto to make the Afram Plains a region in its own right, allowing it to benefit from Government funding. Traditionally an NDC stronghold anyway, the Plains area was strongly backing the party for the upcoming election.

Samuel also mentioned the possibility of opening the wildlife reserve at the northern end of the Afram Plains, the Digya National Park, to the public. Digya, he said, has the same sort of wildlife as Mole National Park in the north. Samuel reckoned that, were it properly organised, opening the park up would boost the Plains' economy, in the same way that Mole generates tourism in the Northern Region. He added, with a note of caution, that this would take time. Much infrastructure would have to be constructed to cope with visitors, even in modest numbers.

Waiting in Ekye the following afternoon for the ferry back across the lake, I went to have a look at the fishing boats which were moored up. They had wonderful names such as 'Judgment Day' and 'Oh Lord Help Me'. Stepping back from the edge of the water I tripped and went arse over elbow onto the rocks. A couple of blokes standing some distance away laughed once they realised that I was unhurt. We got chatting; the more talkative of the pair was a chap called Peter, who turned out to be the head of languages in a school on the other side of the lake, in a town near Adawso. He told of how his father had owned a cocoa farm on land which is now under the water. When the Akosombo Dam was constructed in the 1960s, creating the lake, the plantation was lost. He was one of many thousands who lost their livelihoods for little or no compensation. Despite this, Peter was not remotely bitter towards the lake; in fact, he welcomed it. He reckoned that, contrary to what Suzy and I had previously been told, the lake made the Plains more, rather than less, accessible, because of the ferry service.

Pastor Robert appeared in the doorway of Form 3's room shortly before the end of lesson three. The Rev wanted to speak to all of the teachers in the library during the following lesson, which preceded Second Break. Since the meeting concerned their wages, Pastor added, my presence was voluntary.

Discussion of the teachers' meagre earnings (only eighty cedis a month) was none of my business, and I wanted to get my scheduled lesson with Form 2 in. I took him up on the offer of giving the meeting a miss.

Whilst the rest of the children had a lesson off, I gave Form 2 a recap on their Maths topic, about enlargement of shapes, in readiness for a class test the following week. We worked through a few examples together and then the children set off, heads down, on their own. Daniel, the boisterous nineteen-year-old from Form 3, poked his head through the window and looked with interest at the chalkboard and the general scene in Form 2's room.

Sometime later, I heard a voice next door in Form 1's room, beginning what sounded like a lesson. That was strange, I thought, since the other teachers were, hopefully, being told that a backlog of late wages would shortly be paid. Moreover, the small bits of dialogue that I could make out seemed also to be concerning the enlargement topic. That too was weird, since it was not on Form 1's scheme of work, and *I* was their Maths teacher.

I helped a girl called Rebecca find the area of an enlarged triangle, and forgot about it as I buzzed around the classroom assisting the children.

"You have one minute left," I advised Form 2 a while later. "Please get ready to stop work."

Pens and pencils scratched away in books as the children completed their last bit of working out. We would, I explained, go through the answers one by one. Next door, I could hear the voice telling Form 1 the same.

Something still did not seem quite right, though. Was it Daniel who was conducting the lesson? Surely not.

I popped my head around the doorframe. The Form 3 student stood buoyantly at the front of the room, with a piece of chalk in his hand and his chest puffed out.

"Are you teaching?" I asked.

"Yes!" he beamed in response. "I taught them enlargement."

Looking at the board, it turned out that not only had he been teaching them the same topic, but had set the same questions. He must have memorised them from Form 2's board. I was somewhat impressed, as much by his memory and willingness to teach, as his gumption to actually try it. A more practical thought overtook me once I was back with Form 2. The standard of Daniel's Maths work, whilst reasonable, was rarely anything to boast about. Had he been teaching them correctly?

Shortly afterwards, Peace, Bernice and friends were offering their workings-out and final answers for the questions which I had set them. As they did so, I heard Daniel's voice through the wall, working out the answers for 'his' class; thankfully, the methodology sounded correct. When Caleb had rung the bell for Second Break, I found Daniel and quizzed him further.

"Did you get these answers?" I held out the workings-out that I had done before the lesson.

He began to answer, but a fit of giggles stopped him. After a few attempts, he had recovered his composure sufficiently. He explained that he had simply waited for me to go through the answers with my class, listened to what had been said, and repeated it to the Form 1s. The cheeky devil probably had them thinking that he was a mathematical expert. I had to hand it to him, though. He had pulled it off very well, and, glancing at the chalkboard, his sums were exact copies of those on Form 2's board next door.

It was a story that I related to Martinson and the other teachers over Second Break. They laughed cheerily at Daniel's audacity and called him over to rib him for it. They were especially chipper that lunchtime, since they had been paid up to date by the Rev (I had not realised that many of them, including Pastor Robert, had not been paid for the previous two months, largely because of a shortfall in payment of school fees) and had also been told that their salaries may increase to a hundred cedis a month in the near future. To cap off their excitement, the Rev had relayed the news that the Government had declared a public holiday for the coming Friday, in two days' time, for the start of the Muslim festival of Eid-al-Adha.

This was news to me as well. A three-day weekend was as welcome in Kwamoso as it was anywhere else. A trip was in order.

Chapter 16 – Jaunts away, and meeting the police

The guidebook claimed that the coastal town of Senya Beraku, which lies between Accra and Cape Coast, contains "Perhaps the noisiest children in Ghana." As much as anything, this was an accolade that reflected that the author had never met Peace in Kwamoso; even so, the local kids must have quietened down a bit since the book had been researched. The numerous groups of youngsters that I passed as I walked along Senya's stall-lined streets were if anything less expressive at seeing a foreigner than those in other towns.

It was bank holiday weekend, for Eid-al-Adha, and I intended to enjoy the three-day break by looking around this picturesque little town and relaxing on the beaches that extended beyond it. After a stop-off in Accra, I arrived in the afternoon. The shadows were just beginning to lengthen over the streets.

Very excitingly, I had booked a room at the colonial-era castle. Having been restored, it now serves as just about the only accommodation in the town. Originally built by the Dutch, in 1724, as an outpost for gold merchants, the name Fort of Good Hope became somewhat inappropriate once it became a centre of the slave trade. More appropriate, however, is that despite the fort's transformation into a guesthouse, it retains its grim aura, and is a monument of the horrors faced by the captive people.

The first task was to find the place. Without a map of the town, and no visible sign of the fort, common sense had to take hold. It would be near to the sea, and therefore down the slight slope upon which the town was built.

Arriving there after taking a left at the end of the town's main street, I was led up to the rooms which used to serve as the Dutch soldiers' quarters. A friendly bloke called Sebastian ran the place, along with his wife and family. Standing with him on the ramparts, a picturesque urban scene stretched out in front of us. To the right lay a small and crowded fishing beach. On the near side, the fishermen were beginning to pack up after a day in their boats or on the shore. The empty far end looked good for an evening swim. Ahead was the town, with various buildings dotting the view of the gently inclining landscape, but none dominating it.

Sebastian broke off his questions about what had brought me to Ghana in general, and Senya in particular.

"You found this place easily?" he asked.

"Yes, no problem," I replied. It was a puzzling question, since the walk from town had been both short and straightforward.

"People sometimes do not know the fort," he explained. This did not surprise me; many tourists often do not know much about the places they visit. I was just about to articulate this thought, when Sebastian continued.

"The local people, I mean. They call this place the 'castle'. The word 'fort' means nothing to them. You have to ask the way to the 'castle'."

Once Sebastian had put me in the know about the phraseology, he resumed his casual questioning and told me a bit more about the fort, sorry, the *castle*.

"Slaves were held in the dungeons. Males on that side," he said, pointing in the direction of the western wall, "And females on the opposite side. The Dutch people, sometimes they died of diseases. These two graves are soldiers who had malaria." He gesticulated towards two stones next to our feet which I had not noticed, on which epitaphs were chiselled.

"The Dutchmen remembered what had happened in Elmina," he explained as he directed my attention to the cannons that poked out through gaps in the wall on the land-facing ramparts. Clearly Sebastian knew his history well, and we had a laugh about the Portuguese losing St. George's Castle to the Dutch, who had attacked from the too-lightly defended St. Jago Hill.

Presently, Sebastian excused himself and returned to his task of drawing water from the well in the castle's courtyard. He left me to take in the view of the beach and town. The sun was edging towards the horizon. A dip in the sea was a most pleasant prospect.

It looked like one that I would not be able to enjoy, however, as I finished descending a set of steps leading from the castle to the beach – several boats were blocking the way onto the sand. I turned around, and was about to head back up the steps, when I heard a voice calling.

"*Obruni!*"

Clearly he was addressing me.

"Pass here!"

I turned and found that the voice was that of a rugged fisherman, who was moving an enormous fishing net from inside his boat, and inviting me to climb through his vessel and a couple of others that were beached next to it.

"*Meda ase pa pa!*" I beamed as I made my way onto the sand. Thank you very much!

The Gulf of Guinea's water was beautifully warm as I splashed around and dived under the waves, which lapped up onto the shore with the rhythmic scrape of the sand and pebbles. It felt so refreshing to be back in the sea again.

Mooching back later, the kind fisherman was still there. He told me about the crabs and anchovies that he and his colleagues fished for, and which of the street traders to go to for the best fish or bean stew.

As night fell, Accra's lights and, higher up, the nearly-full moon illuminated the sky to the east. Gazing out at the scene, with the sound of the waves breaking to my right, I once again felt so privileged to be living in this wonderful country.

A few miles along the coast from Senya, the village of Fete has been gentrified and is, I had heard from Sebastian, now more of an upmarket tourist resort. The sort of place, in short, that I had no intention of visiting. From the Fort of Good Hope's walls that morning, though, it looked as though there was a deserted beach lined with palm trees right along the expanse of coastline between these two diverse settlements. Not only would it be a good-length walk to get there, it would be a picturesque one as well.

I was not disappointed. Walking to the beach, sitting on its sand and diving under the breakers during numerous spells in the sea, the day passed in no time. A lagoon just inland was a pure, clear blue. It was thoroughly relaxing, the only drama being the sight of a teenage boy shinning up the trunk of one of the palm trees. A machete was tied around the lad's waist, which he used to cut loose a few coconuts. He threw them to the sand and shinned back down the trunk. The speed with which it happened was incredible.

Once again, the area around the school buildings had become rather too overgrown for Mr Martinson and Pastor Robert's liking, and the children were weeding it. I sat with Mr Daniel and Mr Sam, back in school after the deaths of his sisters and nephew, in the 'office' under the tree. We nattered away about this and that as Daniel marked his Science books, and Sam and I prepared our lessons for later in the week. Sam's phone played the favourite local songs and almost covered the sound made by a gaggle of the other teachers near the primary school buildings. Unsurprisingly, it was Martinson who was doing the talking.

I picked Daniel's brain about photosynthesis, having found out from Madam Pat that this was the next topic on Class 6's Science curriculum. I had forgotten much of what had seen me through GCSE Biology more than a decade earlier. An expert's pointers were needed for my next lessons with Yarro's class at Mount Zion, and Daniel's knowledge was beginning to ring bells.

"So water and carbon dioxide are transformed, by the energy of the sunlight, to make what?" Daniel asked me quizzically, in the way that teachers do. Clearly he was seeing what he was working with.

"Mmm, I know that one is oxygen, but I forget the other thing. Something that makes the plant grow?" I offered.

"Glucose!" Daniel cried. "Glucose is the food of the plant!"

"Of course," I joined in. "And it's made using that chloro-whatsit in the leaves." I hoped that Daniel would not be too harsh on my ignorance.

"Chlorophyll," he corrected, smiling. "That's a pigment that gives the leaves their green colour," he added, probably suspecting – correctly – that I had forgotten this as well. Words flowed out of his mouth, as if they were water from the fountain of knowledge. It gave me a great basis for my lesson preparation, and plenty to think about in terms of re-familiarising myself with all things scientific. Daniel was a fantastic scientist. Holy Hills' classes doubtless miss his insights now that he has left the school to take up medical training, which he did a year or so later, having saved enough money to secure a place in college.

It was a shame, in fact, that so few of the teachers' long-term career plans involved teaching. Madam Paulina and Madam Pat, for example, had their hearts set on joining the police force. Mr Sam aspired to follow in his uncle's footsteps and become an officer in the army. Only Martinson held definite aspirations of going to training college and becoming a qualified teacher. For the others, the money was not enough, long term. Qualified teachers are paid a little over three hundred cedis a month, about £120, a sum far less than other jobs which require an education beyond school level. Those teachers in Britain who complain about their relatively modest, although far from low, salaries, should remember how lucky they are to take home what is, at worst, a great deal more than just a 'living wage'.

To put it into context, schooling at Senior High School costs students four hundred cedis a term – just over a hundred per month – even at state-run schools. SHS is not compulsory; children choose whether or not to continue their education following Form 3. Only in the three northern regions is senior education free. The previous government had abolished SHS fees there some years ago, in order to further the development of the poorer part of Ghana, and give its population a greater opportunity to have a share in the relative prosperity of the rest of the country.

Free SHS is something that may be extended nationwide in future years. It was included in the election manifesto of the governing National Democratic Congress. Meanwhile, the main opposition, the New Patriotic Party, placed it as one of their central planks of policy, along with free healthcare.

One morning I was sorting a few things out in my bedroom. Florence's radio was on, but I was not paying particular attention to what it was playing. Suddenly, a tune started up which was somehow familiar. It had been a long, long time since I had last heard them, but were the *Venga Boys* being aired on the local station? I listened carefully.

The song had reached its tell-tale chorus which begins, "The Venga Bus is coming." I was beginning to wonder what this remnant of the nineties-into-noughties pop scene was doing on Mamfe's *Green FM*, when I noticed that the words were slightly different to how I remembered them. In fact, as the music petered out after twenty seconds or so, I realised that it was not a song at all. A woman's voice was persuading listeners that they should vote for the NPP's presidential candidate, a gentleman called Nana Akufo Addo. Hearing it again the next day, I realised that the main NPP slogan formed the advert's lyrics. It proclaimed that, rather than the Venga Bus, "Free SHS is coming."

The election race was hotting up now, with not much more than a month to go until Ghana went to the polls. Across the region, and, I presumed, across the nation, posters were displaying the 'Free SHS' slogan. The radio frequently played the NPP jingle. Debra took a particular liking to the catchy melody, racing to the radio and dancing to its beat.

Many a discussion was struck up among people in the complex, and the teachers at Holy Hills and Mount Zion, about the likely outcome of the election. Most people around Kwamoso supported the NPP, feeling that the Government had not fulfilled many of its pledges. The Rev and family, for example, had expected electricity to be installed much earlier than it had been. The delay, I was informed by a great many people, was the fault of the NDC council in Koforidua. It also helped the NPP that Nana Akufo Addo was a local man; he came from a town, Kyebi, in the Eastern Region. Finally, many people, particularly among the teachers, were genuinely in favour of the party's education policy.

Over First Break one morning, Madam Paulina and I were discussing the likelihood of free SHS becoming reality. We were on the way back to school, after she had insisted that I come to see the house that she had recently moved into in Kwamoso (until a few weeks earlier she had lived in Akropong). I mentioned a trip that Suzy and I had made a while before, to Larteh, a small town a few miles east of Mamfe. Its church boasts a tall tower, which we had ascended to look at the landscape. We had hitched a lift with the headteacher of the local SHS. He hoped for the scrapping of the fees, as so many of his students had fallen behind with payments, to the tune of hundreds of cedis. Paulina, too, was in favour, and was cautiously optimistic that, if the NPP were elected, fees would be abolished. "But it will take time," she added.

I nodded; of course it would take time. Paulina then expanded, along a line that only a minority of people had taken. "If we have free SHS, then more people will want to go to school. So we will need more classrooms, more teachers, and more of everything else. Whatever the NPP says about opening more colleges and training more teachers, it will take longer than they think."

The question of how long Paulina thought that this would be remained unanswered. The sight of Mr Martinson, Mr Sam, Madam Pat and some of the other teachers walking towards us broke the conversation.

They were going to Benedicta's house. A Tuesday, this was a second day in a row that she had been absent from Form 1; her two younger brothers said that she had malaria. Paulina and I turned around and joined the others in heading towards Benedicta's parents' place. We arrived at the shaded terrace under the overhanging section of the roof and looked on at poor Benedicta, who sat weakly on a chair. Her mother explained that she had become ill on the Friday evening and deteriorated thereafter. Now that she had some tablets from the hospital, she was beginning to get better. All the teachers wished her a speedy recovery, and most gave her a blessing as well.

A couple of days later, I approached Quarters Junction having walked back from Mount Zion. A familiar figure was crossing the road ahead of me.

"Martinson!" I called. "*Wo ko en?*"

"Lawrie, Lawrie!" he called back. "I am going to Benedicta's, to see how she is. Will you come?"

I most certainly would. It was most caring of Martinson to do this, and quite typical of him. Much as he swished the cane around in the mornings, he took a genuine interest in the children, especially those who had been in 'his' Class 6 during the previous academic year.

Benedicta was much more chipper than she had been two days previously. She was even at the stage where she could again boss her brothers about as they did the family laundry. Benedicta's mother came out of the house to welcome us.

"Mr Martinson, Mr Lawrie! *Ete sen?!*" she greeted.

She thanked us for coming, and then spoke to Martinson in Twi, which he translated for me every so often. The gist of it was that Benedicta was recovering well, as we could see. Benedicta's mother nodded in the direction of her daughter, who was scolding the smaller of her siblings for neglecting to rinse a shirt properly. Benedicta would be back in school, her mother hoped, at the start of the following week. Our student was delighted to see us, and smiled up at us as we asked after her health anyway. Sure enough, on the Monday, Benedicta was back with the ranks of Form 1, and being caned along with the others who were not wearing their uniform correctly.

I was eating breakfast one morning along with Roelanda, Robin and a new volunteer called Jodie, who had begun at the Mount Zion children's home.

"I'm going to Akosombo on Saturday," I told them. "The dam and Lake Volta are meant to be really interesting. Does anyone want to come with me? We'll get going after breakfast." There was a general mutter of approval. I joked, possibly inappropriately, but to satisfactory amusement, that we could whistle the *Dam-busters* tune, before conversation moved on to something else.

The next few days passed by without a great deal of fuss. I was woken up by Nana in the mornings with his blasted loudhailers, then taught my lessons, shot the breeze with the other teachers and chuckled through the evening gatherings in *Obruni Castle*.

It came to Thursday. Roelanda was, as had begun to be customary, the first out for breakfast. "I was talking with the volunteers in the Blue Bar last night, about Akosombo," she said.

I looked at her, mildly curious.

"We are going there on Saturday," she continued. "Do you want to come? Someone mentioned earlier in the week that the dam and Lake Volta are worth seeing." She paused. "We could even whistle the *Dam-busters*."

I rolled my eyes.

"That's a nice idea, Roe. I'd like it," I answered, with a wry smile. "Shall we set off after breakfast?"

So I met a whole new crowd of westerners who had come over to work with the volunteering company. Other than Suzy and those that I lived with, I had come across few *Obrunis* in the previous weeks.

The lake and dam, which was built as Kwame Nkrumah's flagship hydro-electric power station, are a few miles north of Akosombo. All visitors must report to the visitor centre located in the town itself.

Arriving there, we were asked by a stern lady with glasses if we had booked a tour. Her cold expression turned almost glacial when we answered that we had not. We had to find transport to get up to the lake, she instructed, before we could buy tickets to be shown around the dam. Robin and I were unsuccessful in our attempt to wangle the group's way onto one of the tour buses that were going there. They were all full to, and in some cases beyond, capacity. Much as we tried, no amount of persuasion could encourage a bending of the rules.

In the end, we found three other visitors who were in a similar position to us. They lived in the Western Region, and were passing through Akosombo on the way to visiting relatives further north. We found a tro driver, negotiated a price for a ride up to the dam, and scuttled back to the stern lady's desk to secure our places on the tour.

The dam is built on the southern-most tip of the lake; on its other side, the River Volta flows towards the sea. Walking along the dam's length, it was easy to imagine that the rocky hills which provided the backdrop to this part of the lake were once the boundaries of the River Volta's fertile valley.

That all changed in 1961, when Nkrumah decided to flood the area and create the dam. Over four years until 1965, American, Canadian and Italian companies worked on its construction. Today, the power station generates sixty percent of Ghana's electricity. Six massive chutes direct water from the lake to feed an equal number of turbines, which use the fast-flowing current to turn a mighty generator.

Nkrumah was most proud of the completed dam, and ordered a Presidential house to be built overlooking it. In contrast, many local residents, having lost their livelihoods beneath the new lake, were considerably less thrilled with the facility. Ten thousand of them filed a petition and won compensation. Other affected people, inspired by this, applied for, and in some cases received, redress. This took either the form of direct payment or a waiving of their children's school fees. I looked across the water and remembered talking to Peter, the teacher who I had met at Ekye: clearly his father had not been one of successful claimants.

In the days before going, I had, somewhat unrealistically, harboured hopes of mooching around the lake and having a little swim in the water; perhaps an ice cream would round the day off. My bubble had been burst, however, even before I left the tro. Numerous security personnel guarded the high metal fence which prevents unauthorised access to the lake. It made perfect sense, really; this was Lake Volta, not the Lake District! The authorities would not have wanted anyone, least of all a silly tourist out for a dip, to be getting on the way of such an important part of the national infrastructure. Instead, after the walk up and down the dam, we *Obrunis* and our Ghanaian acquaintances piled back into the tro and headed into Akosombo once more. The westerners bade a safe journey to the three with whom we had shared the tour, and made a plan for the rest of the day. There was time to find something to eat, in a little place overlooking the river, before returning to the Akwapim Hills, significantly more knowledgeable for the day's activities.

At school, we were nearly two-thirds of the way through the term; Pastor pointed out to the Rev that a break was in order. He was in agreement, and declared a day's holiday at Holy Hills and Mount Zion. This seemed rather mean, when compared with the half-tem weeks that schools in Britain enjoy. It was usual allowance, though, and the children and teachers would be able, however briefly, to recharge their batteries.

Except for Form 3; the Rev reckoned that their batteries had not been used sufficiently to require re-charging. They had still not cottoned on to the idea that they should do some studying outside lessons, or revise for tests. Martinson announced to a rather grumpy Ishmael and co. that they would have to come in for the morning, and crack on with their lessons. The Rev asked me to help out. I had intended to go to Cape Coast in the mid-term break, but I was glad to stay behind; there was plenty of Maths that Form 3 needed to practice before their end of term exam from the Education Service. Martinson and I would have the class for half the morning each.

Since we had not talked about who would teach first, I made my way over to school before eight o'clock. I hoped to teach the first half, when the children's minds were fresher. Martinson had beaten me to it, though; his intention had been the same as mine. It was fair enough, I reckoned. We had a chat until the children arrived, whereupon Martinson began teaching.

I filled the time with the laundry and planning the next week's lessons. At the time that First Break was usually coming to an end, I got ready to go back into school. Crossing the complex, there was no sign of any of the Form 3s. There could have been any number of reasons for that, though. Whilst unexpected, their absence certainly did not trouble me.

Rounding a corner to Form 3's room, I could make out some figures through the doorway. Coming closer and peering in, it looked as if the eleven members of the class were all there, standing around Martinson's desk. They were engaged in a rather heated discussion, in Twi.

What could be happening?

I quietly walked into the room and discovered that the main protagonists were Daniel, Kwasi Owusu, and Martinson. There were numerous finger-pointings, interruptions, and a great deal of '*Ah's*' being grunted in disproval of something or other. Whatever it was, it seemed to be of vital importance. Arguments and counter-arguments – or were they accusations and counter-accusations? – were bandied back and forth with a good deal of passion. Periodically one of the onlookers chipped in, on one side or the other, with some related point that brought on another bout of verbal jousting between the three main participants.

I snapped out of the stunned state that I had dropped into, standing motionless near the doorframe, and laid my Maths textbook on a table next to Ishmael.

"What's going on?" I asked him.

"There is a disagreement," he advised me, and appeared to leave it at that.

Rather helpfully, though, after a moment he carried on. "It is between Sir Martinson and Kwasi Owusu, about money."

Crikey, this sounded unpromising. I tried to make my presence as discreet as possible, although I was actually intrigued to see what was happening and how it would be resolved. Whatever it was, breaktime was going to have to be extended.

As if a switch had been flicked, the tone of the debate around the teacher's desk changed. The mildly confrontational atmosphere became relaxed and cheerful. There was a great deal of backslapping; Martinson, Kwasi Owusu and Eunice clapped each other's hands and clicked each other's fingers, whilst Bismark, Ishmael and Leticia did a little dance in the doorway. Daniel leant on a table and joked with Collins about something.

I caught up with Martinson as he mooched out of Form 3's room, in discussion with Grace.

"What was that all about?" I asked, nonplussed, when they had finished.

"Kwasi Owusu, *ah!*" Martinson snorted. It was the type of response that Ghanaians give when they have claimed the high moral ground from someone. "Yesterday, after school, I went with the Form 3s to watch football at the town park," Martinson began explaining, referring to the pitch in the middle of Kwamoso. As if it were an epic of heroism and spurned love, Martinson told me what had happened. Kwasi Owusu had seen a man selling ice creams, and decided that he fancied one. Not having any money, he borrowed some from Daniel and bought all of the girls a chocolate flavoured cone. "But he did not buy me one!" lamented Martinson. "So today I had to tell him off!"

"So," I began my lesson when everyone had returned from break. "If there is a full ice cream cart of eighty-four ice creams, and a boy buys seven of them, what is the fraction that he buys?" I asked Form 3 to get their mathematical minds ticking over.

Bismark was lightning with mental arithmetic. His hand shot up in the air.

"Seven over eighty-four, you cancel it to one twelfth," he fired at me.

"Good lad," I replied. "Tell me, would you have been kind and shared one of the ice creams with Mr Martinson, or given them all to the girls because you fancy one of them?"

"*Ah!*" grunted Kwasi Owusu, jumping to his feet whilst everyone else hooted with laughter. He began to say something, realised that he would only be digging himself a hole, and sat down again. He sheepishly twiddled his pen between his index finger and thumb whilst I wrote some algebra on the board.

"Expand these equations," I instructed them. "Take them out of the brackets, like you would take ice cream out of its wrapper." Kwasi Owusu put his head in his hands, groaned and peered at the sums through the gaps between his fingers.

With the exams beginning to loom on the horizon, I offered to help Martinson with the class that he ran for all the JHS students on a Saturday morning. He had always assured me that he was managing fine with these classes whenever I had asked him earlier in the term. Now, though, I reckoned that he would be willing for me to take some of the children for lessons on topics specific to their year group. It was getting to the stage, moreover, where I could do with all of the teaching time that I could get, particularly with Forms 2 and 3.

I intended to give them class tests for Maths over the coming week, and wanted to hammer in the details and methodologies of the various topics that would be examined. They did well in that Saturday's lesson, which made it all the more infuriating when, three days later marking their tests, I found that most papers were littered with wildly inaccurate or half-finished answers.

BraKofi was sitting with me when I was half-way through Form 3's papers.

"How am I going to get them to learn things? What does Eunice think she's doing here?!" I grumbled, holding her test up. It was more in exasperation than any hope that BraKofi would give me a detailed breakdown of exactly why she had subtracted a number that she should have multiplied.

I cast my mind back to the school in Britain where I had worked. Doubtless, there, numerous people, with fancy job titles beyond 'subject teacher', would have flapped around. They would have compared numerous data (both relevant and irrelevant) with the test scores, before setting up all sorts of different strategies that would have been branded 'Intervention'. Additional classes would have been set up and official letters sent home, and that would only have been the start of it. Old sandpaper voice would probably have co-ordinated the whole thing, whilst personally doing as little as possible.

"Cane them." BraKofi was looking at me as though I had just finished watching *Back to the Future* and not noticed that there had been some time-travel.

He paused, and then elaborated. "They only respect their work if you cane them."

"Mmm, we'll see," I replied evasively. I doubted that it would have had any effect. BraKofi had caned the children several times himself without transforming any of them into Carol Vorderman. "We'll come back to these topics in class."

We did. Form 3 got a rollicking the next day, and re-wrote their tests over Second Break the day after that. They were little better, but it served notice to them that they needed to work harder. Martinson had ambled into the classroom during the enforced re-sit.

"What is this?" he asked. "It's Second Break."

I explained; Martinson grunted an acknowledgement. I hoped that he and the other teachers would take note. Either way, when Eunice complained in passing to BraKofi that evening about what I had done, he sent her packing with a flea in her ear.

It was revealing, and amusing, to see the different worldly perceptions of the children. One morning, as I was walking over to begin Form 2's French lesson, Peace, Bernice, Belinda, Rebecca and a new student called Solomon were walking the other way.

"Where are you going?" I asked them, a little indignantly.

"Please, Sir Lawrie, we are coming," Peace replied, without breaking stride.

I knew that they would, so it was no particular problem. I also knew, although the children did not, that there would be no French exam at the end of term. There was no sign of a new French teacher coming to replace me after Christmas, and so I was privately on a bit of a wind down with the subject.

In the meantime, I hovered around and took in the sunshine. Mr Daniel's voice rasped through the humid air from Form 3's room. "Mr Lawrie! Please come!"

I wandered over. Daniel stood before the class, looking rather amused. They had been discussing the composition of the atmosphere, I could see from the notes on the board.

"Leticia wants to know if you white people live in the atmosphere," Daniel told me, doing mightily well to keep a straight face.

"Sir Lawrie," she cut in, her voice laced with curiosity. "You always say that your place is very cold, and that you think that this place is hot. Well, I know that the atmosphere is cold, so do you live there?"

It was logical enough, I supposed. Daniel mentioned the seasons. I explained about how the tilt of the earth's axis makes the northern hemisphere much colder in the winter compared to the equatorial climate.

"You would hate the snow that we get in my place," I told Leticia, noticing out of the corner of my eye that Peace and Belinda were coming back towards their classroom, and the other three were following some distance behind. "It's cold, cold, cold. But I'll tell you about that another time."

My final weekend away from Kwamoso took me back into the Volta Region, to the town of Amedzofe in the Avatime Hills. From there, I would walk up the highest of them, Mount Gemi. A series of tro rides took me to a village called Fume at the base of the hills, and I walked the rest of the way. It was a delightful day, hot and sunny, yet with a slight breeze: perfect for a ramble. Gazing at the scenery, it was easy to pick out Mount Gemi, as it has a large metal cross marking its peak.

The route through the hills passed through a tiny village called Biakpa, and on to a junction town, Vane. Dramatically, the road was undergoing massive maintenance. Being a Saturday, there was no work ongoing, so the massive Chinese-built diggers and bulldozers stood idle on the verge. Passing cars kicked up huge quantities of dust as they passed. It was an incredible scene, even without the stunning views of the hills, and a plain which stretched to the River Volta. At one point, a taxi pulled up next to me. A middle-aged lady wound down the back window and asked if I wanted to get in, so I did not have to walk. I politely declined, and she cautioned me to "Drink water, the sun is too, too hot!" It was all very sweet and caring.

A steep incline for a mile or so led to Amedzofe itself. The guidebook had made a song and dance about going to the tourist office, to register myself as a guest in the town and seek either directions or a guide to the summit of Mount Gemi. It all seemed a trifle unnecessary, since the path to the mountain was not only visible along its slope but also signposted. I reckoned that it would be courteous, though, to let the tourist office know that I was around. Dropping in turned out to be a great decision, for I got chatting to a wonderful fellow called Godwin. Working with the local tourist board, he had published a book about the area, which he intended to distribute around Ghana.

Godwin's knowledge was fantastic. The Avatime Hills had been part of German Togoland, he said, until Gold Coast soldiers expelled the Germans during the First World War. Mount Gemi's name is based on the acronym of the German Evangelical Missionary Church. The cross at its peak was erected in November 1939, when the church celebrated its fiftieth anniversary; Germany's religious influence had long outlasted its colonial one. Godwin was convinced, although I was less sure, that there was a secret German communication post somewhere on the other side of the mountain. During the Second World War, Godwin persuaded me, it had been used to keep in touch with the high and mighty in Berlin.

Godwin moved on from the history of the mountain, and told me about his latest work. He pulled out of a desk drawer an exercise book containing a handwritten set of notes on Rasta-culture which was, apparently, three-quarters finished. Although he did not look it, having short hair and being clean shaven, Godwin was a Rasta-man himself. He was aware that Rastafarianism is frowned upon by some people. The book, he explained, was to put the record straight that it is about more than simply music and marijuana.

"Even in the Bible, they had Rasta-men!" he exclaimed. I looked blankly at him.

"They were the Nazarites," Godwin added. "Samson was one of them!"

Breakfast at the summit of Mount Gemi the following morning was breath-taking. Up in the patchy cloud, the Volta Region was laid out below me like a map. To the west, Biakpa, Fume and other, more distant settlements lay dotted around the largely green landscape; roads, visible as little more than lines, connected them. North and east, beyond a valley, lay the hills which bordered Togo. I cast my mind back to Wli and Mount Afadjato earlier in the year, before the sound of Ghana's pop music returned me to the present. Catchy lyrics floated up from a village called Gbadzemi, which was nestled, almost beneath me, in the valley. This was Ghana at its finest.

"Oh, Sir Lawrie, why?!"

Leticia had just found out about snowball fights. She did not ever want to have one.

It was shortly after closing at Holy Hills, and I was explaining British winters to her and Eunice. As I was telling them, to their horror, of how one's breath becomes visible in the cold air, Augustine from the volunteering company wandered over. I had not seen him for a long time. We shook hands, and got chatting whilst the two teenagers skipped away. He was ostensibly here to see the Rev, but decided that the chief could wait a while. He had been working very hard, he said, with the other volunteers for whom he was responsible, and was looking forward to having a week off soon to go to Bolgatanga to visit his family.

There had been an accident on the road into Mamfe, Augustine said. A tro had overturned and caught fire. Fortunately, no-one had been hurt, but it looked bad.

Augustine reckoned that the Government and police were to blame for the frequency of accidents, through not clamping down on dangerous drivers.

"What happens in your country if people are driving dangerously?" he asked.

I explained about driving bans and the variety of offences that receive lesser punishments. Augustine was pleased, albeit slightly surprised, that points are put on driving licenses for minor speeding offences, or going through red lights – "In Accra, everyone does that, now and again. We wouldn't be able to keep up!"

There was nothing unexpected about this comment. Several months before, it had been mentioned to me that a sign on the Mamfe-Koforidua road, which I had assumed to be indicating the speed limit, was in fact simply advisory; an enforced restriction did not exist. The police also deal rather unsatisfactorily with the issue of overload on public transport. Officers turn a blind eye once the driver has slipped a cedi note into their hand. This represents good business for the driver, since tickets from Koff-Town to Akropong sell for two cedis a pop. Another day, a chap who gave me a lift back to Kwamoso in his car told me how a similar process allows drivers to obtain the equivalent of an MOT certificate for their vehicle, regardless of its roadworthiness. The banger in question does not even need to visit the garage, provided a few extra bank notes are passed across the front desk.

Pastor Robert walked into Form 3's classroom during their Maths lesson. It was the most inopportune moment. Working out median averages from a frequency table of statistics is neither intrinsically interesting nor easy. I had fired some of my best bolts earlier in the lesson in an attempt to inspire the teenagers, working out the average number of containers of water that the class had fetched the previous day, and of goals that they had scored in their most recent game of football. They had struggled with the process thus far, and were flagging. I was beginning to run out of ideas as to how to bring the methodology across to them; this was the first time since algebra in July that it had been painfully clear to me that I was no Maths teacher. To make matters worse,

I was rather tired. Nana had clocked in to work early that morning. His voice had boomed through the village from half past three, with such vehemence that it was a wonder that the metal of the information centre's loudhailers had not cracked.

"Good morning Pastor," chirped Form 3. They rose to their feet as much in relief that they had a break from finding the total frequency as from the formality of greeting.

"Good morning class. Ooh, sit down, sit down!" Pastor's voice was as silky smooth as ever. He turned to me.

"Good morning Lawrie," he greeted me warmly. I reciprocated.

"Proprietor would like to see you at First Break," Pastor continued.

I wondered what was coming. Visiting the Rev in school hours usually meant more work. Usually I was quite happy to oblige, as with the teacher training. It had been rather more awkward, however, the two times when he had asked me to interview potential students – Solomon in Form 2 had been the more recent of these. The first interview, the Rev had insisted, was to be done in French, as it was the favourite subject of the interviewee. Victoria was in Form 3 at another school, but wanted to attend Martinson's Saturday classes as well. To my knowledge, not a thought of uttering a word of French in these lessons had ever crossed Martinson's mind. He could manage *comment t'appelles-tu?*, but that was about his limit. Despite this, and Victoria's apprehension at conversing with a stranger in what was – at best – her third language, the girl was apparently an ever-present at the weekend.

Half an hour after Pastor's visit, Caleb rang the bell for First Break. With Form 3 not much more clued-up on the median than they had been earlier, I knocked on the Rev's office door. He invited me to sit down.

We chatted about the forthcoming exams, and then the Rev got to the point. Fortunately, he was talking about something that I had requested from him a while back. In order to get on the supply teaching register, my first step back into teaching in Britain, I required written confirmation from the police that I had a clean criminal record. The Rev informed me that Pastor Robert would accompany me to the police station in Mamfe after school had closed, and help me to explain what I needed.

That afternoon, Pastor and I took a tro up the hill and walked through the gates of the office of the law. We said hello to two security guards, who were sitting under an awning in the courtyard, embroiled in a game of draughts. They knew Pastor well and gave us the standard pumping handshakes, before showing us through to the administrative office. There, a kind-looking lady called Mrs Brago listened, as I explained why I needed an official letter stating something to the effect that I had behaved myself since arriving in her country.

Mrs Brago hesitated, and told me that I would need to speak to the inspector. She got up, left, and returned a few minutes later. She was sorry, she said, but I would have to wait a short time. The inspector was having a bath.

It was no problem. Pastor and I sat and chatted, about the difficulties of Twi as a foreign language – which it was for him, as a Nigerian, as much as it was for me – and about Ruth, Pastor's wife. She was going to America in the coming days, in order to begin a hairdressing course there. She would be away for a year. Pastor was torn between delight that she would advance her skills, and sadness at losing her for so long. His face lit up as he talked about her many qualities.

Presently, the now-clean inspector arrived. He exchanged cheery handshakes with Pastor and me, and asked after the Rev. However, he could not access criminal records; I would have to go to Police HQ in Accra for what I wanted. It would be no problem, though; I had all the documentation – passport, and a letter of explanation (on headed paper) – that I needed. It would be done in a day.

Police HQ provided a stark contrast with Mamfe police station. I climbed off the tro whilst the mate yelled *"Cra-cra-cra"* once more, and made my way along the ring road that led to this imposing building. It was ginormous! At the gate, two armed guards were bellowing at the driver of a car, who must have committed some transgression or other whilst entering the site. One of them, a bear of a man, carried on his finger-pointing tirade whilst the other, much smaller in stature, approached me. Up close, I realised that he was probably not long out of his teens, with a gentle face that was at complete odds with his job description.

We shook hands, and he explained the complex route that I would have to follow to find the Criminal Records Department. Several lefts and rights were involved, as junctions linking corridors of varying lengths. I knew that I had no hope of remembering it all – even before he threw in something about carrying on past a flight of stairs – but thanked him anyway, and shared a joke about how hot it was.

With more than a little extra guidance, I managed to find my way to Criminal Records. It was packed. I queued, signed in, and was pointed to a desk where I had to show my passport. It was quickly apparent that what I would receive would be far more official than simply a letter. I was applying for a full blown Criminal Records Bureau certificate. I felt foolish for assuming that Ghana's police force would not have such things.

A fair-skinned chap with glasses awaited me.

"Do you have a residency permit?" he asked me.

I shook my head. "I have never been told to apply for one," I answered, feeling slightly fraudulent: the memory of being let off in Koforidua's Immigration Office in August had come rushing back. However, I reminded myself, it was technically true – the young immigration official hadn't actually *made* me buy one.

"It costs $200 without a residency permit; and twenty cedis if you have one," he explained.

I blanched. "How much?!"

"Make a photocopy of your visa, and I'll see what I can do," he smiled.

I made a trip out of the back of Police HQ to a tiny shack. The copier which it housed more than half-filled it. I returned to the fair-skinned man clutching the copy.

"I have managed to get it for you, twenty cedis," he beamed. He handed me some papers, one of which apparently was the receipt. Before I had time to look through them all, he was sending me away to have my picture taken in a second room, and my fingerprints done in a third.

This was indeed a serious business.

"Come back in three weeks," the receptionist told me when all this was completed, and I handed the various parts of my application to her.

Three weeks?

"Er, in three weeks I'll be in Britain," I uttered, a touch falteringly. It would not have helped to joke that Accra was a bit of a way to come to collect a piece of paper, so I left it at that.

I was sent off to an office on the third floor, where two well-heeled women looked me up and down, and carefully read my application.

"Do you have any small thing for me?" one of them asked.

She was almost certainly asking for a bribe. I played dumb. "What do you mean?" I asked, sweet and innocent.

She tutted, and told me to return in five hours.

I had plenty of time, then, to have a last look around Accra. I sat in the stand at Independence Square. It was as peaceful as it had been all those months previously on my first visit, when Kwamoso was new to me, and I had never heard of Lene, Martinson and so many of the other wonderful people I had had the pleasure of meeting over my time in Ghana. I noticed that 28th February Avenue had been renamed 'John Atta Mills High Street'. It was a poignant way to remember the former President.

Walking through the capital, business was in full flow. Traders sold, either from stalls or basins on their heads. Vehicles painted in the liveries of the political parties drove past. Megaphones attached to them blared slogans encouraging voters to choose their party's leader at the polling station. Various election posters adorned billboards, doing the same job more quietly. Just as many posters bore cross-party messages urging peaceful elections and acceptance of the result, whatever it may be.

Strolling around, it struck me how there were far fewer people calling out *'Obruniii!'* now than there had been earlier in my stay. Children still did it everywhere, of course, because seeing a white person was still exciting for them. In the eyes of adults, however, I must have acquired a more casual, less foreign manner as I walked around, knowing a little more of the way that life worked in their country.

I still had time to be shocked though. Often when I had been to Accra in the previous few months, I had seen the occasional person lying on the pavement. I had come to the conclusion that they were homeless and sleeping rough. In Tamale and Kumasi in August there had been one or two as well. Along the ring road on the way back to Police HQ, though, I passed one man who was, unquestionably, dead. From the angle of his ankles, *rigor mortis* had begun to set in; he had probably lain down the previous night and not woken up. It was a shocking and shameful scene that put a few things firmly into perspective. I was not alone in just walking on past the body; a man and a woman in front of me had done the same, as had a woman who had gone past me in the opposite direction a few minutes earlier. So too, clearly, had every other pedestrian on the ring road that day.

It was something to consider on the tro ride home. I was returning to Britain soon; my new CRB certificate removed one of the difficulties that I knew I would face as I looked for work again. Thankfully, the prospect of dying on the street, alone and homeless, was not one of them.

Chapter 17 – The exams and the election

"So when you get back to your place, will your family kill a goat for you?"

I was having a chat with Martinson a few hours after school had closed. He was curious to learn how people celebrated the return of a family member in Britain.

"Er, no. I'll probably have a nice meal though," I replied.

"You mean they won't make you goat and banku?!" Martinson was horrified.

"If they made me banku, I doubt I'd ever speak to them again!" I laughed. The very prospect of being given this cassava and corn-based lump of stodge as a treat was enough to put me off family occasions for good.

On second thoughts, it would have been an excellent idea to have served it to the mother of one particular ex-girlfriend.

I was about to share this thought with Martinson, but then he began to explain that, in Ghana, goat with either banku or rice is the customary meal for special occasions. I remembered the festival in Akropong for the King of Kwamoso back in September, where some of these animals had been slaughtered and cooked. Christmas, especially, is a time when people in the countryside would sharpen their knives and look hungrily at their goats. Served in a stew with rice, goat is the equivalent of our roast turkey and trimmings.

It was revision week at Holy Hills and Mount Zion. With the JHS classes, I and the rest of the teachers were trying our best to persuade and coerce the teenagers to do some studying outside the school hours. To be fair, we were beginning to have some success. The Form 2s and 3s who lived locally would frequently gather, sometimes in *Obruni* Castle, and bring their books with them. They would even open them and begin some writing, before their social side overtook them and the studying session descended into a natter.

I intended to go over some of the respective Maths topics with Forms 1, 2 and 3. With the latter, I would give them a break from averages, which they had toiled with to little avail over the previous week, and come back to them during the Saturday class. For the teachers, I would run another training session. It would cover ways of grabbing the attention of children at the start of a lesson and consolidating their learning at its end; things that had been central to my teacher training in Britain.

Everything went swimmingly from Monday to Wednesday. Even Madam Regina was attentive to my suggestions of different starting and finishing activities. This was possibly in part because the Rev had transferred Madam Rebecca, her chief chatting partner during my first session, to the children's home in Tinkong. Rebecca had swapped jobs with a large lady called Elizabeth. Holy Hills' newest teacher was as remarkable for her dry, sarcastic wit as for a pair of sideburns that many a man would have been happy to call his own.

Mr Sam was confident that he had taught all the Social Science and RME that he needed to, although less so that the children had remembered it all. Sitting outside the JHS block during a free lesson, I heard him telling Form 2 what sounded a very interesting story. I moved my chair and table closer to his room, and listened whilst I flicked through the Maths textbook.

Sam was recapping the life and times of a chap called Okomfo Anokye. He was one of the great traditional priests, in the days when the Ashanti kings still had their independence from the British. Okomfo Anokye had been sent to the Ashanti king Osei Tutu, to serve as his priest, and had performed a number of miracles. Among these were bringing down the Golden Stool from the sky, which landed on Osei Tutu's knees and thus conveyed him as all-powerful; throwing a gong-gong so high into the sky that it never fell down; and putting a sword in the ground with such force that no-one could pull it out. I had a vague memory of hearing that story some time before. Did it happen in Kumasi? Sam later confirmed that it did, and that the sword is still in the ground, although sealed off by a fence to prevent vandalism. Theft, I mused to Sam, is presumably not a problem.

At Mount Zion, who knew what lay in store? Class 5 and 6 had not yet finished their schemes of work. I decided to carry on teaching them, unless Madam Mavis displayed particularly vigorous insistence that they should recap their previous topics.

In the event, a shortage of chalk meant that little was done at all. Faustina, Edwin and I were rationed to new piece each. I used mine to put as detailed a set of notes, about the pollination of plants, as possible onto the board before it shortened to nothing. When this happened, we had a quiz about the various different Science topics that they had learned, with and without me. Yarro's understanding proved decisive; his team ran out convincing winners.

Most children were set off weeding after First Break, whilst a small number were tasked with cleaning the chalkboards in some of the classrooms. It looked a rather messy job – some sort of black paste had been mixed, and paintbrushes were being handed out with which to smear it onto the boards. Meanwhile, Mavis phoned the Rev, to arrange for chalk to be brought to Mount Zion the following day. I took the initiative by borrowing her phone when she had finished speaking to him, and suggesting that I deliver the same training that I had given to the Holy Hills teachers earlier in the week. The Rev agreed, and asked to be handed back to Mavis. She accepted the news with a shrug, and ordered the others into her classroom.

Whilst Mavis and, even more so, Selina and Faustina were open to all the tips I could give them, the men slouched and looked generally uninterested. It spoke volumes. Edwin was largely tapping away at the keypad of his mobile phone as I spoke. I probably should have stopped him, but at the same time did not want to create a scene. Daniel the French teacher, on the other hand, appeared lost in a silent daydream.

The following day, few of the children made it to school – Isaac's minibus had developed a fault with the electrics and had not left Kwamoso. Of the other teachers, only Edwin had arrived. Selina and Faustina were ill, and Mavis had called to say that she would be late. Daniel could have been anywhere.

Since Class 5 and 6 were mostly present, I wandered over to their room. After all, it would have been a shame not to have used the chalk that I had brought from the Holy Hills library. We went over the various joints, part of a new topic on the human body. Bright especially enjoyed whirling his arms around above his head as he demonstrated to us all that the shoulder is a rotating joint, in contrast to the knee, which most definitely is not.

"We'll move on to noting this down boys, please, before Bright hurts himself," I counselled, to general amusement. Bright looked slightly sheepish and was the first to pick up his pen.

Half-way through the lesson after First Break, just as Classes 5 and 6 were about to explore the functions of the various internal organs, Edwin came over. Madam Mavis – who had arrived during break – had apparently decided that enough was enough, and that she was closing school. At least that meant that Bright would not try to cough his lungs up to prove that not only did they exist, but that they did so as a pair. The boys packed their things and quickly made their way to assemble. My final taught lesson with what had become my favourite class had ended rather abruptly.

Martinson and I looked at each other more in resignation than anything else. It was the final Saturday class before the exams were due to begin, and a grand total of five of Form 3 had turned up. Many of the other JHS children seemed, by their absence, completely unconcerned that their Assessment for Improving Learning papers were in the library, sitting in a box sent by the Education Service, which would be opened in two days' time.

Dennis eventually showed up in Form 1's room after a good proportion of their lesson with me had passed. In fairness, he had been fetching water for the Rev, and was full of apologies at his lateness. Once little Caleb had consulted his watch for the umpteenth time and convinced me that it was time for him to ring the bell for break – "Twenty seconds left Caleb, time for us to work out another sum," I teased him – I had fifteen minutes or so in order to gear myself up for my latest, and final, attempt to impart the method of finding the median average from a frequency table onto the Form 3s. At least, to what there was of them. I was a little nervous about the topic appearing on the test: Mr Daniel had mentioned once or twice, as we chatted about the exams in his 'office', that these statistics questions came up time and again.

The five students in Form 3 had turned to four by the end of break. Collins had developed a toothache that may or may not have been induced by the prospect of the sums he was about to have to chew on. Since one of the five was Victoria, the 'Saturdays only' girl, there were only three of 'my' Maths class present. Leticia, Bismark and cheeky Daniel braced themselves as much as I did for the struggle that was surely to follow.

A shade under an hour and a half later, pride in the children – and to some extent myself – washed over me in swathes. Not only had they cracked the median with some ease, they had also successfully recapped how to work out mean averages from frequency tables. Walking back across the complex after the children had melted away, I felt a great sense of satisfaction. It was not lessened by the large proportion of the class that had not bothered to show up. If this were to be the last lesson that I ever planned and taught, it was a heck of a way to say goodbye to teaching.

Just as excitingly, for the complex as well as for me personally, German Chris was due back in Ghana that evening. Kofi Bosh and I were to collect him from the airport. He would spend some weeks working with the Rev, BraKofi and Bosh (who the Rev had co-opted to help out), getting the cogs in motion for their foundation.

A taxi drew up, and a bloke who I vaguely recognised got out of the driver's seat and shook hands with Bosh. It turned out that this was one of his friends, a chap called Pascal whom Bosh had got to know by some means or other several years before.

Chris' flight was not due for a few hours yet, so we had plenty of time to get to the airport. We used little of it. Pascal drove along the main road from the hills down into Accra as if his taxi were a racing car. Yet he had a sure touch to his driving, even whilst he was on the phone. Bosh was totally relaxed, as always, and I quickly became comfortable that, despite everything, we would not come to any harm.

On the taxi's radio, a particularly touching election broadcast warmed my heart. John Atta Mills' widow Ernestina delivered it, speaking of how his replacement, John Mahama – referred to throughout simply as 'John' – was a safe pair of hands to carry on with Ghana's development as a nation. There were none of the slogans or rhetoric that political messages always seem to feature, just a moving set of words delivered more as a chat than a speech. It finished with the simple line, "My husband would be proud of John's work," before the DJ recommenced speaking, in Twi, as fast as Pascal was driving. Bosh informed me that this was more speculation on the result of the election, less than a week hence.

I wondered what Ernestina's husband would have made of Pascal's four-wheeled acrobatics through Madina's sidestreets, which he took to avoid a long queue that had formed on the main thoroughfare to the capital. Heading back towards the main road on the other side of Madina, a line of traffic stood motionless. This would have presented a delay for every other driver I knew. Not for our Pascal. He popped his head through the window for a quick peek, saw that there was nothing coming down the other side of the fairly wide road, and gunned the throttle. We zoomed past the stationary traffic. Pascal was in his element. We had gone about a hundred yards, when we met the inevitable oncoming car. Pascal took this in his stride, calmly steering the taxi through the space in the middle of the road that had been created when the approaching car veered to the left.

Before I knew it, we were accelerating up the airport's drive. If Pascal had been in the least bit concerned about the official-looking sign reading 'No taxis', he certainly did not show it.

In the ample time we had to wait for Chris to come out of the Arrivals hall, Pascal and I got chatting. His English was reasonable, although there were a few times when one or the other of us relied on Bosh to act as the interpreter. An instantly likeable guy, Pascal had been driving taxis for years. He knew the Greater Accra region, and the areas around it, like the back of his hand. He commented, without any hint of irony, how many drivers needed to be more careful on the streets, and sounded off about the many drivers that he said were, "Unaware of what is happening on the road, they don't see things." I gave him a few brownie points on that one. Pascal had displayed fantastic awareness, in one sense, of the many situations he had encountered on our journey. We would not have arrived at the airport unscathed – or even at all – if he had not been mindful of the goings-on on the other side of the windscreen.

It was good to see Chris again. Handshakes with rasping finger-clicks were exchanged all round. I mentioned to him, quietly, about Pascal's brand of road craft, but that he needed not to worry. I had developed a massive trust in the guy's instinctive sense for the road. I looked forward, in the way that some people get excited about going on roller-coasters, to the ride that we were about to have back up to Kwamoso.

Nana was in overdrive in the week leading up to the election. He now broadcast for a few hours in the evenings, as well as his usual morning slot. As ever, being delivered fast, in the Twi language, his words sounded like a lot of noise to my still fairly untrained ear.

"It's all about a peaceful election," Bosh explained during one evening broadcast. Jodie, Robin, Chris and I (Roelanda was by now back behind her desk at her branch of *Ikea*) were sitting with him in *Obruni* Castle, chewing the fat. With election violence having marred numerous polls in other West African countries over the previous years, Nana's message was vitally important. None of us minded hearing his loud voice pierce the air.

The exams were in full swing by now. It had been, particularly for Form 3, an incredibly formal beginning to exam week. Bismark, Eunice and their classmates had had to sign a form each, which bore their photograph and the list of exams that they would be sitting, to confirm their presence. Kwasi Owusu nearly put a spanner in the works by signing Ishmael's form; Madam Paulina stopped him just in time.

The school fell virtually silent for long periods over the course of the week, as all classes wrote their exams. As in July, the silence was periodically broken: Martinson's voice rasped out to the JHS classes, telling them, "Five minutes more!", "Three minutes more!" and so on, until he signalled the end of the exam by crying out "JHS, stop work!" with an air of finality. Towards the end of Tuesday afternoon's exam session, in which his own English papers were being written, Martinson surpassed himself. He paced around with a massive grin crossing his face, shouting out at the top of his voice, "Write your name on your paper! Sign your paper! Write your question numbers!" Just in case he had missed anything, Martinson gave a final instruction, "Do *everything!*"

I voiced a thought that had crossed my mind several times before: "That bloke will never suffer stress!" Martinson was in his element, he loved the announcements that had to be made within school.

He was full of his usual bluster the next morning too, insisting that all of the children swap places in their classrooms.

"Why are you making them do that?" I asked, as Martinson stepped from one room to the other and the children found new seats.

"The children, *Ah!*" Martinson exclaimed. "They have written notes on the tables!"

I was stunned, momentarily, that they would do such a thing. They had, of course, and not just a few of them either. Fresh bits of writing had appeared on all but a few tables; they were rather unsubtle pointers for the Social Science papers that were due to be written. The youngsters ended up having new seats at the beginning of every exam to cut out the practice of leaving hints for themselves.

I sat in *Obruni* Castle one evening. Some of Form 3 were sitting around one of the tables with their notes, partly studying and partly having a chat. It was not the best preparation for the following day's tests, but right in that instant it hit me that this was just how it was in Kwamoso. The children wanted to do well and had a thirst for knowledge, as Leticia demonstrated by asking me several questions about photosynthesis (thanks to Mr Daniel, I was able to answer her). But they did not realise that it is impossible to open their heads up and pour in the facts as if filling a cup with water. They were kids, after all. They wanted to be spoon-fed. It was just how they were, and just what, I reckoned, kids all over the world are like to varying degrees. Eunice made me laugh, mocking the way that the teachers used the cane to cajole the children into studying. "If you beat me," she hissed through smiling lips, "I'll beat you!" The last words were almost spat at me, with her face screwed up in mock intimidation and accompanied by a slap of her chest.

"We'll see about that," I laughed. We both knew now that it would never happen.

There was silence around the complex apart from their chatter, and the noise of the birds, insects and animals in the long grass which surrounded us. Somewhere, Peace's mother Cynthia called for Dennis. How many times, I pondered, had I heard various people calling him; at home and in school, to perform some task. He was a remarkable fifteen-year-old.

Kwasi, the quiet and affable leader of the volunteering company's building site, appeared over breakfast the following morning. We poured him a cup of tea, and then listened in a rather stunned silence at what he said.

"On Thursday, my friend will cook cat outside his house. I will help him. You are all invited. Many other people will be there."

Chris, Robin, Jodie and I looked at him and at each other. Had we heard him correctly?

Cat?

Kwasi was saying something about how it would actually be two cats that we would be eating, because one would not be enough. He was looking forward to seeing Robin at work and the rest of us in a few days' time, if not before.

Cat.

It sounded interesting, if not altogether appetising. I was quite looking forward to it, though – more out of curiosity than anything else.

A football that Kofi Bosh had acquired also livened up my final week in Kwamoso. He and I, along with Robin, King David – who had been away, studying, for the previous few months – and a few of his other pals who I had met once or twice, played some fiercely competitive games in the late afternoons on the school pitch. They would begin as the shadows were just beginning to lengthen, and end after dusk, when it was no longer possible to see the other end of the pitch. The lights were off; there was a series of planned early-evening power cuts that week. They accommodated the increased demand for electricity later on, as people watched the election coverage on television. Only when I was walking back to the Rev's house, and my eyes had adjusted to looking further than the ball, did I realise just how dark it had become.

"What does it feel like?"

It was just after morning assembly on my final day at Holy Hills, the Wednesday of exam week. Mr Martinson had completed his round of caning for the latecomers and the sloppily dressed. He and I were walking across to the school office to pick up the morning's exam papers, the Maths tests, as I asked the question.

We stopped. "I should cane you?" he asked, somewhat surprised.

I thought about it for a second. That was not quite what I had in mind.

"Yeah, alright!" I held my hand out.

Martinson raised his cane, and then lowered it again.

"No, I can't! It will pain you!"

"It probably will, but go on, let's see how bad it is," I answered. I had suddenly become greatly curious.

Overcome by his scruples, Martinson refused point blank to have anything to do with it. Daniel from Form 3, though, had heard the second half of the conversation and had no such worries.

"You want me to cane you?" he asked. "I'll do it!" He probably thought that it was Christmas come early. Either that, or Mr Lawrie had gone doolally.

He took Martinson's cane and brought it down on the palm of my hand with an immense crack.

Around a second later, I felt a fire begin to rage where he had caned me. I managed to keep a straight face, though, and looked up at Daniel.

"It's not too bad," I said to him as casually as I could manage. Luckily my voice had held. "I don't know what you complain about."

Daniel was most put out. "I hit you as hard as I could!" he complained, before seeing the funny side of having just caned one of his teachers.

It hurt like crazy for a few minutes though, notwithstanding the fact that it had apparently been significantly harder than a normal caning. It brought home to me how brutal a punishment it was, although I stood by my belief that the children knew what was coming when they committed a misdemeanour around school.

It was soon time to get down to the business of the day, however. The Maths exams for the three JHS classes were handed out. I sat with Form 1. I was happy with their test; we had gone through everything that was on it. I nipped out and took a copy of the other two classes' exams. I looked at Form 3's first. It, too, was the sort that I would have settled for, although, to my irritation, there was nothing about averages, the topic with which the class had laboured for so long. Form 2's paper, on the other hand, was horrific. We had not, quite, finished the scheme of work before the exams started, and an unfortunate proportion of the questions covered the final few topics that we had not had time to go over in depth. Of the other questions, a good deal were, to put it mildly, difficult. Many concerned topics that the children had learned in Form 1, and had not given much attention to since. I wondered why that was the case, that frames into me, in the way they had done so many times before. I experienced, once again, the joyful rush as they competed to take hold of my bag. This time, Morgan emerged triumphant. The others took hold of my fingers, wrists and arms and led me impatiently up to the front of school. Daniel sat outside his classroom under the shade of the overhanging roof. It was a truly incredible experience, and so touching. I wondered whether the children had been tipped off by Daniel that I was coming. I had arranged my visit with him and Diana one morning, when I had met them on the tro on my way to Mount Zion.

Daniel confirmed that this had been the case – "I just had to tell them!" he exclaimed in mock regret – but it took nothing away from the kindness and innocence of the children who were now Class 3. To my delight, their English had improved markedly. They could now ask me questions with far more conversational value than 'How are you?'

"This is Madam Eunice, she is our new teacher!" Bentil said excitedly. He gestured animatedly at a pint-sized lady making her way out of Nursery's room, where she, Dorothy and Diana had been having their usual breaktime chat. Eunice greeted me warmly, as I had come to be used to in her country. We chatted about life in general and the children of Class 3 in particular. Eunice, like the Three Ds, exuded genuine warmth towards the children in her care.

It was high time that I saw the two others. Walking into Diana's room, she – in particular – and Dorothy gave me their widest smiles. We clapped each other's hands and clicked fingers.

"You never found me that wife," I joked to Diana.

She feigned bashfulness. "I'm sorry!" she laughed. We talked about Christmas, and our respective family plans for the holiday. Daniel and Eunice came in, and we speculated on the likely result of the following day's Presidential election. Nana Akufo Addo would be a deserved winner, the four voters agreed. Daniel hoped that it would remain dry for the whole day. That sounded like an odd thing to say. I reckoned that he meant that voter turnout would be lower if it thumped down – even briefly – with rain. Conversation had moved on before I could ask him.

The election was mentioned again on the tro that the five of us boarded once we had reached the roadside. As I got off at Quarters Junction, they waved me away with all of their considerable goodwill. I stood and waved back at them for the final time, until their tro jolted into life and accelerated away around the bend.

It was shortly after this that I said hello to Kwasi. In the excitement of the day, I had quite forgotten about the culinary delights that he had promised a few mornings before. Lunch, he beamed proudly, would be ready very soon.

Following him over to his friend's house, the cat lover inside me told me that I really should reconsider what I was about to do. It did not shout loudly enough, though, to stop me from wanting to find out what cat-meat would look like and, more importantly, taste like.

The first thing that I noticed, as I sat on a bench that Kwasi's friend, a chap called Victor, had put in place next to his grills, was a head. Balanced on a spoon, the teeth in the open mouth dominated the skinned, whisker-less face that stared back at me. I was relieved that I was not of a faint-hearted disposition.

Kwasi and Victor began cutting slices off the decapitated animals. People took plates and began chomping away; they were evidently enjoying their meal. Someone passed me a serving; the lightish-coloured meat was accompanied by a dash of spicy sauce.

So I was about to eat cat. I had not seen this one coming when I arrived in Kwamoso ten months earlier.

I apologised to moggies the world over and took a good-sized bite.

It is a much-repeated cliché that many meats 'taste like chicken'. Often that is because the variety in question is a white meat, and so it would be rather surprising if it did not. Added to this list can be added cat. It was a touch tough, but unexpectedly tasty. I even went back for seconds.

On election morning, Nana's loudhailers broadcast various final messages concerning the poll. The government school at the bottom of the village served as the polling station; it would open at eight o'clock. Our man went into overdrive as he explained the process that the voters had surely heard many times before. They were to queue up in an orderly fashion and have their voting cards and ID ready. They would apply a purple dye to their thumb, then mark their ballot paper with their thumbprint. There would be severe penalties for people who voted twice, this was to be an entirely free and fair election.

Whilst this was going on, I wandered over to Peace, Eunice and Leticia. The three were sitting next to Peace's mum's house.

"Sir Lawrie! Tonight, we will water you!" they giggled. I wondered what they meant. If they had to water something, I told them, surely Bosh would not mind if they did his garden instead.

I wandered down to have a look at the polling station a couple of hours later, when the election process was in full swing. The girls had not elaborated on "watering me"; I decided that it was just a case of teenagers being daft.

Bosh headed down with me. He was uninterested in politics normally, reckoning – quite sensibly I thought – that all politicians are as bad as each other, but had resolved to vote nonetheless. I waited a short distance away whilst he went and cast his ballot. Bosh returned to where I still stood a while later in excellent spirits, bearing his purple thumb for me to see. Nana Akufo Addo, he had decided, was marginally less objectionable than John Mahama.

There was an orderly queue of people waiting with their documentation next to a pair of desks, where officials tapped on laptops to register the arrival of each voter. Ballot papers were marked in one of three or four little alcoves, which were curtained off from view. The polling station resembled any that would be found in Britain, with one major exception: the whole process was taking place outside the school buildings, rather than in one of its classrooms. I guessed that this was not exceptional, and the meaning of Daniel's comment about it staying dry became clear. Rain would not only have made people stay at home, it would also have wrecked the organisation of the event. The laptops and ballot papers would have stood no chance in a Ghanaian downpour.

The polling station was crowded for the majority of the day. In the afternoon, I walked down again with Auntie Gifty and Florence, both big NPP supporters. They joined a lengthy line of people in the queue and inched towards the front. BraKofi was standing away from the line chatting to some other people. Presently, he strolled over to me. He mentioned how the police had arrested two men, who had voted in Akropong and then gone to Tinkong to try to have another vote there.

I noticed that his thumb was free of the purple dye. "Oh, the queue is too long now," he explained in his laconic way. "I'll go and vote later."

Results began to come in that evening. Florence's radio had been moved outside so that she, the Rev and Auntie Gifty could keep tabs on Nana Akufo Addo's progress. They and Debra sat on the chairs outside the front door, listening and eating their dinner. There was near silence from them, except for the occasional grunt of either triumph or disappointment as the NPP won or lost in various areas around the region.

Peace, Eunice and Leticia drifted into *Obruni* Castle, where I sat chatting with Bosh, Martinson, BraKofi (now with a purple thumb), Robin and Chris. The girls each carried a couple of water sachets. This made sense; it was still fairly humid. It was no surprise when they opened one each, nor did I bat an eyelid that they had done so at the same moment. The reason behind this synchronisation, however, quickly became apparent. Without warning, they simultaneously squeezed their sachets and fired icy jets of water at me. Once they had emptied their first one, they got going with their second. I roared a mixture of surprise and indignation, which quickly turned to laughter as the girls pointed out that not only had they "watered me" as promised; they had also had great fun whilst doing it.

Peace had enjoyed it so much that she celebrated by filling a bucket with water from the cistern next to the Rev's house. I watched her as she approached me, bucket primed and at the ready. Noticing that the two others had made similar moves towards the cistern, I made a quick calculation. Whether I made a run for it or not, I was going to get wetter. Who cared? It was a warm evening and the water was quite pleasant. I spread my arms and shouted for them to do their worst.

It was not the cleverest idea. I had no sooner opened my mouth than Peace scored a direct hit in the face. My slightly macho cry turned very rapidly into little more than a splutter.

The Rev, Florence and Auntie Gifty had been disturbed by the commotion. When I had regained my sight, I noticed that they were glaring daggers at the three teenagers. The type of pandemonium that had been unleashed in front of them was unheard of – throwing water over their teacher, indeed?! The Rev's guest as well! Outrageous!

Yet their hard expressions immediately turned into laughter when they saw that I was as gleeful as the girls. Now, though, it was time to get my own back. Peace was still standing next to me, looking deeply satisfied. I took a step towards her and gave her an enormous soggy bear-hug. She screamed in astonishment. That took care of her; I chased after Eunice and Leticia, who had quickly taken flight.

Once dry, I resumed my conversation with Martinson, Chris and Robin. Bosh and BraKofi had retired to bed at some point, whilst I was either catching up with the two girls, or changing into dry clothes soon after. We chatted for a while, about this and that. I saw – again – the differences between Europe and Ghana, but in a different way from usual. The Germans asked me about and commented on aspects of home, and what awaited me there. Yet much of what I was saying simply made no sense to Holy Hills' finest teacher, who for the first time in my experience was in the cultural minority. For large periods, for just about the first time since I had known him, Martinson was not talking! It suddenly hit me that we had inadvertently marginalised him.

I felt so stupid for not noticing it happening earlier. We chatted a bit as a four, about more general topics, before Martinson eventually said that he was going to bed. He got up and shook my hand. He wished me good luck and made his way back off to his house. His smile and good humour were intact, but had a touch of his sparkle been lost? Maybe it was nothing, but the feeling gnawed at me that he had been left out.

Chris, Robin and I went off to bed shortly after. Nice as it would have been to have chewed the fat all night, with election results coming in, we reckoned that Nana's broadcast would not be quiet come the morning.

We were right. On the plus side, I realised that Nana would now never wake me up again. A great tide of compassion flowed through my body for him. After all, someone had to man the loudhailers. More importantly, I had in recent weeks seen him a number of times around the complex; he had proved a witty and intelligent bloke.

As *Safnat Panea*, Nana's signing off tune, began to play, I jumped out of bed and put my shoes on. I picked up my pen drive as well. I wanted to have a last chat with Nana, but if he could also give me a bit of his music… well, that would be a bonus.

Having just shut down his computer, he could not share the couple of songs that I had been after. That didn't matter though. We had a good natter about this and that; Nana was pleased that the election results would be in by the end of the next day, after which he would not have to broadcast during the evenings.

"It's nice to see you here again, it's so long since you last came over," Nana said after a while. I could not decide whether he was just being mischievous by bringing up the time when I had arrived at just gone four o'clock, seething about what I had termed his "very noisy" loudhailer.

"Erm, yes. Sorry," I answered.

"No, no. I liked that," Nana smiled at me. "You had a problem with me, and you came to tell me. Not many people would have done that."

His tone was not only kind but genuine. He asked me about how I would get home, and I told him about my plan to go to Cape Coast for a few days before boarding the plane at Accra's Kotoka airport. We walked down the steps that led to the path together, then shook hands and went our separate ways.

Of the rest of the goodbyes, some stand out more clearly than others. Pastor Robert said some very nice things to me, and asked after Lene in Denmark. When would I come back?

"I don't know Pastor. I doubt that I ever will." It was an answer that I knew would disappoint him, even though he did not show it, but it was better to be truthful. I could not just tell him what I suspected he wanted to hear.

Bosh gave me an enormous bear hug and told me to stay safe. I found Yaw standing outside his house, shook his hand, and told him what a fantastic lad he was. There was a trace of sadness in his eyes, but it melted away when I gave him one of my T-shirts that I knew he liked. His sister Mabena was thrilled with a deck of cards that I placed in her hand, and agreed to let the other children use them as well.

Florence had gone out, very early. I was disappointed to have missed her, but the Rev promised that he would thank her on my behalf for her hospitality. For his part, the Rev told me that I had done good things for his schools, and that he had very much enjoyed having me live with him.

Auntie Gifty was last. A lump was building up in my throat as I gave her a hug and thanked her for as many things as I could remember: her daily cooking and her generosity in having let me stay in her house were but two of these. "More than that, though, thank you for looking after Lene that time when she fell down after giving blood," I said. I struggled to get the words out as I looked at her kind, gentle face. They came, but only just. She gazed back at me, and told me to take care on my journey.

I hoped that she had not noticed a little tear forming in my eye as I said goodbye to her for the last time. Doubtless, though, she had done. As I walked off to Quarters Junction, it rolled part-way down my cheek before I brushed it away. Around me, life was going on just as normal: what else would it be doing? Laundry was being washed, conversations were being had, Samson was running around. The radio, which had been on since way before seven o'clock, was still blaring, telling anyone who was listening about the latest electoral outlook. It looked as though President Mahama's NDC was holding a slight advantage.

This buzz of activity turned into background noise, and then became indistinct from that of the Junction. I flagged down a tro, and was taken around the bend and down the road. It was something that had happened so many times in the past. This time, though, I was not coming back. Had I made a difference to any of the people in the complex? I would not be so presumptuous to say one way or the other. They, though, had enriched my life with so many memories which I was, still am, certain will remain.

Epilogue

John Mahama won the election, by a narrow margin. Rolling coverage of the results as they came in had been on television and radio for most of the weekend; by Sunday night the winner had been officially declared. Straight away, the newly re-elected president appealed for calmness during the NDC supporters' celebrations. Meanwhile, Nana Akufo Addo accepted his defeat and was quick to declare that his supporters should follow his lead. On the streets of Cape Coast, late on Sunday night, fireworks were set off, and there was a celebration. President Mahama would have approved though; it was brief and, by Ghanaian standards, very restrained.

All was thus well as I began my final full day in Ghana, except an ache in my knees, which seemed most peculiar. Probably just a bit of tiredness, I decided. I had done a fair amount of walking over the last few months, after all; it was certainly nothing to worry about. Especially not when I wanted to have a look at Cape Coast castle again, and make another trip to Elmina, to see if it were still as beautiful as it had been all those months before. Of course, I was not disappointed.

And so on to the airport. The tro from Kaneshie station was one of the most cramped that I had ever sat on. It was doubly unfortunate that over one of the bumps my backpack slid ever so slightly, but most crucially, from my lap; it had encroached on a spot of my anatomy that it most certainly had no right to. 'Airport Junction' could not come quickly enough. The thought briefly crossed my mind that I would have one of those comedy high-pitched voices when I told the mate that I was getting out.

Fortunately, I did not.

I heard a voice call out as I walked up the road towards the terminal building. "*Obruni*," it enquired. "Are you going to your country?"

I paused. The reality of the answer sank in during the second it took for the word to come out of my mouth. I smiled. "Yes!" I replied. He waved, and I carried on my way. For the first time, I felt a massive excitement about being back in Britain. Of course I had had a wonderful time in Ghana – on many occasions I had reflected that in a number of ways it had been the best year of my life – but this was the first time that my feelings on returning home had been anything other than that it was the next, logical, step.

At the terminal, I had quite a bit of time to sit around waiting. The thought had crossed my mind to find the little patch of tarmac where Lene and I had sat before she had boarded her flight more than half a year earlier. There had been some building and repair work at the front of the Departures building, however, and the spot where we had shared our last minutes was not obvious. Perhaps that was for the best. I did not want to get caught up in thinking about it.

Lene was, however, the last person with whom I had a conversation in Ghana. We spoke on the phone as I waited at the gate, and chatted and laughed as we had done so many times over the course of the previous ten months.

By now, evening had long given way to night. Stepping out of the air-conditioned building, to walk over to where the plane waited, I experienced the same feeling of walking into a wall as I had done the evening that I landed in Ghana. Even now, the intensity of the humidity came as a shock to the system. The only difference was that, by now, it was fully expected. It would be another of the things that I would miss.

Kwamoso lies underneath a flight path from Kotoka airport. As we ascended into the sky, I was hoping that the plane would fly over the village. It was with a tinge of sadness that I noticed that we were flying a different course out of Accra. There were too many lights for us to be flying over the Akwapim Hills. Instead, we were passing over the Greater Accra conurbation, and then the Volta Region, the river just visible as a dark strip. That delightful little community of which I had been part lay to the west. Almost everyone there would be in bed by now. May they all sleep soundly, tonight and every other night. The children, in particular, have the fantastic opportunity that their parents, to a large extent, did not. Their schooling, whilst not perfect by any stretch, is good enough for them to learn the skills vital for success in wider life outside the village. If the likes of Eunice, Peace, and Dennis in the complex and, further afield in Akokoa, Bentil, Abigail, Wisdom and the rest of them grasp the chance that they have, who knows what they will achieve in the future? They live in a country which is modernising as quickly as any in Africa. True, Ghana is not perfect by any stretch. Too many children are unable to attend school. Workers in a number of industries are exploited, in particular those working in the Chinese-controlled gold mines. The nation is dependent on Ivory Coast to supply a significant chunk of its electricity. Yet Ghana will develop, the road building and general stability will see to that. Today's educated children, those who choose to do so, are the ones who will play a leading part in that development.

At some point I must have dozed off, for I suddenly realised from the plane's mapping screens that we were approaching Morocco. What a sight its coastline looked at three o'clock in the morning! The port of Agadir, all lit up, was almost directly below. Further inland, more lights betrayed the presence of other, smaller, towns.

Waiting for my connection in Lisbon, I peered from a distance at a screen which gave information about London. I could make out that the time there was approaching six o'clock. Underneath, the temperature was displayed. Surely, though, this must be wrong? The screen read twenty-nine degrees.

Unseasonably hot, one would have thought, for Britain in the run-up to Christmas.

The answer hit me square in the face about a second later. This was twenty-nine degrees Fahrenheit, which meant... I had forgotten the exact conversion, but it meant that it was blooming cold. Settling back into my book, the tannoy made its '*bing, bing, bong*' noise. The flight to London, the tinny voice announced, was delayed. Freezing fog had apparently prevented the aircraft's prompt departure from Heathrow *en route* to Lisbon. I mentally shivered: if I had not already been fully aware that I was no longer in an equatorial climate, I well and truly was now.

Despite this, it was actually nothing like as bad as I had expected it to be in London's freezing afternoon. I waited at Arrivals for a friend from my university days. Fay would finish work at four o'clock and meet me soon after. That left a few hours, so I bought a newspaper. It was full of the usual bickering and politicking that various members of the government and their shadow counterparts engage in. There must have been some other national and international news contained within its pages as well; suffice to say that none of it was remotely memorable, if only because it was so routine.

After having read the first few stories, my throat told me that I was thirsty. My first instinct was to find someone selling water sachets. Then I remembered that such things did not exist here; they were part of the past.

Later on, when I was near the end of both the paper and the bottle of juice that I had returned to the newsagent for, I spotted Fay walking into the Arrivals hall. I picked up my things and ambled over to her.

Getting to her house in one of the suburbs of London required a train ride, a bus ride and a walk. There were many things that could have felt quite novel – the idea of a functioning rail network for one, and the sight of semi-detached houses with at least one car on the drive for another. Yet it all seemed perfectly normal. As did walking into a traditional pub a few hours later, for dinner and a pint.

I awoke from a deep sleep on Fay's floor the next morning and looked up. My eyes met the type of sideboard and curtains that adorn any living room in the country. Again, everything looked so familiar. In that moment, I took a moment to consider everything. Had I really been away from Britain? Strange as it may seem, for a couple of seconds I had to think about it.

That day, Fay and I had a look around London. The city's streets were as busy as ever, with Christmas shoppers and suits hurrying along around us. This, too, was a scene I remembered as though it was from the week before. There were only the occasional additions to what I remembered, and these did not really come as surprises. In a bookshop on the South Bank, for example, I discovered a work of fiction that, judging by its title, seemed to be all about a dull colour, in a certain number of hues. Fay assured me, giggling, that it was rather more *risqué* than that. If I wanted a cheap thrill, she said, I should turn to chapter *ahem*. Fay delivered the relevant number over an induced cough. Whilst what little I read was definitely cheap, it was certainly less than thrilling, and I returned it to the shelf.

A brand which I remembered – vaguely – from before I had gone to Africa had extended into a whole series of trendy shops. Its range of Union Flag-themed merchandise had no doubt made its parent company a heap of cash on the back of the summer's Olympics. Most of the expensive products bearing its label seemed unimpressive, to say the least.

Yet nothing prepared me for one of the more extravagant chocolate shops in Piccadilly Circus. Fay insisted that we go in for the sole purpose of taking the Mickey out of the various humdrum products which had the company's logo emblazoned on them. I wondered, briefly, what the likes of Bosh and Auntie Gifty would make of a foot-high model of a sugar-coated sweet riding a motorcycle. Nothing coherent, I reckoned. They would probably ask the point of something so tacky, especially if they had discovered that it was priced at the equivalent of a few weeks' wages. Of course, I realized soon after, this was part of the difference between lifestyles in Britain and Ghana. In our country, not only can we afford these quirky luxuries, but they are seen, by enough people, as semi-important commodities. Is it better, or worse, to live in this type of society? Who am I to make judgments? It is simply different.

My adventure should have been over when I was back at home in the North-West, and in the process of being taken on by a supply teaching agency. Stories could be, and were being, told, and photographs shown. Except that it was not over, not quite. There was one, final, sting in the tail.

The sore knees that I had experienced in Cape Coast came back just over a week later, over the course of the day. I considered them merely a nuisance until later the same evening. Sitting in the pub with friends, a sharp headache also began. Straight away I remembered where and when I had experienced this combination before, and what the result had been.

The local pharmacy did not sell anti-malarial tablets. Instead, on Christmas Eve morning, I dragged myself to A&E and announced myself to the receptionist. I spent the afternoon on a Quinine drip, feeling my condition improve from 'lousy' to 'reasonably good' with surprising rapidity.

Come the evening, on another Quinine drip, I felt I should leave the hospital. The doctor who had been assigned to me concurred. That, sadly, was all that we agreed on. Whilst my preferred destination was home (with a pack of tablets), his was the Tropical Diseases Unit in a different hospital, twenty-odd miles away. A debate ensued, in which he prevailed. I and my drip found ourselves in the back of an ambulance shortly after.

Waking up on Christmas morning, hooked up to yet another bag of liquid Quinine, in a side ward for one, I considered the situation. I had had the experience of a lifetime, yet now here I was with malaria. Alone. In hospital. On Christmas Day.

Had it been worth it?

Absolutely.

Printed in Great Britain
by Amazon.co.uk, Ltd.,
Marston Gate.